The Making of the Bible

The Making *of the* Bible

FROM THE FIRST FRAGMENTS
TO SACRED SCRIPTURE

Konrad Schmid and Jens Schröter

Translated by Peter Lewis

THE BELKNAP PRESS OF HARVARD UNIVERSITY PRESS

Cambridge, Massachusetts, and London, England · 2021

FIRST PRINTING

First published in German as *Die Entstehung der Bibel: Von den ersten Texten zu den heiligen Schriften* by Konrad Schmid and Jens Schröter, © Verlag C. H. Beck oHG, München 2019

The translation of this work was funded by Geisteswissenschaften International—Translation Funding for Humanities and Social Sciences from Germany, a joint initiative of the Fritz Thyssen Foundation, the German Federal Foreign Office, the collecting society VG WORT, and the Börsenverein des Deutschen Buchhandels (German Publishers & Booksellers Association).

Library of Congress Cataloging-in-Publication Data

Names: Schmid, Konrad, 1965– author. | Schröter, Jens, 1961– author. | Lewis, Peter, 1958– translator.
Title: The making of the Bible : from the first fragments to sacred scripture / Konrad Schmid and Jens Schröter ; translated by Peter Lewis.
Other titles: Entstehung der Bibel. English
Description: Cambridge, Massachusetts : The Belknap Press of Harvard University Press, 2021. | First published in German as Die Entstehung der Bibel: Von den ersten Texten zu den heiligen Schriften by Konrad Schmid and Jens Schröter, © Verlag C. H. Beck oHG, München 2019 | Includes bibliographical references and index.
Identifiers: LCCN 2021009296 | ISBN 9780674248380 (cloth)
Subjects: LCSH: Bible—History. | Bible—Criticism, interpretation, etc.
Classification: LCC BS445 .S29613 2021 | DDC 220.1—dc23
LC record available at https://lccn.loc.gov/2021009296

Contents

The Making of the Bible

1

What Is "the Bible"?

At first sight, the question "What is 'the Bible'?" might sound surprising. You might answer it by simply taking from your bookshelf a volume with the title *Bible* on the cover. But if you were to pose the question to people from diverse language groups, religions, and denominations, they would show you very different works. Among German speakers, for example, a Lutheran would likely present a Luther Bible, perhaps a family heirloom dating back to 1912 or a new edition from 2017, while a Roman Catholic would choose a standard translation from 2016, and a member of the Swiss Reformed Church a Zurich Bible in its revised edition of 2007. These Bibles differ from one another not only in how they have been translated and revised, but also in the number of books they contain and the order of those books. The picture grows more complicated if we broaden our scope to English-language translations: the King James Version and the New Revised Standard Version each have their own distinct linguistic profile and theological character. And an even more varied picture emerges if we expand to the whole of Western Christianity. The Old Testament of an Orthodox Christian from Armenia or Russia, say, includes books that do not appear in Western European editions. If we look at other eras in the history of Christianity, the panorama becomes still more complex: in place of the four gospels, the New Testament of a Syrian Christian of the third century would have had a book entitled Diatessaron, which combined an account of the life and work of Jesus Christ with stories from all four gospels of the New Testament that we are familiar with. Jews from the Middle Ages would bring a Hebrew or Arab Bible to the mix, whereas those from ancient Alexandria would contribute one in Greek. All of these Jewish Bibles would differ from one another in both their scope and the sequence of books.

It should be clear, then, that there is no such thing as *the* Bible. Rather, there have always been Bibles that differed in extent, arrangement, and language.[1] The question "What is the 'Bible'?" would therefore best be answered by assembling an entire bookcase of these different volumes to provide a vivid display of the great variety of Jewish and Christian Bibles that have existed from ancient times to the present. This variety would demonstrate the living history of the relationship between Judaism and Christianity, faiths that are bound together and yet separated by their relation to the biblical texts. It would also present a fair reflection of the history of Christianity, including its historical forms and different denominations. "The Bible," as a collection of the authoritative texts of Judaism and Christianity, not only constitutes the foundation of those religions but also bears witness to their shared yet distinct histories. Those histories are reflected in the diversity of these religions' ways of life and kinds of faith today.

Indeed, the very word "Bible," which comes from *biblía*, the Greek term for "books" (singular *biblíon,* meaning "book, text, or document"), encapsulates these commonalities and differences, this unity and diversity of Bibles.[2] This name makes it clear that the Bible is *a book,* yet one that gathers together *several books.* Indeed, it is sometimes referred to as the "Book of Books." This designation has the quite intentional and welcome ambiguity of meaning both "a book composed of several books" and "the most significant and authentic book of all time."

This terminology is found within the Bible itself. The Greek translation of the Hebrew term *sepharim* ("books") in Daniel 9:2 calls the biblical texts *biblía.* In 1 Maccabees 12:9 they are called "sacred books" (*tà biblía tà hagía*), while in works of the Jewish authors Philo of Alexandria and Flavius Josephus, we find the designations "sacred books" (*hieraì bíbloi*) and "sacred writings" (*hieraì grafaí*) in reference not just to the Torah, but also to other writings that had by the first century CE attained an authoritative status within Judaism.[3] With similar emphasis, Paul calls the writings of Israel "sacred writings" (*grafaì hagíai,* Romans 1:2). This is related to the term "sacred books" (*hierà grámmata*) in 2 Timothy 3:15. Later, in the second century CE, reference is made to "books of the Old Covenant" and "books of the New Covenant." In the fourth century, the church father Jerome wrote of owning "many books of the sacred library."[4] From the ninth century onward, the term "Bible" was commonly used as a collective noun for the books of the Old and New Testaments.[5] Thus, from earliest times, there was an awareness that the Bible consisted of several books and that the term had a plural meaning.

The Bible, then, is not a single book but a collection of books, or a "library." And it was in this form—as an assemblage of mostly multipart books, such as the five books of the Torah (or Pentateuch) or the four gospels—that it was produced and also represented pictorially for a long time. An example of this is an illustration from the Codex Amiatinus, one of the most important biblical codices of the early Middle Ages, in which the prophet Ezra is shown seated in front of a cabinet containing the Bible in nine volumes (Figure 1).[6] The model for this illustration may have been the scriptorium of a monastery and the monk in charge of it.

Not until the invention of printing in the late fifteenth century did a single book (or codex) containing the entire Jewish or Christian Bible become the most widespread form to be produced and disseminated. Indeed, we have extensive evidence of a great diversity of forms of the Bible in the preceding centuries. This diversity reflects the complex history of its genesis, which began with the writing of individual texts. Through a series of interwoven and mutually influential processes, these texts then became the Jewish and Christian Bibles. It is vital to recognize this multifaceted nature of the Bible, not least because it makes us aware that we are dealing not with a clearly circumscribed collection but with a compilation that varies in extent and configuration and whose boundaries with other texts are often very fluid.

The Jewish and Christian Bibles

The most striking difference between the Jewish and Christian Bibles is that Christian Bibles consist of two parts: the Old Testament (a term used exclusively by Christians) and the New Testament. In contrast, Jewish Bibles contain only the texts that are found in the Old Testament. But a Jewish Bible cannot be considered identical to the Christian Old Testament. A Christian Bible without the New Testament is not a Jewish Bible, but merely an Old Testament.

Jewish and Christian Bibles also differ in their external form. In antiquity, biblical texts in Judaism were written on scrolls, the prevalent book format up to the third century CE in both Jewish and other ancient civilizations,

Figure 1. The Prophet Ezra, from the Codex Amiatinus. This codex, which was produced in the early eighth century CE at a monastery in Northumbria, England, is the earliest surviving manuscript of the Latin Vulgate Bible.

like those of Egypt, Greece, and Rome. Important parts of the Bible were written on scrolls—these include the Torah, the books of the Major Prophets (the Great Isaiah Scroll, one of the Dead Sea Scrolls from the archeological site of Qumran, is over eight meters long), and the Book of the Twelve, a collection of the shorter books of the Minor Prophets.[7] Scrolls continued to be produced well into the medieval period, although the codex format became increasingly prevalent from the fourth century onward. Codices were composed from sheets—made from wood or wax at first, and later from papyrus or parchment (vellum)—laid on top of one another. Like modern books, these sheets were sewn together at the edge, which made them far more practical to handle than scrolls. Once this format became more common, the scroll took on a special status. This is evident in Judaism today; during synagogue services, readings are done from Torah scrolls.

Unlike the Jews, Christians used codices for their scriptures from the outset. This is quite remarkable because the liturgical practice of reading the scriptures of Israel from scrolls was familiar not only to Jesus and his early followers but also to Paul and his collaborators, all of whom had their roots in Judaism. Luke 4:16–20 tells of Jesus in the synagogue at Nazareth reading from a scroll containing the book of the prophet Isaiah. As Luke recounts, this scroll was unrolled before the reading and rolled up again afterward. Whether this story is based on a specific historical event or not, it accurately reflects the use of sacred texts in a first-century synagogue.

From the second century onward, Christian manuscripts are almost exclusively codices rather than scrolls.[8] There has been much discussion about the possible reasons for this. A number of potentially overlapping factors may have played a part. It could be that the pronouncements of Jesus or collections of his sayings were written down early on, so that they could be preserved and disseminated. And codices, because they are easy to handle and carry around, may have provided the ideal vehicle. Itinerant missionaries and apostles may also have taken codices containing the gospels or letters with them on their mission journeys so that they could read aloud from them at the places they visited. In addition, the letters of Paul or several gospels may have been bound together in codices to create a body of scriptures for use in meetings of early Christian communities. Whatever the case may be, codices were cheap to produce and would have been highly practical items to read from in gatherings of early believers or on missionary journeys. Not least, codices, because they were inexpensive products, may have been more suitable than expensively produced scrolls, given the lowly status of most Christian communities at the time.

Even in their external appearance, then, Christian texts from these early centuries were quite different from Jewish scrolls. The codices were small books around 15 to 25 centimeters high—about the size of a paperback. The first ones generally contained just a single text (a gospel or a letter, say), but later they held multiple texts, such as two of the gospels, or even all four, or several of Paul's letters. These books were used in Christian services, which were then held in private dwellings, and were also kept in private collections, where they could be read at home.[9] From the fourth century onward, larger (and in some cases lavishly produced) codices of biblical texts began to appear. Famous examples of these are the Codex Sinaiticus and the Codex Vaticanus, both dating from the fourth century. A similar development took place in the non-Christian realm during this same period, when beautifully designed codices of secular texts, such as the works of Homer and Virgil, were also being created.[10]

Nothing about the Christian Bible at this early stage, at least from its external appearance, would have given the impression that it would one day be a book containing the authoritative Jewish and Christian texts under one cover. The notion of a New Testament and that of a connection with the Jewish scriptures—seen as a contrasting Old Testament—were first mooted primarily on the level of theological debate and found expression only much later in the creation of books containing both of these texts.

The texts of the Jewish Bible are written in Hebrew for the most part, though some are in Aramaic.[11] Scriptures that were originally written in Greek, or which survived only in a Greek translation, did not feature in it. The Jewish Bible was compiled at a time when Judaism was transforming itself after the destruction of Jerusalem and the Second Temple in 70 CE. Although the Jewish Bible that evolved during this period, like the Christian Bible, has its roots in developments that go far back in the history of Israel, the form in which it has gained recognition and authority in Judaism up to the present day did not take shape until the end of the first century of the Christian era.

This process is sometimes linked to a supposed synod that is said to have been held at Jamnia (Jabneh or Yavne), around 20 kilometers south of the modern city of Tel Aviv. In 1871, the German historian Heinrich Grätz suggested that such an event had taken place, on the basis of information gleaned from rabbinical literature.[12] Jamnia was certainly a site of great significance in the formation of Rabbinic Judaism in the period between the two Judeo-Roman Wars of 66–70 and 132–136 CE. Yet we can be sure that there was never any synod held here at which the content of the Hebrew Bible was determined. The very term "synod" wrongly imputes to ancient Judaism a form of ecclesiastical council that did not develop until later. The supposition that an authoritative collection of scriptures was laid down at a synod of Jews is anachronistic and does not do justice to the complex processes behind the creation of the Jewish Bible.[13] It is much more likely that the traditions and texts that formed the basis of Jewish self-perception were collected by Rabbinic Judaism after the fateful year 70 CE. Among these texts, the status of the Torah and the prophetic scriptures was undisputed, whereas that of the Ketuvim, or Writings, was as yet unresolved. This same period witnessed the development of the Mishnah, a written record of oral doctrines expounded by ancient Jewish scholars (the Tannaim, or teachers). This compendium of biblical exegeses would soon surpass the Jewish Bible in its practical importance. The Mishnah was itself the subject of wide-ranging interpretations, which are contained in the Gemara, the "elucidation" of the analyses and commentaries offered by the Tannaim. The Mishnah and the Gemara together form the Talmud, the principal focus of study in Judaism of late antiquity, the Middle Ages, and the present day.

One important difference between the Christian and Jewish Bibles is that the former included certain texts that were originally written in neither Hebrew nor Aramaic or that existed only in Greek translation. In the Orthodox and Roman Catholic churches, these have the status of either canonical or deuterocanonical (secondary) texts, whereas in the churches of the Reformation, they are treated as Apocrypha.[14] These texts are the books of Judith, Wisdom, Tobit, Ecclesiasticus, and Baruch, the first and second books of Maccabees, additions to the book of Daniel (the Song of the Three Children, the Story of Susanna, and Bel and the Dragon), additions to the book of Esther, and the Prayer of Manasseh.[15] They arose from Judaism during the Second Temple period, but after 70 CE they were handed down further only through Christianity because, as documents written in Greek, they were not considered in Rabbinic Judaism to be of equal ranking with the Hebrew texts.

Their designation as apocryphal in the Protestant churches is explained by the fact that the reformers wanted to scale back the preeminence of the Latin Bible translation (the Vulgate). They returned to the original languages of the Bible—namely, Hebrew for the Old Testament and Greek for the New Testament—and translated the texts anew from those languages. In doing so, they were guided by the humanist emphasis on basing the reading of ancient texts on original sources rather than relying on later translations. Before the Reformation, these texts formed an integral part of the Bible in all Christian churches and were not considered any different from the other scriptures. They were included in the Vulgate, which in turn took its cue from the first Greek version of the Hebrew Bible, the Septuagint, which contained the Hebrew and Aramaic texts in Greek translation alongside those texts for which no Hebrew or Aramaic original was known.[16] These books are also missing from lists of the books of the Old Testament compiled by certain ancient Christian theologians who gave precedence to texts with a Hebrew provenance (see the following section on the Tanakh, the Old Testament, and the New Testament). Thus, the status of these texts was already questionable in ancient Christianity, which may have played a part in the decision of the Protestant reformers to consign them to the Apocrypha.[17]

Finally, the Jewish and Christian Bibles differ in the sequence of the books, with the variability among Christian Bibles being greater than among Jewish ones. Jewish Bibles have been relatively consistent in content and order, especially since the advent of printing.[18] Although there are some differences between the various Bible manuscripts, a certain standard order has become the norm. The Bible invariably begins with the Torah, or Pentateuch (the five books of Moses: Genesis, Exodus, Leviticus, Numbers, and Deuteronomy). In the Jewish Bible, these are followed by a section called Nevi'im (Prophets), which contains the historical books from Joshua through 2 Kings (the Former Prophets), along with Isaiah, Jeremiah, Ezekiel, and the Book of the Twelve (together known as the Latter Prophets). The third section, the Ketuvim (Writings), includes the book of Daniel and the Five Megillot (scrolls), which are all associated with Jewish feasts: the books of Ruth, Song of Songs, Ecclesiastes (or Qohelet), Lamentations, and Esther. While some variation exists within the Ketuvim, the sequence that was established in the sixteenth century is rarely deviated from now. Jewish Bibles customarily conclude with the books of Ezra and Nehemiah along with the two books of Chronicles.

Christian Old Testaments exhibit a different arrangement (with some variation among denominations). The Pentateuch is followed by the historical books, which include the books of Chronicles and two of the books of Ezra (roughly corresponding to the Hebrew books of Ezra and Nehemiah) as well as other books with a historical content: Ruth, Judith, Tobit, and the two books of Maccabees. Next come the wisdom books: the Psalms, followed by the Odes (a compilation of eulogistic texts from the Old and New Testaments), Proverbs, and the books of Job, Wisdom, and Sirach. The prophetic books, including the book of Daniel (with additions that have come down to us only in Greek), are at the end.

This arrangement may derive from the Greek-Jewish tradition in Alexandria.[19] If so, it is possible that the librarians there gave the biblical books a structure that reflected existing literary genres. It is also possible that the arrangement is Christian in origin, with the prophetic books positioned at the end because of the Christian perspective on the scriptures of Israel, in which the Old Testament and New Testament are seen, respectively, as prophecy and fulfillment. This order of books is used in the Codex Vaticanus, one of the earliest biblical codices from the fourth century, whereas the Codex Sinaiticus and the Codex Alexandrinus place the wisdom books at the end of the Old Testament. The sequence with the Prophets at the end is also evident in the writings of the ancient Christian theologians Athanasius and Cyril of Jerusalem.

In light of the differences between the Jewish Bible and a Christian Old Testament, any claim that Judaism and Christianity are linked by virtue of a shared Old Testament is insufficiently nuanced. In terms of the language, composition, and arrangement of the scriptures of Israel, each faith tradition has its own unique perspective. Christians have taken up and carried forward the Greek translations of the scriptures of Israel, along with Jewish interpretations of them. In Judaism the Greek texts were not handed down, and the Hebrew scriptures in the sequence outlined above came to form the basis of Jewish self-perception.

Regardless of the differences between them, Judaism and Christianity share convictions that are expressed in the authoritative Jewish texts. These include the belief in the God of Israel as the creator of heaven and earth; the belief that the Israelites are God's chosen people and that God has preserved them throughout history; the view of God as a being to whom one can direct one's prayers and turn in times of need, from whom one can expect comfort and help, but to whom one can express one's suffering and with whom one can argue; the setting aside of one special day per week to devote to rest and worship; and liturgical formulas and prayers. These commonalities find expression in the fact that Jews and Christians both call upon God through the Psalms of Israel, that they refer to the proclamations of the prophets of Israel (albeit with differing interpretations), and that they see the history of Israel as a template through which to interpret their own history. Finally, the idea of a second divine figure, variously described as the "Son of Man," "Son of the Most High" or "First-born of all Creation," is a prominent feature of early Judaism.[20] This presents an important background for early Christian ways of speaking about Jesus Christ, which tie in with Jewish usage and form the basis for the relationship between God and Jesus Christ.

By analogy with the Old Testament, groups of texts also coalesced within the New Testament, which were then assembled into the Bible codices of the fourth and fifth centuries (see Chapter 6). The corpus of the four gospels developed over the course of the second century, when they became differentiated from other gospels that were labeled "apocryphal." The collecting of Paul's letters also began in the second century, or possibly as early as the end of the first. The collection that finally made it into the New Testament comprises fourteen letters, which include both "genuine" epistles (those written by Paul himself) and letters composed later in his name, as well as the Letter to the Hebrews. The collection called the Catholic Letters (the letters of James, Peter, John, and Jude) has a somewhat different history. They were not compiled until some time later, when they were bound together with the Acts of the Apostles into the so-called Praxapostolos, as testimonies of the apostles. Finally, the book of Revelation was added to this collection.

Christian Bibles differ depending on denomination and language. Nevertheless, it is not hard to identify a Christian Bible as such. It must consist of an Old Testament, generally containing at least thirty-nine books, and a New Testament with twenty-seven. The numbering of these texts can vary, since in some Bibles a group of books is aggregated into a larger unit, as for example the twelve Minor Prophets of the Old Testament, which are combined to form one book, or the four gospels. Deviations from this pattern are most apparent between the Eastern and Western churches. In the Western churches, the Apocrypha, or deuterocanonical scriptures, of the Old Testament can also be included. In the Eastern churches, right up to late antiquity, the canon of biblical texts could look very different. Until the fifth century, for example, the Syrian New Testament contained the so-called Diatessaron instead of the four gospels. This work was composed by the theologian Tatian of Adiabene in the second century. It conflated the four gospels, the Acts of the Apostles, and the letters of Paul into a single account. The biblical canon of the Ethiopian Orthodox Tewahedo Church recognizes eighty-one books, including some that are regarded as apocryphal in the Western tradition. Although the number of books in the Ethiopian Bible is strictly circumscribed, their selection is not.

Biblical texts are not only found in compilations of different content and configuration, but were produced and employed in different ways: as single texts; as scrolls containing the Torah, the Prophets, or the Psalms; as codices with the Gospels or the letters of Paul; or as amulets or miniature codices. A Jewish Bible of the first century BCE looked unlike one from a later period. One cannot draw a firm boundary between biblical and nonbiblical texts for the early years of Christianity—nor indeed for later eras. Rather, the authorization of biblical texts and the process by which they became canonical involved certain texts emerging as essential to Judaism and Christianity, while others became regarded as not authoritative in the same way. Some of those in the latter group were nonetheless still used for private study and devotional purposes. What led to these distinctions and what they imply for "the Bible" in relation to other texts—the Apocrypha, the pseudepigrapha, and the deuterocanonical texts—is examined in greater detail below.

The Tanakh, the Old Testament, and the New Testament

There is no firmly established technical term for the Bible in Judaism. The Hebrew scriptures may simply be referred to as "the Bible," and the term "Jewish Bible" is sometimes used to distinguish it from the Christian Bible. In Hebrew, terms such as *miqra* ("scripture") or *kitve haqqodesh* ("sacred texts") are also common.[21] In allusion to its tripartite division into the T̲orah (Law), N̲evi'im (Prophets), and K̲etuvim (Writings), the Hebrew Bible is also called the Tanakh.[22] This acronym, however, did not appear until the Middle Ages.

The terms "Old Testament" and "New Testament" for the two parts of the Christian Bible only emerged over time. The point of departure was the Greek term *diathéke* (*testamentum* in Latin). This word was used in the Septuagint to translate the term *berit,* which denotes the covenant that God made with Israel or with humankind. The New Testament picks up this language, as in those passages where the term is used to describe God's covenants with the Israelites.[23] The point at issue is the nature of the relationship between God and his people, which is defined by the Torah as God's settlement. The broader sense of "testament," or "compact," can be seen in Paul's Letter to the Galatians. Here, Paul illustrates God's promise to Abraham, which is fulfilled through Christ, with the image of the testator, the provisions of whose testament (*diathéke*) remain in force until they are finally redeemed. The contrast between the old and the new covenant is also to be understood against this background. Its origins can be seen in the third chapter of Paul's Second Letter to the Corinthians. In this passage, Paul contrasts his own service on behalf of Christ with that performed by Moses and emphasizes that "ministry of the new covenant," as a "service of the Spirit," is more glorious than that which, as "a ministry of death," is only engraved on "stone tablets":

> Not that we are competent in ourselves to claim anything for ourselves, but our competence comes from God. He has made us competent as ministers of a new covenant—not of the letter but of the Spirit; for the letter kills, but the Spirit gives life. (2 Corinthians 3:5–6)[24]

In the same context, Paul also speaks of the "reading of the old covenant" and remarks that "Moses is read"; these are references to the practice of reading aloud from the Torah in synagogue services:

> For till the present day, the same veil remains over the reading aloud of the old covenant, and it is not uncovered because it is [first] removed in Christ. But till today, whenever Moses is read, a veil is placed on their hearts. (2 Corinthians 3:14–15)[25]

Paul is drawing a polemical contrast between the old and the new covenant.[26] The old covenant is represented by the Torah, for which he uses "Moses" as a metonym. A similar contrast of the two covenants appears in the Letter to the Galatians (4:21–31), where Paul interprets the sons of Abraham, one of whom he had by a slave woman, the other by a free woman, as two "covenants," one of which leads to servitude, the other to freedom.

The "new covenant" (*kainé diathéke*) is also mentioned in the accounts of the Last Supper in Paul's First Letter to the Corinthians and in the Gospel according to Luke. Both describe the chalice used at the Last Supper as the "new covenant" (1 Corinthians 11:25; Luke 22:20). This image succinctly expresses the new bond that is forged between God and humanity in the celebration of the Eucharist. The idea of a new covenant recalls Jeremiah 31:31 (38:31 in the Septuagint):

> "The days are coming," declares YHWH, "when I will make a new covenant with the people of Israel and with the people of Judah."[27]

In the passage that follows, this new covenant is contrasted with the one God made with the "ancestors," or "fathers," when he led them out of Egypt. In the new covenant, God will make his law intelligible to people's reason as well as writing it on their hearts.

The new covenant identified in the account of the Last Supper, and symbolized by the chalice, stands in this tradition. At the same time, the image of the "blood" of Jesus Christ (which is central to the doctrines of transubstantiation and consubstantiation in the communion service) harks back to the idea of a covenant sealed with blood first mentioned in the Bible in Exodus 24:8.

These two Old Testament texts from Jeremiah and Exodus also play a role in the Letter to the Hebrews, in which another mention of a "new covenant" appears. The text from Jeremiah 31:31–34 (38:31–34 in the Septuagint, from which the Letter to the Hebrews quotes) is cited verbatim in Hebrews 8:8–12, where it is hinted that God has, through his proclamation of a new covenant, declared the existing one to be "obsolete" and therefore about to disappear (Hebrews 8:13). We also encounter in Hebrews the notion of the "blood of the covenant" from Exodus 24:8: "This is the blood of the covenant that YHWH has made with you." This verse, which in Exodus refers to the sealing of the covenant between God and Israel through the blood of young oxen, is quoted in Hebrews 9:20, where it is linked to the blood of Jesus Christ—the blood that has been shed for the remission of sins once and for all time and which has established a new order. For this reason, Christ can be called the "mediator of a new covenant" (Hebrews 9:15).

Thus, whenever the New Testament mentions the old and new covenants, or testaments, it is not juxtaposing two "books," but two orders. Talk of a "new covenant" or "new testament" picks up on the proclamation of a "new covenant" in Israelite-Jewish texts and relates it to God's actions through Jesus Christ. Christ's blood can thereby be interpreted as the "blood of the covenant"—in other words, the blood that seals the new bond.

The theme of the covenant also plays an important role in the Letter of Barnabas, a theological treatise written in around 130 CE. The principal content of this work is an explanation of how God's covenant has been fulfilled through Jesus Christ. The treatise does not use the terminology of the old and new covenants, but it does refer to the "new law of Our Lord Jesus Christ," which does not demand any burnt offerings or sacrifices but instead requires a person's heart to offer praise to God.[28] In a polemical way, the writer explains that Israel lost the covenant by turning to false gods. That is why Moses smashed the tablets of the law—so that the covenant of "our dear Lord Jesus might be sealed into our hearts."[29] As a result, the Christians are the heirs to the covenant that the Israelites had shown themselves unworthy of.[30]

The juxtaposition of old and new covenants reappears later in the works of Justin Martyr, an early Christian theologian from the first half of the second century, and Irenaeus, who wrote his main work, *Adversus Haereses* (*Against Heresies*), in around 180.[31] In the writings of both of these scholars— as in the New Testament texts—the two covenants denote, respectively, God's actions in Israel and God's actions through Jesus Christ. Using biblical references, they both refer to the gospel of Jesus Christ as the "new testament," which has taken the place of the old one but has been instigated by the same God. These writers were not yet using that term to describe collections of biblical texts, however.

The first use of "Old Testament" (or "Old Covenant") to designate the first part of the Christian Bible occurs in a letter written around 170 by Melito, the bishop of a town in Asia Minor called Sardes. Eusebius of Caesarea refers to the letter in his *History of the Church*.[32] It contains a list of the books of the Old Testament (or the Old Covenant) which corresponds in large measure to the list found somewhat later in the works of Origen of Alexandria, Cyril of Jerusalem, and Athanasius: the five books of Moses, Joshua, Judges,

Ruth, the four books of Kings (that is, the first and second books of Samuel and the first and second books of Kings), two books of Chronicles, the Psalms of David, Proverbs, Ecclesiastes, the Song of Solomon, Job, Isaiah, Jeremiah, the book of the twelve Minor Prophets, Daniel, Ezekiel, and Ezra.[33] Nehemiah is not named in its own right since it was presumably counted along with Ezra as a single book, which was the case in the Hebrew tradition until the early Middle Ages.[34] Similarly unnamed is the book of Esther, which continues to be omitted from lists of biblical books from the fourth century, such as those drawn up by Athanasius and Gregory of Nazianzus. Thus, Melito's list, like those compiled by other Christian theologians, includes only books with a Hebrew basis, and excludes the apocryphal or deuterocanonical books.[35] Some early Christian writers made an explicit connection between the count of twenty-two books and the twenty-two letters of the Hebrew alphabet.[36] This tradition is also found in Jewish texts.[37]

Melito's letter, nevertheless, introduces no firm linguistic usage for the term "Old Testament," nor does it contrast the "Old Testament" and the "New Testament" as two distinct books. Melito's formulation "books of the Old Covenant" should be taken to mean that God's "old covenant" with Israel is represented by the texts Melito cites, not that these texts themselves are called a "covenant" or "testament." Melito does not use the expression "books of the new covenant" because he is responding in the letter to his friend Onesimus's specific request for information about the number and sequence of the books of the Old Testament.

The designation "New Testament" for the books whose content reflects God's new covenant with humanity first occurs in the writings of Clement of Alexandria and Origen, around the end of the second century and the first third of the third century.[38] Some scholars have argued that the term can be traced back as far as about the year 140, to the works of the early Christian thinker Marcion of Sinope.[39] Because Marcion's writings have not survived, however, this theory relies upon Tertullian's critical analysis of Marcion from the early third century.[40] Even supposing Tertullian's claim to be true, there is still no proof that Marcion used the term "New Testament" to denote an authoritative group of scriptures for the church. We know that Marcion compiled his own collection of scriptures, which consisted of a particular version of Luke's gospel and the letters of Paul that he had edited, and that this collection was roundly rejected by early Christian theologians.[41] Even if he had indeed called this group of texts the "New Testament," we would not be justified in taking this to refer to a particular section of the Christian Bible, in contradistinction to the "Old Testament," for the simple reason that Marcion utterly repudiated the latter. Consequently, Marcion plays no significant role in the history of designations for the parts of the Christian Bible.

Around the end of the second century, the terms "Old Testament" and "New Testament" shifted from signifying two covenants to referring instead to the collections of scriptures that represent those covenants. We can see this process clearly by comparing use of the term "testament" by Irenaeus, who applies it to the covenants, with its use by Clement and Origen, who also apply it to the scriptures. In the Latin-speaking realm, the works of Tertullian still contain both *testamentum* and *instrumentum* as translations of the Greek *diathéke,* though *testamentum* subsequently won out. The former polemical or negative use of "testament" in the sense of "(old) covenant" which we find, say, in the letters of Paul, the Letter to the Hebrews, and the Letter of Barnabas had now changed. Henceforth, the term came to refer exclusively to books, while the older meaning of "testament" as "covenant" receded.

From this starting point, "Old Testament" and "New Testament" became well established as the names of the two parts of the Christian Bible. Controversy did not arise again until the late twentieth century, when some scholars called for the term "Old Testament" to be dropped as an alternative name for the Hebrew Bible on the grounds that the adjective "old" was pejorative. The name "First Testament" was put forward instead, though this suggestion has failed to catch on.[42] First, it flies in the face of a long tradition; second, it does not take account of the ancient logic that old things, not new ones, were to be preferred; and third, the contrast of old with new—notwithstanding the judgmental presentation of the old and the new covenant in Paul's letters and the Letter to the Hebrews—was not fraught with disparaging connotations when the Christian Bible was created. Throughout the history of Christianity, both the Old *and* the New Testaments have been interpreted as evidence of God's acts of salvation. The term "First Testament" is therefore an unnecessary neologism. What's more, it would seem to imply that the New Testament should be renamed the "Second Testament," a move that would be both historically and theologically questionable and misleading. Today, the terms "Hebrew Bible," "Jewish Bible," and "Old Testament" are used in a nuanced way that makes clear that the scripture collections of either Israel or Judaism are being referred to as great literature and as the Holy Scripture of both Judaism and Christianity.

How the Text of the Bible Is Structured

The Jewish and Christian Bibles are collections of books. As a general rule, each individual book in biblical codices begins on a new page. In a scroll, there is usually only one book to each scroll. On scrolls with several books, such as Torah scrolls or scrolls containing the book of the twelve Minor Prophets, the original configuration is often hard to determine because of the fragmentary state of preservation, though it may be assumed that each new book began with a new column. In Jewish Bibles each book concludes with a final masorah: notes written in the margins or at the end of codices that provide statistical lexical information such as the number of verses in a book, or the identity of the middle verse, middle word, or middle letter of the book. This was important for monitoring purposes, making it easy to check whether a copyist had left anything out.

In ancient codices containing complete Christian Bibles, there is no special marking to indicate the start of the New Testament. Instead, the Gospel according to Matthew begins directly after the final book of the Old Testament (which varies depending on the codex). Even in the Zurich Bible of 1531, the book compositors did not place a prominent break at this point. The New Testament does not even begin on a new page. Although the heading *"Das neüw Testament"* does appear after the book of Malachi, it is set in the same type size as all the other book titles, while the heading *"Das Evangelion Sanc Matthes"* is, uniquely, set in smaller type. The break between the Old and the New Testament is marked much more clearly in modern editions of the Bible, usually by means of one or more blank pages at the end of the Old Testament and a subheading.

One important aid to orientation within the books of the Bible is their division into chapters and verses. In 1205, the English archbishop Stephen Langton introduced the division into numbered chapters, while the numbering of verses was an innovation of the French book printer Robert Estienne (Stephanus), in a Greek-Latin 1551 edition of the New Testament. Accordingly, the Bibles of the Reformation period still did not have numbered verses. The system of numbering chapters and verses varies between Bible editions. In the Anglo-Saxon world, the numberings of certain books and parts of books of the Old Testament differ from one another (as for instance at the end of the books of Joel and Malachi). The first Luther Bible to be officially reviewed by the church authorities, which appeared in 1892, and the Zurich Bible of 1931 are numbered differently than most Bibles are nowadays. The numberings in present-day German editions of the Old Testament result from a conscious effort to take into account the supposed original Hebrew numbering. However, this system dates back no further than a Hebrew Bible printed by Joseph Athias in 1667; there is no evidence of such a numbering system in rabbinical Bibles of the sixteenth century.[43] The most significant system of organization in those Bibles is the subdivision of the text into paragraphs and verses. The ends of paragraphs are marked with typographic final characters (called "alineas" or "pilcrows"), while the ends of the verses are marked with the *Soph pasuq* or the *Silluq*. The *Soph pasuq* takes the form of a colon, while the *Silluq* is a small vertical stroke beneath the final stressed syllable of a verse. The *Soph pasuq* and the *Silluq* were inserted by the Masoretes, scholarly transmitters of the Bible in late antiquity. Working between the fifth and eighth centuries, these scribes furnished the Bible text with its ancient Hebrew consonant script and vowel notations. They also commented in marginal notes on unusual word forms and combinations and recorded how frequently these occurred within a book.

Because textual evidence for the Hebrew Bible from biblical times does not exist, we can only indirectly deduce how the books were organized internally. The best indication is provided by the Dead Sea Scrolls, especially the large Isaiah scroll. This scroll contains not only various elements of text structuring—blank lines, free line endings, indentation of the first word at the beginning of each new paragraph, spaces (larger gaps within a line)—but also special characters written in the margin.[44]

Considering the period of their presumed creation, we may assume that the texts of the Bible composed in Hebrew were not written—or at least not exclusively so—in *scriptio continua,* a style of writing without any word breaks, punctuation marks, or other forms of division. In the Dead Sea Scrolls, the words are clearly separated from one another by gaps.

Inscriptions on pottery from the period before the Babylonian Exile of the Jews—that is, from the tenth to the sixth century BCE—reveal a mixed pic-

Figure 2. An ostracon from Meṣad Ḥašavyahu, seventh century BCE.

ture of writing styles. (Due to the predominance of Aramaic, hardly any Hebrew inscriptions have been preserved from the post-exile period.) Some of these potsherds, or ostraca, such as those from Tel Lachish and Arad, string letters together without gaps or breaks between words. Others, however, such as the ostracon from Meṣad Ḥašavyahu, contain dots separating some of the words (Figure 2).[45]

In contrast, the earliest texts of the New Testament were written in *scriptio continua* (see Figure 3 for an example). They consist exclusively of majuscules, or capital letters. This style of writing is not specific to Bible manuscripts; it occurs in many manuscripts of Greek and Latin antiquity and continues into the Middle Ages. Many ancient manuscripts contain reading aids. These include characters (*paragraphoi*) placed between individual sections of a work (such as in collections of aphorisms or in dialogues of dramas), divisions between words and syllables, and marks (*coronides*) at the end of either individual paragraphs or an entire work. Such aids to understanding and reading do not occur in Bible manuscripts.

Scriptio continua could easily result in errors of comprehension because it was not clear where the division lay between one word and the next.[46] Manuscript configurations that facilitated reading, for instance by including word breaks or accents, gradually began to gain ascendancy. The tendency to divide books up into pericopes—that is, discrete thematic units distinguished from each other typographically—is in evidence from the eighth century onward.[47]

From the ninth century on, majuscule texts were supplanted by manuscripts written in lowercase letters, or minuscules. Minuscule manuscripts also introduced syllable and word breaks. This did not happen in any systematic way, though, and changed according to the whim of the particular scribe. Word breaks become more prevalent in later manuscripts. This practice remained in use until the invention of printing in the fifteenth century. Yet book printing did not put an end to the manuscript tradition. Manuscripts were still produced in the fifteenth and sixteenth centuries, and sometimes even later, but the handwriting in them was adapted to appear like a typecast font.[48]

Figure 3. Papyrus 66 (Papyrus Bodmer II) with the beginning of the Gospel of John, ca. 200 CE.

The Transmission of the Bible Text

Whenever we open a Bible, be it Jewish or Christian, we are faced with texts that have been translated from ancient Hebrew, Aramaic, or Greek and have been copied over and over again through antiquity and the Middle Ages. The oldest German-language Bible was created between 1300 and 1320 in Zurich. It is believed to be the work of the Dominican friar Marchwart (or Marquard) Biberli and was based on the Latin Vulgate Bible.[49] The Mentelin Bible of 1466, the first Bible printed in German, was also based on the Vulgate. People did not begin to translate the Bible from the languages in which the texts had originally been written until the sixteenth century. But how were biblical scriptures transmitted before that date?

Up until the early twentieth century, translations of the Hebrew Bible or the Old Testament that are based on the original Hebrew text took as their basis the text of the Second Rabbinic Bible, which was prepared by Jacob ben Hayyim and printed by Daniel Bomberg in Venice in 1524–1525 (Figure 4). This text was used for the first two printings of the scholarly edition of the *Biblia Hebraica* (1906, 1913). The third edition of this work, which was prepared by Rudolf Kittel and appeared in 1929–1937, used the Codex Leningradensis instead. This codex, dating from the year 1008, is the oldest complete manuscript of the Hebrew Bible (Figure 5). Since 1991, the Codex Leningradensis has been known by its former name, Codex Patripolitanus, or—in reference to its catalog number in the library in St. Petersburg where it is kept—simply as Codex B 19 A. Most modern scholarly editions of the Hebrew Bible, such as the *Biblia Hebraica Stuttgartensia* and the *Biblia Hebraica Quinta,* are based on this manuscript.[50] This codex originates from a Jewish sect called the Karaites, who rejected oral tradition in favor of the Hebrew Bible as the only genuine source of religious authority. This group therefore had a keen interest in a Bible text that was accurately transmitted.

Unlike the ancient Bible manuscripts from Qumran, the medieval manuscripts of the Hebrew Bible include vowels and thus, in the view of the Masoretes, ensured a proper reading and vocalization of the text. The punctuation of the text of the Hebrew Bible is estimated to have come into use between the fifth and eighth centuries. Of course, the Hebrew Bible text is much older than its oldest complete manifestation in the Codex Leningradensis.

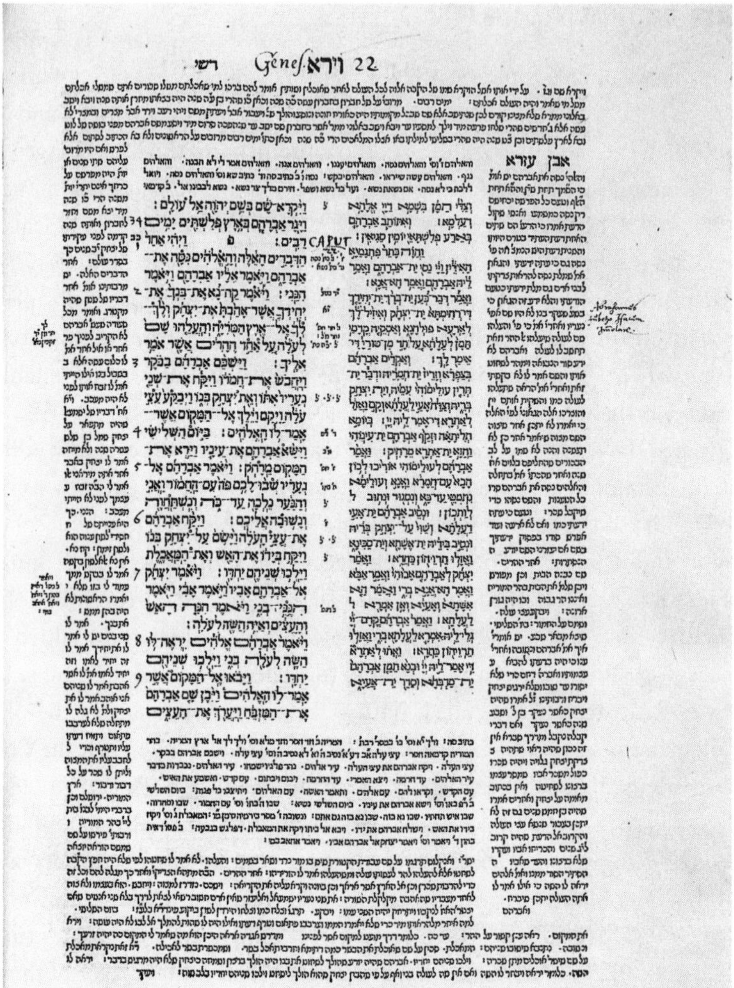
רשי Genes. וירא 22

Figure 4. The Second Rabbinic Bible of Jacob ben Hayyim (Venice 1524–1525). This is thought to have been used as the source text by the translators of the King James Version of the Bible in 1611. Seen here is a section from Genesis 21:33–22:9. The Hebrew text and the Aramaic translation are in the center, surrounded by commentaries by Rashi and Ibn Ezra.

Figure 5. A page from the Codex Leningradensis (B 19 A), the oldest complete manuscript of the Hebrew Bible, dating from 1008. This page contains the text of Genesis 14:12–15:13.

The oldest Greek texts of the Bible are the Septuagint codices of the fourth and fifth centuries: the Codex Sinaiticus, the Codex Alexandrinus, and the Codex Vaticanus. These are all complete Christian Bibles containing both Old and New Testaments (Figures 6 and 7).

Up until 1947, a fragment called the Nash Papyrus, from the first century BCE, was thought to be the oldest example of a biblical text (Figure 8). It was named for its purchaser, W. L. Nash, secretary of the London-based Society of Biblical Archaeology, who acquired the fragment in 1898 and bequeathed

Figure 6. The Codex Sinaiticus from the fourth century is the oldest surviving Christian Bible containing the Old and New Testament. This page shows the end of the Gospel of Luke.

it to the University of Cambridge in 1903. This textual fragment contains the Ten Commandments (Decalogue) in Hebrew along with the prayer *Shema Yisrael* ("Hear, O Israel!"), with the Decalogue transmitted in a hybrid form from Exodus chapter 20 and Deuteronomy chapter 5. The Nash Papyrus cannot, however, be regarded as a true Bible text because of the hybrid nature of the Decalogue and because the Decalogue and the *Shema Yisrael* do not follow on directly from one another even in Deuteronomy.

Figure 7. The Codex Vaticanus from the fourth century, with the end of the Gospel of Luke and the beginning of the Gospel of John.

A completely new era for the reconstruction of the ancient text of the Bible began in 1947, when a cache of ancient scriptures was discovered at the Dead Sea.[51] Over a period of nine years, from 1947 to 1956, the remnants of some nine hundred scrolls were found in eleven caves along the northwestern shore of the Dead Sea. Scholars divided these finds into three groups: texts from the Hebrew Bible, texts that are now counted among the apocryphal or pseudepigraphic scriptures of the Old Testament, and texts that originated within the group, often known as the Essenes, who lived in the settlement of Qumran.

Figure 8. The Nash Papyrus from the first century BCE.

The majority of these scrolls were preserved only in the form of small frag-ments (Figure 9).[52]

One major exception is the Isaiah Scroll from Qumran Cave 1, which has been preserved almost complete throughout the intervening centuries because it was stored very carefully inside a sealed earthenware jar (Figure 10). It dates from around 125 BCE and contains all sixty-six chapters of the book

Figure 9. Fragments of the Dead Sea Scrolls, with texts from 1 Samuel 23:9–13 (*left*) and Deuteronomy 32:43 (*right*).

of Isaiah. Comparing this Hebrew text with that of the Codex Leningradensis, we can see that the text of the book of Isaiah was transmitted extremely faithfully over the more than one thousand years that separate the Qumran scroll from the medieval codex. Although there are 4,500 orthographic variations and 1,375 variations in content between the two, the orthographic differences can mostly be traced back to the fact that the Isaiah Scroll is written in unvocalized Hebrew (vocalization by means of vowel pointings did not arise until the fifth century) and often displays a so-called *plene* form of spelling, in which certain consonants assume the role of vowels (such as the Hebrew letter *w* also standing for "o" and "u"). The variations in content relate to certain differences in vocabulary that do not generally result in any change of meaning. Even so, in a few places, some striking differences are apparent. Among the most important of these is the hardening passage in Isaiah 6:9. In the text of most Bible manuscripts, including the Codex Leningradensis, when God himself calls on Isaiah to become a prophet, he gives Isaiah the following instruction:

And he [God] said: "Go and say to this people: 'You shall hear, hear continually, but you will not comprehend! And you shall see, see continually, but you will not perceive!'"[53]

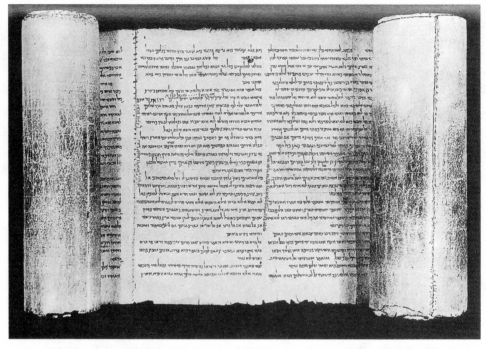

Figure 10. A section of the Great Isaiah Scroll from Qumran, showing Isaiah 38:9–40:28.

This text is remarkable. Isaiah is actually being called upon to become an anti-prophet: the message that he must convey to the people is not supposed to be understood by them. The instruction to the people that they should remain stubborn and unrepentant is a theological formulation after the fact; it envisages the effect of prophesying a day of judgment at the same time as issuing that prophecy. This creates the impression that the rejection of God's prophecy by those to whom it was imparted was intended or at least foreseen from the outset by Isaiah 6:9. But in the Isaiah Scroll, Isaiah 6:9 reads differently:

> And he [God] said, "Go and speak to this people: 'You shall hear, hear continually, in order that you comprehend! And you shall see, see continually, in order that you will understand!'"

In Hebrew, the difference between these two passages comes down to the substitution of a single letter. The Codex Leningradensis uses *we'al* ("and not"), while the Isaiah Scroll uses *we'al* ("in order that"). It is far more likely that the medieval codex has retained the original reading, while the Isaiah Scroll, with its theologically smoother version, represents a correction to the original text. This is because it is easier to explain how a straightforward utterance might be created from a problematic one than vice versa. This case demonstrates that the actual age of a manuscript has no material bearing on the quality of its textual transmission.

No manuscripts of Bible texts predating those discovered at the Dead Sea have been found. Although only a few decades separate the oldest manuscripts of the book of Daniel found at Qumran from the final formation of the biblical book of Daniel and the most recent texts in it, there is no overlap in time between the literary production of the book and its earliest attestation in a manuscript.[54] In biblical times, the scriptures of the Bible were written on either papyrus or hide (vellum), and these materials cannot normally survive for more than two or three hundred years. The texts found at the Dead Sea are an exception because they were stored in a desert climate in sealed terracotta jars.

Almost all inscriptions from biblical times that have survived are those written on potsherds, or ostraca.[55] Broken pieces of pottery jars and other vessels were used for writing notes, keeping records, making copies of letters, and so on, and these writing surfaces were of course perfectly durable.

Just a single fragment of papyrus—the cheapest and therefore most widespread writing material—has been preserved from the reign of the kings of Israel and Judah in the area once occupied by the ancient state of Israel. This too comes from the region around the Dead Sea.

There is one possible example of a Bible text that has survived from biblical times: the silver amulets from Ketef Hinnom in Jerusalem, which were discovered at a burial site and are thought to date from the seventh century BCE (Figure 11).[56] These small silver scrolls are inscribed with the remnants of a text that is somewhat akin to the "Aaronite blessing" in Numbers 6:24–26:

YHWH bless you and keep you; YHWH make his face shine on you and be gracious to you; YHWH turn his face toward you and give you peace.

- - הברו (כ)

-אֶנִיהו -

- ר יה)ו(

- - בָעה -

- שיברכ

יהוה ו

(י)שמרכ

יאר   יה

(וה)   פניו

(אל)יכ וי

שמ לך ש

לו (מ) - -

- - - - -

- -   - -

- - כמ - -

- - - - - -

-ור-נ-

- - - - -

Figure 11. Silver amulet from Ketef Hinnom. *Left to right:* the amulet, a tracing, and a transcription.

The text is very fragmentary, however, and it displays some differences from Numbers 6:24–26. Thus, although we may talk in terms of a common tradition, we are not justified in regarding this as a Bible text from biblical times.

The oldest surviving manuscripts containing New Testament texts come from the second century. They are papyrus fragments that contain individual scriptures of the New Testament, indicating that these scriptures were originally composed and transmitted as single texts. The oldest of these is usually considered to be Papyrus 52, presumed to date from the second half of the second century, which contains some verses from the Gospel according to John. The first manuscripts containing several texts date from the third century. These are compilations of either Paul's letters or the Gospels (sometimes including the Acts of the Apostles). There is no sign of any consolidation of these collections prior to the great Bible codices of the fourth century. This, then, is clear proof that the New Testament arose from individual collections, which in their turn are based on the compilation of what were originally single texts.

The earliest evidence of a more extensive collection of the letters of Paul is a papyrus codex from the early third century (Papyrus 46), while the four gospels and the Acts of the Apostles can be found in a codex dating from the mid-third century (Papyrus 45) (Figures 12 and 13).

Other codices have been found that contain two letters of Paul (e.g., Papyrus 30 from the third century, with the two Letters to the Thessalonians) or two gospels (e.g., Papyrus 75, likewise from the third century, with the Gospels of Luke and John).

One important distinguishing feature of Christian manuscripts is the presence of *nomina sacra,* or sacred words.[57] This term describes an abbreviated way of writing key terms that appear frequently in the texts, principally "God," "Jesus," "Christ," and "Lord"—to which were later added "Father," "Cross," "Heaven," "Man," and a number of others. The terms were mostly abbreviated to just two or three letters (the starting letters, the letters beginning and ending the word, or even the first letter, a middle letter, and the final letter), above which a line was drawn (Figure 14). The scribes who wrote the manuscripts had different ways of executing these *nomina sacra.* They are also found in other Christian manuscripts such as the Egerton Papyrus, which is thought to date from the late second or early third century and belongs to the Jesus tradition outside of the New Testament. *Nomina sacra* are also found in non-Greek manuscripts, such as those in Coptic and Latin. The staurogram is a very particular form of *nomen sacrum* that combines the Greek letters *tau* and *rho* to represent the words "Cross" (*staurós*) and "crucify" (*stauróô*) (Figure 15).

Although it has been much discussed, it is still unclear why Christians used *nomina sacra.* In any event, we know that the term for these abbreviations was not introduced until the early twentieth century. This form of writing was evidently intended to emphasize certain concepts. The background to it may lie in the adoption in some Greek manuscripts of the Hebrew name for God written in the form "YHWH," without vowels, to indicate its special nature. Another factor that may have played a part was the tendency during

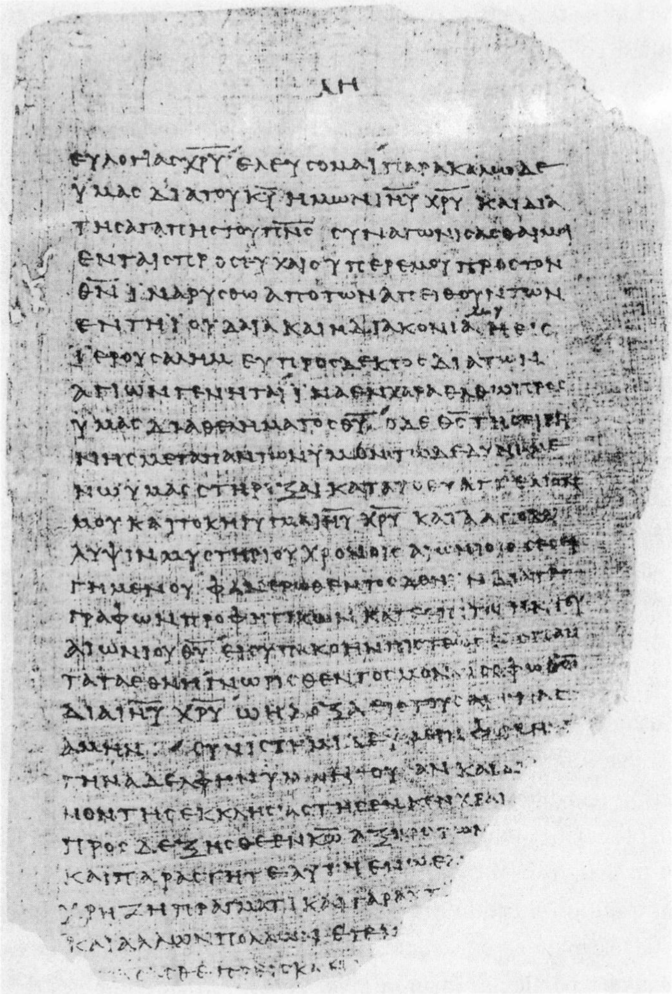

Figure 12. Papyrus 46 (Papyrus Michigan 6238), dating from the early third century, contains letters of Paul. Seen here is part of his Letter to the Romans, 15:29–33 and 16:25–27.

the period of the Roman Empire to write the names and honorary titles of rulers in abbreviated form on inscriptions and coins. The name of Jesus as the *nomen sacrum* IHS (the first three Greek letters of the name "Jesus": *iota, eta,* and *sigma*) and as the symbol ☧—formed by superimposing the first two letters, *chi* and *rho,* of the Greek word *Christos*—both came to be used in

Figure 13. Papyrus 45 (Chester Beatty Papyrus I) from the mid-third century contains the four gospels and the Acts of the Apostles. The section shown here is Matthew 25:41–26:18.

Figure 14. Papyrus 72 (Papyrus Bodmer VIII) from the third or fourth century, with the end of the First Letter of Peter and the beginning of the Second Letter. This codex is an arbitrary collection of texts, which includes, alongside the letters of Peter, the Birth of Mary (or Protevangelium of James), the Third Letter to the Corinthians, the Letter of Jude, and various other early Christian texts. The writing of the *nomina sacra* for God and Jesus Christ is clearly visible. The codex thus demonstrates that this system was not used just in "biblical" manuscripts in the narrow sense.

many contexts other than Bible manuscripts, for instance on gravestones, as ornamental features in rooms of state, or on church buildings.

Scriptures or individual verses of the New Testament have been found in the form of amulets, or miniature codices.[58] For example, an amulet dating from the third or fourth century that was found at Oxyrhynchus in Upper Egypt was inscribed with the opening words of the Gospel according to Mark.[59] Prefacing this is the exhortation: "Read the beginning of the Gospel and behold!" Then come the first words of Mark's gospel: "The beginning of the gospel of Jesus, the Christ," with the words "Jesus" and "Christ" written as *nomina sacra*.[60] The beginning of Mark's gospel on the amulet is represented as the literal start of the gospel, and accordingly the meaning of the text that follows changes. The sentence "As it is written in Isaiah the prophet: 'I will send my messenger ahead of you, who will prepare your way,'" which in the Gospel of Mark refers to John the Baptist as the forerunner of Jesus Christ, becomes here an assurance to the wearer of the amulet of protection by a messenger (or angel) of God.

Figure 15. Papyrus 75 (Papyrus Bodmer XIV–XV) is thought to date from the third century. Seen here are the end of the Gospel of Luke and the beginning of the Gospel of John. The papyrus is an early example of two gospels contained in the same codex. Luke 14:27 in this manuscript includes an example of the staurogram.

A second example concerns a small (5.2 × 4 cm) amulet, inscribed on both sides with the text of the Lord's Prayer.[61] On the papyrus, which is preserved in only fragmentary form, are the pleas, "Your will be done, on earth as it is in heaven. Give us today our daily bread. And forgive us our debts." The text stops after the plea for forgiveness, which may indicate that shorter versions of the prayer were in circulation at this time. The Lord's Prayer is often found on Christian objects—amulets, wooden tablets, potsherds, and the like—which points to the great popularity of this prayer and the protective role associated with it.[62]

Early Christian codices were small-format books, generally no more than 10 cm in height, which contained verses from Christian writings (both canonical and noncanonical) and from books of the Old Testament, especially Psalms.[63] Because of their fragmentary state of preservation, it is no longer possible to determine how much text was on these codices. Nonetheless, in spite of their small format, they could contain quite a lot. Of the fifteen extant miniature codices with texts from the New Testament, four contain verses from the Gospel of John and three contain verses from the book of Revelation, while the remainder derive from a variety of sources: two from the Gospel of Matthew, and one apiece from the Gospel of Mark, 1 Corinthians, Galatians, James, Jude, and 2 John.

A well-known example of a noncanonical text is Oxyrhynchus Papyrus 840. "Papyrus" is something of a misnomer, since the document is actually a small parchment (vellum) sheet from the fourth century, on which is written the episode of an encounter between Jesus and a high priest and Pharisee named Levi on the temple square in Jerusalem. Forty-five lines of text occupy an area of 5.5 × 5.2 cm on this sheet, which measures 8.6 × 7.2 cm overall. Twenty-two lines are written on the hair side of the vellum, and twenty-three on the flesh side.

These miniature codices provide proof that "pocket books" with biblical or nonbiblical texts were produced for personal use in early Christian times. They were clearly meant for private reading and possibly, like amulets, were carried around as a way of ensuring divine protection. More miniature codices with nonbiblical texts have survived than those with biblical scriptures.[64] This may be purely fortuitous. It does, however, indicate that the distinction between "canonical" and "apocryphal" texts did not play a significant role for early Christians in their personal worship.

Canonical, Pseudepigraphic, and Apocryphal Texts

The biblical scriptures were not written as canonical texts. Rather, they developed from particular situations in the history of Israel, Judaism, and early Christianity and were created for a variety of purposes: to preserve traditions, to interpret history, or to convey guidelines on how to live according to the will of God. They did not attain binding authority until they came to be seen as fundamental to the self-conception of Jews and Christians, as well as to their religious, social, and private lives. At that point they began to be collected, copied, translated, and disseminated. They were, and continue to be, read aloud during religious services, analyzed historically and philologically, and interpreted in sermons. In this way they acquired a significance in Judaism and Christianity that distinguished them from all other texts. This special nature is expressed in their designation as "canonical books."

The term "canon," which is more firmly anchored in Christianity than it is in Judaism, occurs twice in the New Testament in the sense of "standard, rule."[65] In his Letter to the Galatians, Paul uses it to summarize the core of the Christian faith:

> Neither circumcision counts for anything nor uncircumcision, but: new life. And those that live according to this standard [canon]: peace and mercy upon them and upon the Israel of God. (Galatians 6:15–16)[66]

A little later the term is used more generally to describe the precepts of faith, that is, the standards by which Christians live their lives.[67] From the mid-fourth century onward, the term "canon" was also used for the decrees issued by church councils (synods) and for the scriptures seen as having authoritative force within the Christian church.

Important evidence of the word's use in this latter sense comes from the thirty-ninth Festal Letter of Bishop Athanasius of Alexandria, written for Easter in the year 367. The letter deals with the disputes that raged throughout the fourth century about church doctrine. These arguments primarily concerned the relationship between God and Jesus Christ: Are God the Father and God the Son of the same substance (*homoousios*), or of similar substance (*homoiousios*)? Is there a hierarchy between God and Jesus Christ, or are both on the same level? Athanasius accuses his adversaries of having authored "so-called apocrypha" and draws a clear distinction between such writings and the "canonical and traditional scriptures attested as divine." He ends his letter by listing these latter texts, including twenty-two "Books of the Old Testament" and twenty-seven "Books of the New Testament." Athanasius also mentions works that, while "not included in the canon," may still be recommended to "those who newly join us, and who wish for instruction in the word of godliness." These are the books of Wisdom, Sirach, Esther, Judith, and Tobit, the *Didache* (Teaching of the Apostles), and the Shepherd of Hermas. Some years before, around 350, Athanasius had already voiced the opinion that the Shepherd of Hermas was "not part of the canon." The primary aim of this long text is to explore ethical questions. Its subject matter is presented as the revelation of an angel called "the shepherd" to the author Hermas.

In the 360s, the Council of Laodicea ruled, in its fifty-ninth Decree ("Canon"), that neither psalms composed by private individuals nor "any noncanonical books" could be read in church, but only the "Canonical Books of the Old and New Testaments." A sixtieth Canon was later added, containing a list of these approved scriptures.

The term "canon" thus served the purpose of identifying suitable writings to be read in church.[68] The main objective was to ensure the unity of the church and its teachings and to distinguish these from other beliefs denounced as heretical. As a consequence, the distinction between "canonical" and "apocryphal" in the history of the emergence of the Christian Bible is closely bound up with controversies about the legitimacy of doctrine and the authority of bishops and synods.

Where the origins of the Bible are concerned, the designations "apocryphal" and "pseudepigraphic" are not unproblematic. A number of factors come into play when assigning texts to these categories, and the process is not nearly as clear-cut as it might appear at first sight. In antiquity, many texts were published and distributed with a false author's name attached to them; these are called pseudepigraphic texts. Numerous Bible texts and other works, for example, have been wrongly attributed to Homer, Plato, Aristotle, or Hippocrates. Deuteronomy is presented as a farewell address by Moses to the Israelites, though its authorship has no more to do with Moses than does the "Assumption of Moses," a Jewish pseudepigraphic text dating from the first century CE. Some texts were retrospectively attributed to a famous person. This is the case, for example, with the biblical books of Proverbs and Song of Songs, as well as the later book of Wisdom, which was written in Greek. These all designate the name of the Israelite ruler King Solomon as their author. In the New Testament, some of the letters of Paul are pseudonymous, as are the letters bearing the names of Peter, John, James, and Jude. Other ancient Jewish and Christian scriptures, such as the apocalypses ascribed to Enoch, Ezra, and Baruch, as well as the epistles under the names of Clement and Barnabas, are pseudepigraphic.

The distinction between "canonical" and "pseudepigraphic" does not tell us which of these books were actually pseudepigraphic in origin. Rather, the category has been used since the eighteenth century to gather together a group of Jewish texts, only some of which are of a pseudepigraphic nature. They share this characteristic with many other texts, including biblical ones. This terminology served to demarcate them from the biblical Old Testament books as well as from scriptures designated as the Apocrypha. The Jewish Pseudepigrapha include the writings attributed to Enoch, the book of Jubilees, the *Letter of Aristeas,* the third and fourth books of Ezra, the third and fourth books of Maccabees, the Testaments of the Twelve Patriarchs, the Life of Adam and Eve, the conversion narrative Joseph and Aseneth, the Odes of Solomon, the Psalms of Solomon, the Apocalypse of Abraham, the Assumption of Moses, the Syrian Apocalypse of Baruch, the Sibylline Oracles, and several other writings.

The word "apocryphal" means "hidden," and it refers to books containing esoteric teachings.[69] The term was used in this sense in early Christian texts as a self-designation. For instance, at the beginning of the Gospel of Thomas, the scripture is characterized as containing the "hidden words of the living Jesus." Another early Christian text has the title "Apocryphon of (or according to) John." Early Christian theologians, however, invariably used the term to signify repudiated, "counterfeit" scriptures (see Chapter 6).[70] It was in this sense that the term found its way into lists of Christian canonical works.

In the Lutheran tradition the "Apocrypha of the Old Testament" currently denotes the scriptures (listed above) that were assembled as a discrete group by Martin Luther and are referred to as "deuterocanonical" texts in the Roman Catholic Church (following the model of the Septuagint). By contrast, the "Apocrypha of the New Testament" encompasses a wide range of texts; some were decried as "counterfeit" or "heretical" in ancient times, while others update the New Testament texts and enrich them with legendary traditions. These New Testament Apocrypha have been compiled since the eighteenth century, and various collections differ in their scope.

The terms "apocryphal" and "Apocrypha" should be used in a nuanced way when discussing the making of the Bible. For one thing, the Apocrypha of the Old Testament should be viewed differently from the Apocrypha of the New Testament in the history of the biblical canon. Furthermore, "apocryphal" did not have a consistent meaning in antiquity and the Middle Ages. Sometimes it denoted a text considered forged or heretical, while on other occasions it was used to draw a line between canonical and noncanonical scriptures. Finally, we must take into account the pejorative connotations that have long clung to this term. Thus, use of the term is problematic and misleading both historically and ecumenically in relation to the Old Testament. Where the nonbiblical books of the Old Testament are concerned, it would be more appropriate to refer to them not as apocryphal texts but as "deuterocanonical and related literature" or "Jewish texts from the Hellenistic-Roman period."[71] As for the New Testament, it would be more accurate to refer to "ancient Christian Apocrypha"—an umbrella term covering those texts that evolved within the same milieu as the New Testament but were not included in the Bible.

The different Christian denominations have approached the configurations of the books of the New Testament in a variety of ways. One early, major divergence divides the Eastern and Western churches. In the West, the Vulgate, which derives chiefly from the translations and revisions carried out by Jerome, is generally seen as the authorized version of the Bible, whereas the Eastern churches continued to use Greek Bibles—a situation that still pertains in part today. Moreover, in the Eastern churches, the exegeses of the church fathers—which are not restricted to a certain number, as they are in the West—continue to play an important role. On the question of which writings should be included within the Old Testament, differences have existed since the Reformation over the deuterocanonical, or apocryphal, scriptures. Luther made fundamental interventions in the biblical canon. Apart from the group of Apocrypha that he compiled himself, by picking the texts and assembling them in an arbitrary sequence, he also changed the order of the New Testament books.[72] He grouped together four texts—the Letter to the

Hebrews, the Letters of James and Jude, and the book of Revelation—placed them at the end, and did not give them sequential numbers, unlike the other New Testament writings. He did this because he believed that these books did not convey the central message of the Bible clearly enough (or, as he put it, did not "put forth Christ"—*Christum nicht treiben*).[73] The result was that Luther created an idiosyncratic and arbitrary order of biblical books, which today exists only in Lutheran Bibles.

In Judaism, a comparatively consistent view of the canon of holy scriptures has evolved since the late first century. Of the various different groups that emerged in Judaism from around the second century BCE—the Pharisees, the Sadducees, the Essenes, and the Zealots—only the Pharisees survived the destruction of Jerusalem and the Second Temple by the Romans in 70 CE.[74] As a result, the Pharisees had a decisive influence on the development of Rabbinic Judaism, and their view of what constituted the authoritative texts of Judaism prevailed. There is strong evidence that the Sadducees and the Essenes took a different view of what should be seen as Holy Writ. Because they rejected the belief in the resurrection that was rooted in the prophetic and apocalyptic scriptures (for example, Mark 12:18; Acts of the Apostles 23:8), the Sadducees focused on the Torah.[75] On the other hand, the Jewish community living in Qumran, widely regarded as having been a group of Essenes, considered other scriptures that went beyond the later Hebrew Bible as authoritative—for example the book of Jubilees and the writings attributed to Enoch (see Chapter 4).[76]

Hence, in pre-Rabbinic Judaism, there was no generally accepted biblical canon. Although the concept of an authoritative collection of scriptures did exist at the time, the process of interpretation and appropriation is of fundamental importance for Judaism. The creation of a firmly circumscribed canon of authoritative texts is more characteristic of Christianity than Judaism, which is based on a living tradition that has to be repeatedly assimilated. Admittedly the two faiths are not diametrically opposed on this question, since a multitude of traditions that update the "canonical" texts are inherent within Christianity, too. In certain historical situations, as in the Reformist tradition, we may be justified in describing a strict antithesis between canonical and apocryphal texts, as well as between scripture and tradition. But we must also recognize that both Judaism and Christianity are ultimately based on a stock of tradition that was at no stage ever confined to "canonical" scriptures. When a particular body of writings becomes established as authoritative, this sets certain boundaries within which religious belief and a corresponding religious practice should operate. Yet within the environment of such scriptures, there have always been other texts and traditions that have played a significant role in the faith and lives of Jews and Christians and that placed the canonical scriptures on a broader base.

2

Scribal Culture

The Beginnings of the Hebrew Bible

The "books" of the Bible were not written as books of *the Bible* as such. These texts and collections of texts only gradually became books, and these in turn only became "biblical" over the course of time. In other words, the Bible's development as a book, its literary history, and its canonical history do not coincide, although they do overlap.[1] The scriptures of the Bible came into being in extremely diverse contexts. They were written down, collected, assembled, edited, and ultimately canonized during the first millennium BCE.

The Bible itself paints quite a different picture of its own creation. The heart of the Old Testament, the Torah, contains the revelation that God imparted to Moses on Mount Sinai. The Bible thus ascribes what it portrays as its oldest texts to divine authority. In this view, the canonical history and the literary history synchronize. Through the image of the revelation on Mount Sinai, biblical tradition presents Moses as the author of the Torah. Yet the Torah itself acknowledges Moses's authorship of only certain sections of biblical scripture. For instance, according to Exodus 17:14, Moses supposedly recorded the battle of the Israelites against the nation of Amalek, and in Exodus 24:4 he is cited as writing down the Covenant Code. Exodus 34:28 states that Moses wrote the second version of the Ten Commandments after he destroyed the first, which God himself had inscribed on tablets of stone. Numbers 33:2 recounts how Moses documented the stages in the journey of the Israelites through the desert. He is described in Deuteronomy 31:9 as writing down the Deuteronomic Code (the law code set out in chapters 12–26 of that book), and in Deuteronomy 31:22 as composing the Song of Moses (Deuteronomy 32).

The Torah itself does not take the view that Moses wrote the entire Torah. This conclusion is, rather, implied in the formulation used by later biblical texts, which speak of the "Torah (Law) of Moses" (see, for example, Daniel 9:11 and 13, Ezra 3:2 and 7:6, and Nehemiah 8:1). But even the Babylonian Talmud, which came into existence between the second and sixth centuries CE, maintains that the last seven verses of the Torah (Deuteronomy 34:6–12) originated not from Moses but from Joshua (bBB 14b–15a), since Moses's death and burial are described in them. However great a figure Moses may be in the Torah, he cannot possibly have recorded his own death. And so, on the grounds of the logic of the narrative alone, the Torah cannot derive in its entirety from Moses.

It is also impossible to historically attribute certain parts of the Torah to Moses. Moses was in all likelihood a historical figure, but during his supposed lifetime there was no such language as Hebrew, whose alphabetic script first developed from Phoenician.[2] In addition, literary and historical analysis of the Torah has demonstrated beyond doubt that its texts come from the first millennium BCE, not the second.[3] That means that the production of biblical literature could not have begun during the pre-state era of Israel and Judah. Nonetheless, it is highly likely that extensive oral transmission of proverbs, stories, and songs took place during this period, and that these may well have found their way into the Bible in one form or another.

The Bible describes the reigns of Kings David and Solomon (ca. 1000 BCE), the first rulers of Israel and Judah, as being especially culturally vibrant. This period is regarded as the golden founding age of Israel. According to the Bible, David and Solomon presided over a politically, militarily, economically, and culturally successful major empire. David and Solomon are depicted not just as monarchs, but also as authors: no fewer than seventy-three of the psalms are ascribed to David, while the scroll of psalms found in Cave 11 at Qumran attributes over four thousand texts to him.[4] The scroll passage reads:

Now David, son of Jesse, was wise, and he shined like the light of the sun. And he was a scribe and discerning, and blameless in all his ways before God and humankind. YHWH gave him a discerning and shining spirit, so that he wrote: psalms: 3,600; songs to sing before the altar over the daily perpetual offering for all the days of the year: 364. For the Sabbath offerings: 52 songs. For the new moon offerings, all the festival days, and the Day of Atonement [Yom Kippur]: 30 songs. The total for all the songs that he composed was 446. Also, songs for making music on intercalary days: 4. And the sum total was 4,050. (11QPsalm[a] 27:2–10)[5]

The first book of Kings asserts that Solomon composed three thousand proverbs and that his songs numbered one thousand and five (1 Kings 4:32). In addition, the opening lines of three scriptures traditionally identify him as their author: Proverbs, Ecclesiastes (Qohelet) and the Song of Solomon.

The archeological and historical reconstruction of the period of David's and Solomon's reigns reveals a very different picture from that painted in the Bible. There is no evidence of a grand, flourishing empire capable of producing great literature. No discoveries have been made of monumental edifices that would point to a sophisticated state infrastructure, nor have any extensive epigraphic primary texts come to light suggesting the existence of an advanced system of writing. The political and military expansion that the Bible claims for the reign of David (2 Samuel 8:2–10) is inconceivable for this period. The total population of Israel and Judah at that time, likely about 55,000, would have raised an army of at most 1,500 men, an insufficiently large force to conquer or control a region of this size. The supposed expansion is based on a retrospective extrapolation of later circumstances, most probably under Jeroboam II (781–742 BCE).[6] David's and Solomon's reigns represent an important founding idea for the Bible—but one which is based more on creative recollection than on historical truth.[7]

Having said that, there is no reason to doubt that David and Solomon were real historical figures. Even from an internal Old Testament perspective, to claim otherwise would be unjustified, given that they form the basis of several bodies of tradition, above all the books of Samuel and Kings. Also, in 1992 researchers discovered an inscription from Tel Dan, dating from the ninth century BCE, which explicitly names the "House of David" (*byt dwd*), the dynasty initiated by David (Figure 16). It is out of the question that David would have been invented as the progenitor of a royal lineage a mere century after the time of his supposed reign. The Tel Dan inscription is an important piece of evidence for the historical reality of King David.[8]

The beginnings of a historically significant scribal culture in Israel and Judah can only be identified one or two centuries after David and Solomon.

Figure 16. The Tel Dan inscription from the ninth century BCE, in which the House of David is mentioned.

Surviving epigraphic evidence has enabled scholars to reconstruct at least the bare bones of this development, as described later in this chapter. First, however, we must cast an eye over the religious-historical climate within which biblical literature first emerged.

From Cult Religion to Book Religion

The oldest scriptures that eventually became the Bible were created within an environment where no appreciable religious function was assigned to texts. The stories, proverbs, songs, and prayers dating from the ninth and eighth centuries BCE that researchers have managed to reconstruct from the Bible are examples of literature rather than holy scripture. They evolved into scripture through a lengthy process. What scholars call a "cult religion" was practiced in Israel and Judah in the period before the Babylonian Exile (586–538 BCE). Religious observance centered on local shrines, and contact with the deity was maintained through sacrifices, votive offerings, and prayer. In the late pre-exile period, that is, the final decades of the seventh century BCE, cultic activities in Judah came to be focused on a single temple in Jerusalem. The Bible portrays this process as part of the religious reforms undertaken by Josiah (2 Kings 22–23).[9]

Of course, religious texts also had their place within this cult, but they did not play a key role in either its foundation or its normalization. Instead, like the religious paraphernalia in the temple, they simply formed one aspect of cultic activities. An example of this appears in Psalm 24:7–10:

> Lift up, oh gates, your heads, and become high, eternal entrances,
> and the king of glory enters.
> Who is the king of glory? YHWH, the strong and heroic, YHWH,
> the hero of the battle.
> Lift up, oh gates, your heads, and become high, eternal entrances,
> and the king of glory enters.
> Who is the king of glory? YHWH Sabaoth, he is the king of glory.[10]

This psalm clearly reveals its roots in cultic rites. It describes a procession—the entrance of God into his sanctum—accompanied by a cultic antiphony. The imagery used in this psalm suggests that God was symbolized here in the form of an effigy. Whether we can infer the presence of such a cult statue in the temple in Jerusalem is the subject of fierce debate and will no doubt remain forever unresolved. Another possibility is that Psalm 24 is couched in metaphorical language, evoking an object that was customary in the history of religion but was not physically present in Jerusalem. There is no disputing the fact that effigies of deities did exist during the period of monarchical rule in ancient Israel and Judah.[11] For instance, the goddess Asherah appears on numerous seal impressions and so-called pillar figurines, and in inscriptions from the ninth and eighth centuries BCE she is named as the partner of YHWH. In the Bible, she is known primarily as a figure to be shunned:

> Do not set up any wooden Asherah pole beside the altar you build to
> YHWH your God. (Deuteronomy 16:21)

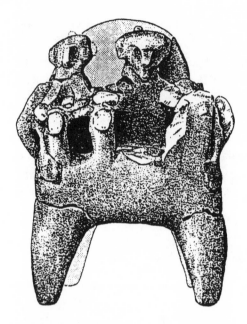

Figure 17. Terracotta figure from
the Judean Hills, possibly showing
YHWH and Asherah, eighth century
BCE.

A terracotta figure dating from the eighth century BCE that was found in
the Judean Hills may possibly depict YHWH and his partner Asherah
(Figure 17). However, this find came to light through the trade in ancient ar-
tifacts and has not been well documented archeologically.[12]

The tradition of the bull figures erected by King Jeroboam in the temples
at Bethel and Dan, in the kingdom of Israel, might suggest that YHWH was
also portrayed in the guise of a bull (Figure 18). The identification of these
bull effigies as "golden calves" in 1 Kings 12:28 (see also Exodus 32:4) is part
and parcel of the Bible's treatment of such graven images as abominations.
An Assyrian inscription of King Sargon II implies that the shrine at Samaria
(conquered by Sargon in 722 BCE) also contained cult statues:

> I [Sargon II] took as war booty 27,280 people, along with their chariots
> and their gods in whom they [the Samarians] trusted.[13]

As for Judah, YHWH was venerated at the shrine at Arad in the northern
Negev Desert in the form of a *matsevah*—a stone stele. Although the archeological evidence is not entirely clear, a ca. 90-cm-high red stone pillar may
well have served as the representation of a deity.[14]

Figure 18. Bronze statuette of a bull from the Samarian Hills, twelfth–eleventh centuries BCE.

Whichever interpretation of the imagery in Psalm 24 we opt for, it is evident that the religious cult, which operated through ritual objects, implements, and observances, gave rise to the text rather than vice versa. Moreover, a long religious-historical road lay ahead before this text was written: Judaism only became a "religion of the book"—that is, one whose core entailed the study of sacred texts—following the destruction of the Second Temple by the Romans in 70 CE. With the demise of the sacrificial cult of the temple, the faith shifted entirely to the study and celebration of the scriptures. And it was not until that stage that the concept of the Bible as a complete, authoritative collection of texts arose (see Chapter 6). Its texts had almost certainly been in religious use before this, but alongside many other documents. A strict dividing line between biblical and nonbiblical literature did not exist at that time, since there was as yet no such thing as the Bible.

And so the belief system of Israel and Judah changed gradually over the course of the first millennium BCE from a cult religion to a religion of the book. The destruction of the First Temple in 587 BCE played an important role as a catalyzing factor in this process.[15] The loss of the central place of worship laid the foundations of a religion that was no longer reliant upon ritual activity. The period of the Babylonian Exile was of fundamental significance for the emergence of the Bible and is often seen as the beginning of the era of "Judaism"—that is, the text-based form of the religion of ancient Israel and Judah, which committed these kingdoms to the Torah and to a belief in a single God (monotheism).

Although one might say that the Babylonian Exile is still going on, with a Jewish diaspora throughout the entire world, strictly speaking, it came to a close with the end of Babylonian (Assyrian) rule and the rise of Persian hegemony in the region. At that time, the people who had been deported from Israel and Judah were allowed to return home and rebuild the ruined temple in Jerusalem. The reconsecration of the new building marked the start of the Second Temple period (515 BCE–70 CE), whose most characteristic feature was the restoration of the practice of sacrificial offerings. Indeed, the business of sacrifice was probably organized on a far more extensive scale in the Second Temple than it had been in the First. Whereas beforehand sacrifices had mainly been confined to feast days, animals were sacrificed in large numbers on a daily basis. The practice of ritual sacrifice in Jerusalem became the central economic driving force of the city. Livestock merchants transported sheep and goats to the city, where prominent individuals wishing to make votive offerings purchased them and then handed them over for sacrificial slaughter at the temple. Because this activity was centralized in Jerusalem it was impossible for all but a few people to bring their own animals to be sacrificed at the temple. Everyone else was obliged to acquire their sacrificial offerings in the city. This temple-based economy forms the basis for the well-known scene of Jesus clearing the temple precincts of merchants and moneychangers:

> The Passover of the Jews was near, and Jesus went up to Jerusalem. And in the temple he encountered those selling cattle, sheep, and doves, and the moneychangers that sat there. Then he made a whip from cords and drove them all out of the temple, also the sheep and the cattle, and the money of the changers he poured out. He overturned the tables;

and to the sellers of doves he said: "Take this away from here! Do not make my father's house into a marketplace!" (John 2:13–16)[16]

Such clashes during the time of Jesus were clearly concerned not with holy scripture but rather with the ritual sacrifice practiced at the temple. By that time the books of the Hebrew Bible had already been completed and were no doubt present in the temple, yet they were not yet of central importance within the framework of the Jewish religion. That central position was still occupied by the temple in Jerusalem.

Apart from a hiatus from 587 to 515 BCE, then, the biblical period was characterized by the presence of a temple cult (a religion based on ritual sacrifice at the temple). Yet also in evidence at this time were a variety of texts and text collections, some of which gradually gained in significance while others sank into oblivion or were deliberately expunged. Only the most recent parts of the Hebrew Bible express the idea that texts could be granted sacred status and themselves become the subject of veneration. Nehemiah 8:5–8, for example, recounts a public reading of the Torah by Ezra. Because of its similarity to synagogue worship today, it is highly unlikely that this account dates from earlier than the second or third century BCE:

> Ezra opened the book. All the people could see him because he was standing above them; and as he opened it, the people all stood up. Ezra praised YHWH, the great God; and all the people lifted their hands and responded, "Amen! Amen!" Then they bowed down and worshipped YHWH with their faces to the ground. The Levites—Jeshua, Bani, Sherebiah, Jamin, Akkub, Shabbethai, Hodiah, Maaseiah, Kelita, Azariah, Jozabad, Hanan and Pelaiah—instructed the people in the Law while the people were standing there. They read from the Book of the Law of God, making it clear and giving the meaning so that the people understood what was being read.

One consequence of the biblical texts assuming an increasingly authoritative role within Judaism is that other writings produced in ancient Israel and Judah were not preserved. For instance, it is highly likely that the traditions of prophetic soothsaying from the pre-exile period were recorded in written form. Jeremiah 28 gives an account of a disagreement between the prophets Jeremiah and Hananiah. Unlike Jeremiah, Hananiah believes that the Babylonian occupying forces will withdraw from Israel and Judah. It is quite conceivable that Hananiah's prophecy was once committed to writing but was not handed down. The Bible itself acknowledges and names several texts that are lost today, such as the book of the Wars of YHWH (Numbers 21:14), the book of Jashar (Joshua 10:13; 2 Samuel 1:18), the Book of the Song (1 Kings 8:53 in the Septuagint), and the books of the Annals of Solomon (1 Kings 11:41), the Annals of the Kings of Israel (1 Kings 14:19), and the Annals of the Kings of Judah (1 Kings 14:29).[17] Even though some of these titles may be fictitious, they are surely not all invented. We do not know why these scriptures no longer exist. It may be that they were eliminated because they did not harmonize with the fundamental theological beliefs of post-exile Judaism.

Thus, although the Hebrew Bible contains an important part of the literature produced in ancient Israel and Judah, it represents only a sample of that body of work. The existing texts must have survived because of their historical influence. In other words, the scriptures that found their way into the Bible are those that proved their worth as working texts in the Second Temple in Jerusalem and as Holy Scripture in the temple school.

The Rise of a Scribal Culture in the Levant

The growth of a scribal culture in Israel and Judah forms the cultural and historical background to the genesis of the Bible and its evolution into Holy Scripture.[18] The kingdoms of Israel and Judah were relative latecomers in the Near East. The great empires on the Nile, as well as on the Tigris and Euphrates Rivers, were some two to three thousand years older and thus shaped the cultural history of the region far more definitively. The American Egyptologist James Henry Breasted coined the term Fertile Crescent to refer to the arc of cultivated land between Egypt and Mesopotamia, in the middle of which were Israel and Judah.[19]

The preeminence of these older civilizations was largely overlooked in the theological and historical research of the nineteenth and early twentieth centuries. Thanks to the powerful historical influence of the Bible, the ancient

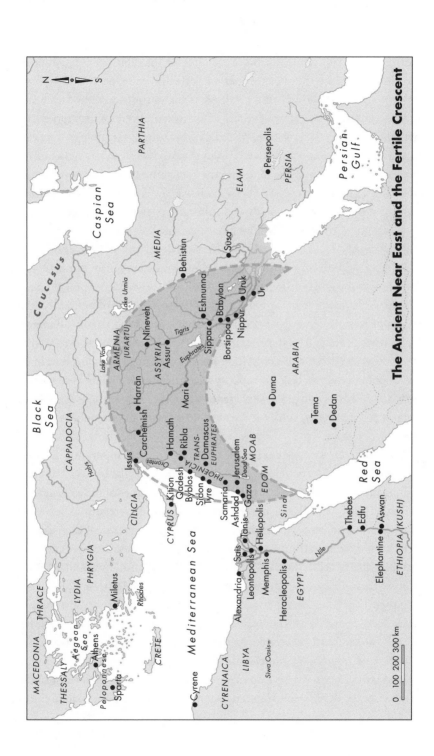

The Ancient Near East and the Fertile Crescent

MACEDONIA

THRACE

THESSALY

Athens
Sparta
Peloponnese

Aegean Sea

PHRYGIA

LYDIA

Miletus

Rhodes

CRETE

Black Sea

CAPPADOCIA

Halys

CILICIA

Issus

CYPRUS

Kition

Mediterranean Sea

Cyrene

CYRENAICA

LIBYA

Siwa Oasis

Alexandria

Sais

Leontopolis

Tanis

Heliopolis

Memphis

Heracleopolis

EGYPT

Nile

Ashdod

Gaza

Samaria

Sidon

Tyre

Byblos

PHOENICIA

Jerusalem

Dead Sea

MOAB

EDOM

Sinai

Red Sea

Thebes

Edfu

Aswan

Elephantine

ETHIOPIA (KUSH)

Qadesh

Damascus

TRANS.
EUPHRATES

Hamath

Ribla

Orontes

Carchemish

Harrān

Mari

Euphrates

ASSYRIA

Assur

Nineveh

Tigris

ARMENIA
(URARTU)

Lake Van

Lake Urmia

MEDIA

Behistun

Caucasus

Caspian Sea

PARTHIA

Susa

ELAM

PERSIA

Persepolis

Persian Gulf

ARABIA

Duma

Tema

Dedan

Eshnunna

Babylon

Sippar

Borsippa

Nippur

Uruk

Ur

N

S

Near East was viewed chiefly as the backdrop to the Bible. Its designation as the Holy Land in writing of this period perfectly expresses this viewpoint. Egypt and Mesopotamia were regarded as the periphery, while Israel and Judah occupied center stage. Biblical scholarship concerned itself primarily with the literature of revelation, while Egyptology and Assyriology were cast in the role of ancillary disciplines. But in the twentieth century, scholars researching the history of the Bible and the ancient Near East showed that the historical significance of these two regions was the exact opposite. Israel and Judah did not become politically and culturally relevant until after the great civilizations of the region had long been established and were already setting the agenda for the cultural and historical development of the region.

Writing systems appear to have developed independently in Egypt and Mesopotamia during the fourth millennium BCE. Their development marks what is perhaps the most significant break in the history of humanity. The advent of writing demarcates prehistory from history, which is to all intents and purposes defined by the existence of written sources for its reconstruction.[20] Yet the introduction of writing was of fundamental importance in an anthropological sense, too. The capacity to consign human memory to written texts and to amass and preserve these texts for future generations broadened human potential enormously and lent rapid impetus to the evolution of the human species.

The forms of writing developed in Egypt and Mesopotamia utilized logograms—characters that signify entire words or syllables. With the development of the alphabetic writing system, which was established primarily by the Phoenicians, writing became a much simpler exercise.[21] Now people only needed to learn around twenty or so characters instead of thousands.

Hebrew developed from Phoenician and, at first, existed in a variety of dialectal forms (Israelite, Judaic, Gileadite, Moabite, Ammonite, and so on).[22] Both in their form and their naming, the letters of the Hebrew alphabet reveal their origins in a hieroglyphic script. For instance, the letter *aleph* signifies "cattle" and takes the form of a cow's head (rotated 90 degrees), *bet* means "house" and takes a corresponding form, and *gimel* derives from "camel" and resembles a camel's hump.

As Aramaic began to develop into a lingua franca in the Near East in the ninth century BCE, Hebrew became standardized and transformed into a language of the educated classes, with a corresponding degree of uniformity. This explains, at least in part, why the Hebrew of the Hebrew Bible, for all its many variations in detail—particularly the distinction between Classical Biblical Hebrew and Late Biblical Hebrew—displays a remarkable consistency over the centuries during which its texts were composed.[23] Hebrew is written in a script where only the consonants are shown. In late antiquity, starting in the fifth century BCE, the practice began of filling in the missing vowels by adding dots to the consonants. This was done in order to ensure the correct pronunciation and interpretation of biblical texts. Other symbols aimed at giving the text greater structure were also added at this time. Because Hebrew texts had previously been entirely unpunctuated, we cannot be absolutely certain how biblical Hebrew was pronounced.[24] Here is the first sentence of the Bible, "In the beginning, God created the heaven and the earth," shown in unpunctuated and punctuated Hebrew:

בראשית ברא אלהים את השמים ואת הארץ

בְּרֵאשִׁית בָּרָא אֱלֹהִים אֵת הַשָּׁמַיִם וְאֵת הָאָרֶץ

Scholars have determined, based on surviving inscriptions, that the writing direction of Hebrew (from right to left) was established in the ninth century BCE. This is an indication that longer texts, which demanded such a convention, were being created at this time. Up to the third century BCE, Old Hebrew script, which took many different forms, was in widespread use. This script was still occasionally used in later periods, for instance by the Samaritans, the descendants of the former kingdom of Israel (Figure 19). The Old Hebrew script featured Phoenician-style letters that were later transformed into the blocky characters of Hebrew square script.

The scrolls found at Qumran on the Dead Sea, which were written in the period between 200 BCE and 68 CE, contain some texts that use the Old Hebrew script in a consciously archaic manner. In addition, some of the scrolls include the tetragrammaton YHWH in Old Hebrew script (Figure 20). This script is used consistently in only a few scrolls—in particular, Leviticus and Job (Figure 21). The fact that these two books are written in Old Hebrew no doubt has to do with their legendary antiquity: Leviticus goes back to Moses, while Job is a figure whom the narrative setting of the book places in the time

Figure 19. Text of the Samaritan Pentateuch of 1215–1216 CE. Shown here is Numbers 34:26–35:8.

of the Patriarchs—the world of Abraham, Isaac, and Jacob. The appearance of YHWH in Old Hebrew within a text that is otherwise composed in Hebrew square script suggests that the name of God was no longer uttered at that time. The change in script style indicates to the reader to pause and then resume reading again after the name of God. This convention was not yet standardized, however: many texts from Qumran also display the name of God in square script, while others insert four dots within the text to symbolize the tetragrammaton.

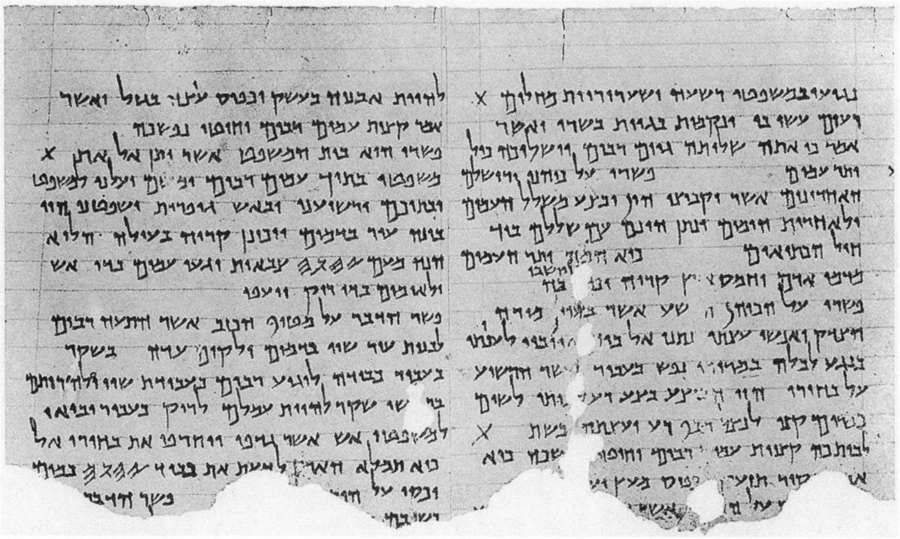

Figure 20. The Habbakuk Commentary from Cave 1 at Qumran, showing the tetragrammaton in Old Hebrew script (see left panel, line 7 and last full line).

Hebrew square script likely started to gain ground gradually along with the spread of Aramaic, which was widely used as a language of administration throughout the Persian Empire. The oldest example of square script can be found in the "Tobias" inscription in a cave at Iraq al-Amir in eastern Jordan (third century BCE) (for comparisons of different scripts, see Figure 22).

The preliminary stages of this process can be observed in texts from the Jewish military colony on the island of Elephantine in the Nile near the modern city of Aswan (Figure 23). These texts date from the fifth and early fourth centuries BCE.[25]

Based on the inscriptions that have been discovered from the tenth and ninth centuries BCE, it is clear that the cultural evolution of script was not very far advanced in Israel and Judah at that time. One of the oldest written documents known from ancient Israel is the so-called Gezer Calendar (after Gezer, the location near Jerusalem where it was found), dating from the tenth century BCE (Figure 24). Its text, in translation, runs as follows:

Two months of harvest,
two months of sowing,

אלהיכם . מפנני]
מאלהיך . אני . יהו[ה]
את[ו] . כאזרח . מכם

ישאו
[א]חיו . נדה . היא . [ער]ות
[ושמרת[ם . את . כל . חקתי . ואת . כל .
אתכם . הארץ . אשר . אני .
תלכו
אל[ה]

ישראל
. בניו .
. אשר .
[לדרתיכ]ם . כל . איש . אשר .
[א]שר . י[קדישו] . בני .
[מלפ]ני . [א]נ]ני]

Figure 21. Fragments of the book of Leviticus in Old Hebrew script from Cave 11 at Qumran.

two months of late planting,
one month of reaping flax,
one month of reaping barley,
one month of reaping and measuring,
two months of vine-tending,
one month of summer fruit.[26]

	Gezer	Inschriften	Kursiv	Buch-schrift	Münzen	Samaritanisch	Quadrat-schrift
1							א
2							ב
3							ג
4							ד
5							ה
6							ו
7							ז
8							ח
9							ט
10							י
11							כ
12							ל
13							מ
14							נ
15							ס
16							ע
17							פ
18							צ
19							ק
20							ר
21							ש
22							ת

Figure 22. Old Hebrew alphabet table. The columns, from left to right, show (including variations), the script of the Gezer Calendar, inscriptions, cursive Hebrew, book script, coin inscriptions, Samaritan script, and Hebrew square script.

Figure 23. Papyrus from Elephantine in Upper Egypt, with the letter to Bagohi,
Persian governor of the province of Yehud (Judah), 408 BCE.

It is unclear whether this text is truly a Hebrew document, since its language
shows strong influences from Phoenician.[27] The individual letters are formed
in a quite rudimentary fashion.

The inscription on a jug found in Jerusalem on the Ophel (the biblical name
for an elevated, usually fortified part of a city) differs markedly from that of
the Gezer Calendar. This text comes from the eleventh or tenth century BCE
and contains eight letters (m, q, p, $ḥ$, n, m, $ṣ$, n), though it is unclear in which
direction it should be read (Figure 25).[28]

Equally puzzling is the so-called Ba'al inscription from Beit Shemesh near
Jerusalem, which scholars have dated to the twelfth century BCE (Figure 26).[29]
The name "Ba'al" is clearly visible, but the rest of the inscription is hard to
decipher. The text displays an inexpert script similar to that found on the
Ophel jug inscription.

An ostracon found at Khirbet Qeiyafa, an archeological site above the
Valley of Elah in the Shephelah region of the Judean Hills, is usually dated
to the tenth century BCE (Figure 27).[30] Although a variety of translations

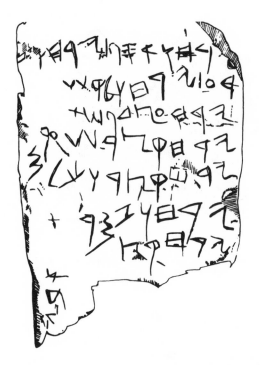

Figure 24. The Gezer Calendar, from the tenth century BCE.

Figure 25. A potsherd from the Ophel in Jerusalem, dating from the eleventh or tenth century BCE.

Figure 26. The Ba'al inscription from Beit Shemesh, ca. twelfth century BCE.

Figure 27. An ostracon from Khirbet Qeiyafa, ca. tenth century BCE.

have been proposed, the content of this ostracon continues to be obscure. Individual words can be made out, but a clear reading is not possible. In any case, since it is debatable whether Khirbet Qeiyafa was a Jewish site at all, no conclusions can be drawn from this ostracon about the evolution of a scribal culture in Judah.[31]

A more significant artifact is the so-called Zayit stone discovered at Tel Zayit, also in the Shephelah region of Judea. This limestone boulder inscribed with an abecedary has been dated to the tenth century BCE.[32] It contains all twenty-two letters of the Hebrew alphabet, though not in the order that later became customary. For example, *waw* is placed before *he, khet* before *zayin,* and *lamed* before *kaph.* Such variations in the sequence of letters are not unknown. Although the switching of *lamed* and *kaph* is the result of an error, the other two differences are known from other abecedaries. This text appears to represent an educational writing exercise—a quite remarkable phenomenon for rural Judah in the tenth century BCE.

Another important find revealing how a scribal culture evolved is the ink wall inscription found in 1967 at Tell Deir Alla, a small settlement in eastern Jordan close to the confluence of the Zarqa River (known as the Jabbok in biblical times) and the Jordan River (Figure 28).[33] Archeologically, the text can be dated to the ninth century BCE. As a result of earthquake damage it has survived in only fragmentary form, but one clearly recognizable feature is mention of the prophet "Balaam, the son of Beor," who is known from the Bible (Numbers 22–24). There is much evidence to suggest that the building where this inscription was found was a school for scribes. Because the inscription is written in a dialect that is close to Aramaic and appears to have no religious or historical affinities with Israel or Judah, we may assume that this school was an outpost of Aram, a region in and around present-day Syria.

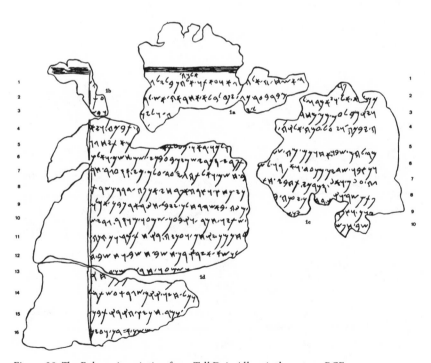

Figure 28. The Balaam inscription from Tell Deir Alla, ninth century BCE.

Even so, the inscription is highly significant for understanding the development of scribal culture in ancient Israel, inasmuch as it demonstrates that quite extensive texts could be produced as early as the ninth century BCE, even in the political peripheries (Figure 29).[34]

The so-called Mesha Stele, which was found in 1868 in Dibon, eastern Jordan, south of present-day Amman, points in a similar direction.[35] The stele, which is dated to the ninth century BCE, contains over thirty-four lines of text that provide information about the history of the kingdom of Moab under King Mesha, who is mentioned in the Bible (2 Kings 3:26–27). The Mesha Stele also names King Omri of Israel and the God of Israel, YHWH. The writing on the stele is in the Moabite language, which is closely related to ancient Hebrew.

The Tel Dan inscription, which likewise comes from the ninth century BCE, is also a triumphal royal inscription.[36] It can in all probability be traced back to King Hazael of the state of Aram-Damascus, who boasts that he killed Kings Joram and Ahaziah of the House of David, though in the Bible this impressive feat of arms is ascribed to Jehu (2 Kings 9). The text is in Aramaic.

The first unequivocally Hebrew inscription from ancient Israel and Judah is the Siloam inscription from the late eighth century BCE (Figure 30).[37] The

Figure 29. Wall inscriptions from Kuntillet ʿAjrud, ninth century BCE.

Figure 30. The Siloam inscription from the eighth century BCE.

text describes the construction of the Siloam Tunnel in Jerusalem, a subter-
ranean watercourse that runs from the Gihon Spring to the Pool of Siloam
and was excavated from both ends. The precise dating of both the tunnel and
the inscription, which was found in 1880 near the eastern mouth of the
tunnel, is uncertain. The Bible attributes the digging of the tunnel to King
Hezekiah of Judah (2 Kings 20:20 and 2 Chronicles 32:3–4, 30; see also Sirach
[Ecclesiasticus] 48:17), which is not out of the question in archeological terms
but is nonetheless unprovable.[38] Because the inscription does not mention a
king and was not installed at a public site, it is highly unlikely that it was created in an official context. This may indicate that the literacy of the Jewish
people was not confined, as is often assumed, to the caste of scribes. On the
basis of evidence such as this, it is conceivable that the process of writing
down biblical texts began in the ninth or eighth century BCE.[39] Even though
one should be circumspect in drawing conclusions from archeological
findings, such as the Balaam inscription from Tell Deir Alla, this general
insight still remains significant, especially since it tallies with two further
observations.

First, written prophecy arose in Israel and Judah at a time when the culture of writing had developed enough to enable the creation of literary texts—
namely, in the eighth century BCE. The nineteenth-century German biblical scholar Julius Wellhausen was the first to note that Elijah does not have
a book of his own, in contrast with Isaiah.[40] The interval between these
prophets saw the rise of a scribal culture so far-reaching that, in addition to
Isaiah, it also embraced Amos, Hosea, and their commentators.

Second, it was around this same time that ancient Middle Eastern sources
began to refer to Israel, and somewhat later Judah, as states.[41] This in turn
implies a certain level of cultural development, including scribal activity.

This stocktaking of the archeological evidence, which is somewhat meager,
should not mislead us into thinking that a scribal culture came about for the
very first time in the geographical region of Israel and Judah some two or
three centuries after the reign of David and Solomon, or that it emerged out
of nothing. Even during the Bronze Age, Jerusalem was a relatively important city.[42] The Amarna Letters—clay tablets found in Egypt that date to the
fourteenth century BCE—indicate that extensive diplomatic correspondence
went on between Abdi-Heba, the ruler of Jerusalem, and Pharaoh Akhenaten
in el-Amarna (Figure 31). This demonstrates the existence of a well-established
scribal culture in Jerusalem by this time.[43]

Figure 31. The Amarna Letters were written in the fourteenth century BCE. The ones shown here come from Jerusalem and were addressed to Pharaoh Akhenaten in el-Amarna.

Figure 32. Fragment of the Gilgamesh Epic from Megiddo, fourteenth century BCE.

During the Bronze Age, an advanced urban civilization existed not only in Jerusalem but in the Levant as a whole, including scribes who had been trained on the basis of classical texts. Compelling evidence of this is provided by a clay tablet fragment of the Epic of Gilgamesh from the fourteenth century BCE that was unearthed in Megiddo, near Nazareth (Figure 32). The fragment was made of clay from that region, meaning that the tablet had not been imported from Mesopotamia but had been manufactured in southern Judah and had therefore in all likelihood been inscribed in Judah itself.[44]

No direct line of descent exists, however, between this Bronze Age culture and scribal activity in Israel and Judah, which, as we have already seen, did not begin to develop until the ninth and eighth centuries BCE. The city kingdoms in Canaan went into decline toward the end of the Bronze Age (late eleventh century BCE). Twentieth-century scholars often associated this demise with the rise of the Philistines, or "Sea Peoples," who invaded this region. A number of other factors are now thought to have played a part, including climatic events such as a prolonged period of drought—a theory that has been corroborated by archeobotanical studies.[45]

The scribal schools that we believe existed in the kingdoms of Israel and Judah would have educated bureaucrats and priests.[46] Their duties involved not only dealing with texts of an administrative nature, but most likely also writing and copying traditional material for the religious and cultural spheres—primarily for educational purposes.[47] Compelling evidence for the existence of such schools is provided by the relatively high degree of standardization (especially in script and orthography) in epigraphs written during the monarchical period, which lasted from the reign of Saul in the eleventh century BCE to that of Jehoiachin in the sixth century BCE. Yet it is unclear quite how we are to picture these "schools." They are mentioned in the Bible only in Sirach (Ecclesiasticus) 51:23 and Acts of the Apostles 19:9. The profession of scribe is well attested, however, both in the surviving epigraphic material and in the Bible.[48] The titles of "royal secretary" or "king's scribe" point to the fact that this form of training was probably carried out in the royal palace.[49] According to Jeremiah 36:12, a "scribe's chamber," or "secretary's room," was located within the palace. Military affairs were also documented by scribes, as witness the position of "scribe of the commander" (1 Kings 25:19; Jeremiah 52:25). New research into sixteen ostraca with a military content dating from the sixth century BCE, which were found in Arad, an important military base in the Negev Desert, indicates that literacy was widespread in the army at that time. Analysis of the text reveals that these ostraca were not the work of one professional scribe but that at least six separate hands must have been involved.[50] Thus, several members of the military unit appear to have been versed in the art of writing.

Literature of the Early Monarchical Period

Even if we assume that the earliest biblical texts were not written down until the ninth or eighth century BCE, this does not mean that their subject matter cannot be older. Many of the stories, songs, proverbs, and legal principles in the Bible are of a traditional nature and hark back to a long history of oral transmission. As a general rule, this history is hard to pin down, let alone to reconstruct in detail. Nonetheless, we should not underestimate the radical break involved in turning into scripture the traditions that have been passed down orally for generations. This process fixes the texts in a certain form of language and a particular sequence. People are then able to refer to them, and they can be interpreted and copied. This is exactly what happened to the literature of ancient Israel and Judah.[51]

The Two Kingdoms of Israel and Judah

To understand the beginnings of literary production during the monarchical period, we must draw a distinction between the two kingdoms of Israel and Judah. The Bible describes royal rule coming about as the result of the twelve tribes of Israel's wish for a king to rule over them after they settled in Canaan. Although this urge is condemned by the prophet Samuel and by God, Samuel finally grants it:

> But when they said, "Give us a king to lead us," this displeased Samuel; so he prayed to YHWH. And YHWH told him: "Listen to all that the people are saying to you; it is not you they have rejected, but they have rejected me as their king." (1 Samuel 8:6–7)

This negative appraisal of royal rule, which is placed in the Bible even before that rule begins, shows earthly kingship as being in direct competition with the rulership of God. The ground for this critical standpoint is laid in Joshua 24, which tells of the Israelites' choice of YHWH as their king: Joshua assembles all the tribes of Israel at Shechem, a traditional site for the election of kings (see 1 Kings 12:1), where they pledge to take YHWH as their God. Yet the theocratic perspective of Joshua is superimposed upon older interpretative passages in the following books, which take an unequivocally positive attitude toward secular kingship. This different, most likely older, perception of monarchy is evident, for example, in 1 Samuel 9:15–17:

> Now the day before Saul came, YHWH had revealed this to Samuel: "About this time tomorrow I will send you a man from the land of Benjamin. Anoint him ruler over my people Israel; he will deliver them from the hand of the Philistines. I have looked on my people, for their cry has reached me." When Samuel caught sight of Saul, YHWH said to him, "This is the man I spoke to you about; he will govern my people."

Monarchy is presented here as a way for God to save Israel from its enemies. Saul was duly anointed as king by Samuel. He was succeeded by David and Solomon, who both ruled from Jerusalem. For the Bible, this is the golden age of the combined monarchy; it is the subject of extensive treatment in the books of Samuel and Kings, as well as in the two books of Chronicles. The era of David and Solomon is presented as a glorious heyday not just in politics but also in culture and literature. According to 1 Kings 12, after the death of Solomon the northern tribes broke away from Judah, and the history of kingship is played out thereafter in the two realms of Israel and Judah. These two kingdoms come to an end respectively in 722 BCE (Israel) and 587 BCE (Judah). The northern kingdom of Israel is portrayed in the Bible as a godless realm. Because its rulers showed no reverence toward the central sanctuary in Jerusalem, not one of them is seen in a positive light. This suggests that the principal narrator of the books of Kings lived in Jerusalem (Judah). The southern kingdom of Judah is viewed far more favorably, even though complaints are sometimes voiced that the people of this realm continued to make sacrifices and burn incense on hilltops, acts that violated the prerogative of the temple in Jerusalem.

With the enormous increase in archeological research over the past four decades, this biblical view of the relationship between the kingdoms of Israel and Judah has been radically altered.[52] The Bible presents Jerusalem, as the site of David and Solomon's royal residence and the center of cult worship, as the capital of their extensive realm. It treats the northern kingdom of Israel as an illegitimate state that had seceded from the empire and bases its greatness on religious syncretism. Archeological finds from Israel and Judah indicate a very different state of affairs, however.[53] Politically and economically, the northern kingdom of Israel appears to have developed earlier, more rapidly, and more robustly than the southern kingdom of Judah. Its architecture, the existence of certain luxury items, the epigraphic evidence, and sundry mentions of Israel and Judah in sources other than the Bible all paint a picture of Israel's advanced development. This finding makes sense in a geopolitical context too, since Israel was far more centrally located as a transportation hub than Judah, which had Jerusalem, in the Judean Hills, at its center. The relationship between north and south is therefore quite different in the historical record than in the Bible.

At the same time, we should picture the beginnings of royal rule in both the north and the south as far more low-key phenomena than the Bible would have us believe. The kingdom of Saul, David, and Solomon and their successors can be characterized as a patrimonial realm guided principally by a military commander and those who depended on his patronage.[54] A more

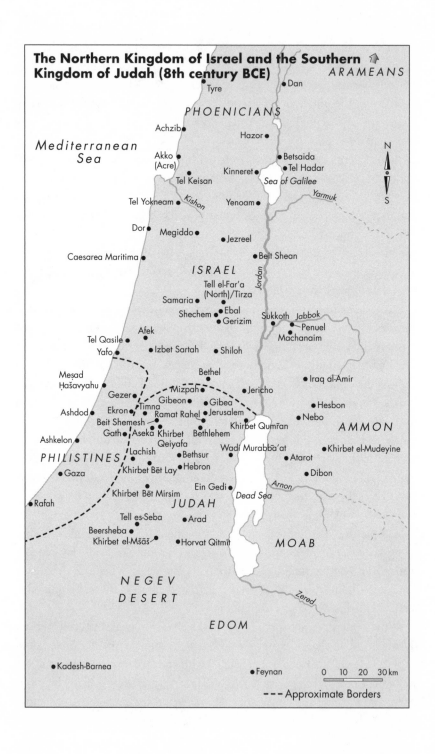

The Northern Kingdom of Israel and the Southern Kingdom of Judah (8th century BCE)

ARAMEANS

Mediterranean Sea

PHOENICIANS

Tyre
Dan
Achzib
Hazor
Akko (Acre)
Betsaida
Kinneret
Tel Hadar
Tel Keisan
Sea of Galilee
Yarmuk
Tel Yokneam
Kishon
Yenoam
Dor
Megiddo
Jezreel
Caesarea Maritima
Beit Shean
ISRAEL
Jordan
Tell el-Far'a (North)/Tirza
Samaria
Shechem
Ebal
Gerizim
Sukkoth
Jabbok
Penuel
Machanaim
Afek
Tel Qasile
Izbet Sartah
Shiloh
Yafo
Bethel
Meṣad Ḥašavyahu
Iraq al-Amir
Mizpah
Jericho
Gezer
Gibeon
Gibea
Hesbon
Ekron
Timna
Ramat Rahel
Jerusalem
Nebo
Ashdod
Khirbet Qumran
AMMON
Beit Shemesh
Gath
Aseka
Khirbet Qeiyafa
Bethlehem
Wadi Murabba'at
Khirbet el-Mudeyine
Ashkelon
Lachish
Bethsur
Atarot
PHILISTINES
Khirbet Bēt Lay
Hebron
Dibon
Gaza
Ein Gedi
Arnon
Khirbet Bēt Mirsim
Dead Sea
Rafah
JUDAH
Tell es-Seba
Arad
Beersheba
MOAB
Khirbet el-Mšāš
Horvat Qitmit

NEGEV DESERT

EDOM

Kadesh-Barnea
Feynan

0   10   20   30 km

- - - Approximate Borders

sophisticated society, with an enlarged royal court and an aristocracy as a class distinct from the free citizenry, did not develop until the ninth and eighth centuries BCE. This period also witnessed the growth of great social and economic disparities, which are reflected, for example, in the prophetic social criticism of the books of Amos and Isaiah.

As centers of scribal activity, the sanctuaries at Bethel and Dan, together with Samaria, the capital city founded by King Omri, are the most likely sites for the production of literature in the northern kingdom of Israel. Throughout the Levant and the rest of the ancient Near East, both the training of scribes and scribal activity were associated with either the royal court or the temple. These institutions required documentation in the form of annals and financial records, work that could only be done by scribes. These scribes were also responsible—especially in the temple—for transmitting religious knowledge. The reign of Jeroboam II (eighth century BCE), which was marked by a cultural revival, is thought to have been a time of intense scribal activity. This was a very fertile period for the compilation and textualization of the northern Israelite oral tradition.[55]

We know little more than this about the literature of the former kingdom of Israel. Many texts must have been lost in the destruction of Samaria in 722 BCE, when the Assyrians overran Israel, and what little material did remain was only preserved by refugees taking it south with them as they fled.[56] In addition, the Hebrew Bible as it existed at that time was heavily influenced by the culture of Judah, which was reluctant to recognize any other site but Jerusalem as having cultic legitimacy (see Deuteronomy 12:13–19). As a result, other texts may have been discarded. These texts had been brought to Jerusalem in the seventh century BCE, but because they were considered heterodox, they were not added to the inventory of books included in the emerging Bible. Thus, there may have been a number of texts that were in widespread use in Dan, Samaria, and Bethel but which are now lost.

The Jacob Traditions

Despite this loss of material, critical scholarship has been able to identify the kind of literature that might have been handed down at the temples in the kingdom of Israel. The texts concerning the ancestor figure Jacob from Genesis 25–35 appear to have been preserved and transmitted at the official sanctuary in Bethel.[57] This conclusion is suggested by the prominent role this shrine plays in the Jacob cycle of stories.[58] Jacob receives a significant revelation from God in Bethel (Genesis 28:12–25), and it is also there that he swears an oath that results in the levying of a temple tax:

> Then Jacob made a vow, saying, "If God will be with me and will watch over me on this journey I am taking and will give me food to eat and clothes to wear so that I return safely to my father's household, then YHWH will be my God and this stone that I have set up as a pillar will be God's house, and of all that you give me I will give you a tenth." (Genesis 28:20–22)

It is very unlikely that a statement of this kind would have been possible following the centralization of cult activity in Jerusalem, which most likely occurred in the late seventh century BCE. As a result, it seems fair to conclude that the substance of the Jacob cycle is older than the reign of King Josiah in the kingdom of Judah (640–609 BCE). Further evidence that the northern kingdom was home to the stories about Jacob comes from the geographical sites mentioned in these texts. Jacob never journeys to Jerusalem, Hebron, Gerar, or Mamre. All of these sites are in the south and appear frequently in the Abraham and Isaac traditions. By contrast, the Jacob tradition plays out in Shechem, Mahanaim, Penuel, and Bethel, all situated in the northern kingdom.

Even though the Jacob stories take the form of family histories and occur at a time when no states yet existed in the Levant, they are nonetheless great works of literature that are politically informed. It is believed that these ancient stories concern the political entities represented by the major ancestor figures: Jacob is Israel, and Esau is Edom.[59] It is possible that the Jacob stories had oral precursors with no political meaning.[60] But even the earliest written versions, which were probably created starting in the eighth century BCE, place Israel in relation to the neighboring states of Aram and Edom.[61]

It has been speculated that certain psalms, which were later taken to Jerusalem, may have originated in the royal shrine at Dan in the northern kingdom. These include the Sons of Korah psalms (42, 44–49, 84, 85, 87, and 88), along with Psalms 29 and 68. Psalm 29, for instance, was clearly composed on the basis of an Ugaritic model.[62] Ugarit was an important city-state in northern Syria, and direct cultural and economic contacts with Ugarit are

far easier to imagine for the northern kingdom, and especially its temple at
Dan, than for the southern kingdom. In the tenth and ninth centuries BCE,
however, Dan was not yet part of Israel; it still belonged to Aram. The founding
legend of the sanctuary in 1 Kings 12, which attributes the building of the
temple there to Jeroboam I, is almost certainly a fictional account dating from
the reign of Jeroboam II (781–742 BCE).[63] Dan probably became an Israelite
possession under his rule. Psalm 20 is a nearly direct copy of an Aramaic
psalm which is attested in a fourth century BCE Egyptian papyrus (Papyrus
Amherst 63).[64]

Finally, we may assume that the sanctuary in Samaria, which was constructed by the Omrides in the ninth century BCE, had its own cultic literature.[65] In around 880 BCE, Omri, a former military commander in the army
of Israel, ascended to the throne of the northern kingdom. Under his rule,
Israel became a serious political force in the Levant for the first time. Although archeologists have not yet found a temple at the site of Omri's city of
Samaria, that does not mean that one did not exist. First, it is more than likely
that the new capital of Israel—if not from the outset, then certainly not long
after its construction—was home to a shrine dedicated to the national deity,
YHWH. Second, the Bible mentions that there was a temple to Ba'al in Samaria, supposedly built by Omri's son Ahab (1 Kings 16:32). This lends weight
to the supposition that a temple was erected in the city. The discrepancy in
its dedication (whether to YHWH or Ba'al) may well result from the books
of Kings having originated in Jerusalem. As a follower of the Jerusalem temple
cult, the writer of these texts would have had a vested interest in discrediting
the temple in Samaria by describing it as a shrine not to YHWH but to Ba'al.
Third, the inscriptions that were found at Kuntillet 'Ajrud in northern Sinai,
dating from the ninth century BCE, confirm the specific wording "YHWH
of Samaria," which cannot be convincingly explained unless a shrine to
YHWH existed in the city.[66] "YHWH of Samaria" is only conceivable as a
ritually distinct and specific manifestation of YHWH who was venerated at
the temple there.

The Exodus Story

Like the Jacob stories, the story of Moses and the Exodus also originally
comes from the north. Its oral precursors are among the oldest materials that

made their way into the Bible, as demonstrated by the many formulaic references outside the Torah to the significance of the Israelites' exodus from Egypt for the identity of Israel.[67] The hero of the story, Moses, was in all probability a historical figure. Evidence of this includes his Egyptian name and his supposed marriage to a foreign woman; both of these details would not have been invented at a later date and so must already have been established as facts by tradition.[68] It is, however, hard to shed any light on the historical background to the exodus itself. On the one hand, it is certain that no such event ever took place precisely as it is described in the Bible. That kind of mass departure would have left behind traces that would subsequently have been found by archeologists. But more importantly, the Israelite people had not as yet become the kind of large-scale cohesive group that could have staged a mass exodus from Egypt. Such a population only emerged gradually in the land of Canaan. The absence of any cultural differences and upheavals of civilization in the late Bronze Age indicate that Israel essentially evolved out of Canaan through a gradual process of internal differentiation.[69]

On the other hand, the Exodus as it is portrayed in the Bible may well be based on a number of historical experiences that coalesced over time into a mythical origin story. Various migrations of Canaanite population groups between Egypt and the Levant are well attested. For instance, documents written by Egyptian border officials mention the transit through the region of nomads who stayed in Egypt on a seasonal basis before returning to Central Asia. The withdrawal of Egyptians from the Levant in the late Bronze Age, which was caused by internal political developments, may also have influenced the Exodus tradition—by presenting it in reverse as a withdrawal of Israel from Egypt.[70] Presumably groups from the north were chiefly responsible for introducing the experience of migration in and out of Egypt into the Israelite tradition.

Within the biblical tradition, there are good reasons to identify the Exodus story as coming from the north. The Bible's account of Jeroboam I's construction of two state temples in the north—one at Bethel and the other at Dan—expressly links the story of the "golden calves" to the Exodus tradition:[71]

After seeking advice, the king made two golden calves. He said to the people, "It is too much for you to go up to Jerusalem. Here are your gods, Israel, who brought you up out of Egypt." (1 Kings 12:28)

Even though this story is probably not historical and belongs to the reign of Jeroboam II rather than Jeroboam I (Dan did not become part of Israel until the eighth century BCE), it still credibly demonstrates the close connection of the Exodus tradition with the official state cult in the north.[72] Another factor pointing in the same direction is the observation that the Exodus plays a far more prominent role in the books of the prophets of the northern kingdom, Hosea and Amos, than it does in those of the southern kingdom, Isaiah and Micah.[73] The story of the two golden calves from 1 Kings 12 is taken up in Exodus 32 and transferred from King Jeroboam I to the entire Israelite people. This latter version emphasizes that idolatry in Israel is a sin not just of the king, but of the entire population. We can almost certainly conclude from the use of the plural ("your gods") in both texts that Exodus 32:4 derives from 1 Kings 12:28 and not vice versa. The passage in Exodus reads:

> He [Aaron] took what they handed him and made it into an idol cast in the shape of a calf, fashioning it with a tool. Then they said, "These are your gods, Israel, who brought you up out of Egypt." (Exodus 32:4)

In 1 Kings 12, two calves are produced, whereas in Exodus 32 there is only one. The plural form was therefore established in 1 Kings 12 and reproduced in Exodus 32.

In the current narrative arc of the Pentateuch, the Exodus story functions as a continuation of Genesis, and in its conclusion—the occupation by the Israelites of the "land flowing with milk and honey" in the book of Joshua— it also points beyond the Pentateuch. At first, however—and this goes for both the oral and the written tradition—it represented a tradition complex in its own right and undoubtedly existed as such until the late exile period or even the early post-exile period.[74] Its original autonomous status may be deduced from its thematic and theological cohesion as well as from the fact that the story of the forefathers told in Genesis 12–50 does not progress seamlessly to the Exodus story.[75] The stories of the forefathers and the Exodus represent two formerly independent traditions that have been yoked together for literary effect. This is particularly noticeable in Exodus 1:6–8:

> [6] Now Joseph and all his brothers and all that generation died, [7] but the Israelites were exceedingly fruitful; they multiplied greatly, increased

in numbers and became so numerous that the land was filled with them. [8] Then a new king, to whom Joseph meant nothing, came to power in Egypt.

These three verses provide a transition between the previously recounted story of Joseph and the Exodus story that is about to be told. All memories of Joseph and the good things that he did for Egypt must first be extinguished, so that the motif of oppression can be plausibly introduced. Exodus 1:8 pays the price for this connection, inasmuch as the new pharaoh supposedly has no recollection of his predecessor's second-in-command, Joseph. This troublesome passage arises from the attempt to link the stories of the forefathers and of the Exodus with as short a narrative arc as possible.

The Exodus story was, then, transmitted independently of the account of the forefathers. It is by no means easy to determine whether its oldest written version came into being before or after the collapse of the northern realm. As with the Jacob tradition, what is noticeable about this narrative is that it dispenses with any royal figure. In any event, the literary form of the Exodus narrative, which begins with the story of Moses's birth in Exodus 2:1–10, was probably written sometime after 722 BCE, in view of its pronounced anti-Assyrian tone. Exodus 2 appears to be a retelling of the legend of Sargon from the Neo-Assyrian tradition.[76] Sargon's autobiography begins:

Sargon, the mighty king, king of Akkad, am I. My mother was a priestess, my father I knew not. The brother of my father lived in the hills. My city is Azupiranu, which is situated on the banks of the Euphrates. My priestess mother conceived me, and bore me in secret. She set me in a basket of rushes, and with bitumen she sealed the lid over me. She cast me into the river from which I was not meant to emerge. The river bore me up and carried me to Akki, the drawer of water. Akki, the drawer of water, drew me out of the river as he lifted up his ewer. Akki, the drawer of water, took me as his son and reared me. Akki, the drawer of water, appointed me as his gardener, While I was a gardener, Ishtar fell in love with me, and I reigned for 54 years.[77]

Sargon reports that his mother was a priestess who was forbidden to marry, while his father was unknown to him. In spite of his dubious origins, however, he is chosen by the gods. This divine providence is shown both by his miraculous preservation in the sealed basket and by the fact that the goddess Ishtar favors him with her love—in other words, that she bestows kingship upon him. The story recounted in Exodus 2:1–10 is very similar to the Sargon legend: Moses's preservation and rescue after being abandoned by the Nile in a basket of bulrushes shows that God is by his side. The Neo-Assyrian background to Exodus 2:1–10 exemplifies the anti-Assyrian focus of the Exodus narrative. In place of Sargon, the Assyrian king of kings, we now have the nonroyal figure of Moses as the object of divine selection, and this divine providence saves the Israelites from a life of slavery under the Egyptian pharaoh.

The Exodus story is the first example of an anti-imperial literary document in Israel. Conversely, though, this same document endows God himself with absolute, "imperial" majesty. The story recounts the liberation of Israel from "servitude" under Egypt into the "service" of God.[78] This underlying motif of the absolutely sovereign design of God, hand in hand with his chosen people's fundamental dependence upon him, is a classic trope in the history of theology. It is of particular importance in the emergence of monotheism. And this motif is borrowed from an Assyrian basic pattern, albeit with an anti-Assyrian twist. In the Exodus story, this anti-Assyrian focus is transposed into an Egyptian backdrop, which is conceived as a prototypical situation. Egypt and its pharaoh (who quite deliberately remains unnamed) do not represent actual imperial power, but rather the institution of earthly empires in general.

Psalms from the Monarchical Period

Another text that may originate from Samaria is Psalm 45. This royal psalm, which recounts the marriage of a king to the daughter of a foreign ruler, recalls the policy of the Omrides, who forged alliances with the Phoenicians through marriage. One particularly well-known instance is the marriage of King Omri's son Ahab with Jezebel, a Phoenician princess. In the biblical tradition, Jezebel is a tyrant and miscreant who exerts a malign influence over her husband. The Bible often portrays foreign women as causing calamity by worshipping other gods and enticing their husbands to do the same. Psalm 45, however, does not follow this pattern. The psalmist lavishes praise on the

bride, a "daughter of Tyre" (the most important of the Phoenician ports), in
all her splendor:

> My heart is stirred by a noble theme as I recite my verses for the king;
> my tongue is the pen of a skillful writer. . . . Daughters of kings are
> among your honored women; at your right hand is the royal bride in
> gold of Ophir. . . . The city of Tyre will come with a gift, people of wealth
> will seek your favor. All glorious is the princess within her chamber; her
> gown is interwoven with gold. In embroidered garments she is led to the
> king; her virgin companions follow her—those brought to be with her.
> Led in with joy and gladness, they enter the palace of the king. Your sons
> will take the place of your fathers; you will make them princes throughout
> the land. (Psalm 45:1–2, 9, 12–16)

Psalm 45 presumably owes its literary survival in the Psalter to the fact that
its paeans of praise were thought to refer not to an earthly ruler but to God
himself receiving the homage of his peoples.

The southern kingdom of Judah was originally less powerful than the
northern kingdom of Israel, but the tradition of Judah has had a much more
significant historical impact. Judah had only one notable cultural and political center: Jerusalem.[79] Unlike the temples in the northern kingdom, the
temple in Jerusalem had an eventful history. Despite being destroyed twice
(in 587 BCE by the Babylonians and in 70 CE by the Romans), it still managed to retain sizable portions of its body of ritual lyric poetry and other elements of its literary tradition. The book of Psalms preserves a series of texts
that scholars have good grounds for tracing back to liturgical use during the
First and Second Temple periods (957 BCE–70 CE). These sit alongside other
psalms that scarcely ever had a ritual purpose (for instance, Psalms 1, 39, 73,
78, 104, 119, and 136).[80] In its present form, the Psalter as a whole must be
seen as a book of meditation for devout scholars of the Torah rather than as
a volume for practical ritual use, say, as a hymn book for the post-exile community.[81] This becomes abundantly clear from the opening of the First Psalm,
which does not have a heading of its own and introduces the Psalter as a work
primarily for reading, with something of the quality of the Torah about it:[82]

> Blessed is the one who does not walk in step with the wicked or stand
> in the way that sinners take or sit in the company of mockers, but whose

delight is in the law of YHWH, and who meditates on his law day and night. That person is like a tree planted by streams of water, which yields its fruit in season and whose leaf does not wither—whatever they do prospers. Not so the wicked! They are like chaff that the wind blows away. Therefore the wicked will not stand in the judgment, nor sinners in the assembly of the righteous. For YHWH watches over the way of the righteous, but the way of the wicked leads to destruction. (Psalm 1:1–6)

In naming the "law of YHWH," the First Psalm is no doubt referring primarily to the familiar Torah while at the same time construing the whole of the Psalter itself as a Torah, similarly divided into five sections (Psalms 1–42, 43–72, 73–89, 90–106, and 107–150). The ideal way to assimilate the Psalms is to meditate upon them or, to translate literally the word used at this point (*hagah*), to "mutter" the words to oneself. In antiquity it was common to read to oneself in an undertone rather than silently. This practice made the act of reading a more intense experience, since it was impossible to skip over words.

Though few people dispute that the Psalter contains poetic texts from different periods, there is still a great deal of uncertainty about the historical order of the texts. This is not surprising, given the themes treated by the psalms. Songs of lament and thanks, as well as hymns of praise, contain hardly any references to actual historical circumstances. Indeed, the character of these texts as liturgical templates requires that they be somewhat vague. In this way different suppliants down the ages could identify their own circumstances in the situations outlined. Psalm 1 itself is undoubtedly one of the later psalms. It presents a view of the psalms as individual texts for reading as opposed to communal songs and prayers for use in worship.

There is only one psalm—Psalm 137—which alludes to a verifiable historical event. Its famous first verse runs as follows: "By the rivers of Babylon, we sat and wept, when we remembered Zion." This psalm refers to the Babylonian Exile and may even have originated in this context. Scholarly opinion on when it was written varies widely. Ivan Engnell, for example, believes it to be the most recent psalm, whereas Bernhard Duhm thinks it may be the oldest.[83] Engnell's work epitomizes early twentieth-century Scandinavian psalm research, which posited a specific ritual celebration behind virtually every psalm. Bernhard Duhm, on the other hand, who was writing around

1900, thought it likely that extensive scholarly activity during post-exile Judaism was the driving force behind the creation of Old Testament texts. On this basis, he dated many of the psalms to the time of the Hasmonean dynasty, toward the end of the second century BCE.

Although dating the psalms is necessarily difficult, since they discuss universal human situations unrelated to specific historical or political contexts, a few points of reference allow us to organize them in rough historical order all the same. To start with, we may assume that the royal psalms (2, 18, 21, 72, and 110) came into existence at a time when Judah was no longer a sovereign kingdom, even though they were subsequently taken to be works depicting an idealized past. In the context of the Near East we might expect the temple cult to provide a foundation for the secular monarchy, and indeed the royal psalms play this role.

It is conceivable that some of the so-called psalms of individual lament (Psalms 6, 13, and so on) were originally royal texts too, since during the monarchical period the king was presumably the only person outside the priesthood who was a full member of the temple cult. The temple in Jerusalem was entirely subsumed within the royal palace complex, and to that extent it was, like the sanctuary at Bethel in the north, a "king's sanctuary and a temple of the kingdom" (Amos 7:13; see also 1 Kings 12:26). Psalm 56:8 and Psalm 59:6, 9 portray foreign peoples as enemies of a person at prayer, meaning that a royal interpretation is also possible here.[84] The opposition of individual and foreign enemies makes sense only if we presume that the individual is a king. We must constantly bear in mind that the First Temple in Jerusalem was nothing more than an annex of the royal court, even architecturally.

Furthermore, looking beyond the Psalter, we can date to the early monarchical period (tenth to ninth century BCE) the words ascribed to Solomon at the consecration of the First Temple. They can be reconstructed from the first book of Kings on the basis of the Greek version, which is placed in 1 Kings 8:53 instead of 1 Kings 8:12–13:

> Then Solomon said, "YHWH has set the sun in the heavens, but has said that he would dwell in a dark cloud; I have indeed built a magnificent temple for you, a place for you to dwell forever." See, is this not written in the Book of the Song? (1 Kings 8:53 in the Septuagint)

This text shows that the sanctuary in Jerusalem, which must originally have been dedicated to the pagan sun god, was occupied by YHWH—who thus took on characteristics of the sun.[85] Jerusalem's traditional affinity with the cult of the sun is hinted at in the very name of the city, which almost certainly originally meant "the city of Šalim," the Canaanite god of the sunset. In the ancient Near East, the solar deity was responsible for law and justice. With the introduction of the cult of YHWH to Jerusalem, most likely during the reign of David, YHWH, who was at first a god of the mountains and the weather, took on this role as the guarantor of law and justice. This theological legacy represented a decisive step toward the universalization of the concept of God in Israel and Judah—a step that was central to the subsequent history of the concept.

The literature of the pre-exile temple cult reveals the basic outlines of an all-embracing theological vision that has become known as the Jerusalem Cult Tradition.[86] At its center stands the powerful God of Zion, who protects Jerusalem and its king and is responsible for the prosperity of the surrounding country and for upholding law and justice. The underlying idea is that God defends the life-giving cosmos against deadly chaos. In the various theologies of the Canaanite city-states, this antagonism was often illustrated by the motif of the struggle against chaos. This motif is also present in the ritual lyric poetry of the Old Testament, but it has been transformed into a scene where the struggle is over and peace has been established:

> YHWH reigns, he is robed in majesty; YHWH is robed in majesty and armed with strength; indeed, the world is established, firm and secure. Your throne was established long ago; you are from all eternity. The seas have lifted up, YHWH, the seas have lifted up their voice; the seas have lifted up their pounding waves. Mightier than the thunder of the great waters, mightier than the breakers of the sea—YHWH on high is mighty. (Psalm 93:1–4)

In this psalm, God is portrayed as an absolute sovereign power. In the mists of time the waters of chaos raised their voices against him, but God had such power that no battle was necessary. Psalm 93 demonstrates that the Jerusalem Cult Tradition was rooted in its environment but had its own distinct theological character.[87]

Scholars developed the idea of the Jerusalem Cult Tradition at a time when it was taken for granted that the contents of the Psalter originated from the pre-exile temple cult. This assumption still has some validity, inasmuch as liturgical texts are usually conservative—that is, they embody traditions from former eras even though, in the form in which they have come down to us, they were actually written later. The best examples of this are the texts from Isaiah 40–55, which are usually referred to as Deutero-Isaiah (from the Latin root *deutero-*, meaning "second"). On the one hand, these clearly date from the period of the Babylonian Exile, since they cite the destruction of Jerusalem (Isaiah 40:1–2) and name the Persian king Cyrus (Isaiah 44:28, 45:1). But on the other hand, they form part of a fixed liturgical tradition that may well date back to the era of the First Temple in Jerusalem. As a result, it is now thought that Isaiah 40–55 may have originated from a group of exiled temple singers.[88] It is certainly the case that the religious ideas contained within the psalms of the monarchical period have a certain similarity that places them within the framework of the cosmos-chaos matrix.

Wisdom Literature

The biblical texts from the monarchical period also include traditional scriptures that are customarily grouped together under the heading "Wisdom literature." In the ancient Near East, Wisdom denoted a structure that helped people get their intellectual bearings. This framework consisted of empirical knowledge that aided practical living and could appear in a variety of linguistic forms, such as proverbs, didactic speeches, and instructive tales. It had an international flavor (embracing knowledge from the entire ancient Near East) and was not explicitly religious. God is often, but not always, mentioned in these texts. In the Old Testament, these sayings and compositions are found primarily in Proverbs 10–29, which are thought to be of great antiquity.[89] Their literary and sociological roots are not entirely clear. The oral origins of Wisdom literature are thought to lie in family tradition. Many of the "wise" pronouncements also reflect common-sense beliefs that were widespread beyond the domain of the Israelites and cannot easily be ascribed specifically to Israel and Judah. In Proverbs 12–14 we also find material that displays a close affinity with Egyptian models, which must have arisen within a learned scribal milieu that had the requisite cultural contacts.[90]

The Destruction of Israel and Its Implications for Judah

The kingdom of Israel existed as a sovereign state for only about two hundred years before it lost its political independence with the conquest of Samaria in 722 BCE and became a province of the Assyrian Empire. And yet "Israel" continued to live on in a multitude of different ways. The Israelite diaspora in Mesopotamia has left behind the fewest archeological traces. The victorious Assyrians did not usually settle groups of people from conquered territories in self-contained colonies but instead dispersed them among the local populace. As a result, although there are a few reports of deported Israelites in Mesopotamia after 722 BCE, all traces of them soon disappear.[91]

Conversely, Assyrians were also typically relocated to conquered territories. We can assume that this was also true of the conquered land of Israel, and, indeed, the Bible states expressly that this was the case (2 Kings 17:24–41).[92] The aim of this practice was to destroy the ethnic and political identity of the regions the Assyrians had subdued. In the case of Israel, this policy appears to have been successful insofar as—in the eyes of Judah and later of the Jews—the people left behind in the territory of the northern kingdom came to be referred to disparagingly in the Bible as Kutim (Cutheans or Cuthites). This was an allusion to Kuta (Kutha or Cutha), the origin of some Mesopotamians who were resettled in Israel by the Assyrians (2 Kings 17:24). In reality, however, it was the community of the Samaritans that developed in the territory of the former kingdom of Israel.[93] From the early Persian period onward, the Samaritans maintained their own shrine on Mount Gerizim (near the present-day city of Nablus).[94] This community still exists today but is very small, with only around a thousand members. By contrast, in ancient times, the Samaritans are thought to have been equal in number with the Jews for long periods, and at times even outnumbered them (see Chapter 4).

After 722 BCE, the former kingdom of Israel appears to have provided the historical setting for some of the stories of judges in the Bible; the oral prehistory of these stories doubtless dates back to the period before the destruction of Israel.[95] In its present configuration, the book of Judges takes the form of an intermezzo between the story of Israel's salvation (extending from the promises made by God to the forefathers through the Exodus to the settling of Canaan) and the ensuing period of the kings. The so-called judges—charismatic savior figures—appear in crisis situations and save Israel through the gift of the spirit with which God has endowed them. And yet Israel continues repeatedly to forsake God, resulting in a recurring cycle of lapses and deliverance (Judges 2:11–19). The book of Judges is followed by the depiction of the monarchical period of Israel and Judah in the books of Samuel and Kings, which no longer recount recurring acts of salvation by God but rather the falling away from YHWH of these two kingdoms, culminating in their demise (2 Kings 17 and 2 Kings 25).

The book of Judges was not, however, originally written as a link between the books of Joshua and Samuel; the pattern of repeated lapses and deliverance is part of the book's reworking during the exile. The literary core of the book is instead to be found in Judges 3–9, which contains a collection of tales of judgment from the Assyrian period. The fact that nearly all of the judges—Ehud, Shamgar, Deborah, Barak, Gideon, Abimelek—come from the former kingdom of Israel (the exception being Othniel [Judges 3:7–11]) suggests that Judges 3–9 is a repository of specifically northern Israelite traditions. These chapters advance the possibility of a non-state existence of Israel, without its own king. A particularly stark warning against establishing an independent kingdom in Israel is evident in the episode of Abimelek's failed attempt to set up such a state in Shechem (Judges 9), which in historical terms surely takes as its model the destruction of Shechem in 722 BCE. The events surrounding the establishment of a Shechemite kingdom in Judges 9 can be read as a catalog of the worst crimes of the kings of the northern kingdom. The story of Abimelek in Shechem distills two centuries of Israelite royal dominion into a single chapter.[96] Even the very specific way in which the enemies of Israel are characterized points to the period of Assyrian ascendancy. For instance, it was not until around 845 BC, under King Mesha, that Moab emerged as a state that could threaten Israel (Judges 3:12–14).[97] The same is true of the portrayal of the clashes with the Midianites, which appears to reflect the Israelites' experiences with the Arabs beginning in the seventh century BCE.[98]

Thus, it seems likely that the core of the book of Judges in chapters 3–9 operated as a kind of manifesto for the postmonarchical period, arguing against an institutionalized monarchy in Israel and in favor of a divinely governed policy implemented by charismatic savior figures. These chapters convey the impression that a theocratic leadership within Israel would not inevitably conflict with the political organizational structures put in place by the Assyrians. By showing that God enacts his will in the former northern kingdom through charismatic savior figures, the stories of the judges refute the implicit criticism that it was a godless realm. The political program of Judges 3–9 is decidedly pro-Assyrian in tone and thus forms something of a counternarrative to the Exodus story.

Circumstantial archeological evidence bears out what we can only surmise about the history of this period—namely, that after 722 BCE a large number of refugees from the kingdom of Israel decamped to the southern kingdom of Judah and settled there.[99] Jerusalem, in particular, mushroomed in the seventh century BCE. The traditional Jerusalem of the monarchical period was located in the part of the city founded by David, on the southeastern spur of the Temple Mount. In the seventh century BCE, people began to settle an area extending to the southwestern spur, which is described in the Bible (2 Kings 22:14) as the "new quarter."[100] The rapid growth of this new settlement was probably occasioned by the need to accommodate an influx of refugees from the north. Of course, these refugees brought with them not only their material belongings but also their texts and traditions. This is the route by which the Hosea tradition and a number of psalms came to Jerusalem, as well as certain traditions that were incorporated into Deuteronomy.

Yet Israel did not live on solely in the diaspora from the northern kingdom and in the people who later came to be called Samaritans—the ethnic and religious group that continued to inhabit the former northern kingdom and is portrayed in the Bible primarily as a rival to the Judaism of Judah in the Second Temple period.[101] Israel also survived within Judah itself. The prestigious and important name "Israel" seems to have been adopted by Judah after 722 BCE. It is a matter of dispute whether this was a new coinage or whether, even before the fall of the northern kingdom, the name "Israel" continued to signify the ten tribes, excluding Judah (and Benjamin).[102] It is perfectly plausible that a pan-Israelite ideology was present even during the era of the kingdom of Israel, under the long and prosperous reign of Jeroboam II—albeit one that was predicated on a leading role for the north rather than the south. The transfer of the name "Israel" to the south can be seen especially clearly in the book of Isaiah: according to Isaiah 5:3, the Song of the Vineyard is addressed to the "dwellers in Jerusalem and people of Judah," while the interpretative verse 5:7 asserts: "The vineyard of YHWH Zebaot is the nation of Israel, and the people of Judah are the vines he delighted in." Israel and Judah are not being seen here as complementary major realms; Judah is designated as a subset of Israel. In other words, the term "Israel" in Isaiah 5:7 encompasses both Israel *and* Judah.

In the prophetic tradition of the book of Isaiah, the identification of Judah with Israel is of key theological importance concerning the coming judgment awaiting Judah. The book of Isaiah does everything it can to emphasize that the judgment against "Israel" did not end with the demise of the northern realm. What are probably the most important theological statements regarding the question of divine judgment against both Israel and Judah can be found in the part of Isaiah called the "refrain poem" (5:25–30, 9:7–20, and 10:1–4). This poem, in referring back to the tradition of the northern kingdom prophet Amos, reflects upon the theme of the judgment against Israel and its significance for Judah. The poem contains a readily identifiable refrain that indicates the poem's stance toward God's judgment against Israel: "Yet for all this, his anger is not turned away, his hand is still upraised" (9:12, 9:17, 9:21, 10:4; see also 5:25). Within the refrain poem, the statement made in Isaiah 9:8–10 is initially the most telling regarding the links to Amos:

> YHWH has sent a message against Jacob, and it has fallen on Israel. All the people will know it—Ephraim and the inhabitants of Samaria—who say with pride and arrogance of heart, "The bricks have fallen down, but we will rebuild with dressed stone; the fig trees have been felled, but we will replace them with cedars."

Isaiah 9:8 explicitly looks back to a prophetic pronouncement that had already been issued against Israel (that is, the northern kingdom, as the references to Ephraim, Samaria, and Jacob make clear). We should note here the use of the present perfect tense, "*has* sent," "*have* fallen," referring to events in the past. In its address to the northern kingdom, the poem must be referring to the Amos tradition. This is suggested by the motif of the earthquake alluded to in Isaiah 9:10, which is also central to the book of Amos (Amos 1:1–2), and by the following text of Isaiah 9:13, which also hints at Amos:

But the people did not return to the one who struck them, and they did not seek YHWH Sabaoth.[103]

This verse is replete with allusions to the book of Amos. The statement that the people did not "return" to God picks up the refrain from Amos 4:6–12, and the claim that God has "struck" Israel refers to Amos 5:4–6, where Israel is implored to "seek" God. The purpose of these references to Amos is to show that the judgment against Judah that Isaiah announces is not a new occurrence; it is based on the wrath of God against Israel, which continues to be directed against its people. The judgment against Judah therefore renews and extends the judgment that was enacted against the northern kingdom of Israel.[104]

Thus, where the impending judgment is concerned, Israel and Judah are seen as a unit. Casting this event in a historical light, however, there is no reason to presume that Judah has already fallen by the time of Isaiah's prophecy. On the contrary, it is far more plausible to assume that the conviction expressed in the Isaiah tradition—that the judgment against "Israel" did not end with the fall of Samaria—actually comes before the fall of Judah. For the book of Isaiah, unlike the other prophetic books in the Bible, does not focus on its prophetic message being rejected by those who hear it. Such an attitude makes sense in a historical situation where Israel has been destroyed as a political entity but Judah still exists. This example illustrates the crucial significance of the period between the fall of the northern kingdom (722 BCE) and that of the southern kingdom (587 BCE) as an era of fundamental theological realignment. The driving force behind Old Testament theology was not the catastrophe suffered by Jerusalem in 587 BCE and the ensuing Babylonian Exile. Rather, these events could only be processed in a way that did not involve the demise of the YHWH religion because that tradition had already been set on a decisive new course in the preceding century.[105]

These developments in the history of ideas are of key importance for the transformation of the biblical texts into scripture. The prophecies in the book of Amos had come true in the eyes of those responsible for passing down the Isaiah tradition, and it was therefore a suitable theological point of reference. For this reason the nascent book of Amos acquired a certain degree of authority, while the emerging book of Isaiah was able to benefit from this authority by forging a connection with the Amos tradition.

The Beginnings of Scriptural Prophecy

Prophecy is not significant only for its role in transforming the Bible into scripture by means of the reception of the Amos tradition into the book of Isaiah. Because the essence of prophecy involves the transmission of messages from God, it plays a decisive part, when put down in writing, in the formation of the concept of normative texts.

The phenomenon of prophecy is known not only from Israel and Judah, but also from elsewhere in the ancient Near East.[106] The most famous examples are the prophetic texts from Mari on the upper Euphrates, which date from the eighth century BCE, and those from Assyria, dating from the seventh century BCE.[107] Ancient Near Eastern prophecy should be seen in the wider context of divination.[108] Through the use of various techniques such as haruspicy (inspection of entrails from sacrificed animals), necromancy (communication with the dead), or the interpretation of dreams, specialist augurs sought to obtain divinely imparted knowledge of the future that they could use to advise the royal court in military, economic, or political matters. Some years ago, the German theologian Manfred Weippert proposed a definition of a prophet in the context of ancient Near Eastern and biblical prophecy: "A prophet or prophetess is a person of male or female gender who (1) is privy to a revelation by a deity or several deities in some form of cognitive experience, be it a vision, an audition, a dream, etc. and who (2) sees him- or herself tasked by the god or gods in question to make this revelation known to a third party, its actual intended recipient, in the form of language or metalanguage (namely, through the use of symbols or other signs)."[109]

This definition is striking in many ways. First, it includes polytheistic contexts, as reflected in its reference to "deities" in the plural. Second, it takes into account female prophets, who played a prominent role in Neo-Assyrian prophecy.[110] Third, it includes nonverbal forms of prophecy of the kind cited, for example, in 1 Samuel 10:5–6. Fourth, it leaves open the aspect of foretelling the future. It defines prophecy as the passing on of a message; foretelling the future is included but given no special emphasis.

Prophecy, then, is the communication of divine knowledge to human re-cipients. Such a process is described in 1 Kings 22:6–22. The king of Judah, Jehoshaphat (ca. 873–849 BCE), and the king of Israel, Ahab (ca. 871–852 BCE), confer about leading a joint military campaign against Ramot-Gilead, and Ahab seeks the expert advice of his court prophets. The fact that they apparently numbered some four hundred speaks to the extraordinary impor-tance of this institution. The prophets provide nearly unanimous advice to King Ahab: he should go ahead with his campaign. Yet one prophet, Micaiah son of Imlah, disagrees, prophesying that Israel will be defeated. Micaiah explains to Ahab that the prophecy of all the other prophets, who predicted the contrary, was the direct result of a deceiving spirit that God himself sent to those prophets. This sophisticated conception does not ex-plain the phenomenon of false prophecy on the level of the prophets them-selves, but instead entertains the possibility of such a thing as a "genuine" false prophecy. God himself has chosen to deceive his prophets and has im-parted a false message to them.

This episode is a one-off occurrence. Yet it clearly demonstrates the basic problem of institutionalized prophecy, which tailors the content of its "ex-pert" assessments to the expectations that are placed, implicitly or explicitly, upon it. We know about this kind of prophecy because the books of Kings recount instances of it. However, it never formed a tradition in its own right; there are no books attributed to any of the four hundred prophets in the ser-vice of King Ahab.

The only books of prophecy that have been preserved are those of the in-dividual figures who now make up that part of the biblical canon known as the Latter Prophets. However prominent Isaiah, Jeremiah, Ezekiel, and the twelve Minor Prophets have become, the figures behind these books must surely have represented a marginal subculture as a result of the messages they imparted, which were critical of political regimes and religious cults. They likely only became authoritative figures after the national catastrophes of 722 and 587 BCE—the destruction first of the northern and then of the southern kingdom. It seems beyond doubt that the majority of these prophets were his-torical figures, in part because of the authenticity of the milieu in their ac-counts, but above all by virtue of their historical influence, which began early on. Only Malachi and Joel are most likely literary constructions. Malachi (lit-erally, "my messenger") is a made-up name, and many commentators have remarked that the core of this book is closely connected to the preceding book of Zechariah and carries it forward.[111] The book of Joel dispenses entirely with any attempt to locate itself historically and is characterized by the scribal nature of its texts.[112] No individual prophetic figure can be identified behind this scripture.

The figures who have become known as the Latter (or Literary) Prophets appear in part to have explicitly broken away from institutionalized prophecy. Amos, for example, reacted to his expulsion from the temple at Bethel in the following way:

> I am not a prophet, and I am not the student of a prophet. Instead I am a shepherd and a tender of sycamore trees. But YHWH took me away from the sheep and said to me: "Go, prophesy to my people Israel!" (Amos 7:14–15)[113]

This answer is only comprehensible when set against the sociological background outlined in 1 Kings 22: Amos does not dispute that he himself utters prophecies, but he is at pains to distance himself from the institutionalized "prophets" who fabricate their predictable expert assessments. Amos claims that he is not involved in any such institutional context; all he does is tend sheep and trees, but he has the Word of God.

The particular problem facing the Literary Prophets is also evident in the book of Isaiah. In the vision in which Isaiah receives his calling as a prophet (Isaiah 6), he is given the following absurd instruction by God:

> And he [God] said: "Go and say to this people: 'You shall hear, hear continually, but you will not comprehend! And you shall see, see continually, but you will not perceive! Make the heart of this people sluggish, make their ears heavy, and close their eyes so that they will not see with their eyes and shall not hear with their ears, so that their heart will not understand, so that they will not repent and become healed.'" (Isaiah 6:9–10)[114]

Biblical scholars, as well as the scribes who wrote the Great Isaiah Scroll found at Qumran, have puzzled over how to interpret this order.[115] The Qumran scribes simply altered the text to make it less incongruous (see Chapter 1). The most plausible explanation for the original reading continues to be the back-projection hypothesis. In this passage, the failure of Isaiah's proclamation to make any impact is expressed in tandem with his calling to become a prophet in the first place. In other words, behind the formulation of Isaiah's calling as a prophet we can already witness his failure in this role.

The reader of the book of Isaiah therefore becomes aware of a double meaning. On the one hand, this text explains why Isaiah was not listened to during his lifetime. On the other hand, fixing his message in writing indicates that it is actually of great importance to future generations—that is, those people who are reading the book that bears his name after the judgment he prophesied has come to pass.

The rise of written prophecy in Israel coincided with the destruction of the northern kingdom of Israel. Indeed, it may even be materially contingent upon this event.[116] At the very least, the loss of statehood in the north may well have contributed heavily to the success of written prophecy. It is reasonable to assume that the main body of prophecy in the Old Testament was originally in oral form. The use of particular formulations and genres typical of oral declamation point in this direction, as does the narrative literature that discusses prophecy. Yet it is virtually impossible to reconstruct the original oral entities. Because the process of committing the very first words to writing must have gone hand in hand with interpretative adjustments, the individual words can only be understood now in their newly created context of being read. This process can be seen especially clearly in Hosea 4–11. Because this section of text is not interrupted by subheadings, it forces the reader to read on from one section to the next. The belief underlying this is clear: the words of the prophet that have now been set down in writing can only be properly received and interpreted when they are considered in their entirety.[117]

The Legal Tradition

In addition to the prophetic tradition, the legal tradition is responsible for the Bible becoming the Bible.[118] The very fact that the Bible contains legislative material places it within the domain of normative texts. The key aspect of biblical legal texts is that, taken as a whole, they represent God's law. In the present version of the Torah they are incorporated narratively into the biography of Moses, from Exodus to Deuteronomy. Most of the regulations are associated with the Israelites' wanderings in the Sinai Desert, while the book of Deuteronomy is configured as Moses's farewell address on the east bank of the Jordan River, before entrance to the Promised Land. Three separate collections of laws can be identified: the so-called Covenant Code (Exodus 20–23), which Exodus 24:4 informs us Moses wrote down; the Holiness Code (Leviticus 17–26); and the Deuteronomic Code (Deuteronomy 12–26). These collections contain very similar legal provisions, including presentations and interpretations of the same laws. This makes it possible to attempt a relative dating of the three bodies of law. The Covenant Code appears to be the oldest collection. It is reinterpreted in Deuteronomy from the perspective of a centralized cult: cultic activities are no longer allowed outside of the temple in Jerusalem. The Deuteronomic Code is itself tempered by the priestly tradition in its reception in the Holiness Code.

Even in the case of the Covenant Code, we are dealing with a collection of laws that are premised upon Israel being a sedentary agricultural society, which is completely at odds with the view that the Bible originated in a nomadic phase of Israel's prehistory. Scholars have determined that the Covenant Code was written in the eighth century BCE, the Deuteronomic Code in the late seventh century BCE, and the Holiness Code in the Persian period (539–331 BCE).[119]

In order to understand the characteristic nature of the earliest biblical legal texts, we must interpret them in their ancient Near Eastern context. The ancient Near East had an extensive tradition of written law dating as far back as the third millennium BCE. This tradition involved sovereign law that was descriptive rather than prescriptive. The great legal books that are associated with the names of Hammurabi, Eshnunna, and Lipit-Ishtar and that came into being around the beginning of the second millennium BCE represented "an aid to securing justice rather than a firm commandment to that end."[120] This non-normative tendency is apparent above all from two observations. First, the provisions of these law codes do not remotely cover all potential legal cases that could arise in private or public life; on the contrary, the cases treated are often very specialized and complex and appear to have served as practice exercises for scholars of jurisprudence. Second, surviving trial documents tally only very approximately, or not at all, with the provisions of the law codes, which are not cited by name.[121] The actual dispensing of justice was apparently not obliged to follow the written collections of laws.

In the ancient Near East, legislative authority resided not with written legal provisions but with the ruler. Hence, far from being an exception, the absence in pre-Hellenistic Egypt of any laws enshrined in writing—apart from a single edict issued by King Haremhab in the Eighteenth Dynasty—only corroborates this finding. The idea of the monarch as the embodiment of the law finds clear expression in the respective Greek and Roman epithets for the king as the *nomos empsychos* and the *lex animata* (i.e., "the living law").

The nature of ancient Near Eastern law books is evident from the Laws of Eshnunna, which were written down in Mesopotamia around 1790–1770 BCE. The first two paragraphs of the code present a price list for various commodities:

§1 600 silas of barley (can be purchased) for 1 shekel of silver. 3 silas of fine oil for 1 shekel of silver. 12 silas of oil for 1 shekel of silver. 15 silas of lard for 1 shekel of silver. 40 silas of bitumen for 1 shekel of silver. 360 shekels of wool for 1 shekel of silver. 600 silas of salt for 1 shekel of silver. 300 silas of potash for 1 shekel of silver. 180 shekels of copper for 1 shekel of silver. 120 shekels of wrought copper for 1 shekel of silver.

§2 1 sila of oil extract (?) equates to 30 silas of grain. 1 sila of lard extract (?) equates to 25 silas of grain. 1 sila of bitumen extract (?) equates to 80 silas of grain.[122]

Up to this point, one would be tempted to categorize the Laws of Eshnunna as a commercial rather than a legal document. The following paragraphs continue in the same vein, by setting prices for various means of transport:

§3 A wagon together with its oxen and its driver, 100 silas of grain is its hire; if (paid in) silver, 113 shekels (i.e., 60 barleycorns) is its hire; he shall drive it for the entire day.

§4 The hire of a boat is, per 600-sila capacity. 2 silas: furthermore, [x] silas is the hire of the boatman; he shall drive it for the entire day.

However, in place of economic lists of prices, paragraph 5 proceeds to set forth legal provisions, couched in the classic "If . . . then" formulation:

§5 If the boatman is negligent and causes the boat to sink, then he shall restore as much as he caused to sink.

§6 If a man, under fraudulent circumstances, should seize a boat which does not belong to him, then he shall weigh and deliver 10 shekels of silver.

From these six paragraphs we can see that the literary genre of the law book had not yet been firmly established. The Laws of Eshnunna regulate prices but also rule on disputes that might arise in commercial life. In the following paragraphs, the codex goes on to treat more common legal cases. But just as prices reflect conditions at a particular time and place, so this law code is geared specifically to life during this period and is rooted in everyday concerns. The law is enacted by the king, and it possesses a divine component only insofar as the monarch follows the cosmic order and reflects it in his lawgiving.

The same is true of the famous Babylonian Laws of Hammurabi (ca. 1750 BCE). The stele on which they are inscribed has on its upper section a bas-relief image of Hammurabi standing before the sun god Shamash, who was traditionally held to be responsible for dispensing law and justice (Figure 33). Hammurabi is shown receiving a ring and a staff from Shamash, presumably as the symbols of his power as monarch, but not the text of the codex, which is inscribed on the lower section of the stele. The stele thus portrays the godly legitimation of the king, but it does not portray his laws as having a divine origin.

There can be little doubt that the various legal codes of the ancient Near East were not composed in "splendid isolation" from one another; rather, they all evidently formed part of a scribal culture of jurisprudence. Both linguistically and in terms of their content, their legal pronouncements are often closely linked to one another. This is demonstrated, for example, by the provisions regarding an ox with a propensity to gore people, which can be found in both the Laws of Eshnunna and the Laws of Hammurabi:

§54 If an ox is a gorer and the ward authorities notify its owner, but he fails to keep his ox in check and it gores a man and thus causes his death, the owner of the ox shall weigh and deliver 40 shekels of silver.

Figure 33. King Hammurabi (*left*) receiving a ring and staff from the sun god Shamash. Bas-relief on the upper part of the Stele of Hammurabi, ca. 1750 BCE.

§55 If it gores a slave and thus causes his death, he shall weigh and deliver 15 shekels of silver. (Eshnunna)

§250 If an ox gores to death a man while it is passing through the streets, that case has no basis for a claim.

§251 If a man's ox is a known gorer, and the authorities of his city quarter notify him that it is a known gorer, but he does not blunt(?) its horns or control his ox, and that ox gores to death a member

of the *awilu*-class [i.e., the son of a free man], he (the owner) shall
give 30 shekels of silver.

§252   If it is a man's slave (who is fatally gored), he shall give 20 shekels
of silver. (Hammurabi)

Although these legal provisions relate to a similar situation, the exposition
and degree of detail differ considerably between the two. We may deduce
from this that certain cases acted as model cases that were framed differently
in different legal traditions.

Biblical law clearly shares in this ancient Near Eastern law tradition.[123] The
Torah, for example, also cites the example of the ox with a propensity for
goring people:[124]

> When an ox gores a man or a woman to death, the ox shall be stoned,
> and its flesh shall not be eaten; but the owner of the ox shall not be liable.
> If the ox has been accustomed to gore in the past, and its owner has been
> warned but has not restrained it, and it kills a man or a woman, the ox
> shall be stoned, and its owner also shall be put to death. If a ransom is
> imposed on the owner, then the owner shall pay whatever is imposed for
> the redemption of the victim's life. If it gores a boy or a girl, the owner
> shall be dealt with according to this same rule. If the ox gores a male or
> female slave, the owner shall pay to the slaveowner thirty shekels of
> silver, and the ox shall be stoned. (Exodus 21:28–32)

This example makes it clear that we should be wary of assuming that laws
become increasingly humane over the course of legal history. The example from the Torah is the only one that provides for a negligent owner to
be put to death in the case of an ox that has a habit of goring, and it is also
the only one to stipulate that the ox should be stoned to death and that its
meat should not be consumed. In the Bible, the act of stoning is a way of elim-
inating an immediate threat (see Exodus 8:26, 17:4, 19:12–13; Joshua 7:24–25;
and 1 Samuel 30:6–7), while the proscription against eating the meat of the
stoned animal seems to be aimed at preventing its owner from gaining any
benefit from it.

This ruling is typical of the literary core of the Covenant Code. God does
not appear either implicitly or explicitly in such provisions. He is neither a

legislator nor a judge but at best a guarantor and guardian of the rule of law. The prevailing impression on reading these texts today—that all of the law contained within the Torah is divine law—derives chiefly from the introduction to the Covenant Code in Exodus 20:22–21:1:

> Then YHWH said to Moses, "Tell the Israelites this: 'You have seen for yourselves that I have spoken to you from heaven. . . . These are the laws you are to set before them.'"

However, this introduction belongs not to the literary substance of the Covenant Code but rather to its secondary framing, which is there to serve its "theologization."[125] It turns secular law, which is formulated in accordance with the ancient Near Eastern legal tradition, into divine law, which is a unique feature of the Bible. How old is this act of theologization? The process is impossible to understand historically without considering how the book of Deuteronomy evolved. For this is where the historical kernel of the idea that law is divine law is to be found.

Deuteronomy and the Later Biblical Canon

The writing down of a first draft of Deuteronomy represented an important step forward in the formation of the Bible.[126] This first draft undoubtedly included chapters 12–28, which form the heart of the book. Because the book refers to itself as "this law (Torah)" (Deuteronomy 1:5, 4:8, 27:3) or "this book of the law" (Deuteronomy 29:20, 30:10, 31:26), some commentators have speculated that Deuteronomy may be the first biblical scripture, and that it was written down on a (parchment) scroll.[127] Before this time, papyrus had been the preferred writing material. Yet the passages cited cannot sustain the weight of this theory, since they belong to the more recently written framework sections of the book and fulfill a particular literary function—to underscore the textuality of the will of God that is laid down in Deuteronomy.

The name "Deuteronomy" derives from the history of the book's reception in Latin, and before that Greek, where it was regarded as the "second" law (see Deuteronomy 17:18)—the first being the set of commandments that were given to Moses on Mount Sinai. According to the narrative logic of the Pentateuch, Moses passes these commandments on to Israel in Deuteronomy, which is framed as his valedictory address on the last day of his life. In all probability, though, Deuteronomy was once a collection in its own right. The fact that it fits so well into its current place in the Pentateuch has to do with its evolution as a new edition of the Covenant Code (Exodus 20–23). The literary placement of Deuteronomy after the giving of the law on Mount Sinai thus mirrors the historical relationship of dependency of this text upon the Covenant Code.

In Deuteronomy, we have before us for the first time in the history of biblical literature a book that conceptualizes itself as a normative text. It is thus in a certain sense a "biblical" text from the very outset, even though this category did not yet exist at the time.[128] This quality in turn is related to its genesis: the writing of Deuteronomy—or its literary core—can be dated to the end of the seventh century BCE, during the reign of King Josiah of Judah (640–609 BCE). This finding is one of the earliest and most durable discoveries of historical-critical biblical scholarship. In his 1805 doctoral dissertation, Wilhelm Martin Leberecht de Wette, following in the footsteps of some predecessors, recognized and substantiated the close connection between the theological claims of Deuteronomy and the reform of religious ritual undertaken by Josiah in Jerusalem, as described in 2 Kings 23.[129] These similarities have been summed up in the phrase "cultic unity and cultic purity." This meant that YHWH could only be worshipped in Jerusalem, and that YHWH alone, and no other gods, could be venerated. De Wette's critical approach was conditioned by his belief that the account of Josiah's religious reforms in 2 Kings 23 was a contemporary document that was based on real historical events. Today, most scholars agree that 2 Kings 23:4–24 is not a homogeneous text in literary terms, but this does not preclude the possibility that its literary core dates back to the late seventh century BCE.[130]

Indeed, the dating of the core of Deuteronomy to the Neo-Assyrian period can be plausibly substantiated even without reference to 2 Kings 23. As far back as the 1960s and 1970s we have known that, in its language and theological ideas, Deuteronomy shows clear affinities to Neo-Assyrian vassal treaties.[131] By means of such treaties, the Assyrian king of kings placed his dominion over conquered territories on a legal footing. Until recently, the only documentary evidence of such agreements came from the east of the Assyrian Empire, but in 2012 an example of one from the west came to light at Tell Tayinat near the border of present-day northwestern Syria and southern

Figure 34. Assyrian vassal treaty from Tell Tayinat, eighth century BCE.

Turkey (Figure 34).[132] This corroborated a fact that was indirectly hinted at in Deuteronomy itself: subdued peoples in the western Assyrian Empire, as well as in the east, were made to pledge fealty to the Assyrian king of kings through such vassal treaties. In the case of Judah it is possible that such a treaty was framed in Aramaic, which at that time was the lingua franca of the Near East. However, there is no direct proof of this.

Deuteronomy adopts the basic structure of the Assyrian vassal treaties but transfers the relationship of fealty between the Assyrian king of kings and his vassals to that of the God of Israel and his people, demanding unconditional loyalty not to the Assyrian ruler but to YHWH. Deuteronomy can thus be viewed as a subversive reception of Neo-Assyrian vassal treaties.[133]

Through this replacement of the Assyrian ruler with God, Deuteronomy introduces for the first time in ancient Near Eastern legal history the concept of a divine legislator and a Law of God.[134] Yet in its present guise, Deuteronomy takes the form of Moses's farewell address to his people on the east bank of the Jordan River. In the context in which we currently read the book, the "I" in the corpus of legislation presented in Deuteronomy 12–28 appears to refer to Moses. But this impression is due to the incorporation of Deuteronomy into the Torah. In certain places, such as Deuteronomy 6:17 and 28:45, the text clearly reveals that the "I" refers not to Moses but to God as the original lawgiver:[135]

Be sure to keep the commands of YHWH your God and the stipulations and decrees *he has given you*. (Deuteronomy 6:17; emphasis added)

All these curses will come on you. They will pursue you and overtake you until you are destroyed, because you did not obey YHWH your God and observe the commands and decrees *he gave you*. (Deuteronomy 28:45; emphasis added)

From Deuteronomy, this interpretation of the law as the Law of God appears to have had a retrospective effect on the Covenant Code, lending it a new theological context and thereby elevating it to the same status as Deuteronomy.

Within the history of ideas, one can hardly overestimate the significance of the concept of divine law being formulated.[136] This idea not only portrayed the law as emanating from God himself but also gave the law an essentially normative quality—an innovation without precedent in ancient Near Eastern legal history.[137] Endowing legal provisions with divine authority, however, also brought with it a fundamental problem. A law of this nature could no longer be replaced or repealed. Only through biblical exegesis was it possible to update such a law or give it a new form, and with the passage of time revisions of this kind proved necessary over and over again as new problems arose.[138] The recasting of the old slave law from Exodus 21:2–7 in Deuteronomy 15:12–18 is a case in point:[139]

Exodus 21:2: When you buy a Hebrew slave, he shall serve you for six years, and in the seventh year he shall go free without pay.	Deuteronomy 15:12–13: When your brother, a Hebrew man or woman, sells himself to you, he shall serve you for six years and in the seventh year you shall set him free. And when you set him free, you shall not let him go empty-handed.
Exodus 21:5–6: But when the slave says, "I love my master, my wife, and my sons and do not want to go free," then his master shall take him before God. He shall take him to the door or the doorpost and there his master shall bore through his ear with an awl, and he will be his slave forever.	Deuteronomy 15:16–18: And when he says to you, "I do not want to depart from you," because he loves you and your house, because it has been good for him with you, then take an awl and pierce him through the ear into the door, and he will be your slave forever. You shall do the same thing with your female slave. It should not be difficult for you, if you must set him free; for in the six years that he was your slave, he cost you half as much as a day laborer. And YHWH your God will bless you in everything you do.

Slavery is seen as a perfectly natural state of affairs in Exodus 21 ("When you buy a Hebrew slave . . ."). By contrast, although slavery is accepted in Deuteronomy 15, it is viewed critically ("sells himself to you" means "is forced to sell himself to you"). Upon release, the slave in Deuteronomy 15 is equipped in such a way that he can make his own way in the world and not immediately slip back into debt slavery. However, if the slave wishes to serve permanently, then this arrangement is sealed through a rite which in Exodus 21 is clearly of a sacred nature ("before God"), whereas this same ritual appears in secular guise in Deuteronomy 15. Finally, one particularly striking element is the closing passage in Deuteronomy 15, which formulates a justification for emancipating a slave while at the same time raising the prospect of a divine blessing for keeping this commandment. The law in Deuteronomy is clearly intended to operate through common consent rather than through the use of executive force.

A further interpretative step is taken in the way both of these provisions are treated in the Holiness Code in Leviticus:[140]

> If any of your fellow Israelites become poor and sell themselves to you, do not make them work as slaves. They are to be treated as hired workers or temporary residents among you; they are to work for you until the Year of Jubilee. Then they and their children are to be released, and they will go back to their own clans and to the property of their ancestors. Because the Israelites are my servants, whom I brought out of Egypt, they must not be sold as slaves. Do not rule over them ruthlessly, but fear your God. Your male and female slaves are to come from the nations around you; from them you may buy slaves. You may also buy some of the temporary residents living among you and members of their clans born in your country, and they will become your property. You can bequeath them to your children as inherited property and can make them slaves for life, but you must not rule over your fellow Israelites ruthlessly. (Leviticus 25:39–46)

This passage forbids the ownership of slaves from Israel, for, as verse 25:42 stipulates, the people of Israel are the slaves of *God,* not of each other. The formulation "rule over them ruthlessly" (*bepharekh*) is taken from Exodus 1:13–14, where it alludes to Israel's subjugation in Egypt.[141] The Israelites must not rule over Israelites in the same way that the Egyptians ruled over the Israelites. According to Leviticus 25, only the keeping of foreign slaves is permitted.

This arrangement of text and commentary is of key theological importance. From a biblical point of view, it is not the law in itself that is normative, but the law *and* its interpretation. In other words, the dynamic of the interpretation is already embedded in the canon itself, and, consequently, points beyond it. There is no such thing as a timeless law of God in the Bible; even the Law of God—indeed, precisely that form of authority—requires constant updating.

3

Emerging Judaism

The Narrated World versus the Authors' World

The narrative passages of the Hebrew Bible are largely set in the pre-exile period. This is true above all of the account that runs from the book of Genesis to 2 Kings, which recounts the history of the world and then of Israel from its beginnings until the destruction of Jerusalem in 587 BCE. It ends with a brief account of the pardoning of Jeconiah, the penultimate king of Judah, by his captor, Nebuchadnezzar II, in Babylon. Only the concluding parts of the books of Chronicles, along with the books of Ezra and Nehemiah, Esther and Daniel cover the Babylonian Exile (586–538 BCE) and the period of Persian rule (539–331 BCE). The prophetic tradition also plays out for the most part in the pre-exile period. The only scriptures that are set exclusively in the period of Persian rule are the books of Haggai, Zechariah, and Malachi. Finally, many of the psalms, along with the Wisdom literature and the Song of Songs, are, by virtue of their attribution to David, Solomon, and other figures from Israelite prehistory, also located in the era preceding the Babylonian Exile.

The narrated time of the Hebrew Bible is thus located primarily in the period between the creation of the world and the destruction of Jerusalem in 587 BCE. But is this narrated world also that of the authors themselves? Even early biblical research considered Moses, rather than Adam, to be the first author of the Bible. So, well before the emergence of critical biblical scholarship in the eighteenth century, it was clear that the narrated world and the authors' world were not the same. We now know that the same is true of the period after Moses as well. These two worlds undoubtedly do overlap, since some biblical texts were composed before the time of the Babylonian

Exile. Yet the Hebrew Bible does not contain a single book that appears in any form other than its post-exile revision. Although the dates of many biblical texts are disputed, most scholars assign not just peripheral but also central sections of these texts to the post-exile period. These sections were not entirely new but rather involved reworkings of previously existing texts. In its present form, the Hebrew Bible is a record of early Judaism.[1]

This historical divergence between the narrated world and the world of the narrators is rooted in the backward-looking nature of the accounts. The narrators explain events of their present by relocating them to an idealized period of the past. The Torah, for example, establishes the basis for monotheism and the laws of Judaism in the revelation on Mount Sinai, which, according to biblical chronology, took place around 1200 BCE. But in historical terms, biblical monotheism evolved at the earliest in the late monarchical period and found its first explicit expression in texts produced during the Babylonian Exile (Isaiah 45:5–7).[2] Even key stipulations of the Torah, such as circumcision and the Sabbath rest, belong to the period of exile at the earliest, though the Torah resolutely maintains that they were instituted by Abraham (Genesis 17) and Moses (Exodus 16, 31:12–17), respectively.[3] Finally, the Torah unfolds for long stretches outside of Israel and Judah. For instance, the narrative from Exodus to Deuteronomy describes the journey of the people of Israel through the desert from Egypt to the eastern bank of the Jordan River and their imminent entry into the Promised Land. This narrative placement, together with the promulgation of the law in its entirety outside of Israel, is only comprehensible as the explication of an Israel "in exile." Thus, the Torah in its present configuration takes the diasporic existence of Israel for granted. In other words, it is a document of early Judaism, but one that presents itself in its spiritual substance as being as old as ancient Israel.[4]

This explains why the book of Genesis describes Abraham as having emigrated from Ur in Chaldea, that is, Babylon (Genesis 11:28–32, 15:7), when historical tradition locates his homeland within Israel itself, in the region of Hebron and Mamre (Genesis 18). For the same reason, Jacob is said to have had a dream in Bethel which predicts that his descendants will people the whole world:

There beside him stood YHWH, and he said: "I am YHWH, the God of your father Abraham and the God of Isaac. I will give you and your descendants the land on which you are lying. Your descendants will be like the dust of the earth, and you will spread out to the west and to the east, to the north and to the south. All peoples on earth will be blessed through you and your offspring." (Genesis 28:13–14)

Behind these texts lies the experience of those who were deported to Babylon, who wanted to see their return to Judah after exile as having been anticipated by Abraham. Similarly—though this is at variance with the view taken by the prophetic tradition (see Jeremiah 24:9–10)—the exiled Israelites interpreted their dispersal not as a token of God's punishment but as a means by which God enacted universal salvation. Seen from this standpoint, Israel had to go into exile in order that the world might thereby earn divine blessing (see Genesis 12:2–3).

The Loss of the Temple Cult in Jerusalem

The destruction of Jerusalem and the First Temple by the Neo-Babylonians (called by their Greek name, "Chaldeans," in some Bibles) in 587 BCE is the most drastic event in the history of ancient Judah and hence, in a wider sense, also of Israel.[5] The last king of Judah, Zedekiah, had rebelled against Babylonian rule over his realm. In response, in the ninth year of his reign (that is, in the year 588 BCE; see 2 Kings 25:10), the Babylonian army laid siege to Jerusalem. A year and a half later, in 587 BCE, Jerusalem fell (2 Kings 25:2–3). One month after that, the city was destroyed, the king was taken prisoner and deported, his sons were put to death, and the temple was sacked and burned to the ground, along with the royal palace and many houses (2 Kings 25:7, 9, 13–17). The city walls were torn down and all the high priests and temple officials were executed (2 Kings 25: 9, 18–21; see also Jeremiah 52:12–14). After the loss of their kingdom, state, and shrine, the people of Judah were forced to reinvent themselves in both political and religious terms. Under Gedaliah, a member of the pro-Babylonian party of the Shaphanites (the family of the royal scribe Shaphan), a small-scale successor kingdom arose with the Babylonians' blessing, though not in Jerusalem but instead in the village of Mizpah, a few kilometers north of the city (Jeremiah 39–41; see also 2 Kings 25:22–26). This did not survive for long, however.[6] The Bible presents Gedeliah, who was assassinated, as merely a governor.

Historically, though, he may well have been a Babylonian vassal king who was murdered in a nationalist insurrection. The establishment of the state at Mizpah did not mark the start of a successful, enduring political venture. Gedaliah's murderers, whose ringleader evidently came from the house of David (Jeremiah 41:1), would not tolerate a person who was not of that lineage occupying the position of king.

Jeremiah 41:5 gives an account of ritual observances at a ruined temple ("the house of YHWH"). It is not clear, however, whether this refers to the temple in Jerusalem or to the shrine at Bethel. The latter is a more likely scenario, as the worshippers came from sites in the northern kingdom, such as Shechem, Shiloh, and Samaria. But in any case, the destruction of the temple, regarded as the central place of worship and as God's residence on earth, must have represented a historical watershed without precedent. The New Babylonian conquest spelled the end of the kingdoms that surrounded ancient Judah—Ammon and Moab (conquered in around 582 BCE) and Edom (553 or 551). Their principal deities, Milqom, Chemosh, and Qôs, did not vanish immediately, but they did not survive antiquity. An inscription in the Moabite language dating from the late fourth century BCE that was discovered at El-Kerak, Jordan, names the Moabite god Chemosh and his wife, Sarra.[7] It indicates that veneration of Chemosh endured into the Hellenistic period.[8] Thereafter all traces of the deities worshipped in Ammon, Moab, and Edom vanish.

Ancient Judaism took a different long-term path from the Moabite, Ammonite, and Edomite religions, as evidenced by the continuing survival of Judaism and the emergence of its daughter religions. Unlike these other ancient religions, Judaism did not go into terminal decline with the end of antiquity but is still very much alive today. The same is true of Christianity, which began as a Jewish sect, as well as Islam, which came into being in late antiquity and was influenced in many different ways by Judaism and Christianity. Even short-term developments were significant for this divergence. The policy of deportation implemented by the Babylonians in 587 BCE was markedly different from that enacted by the Assyrians, who overran the northern kingdom of Israel in 722 BCE.[9] The Jews transported to Babylon were not dispersed but were settled in colonies, and the Jewish communities that grew up there seem to have retained their separate cultural and religious identity.[10] It is possible that a temple was erected for the exile community in Babylon, though there is no firm evidence to substantiate this.[11] Since it was

Figure 35. Clay tablets from Al Yahudu ("Judah Town"), thought to have been located southeast of Nippur, from the period of the Babylonian Exile, sixth century BCE.

predominantly the upper echelons of Jewish society that were deported, influential bearers and recorders of tradition may have remained active in the exile community (Figure 35).

Even though the Bible sometimes conveys the impression that the land formerly occupied by Judah was entirely or almost entirely uninhabited during the Babylonian Exile (2 Kings 24:14, 25:21; 2 Chronicles 36:20–21), archeological finds from Judah during the exile period suggest that significant numbers of people remained.[12] It is hard to determine, however, which biblical texts may have originated there. The traditional body of texts represented by the Psalms and the Wisdom literature must have continued to be handed down and enlarged. Likewise, the books of Kings were supplemented and embellished right up to the end of the monarchical period and beyond.[13] Yet the text that most clearly reflects the situation during the exile period in Judah is the book of Lamentations. This is a collection of five songs, the first four of which are internally arranged so as to form acrostics. That is, the first letter of each of the twenty-two verses or strophes (Lamentations 3 comprises sixty-six verses) follows the twenty-two letters of the Hebrew alphabet. While the fifth lamentation also has twenty-two verses, its opening letters are not in alphabetical order. In the Greek tradition, authorship of the Lamentations is ascribed to Jeremiah (presumably on the basis of the note in 2 Chronicles 35:25, which claims that Jeremiah was responsible for composing a lament for King Josiah).[14] The songs are reflections on the downfall of Jerusalem and develop a theology of guilt for the city, to which the prologue to the Deutero-Isaiah section (chapters 40–55) of the book of Isaiah, in particular, is a response. This prologue (Isaiah 40:1–2) absolves the city of sin. In the Deutero-Isaiah chapters, the city is presented as a figure in its own right and not simply as an agglomeration of its inhabitants.[15] The acrostic form of the Lamentations conveys an impression of insularity and completeness, though it is possible that the more open format of the fifth lamentation is meant to suggest a dynamic for the whole book pointing beyond the blameworthy state of Jerusalem. In any event, the closing proclamation seems to have been chosen with care:

> Restore us to yourself, YHWH, that we may return; renew our days as of old unless you have utterly rejected us and are angry with us beyond measure. (Lamentations 5:21–22)

Because of the Jewish people's continued exile, which lasted for centuries, the Lamentations of Israel have remained topical and thus have been passed down in the tradition.

That the religion of YHWH was able to survive, be it in Babylon, Egypt, or within the land of its origin, has to do primarily with how the catastrophe that befell the northern kingdom of Israel in 722 BCE was resolved. Because Israel and Judah worshipped the same national deity, YHWH, the demise of

Israel had already prompted a decisive reshaping of people's understanding of divinity.[16] An influx of refugees from the northern kingdom must have spread this reinterpretation to the southern realm of Judah. God was no longer seen as simply a guarantor of prosperity and of the political and commercial success of those who worshipped him. After the fall of Samaria, significant portions of the population migrated south.[17] The theological "coping strategies" of the north were almost certainly being used by leadership circles in the south as early as the late eighth and the seventh centuries BCE. Theological recastings of biblical literature during the Babylonian Exile observed these same coping strategies. Reinterpreting the religion of ancient Judah in the light of emerging Judaism, this remodeling process divested the belief system of the confusion of earthly politics and began to conceive of God as independent of the success or failure of political leaders.

Literary Production during the Babylonian Exile

Although the extent of the deportations from Judah to Mesopotamia carried out by the Babylonians remains a matter of dispute, there is no question that sizable, colony-like settlements of Judeans grew up in the land between the Tigris and Euphrates Rivers. It is also clear that these settlements included social classes with sophisticated religious and cultural knowledge.[18]

In depicting the events of the exile, the second book of Kings makes explicit mention of priests among the deportees (2 Kings 25:18). It makes sense, then, that the Babylonian Exile not only nurtured traditional texts but also proved fertile ground for the emergence of new literature. Contact with educated Babylonians led to an enormous intellectualization of literary production. We must bear in mind that Babylon at that time had long been seen as an intellectual center of the Near East, with an academic life dating back some two thousand years.[19]

Texts of the Hebrew Bible that focus on matters relating to priests display unmistakable Babylonian influences. These include the so-called Priestly Source—source material that is considered to be the "original text" of the Pentateuch and most likely ran from the story of the creation to the giving of the law on Mount Sinai. The Priestly Source was first hypothesized by Theodor Nöldeke, and Julius Wellhausen and his followers believed it to have been written during the Babylonian Exile or the Persian period.[20] Other such texts are the Deutero-Isaiah (Isaiah 40–55) and the book of Ezekiel. It is hard to believe that they were not produced in Babylon, or at the very least by people who once lived in Babylon. The protagonist of the book of Ezekiel is described as belonging to a group of Judeans who were deported to Babylon in 597 BCE along with King Jeconiah (2 Kings 24:14). King Jeconiah is mentioned in Babylonian documents that list the food rations distributed to residents of the Babylonian royal court.[21]

Above all, those parts of the Priestly Source text that relate to Genesis 1–11—the chapters that treat the creation of the world and its earliest history—show evidence of a literary interaction with Babylonian scholars. The main features of the cosmology developed in Genesis 1 are taken from the Babylonian epic of creation known as the Enuma Elish, while the theme and the form of the passage describing the Great Flood are clearly inspired by the Mesopotamian epics of Atrahasis and Gilgamesh.[22] It is tempting to speculate that its authors were priests who had returned from Mesopotamia and brought their learning back with them. Yet the conception in the Priestly Source of what constitutes a tabernacle—a portable tent consecrated and erected in the desert as a shrine for the Israelites (see Exodus 25–31, 35–40)—is characteristic of an "exile" mode of thought and gives no hint of prefiguring the Second Temple in Jerusalem. As a result, it is far more likely that its author had lived in Babylon.

However, the Priestly Source did not assimilate Babylonian material just because those stories were well known and widespread in Mesopotamia. The biblical authors who were active in the Babylonian diaspora were apparently open to the intellectual ambience of their surroundings, which surely must have struck them as superior to their own milieu and therefore worthy of consideration. The creation story given in the Priestly Source thus provides early evidence of a dialogue between religious tradition and scholarly insight, however artificial such a distinction may have been to the ancient mind. The authors clearly recognized the necessity of adapting their own traditions to new learning and thereby staying abreast of contemporary intellectual trends.[23]

The tradition of the Deutero-Isaiah (Isaiah 40–55) may be traced back to an anonymous prophet or group of prophets active in Babylon whose work was subsequently incorporated into the book of Isaiah. The prologue, with its image of a mighty and miraculous procession of YHWH through the desert back to Zion, appears to be based on the experiences of exiled Judeans who had witnessed the monumental New Year celebration in Babylon with its magnificent procession of images of deities.[24] After seeing this, they pictured no less splendid a spectacle accompanying the return of their own god to Jerusalem; indeed, they imagined an even more wondrous event:[25]

> A voice of one calling: "In the wilderness prepare the way for YHWH; make straight in the desert a highway for our God. Every valley shall be raised up, every mountain and hill made low; the rough ground shall become level, the rugged places a plain." (Isaiah 40:3–4)

Likewise, the depictions of the visions of Jerusalem and the temple in Ezekiel 40–42 can only truly be understood against the backdrop of the Babylonian Exile. They suggest that the author(s) of the text did not intend the numinous realm of the biblical God to lag behind its Mesopotamian counterparts.[26] In the vision that first inspires him to become a prophet, Ezekiel sees a four-winged creature with the feet of a calf supporting the vault of heaven, above which God is enthroned in majesty (Ezekiel 1:6, 22, 25–28). A comparison of Ezekiel 1 with the iconography of an ancient Near Eastern cylinder seal from the reign of the Neo-Assyrian ruler Ashurbanipal (669–627 BCE) suggests how strongly this vision was influenced by Mesopotamian models.[27]

The scene shows a winged deity in the center, standing on the back of a horse (Figure 36). Around the area of its hips the figure is joined to a plate that is supported by two creatures that are half-human, half-bull. In the upper left is an eight-pointed star, and in the upper right a crescent moon. The scene is framed on the left by a priest dressed in a fish robe and on the right by a man in prayer who is facing the deity. This ensemble clearly indicates that the subject is the Mesopotamian sun-god shown in anthropomorphic form and joined to the heavenly firmament, which is being carried by hybrid beings.

This cosmological constellation forms the background of Ezekiel 1. Like the iconography of the cylinder seal, the book of Ezekiel describes a plate-like vault of heaven supported by hybrid creatures. This firmament separates

Figure 36. Cylinder seal from the reign of Ashurbanipal (669–627 BCE), depicting a deity being carried on the vault of heaven.

the earthly from the godly realm. Unlike the depiction on the seal, the book of Ezekiel describes God as being enthroned above the vault, rather than on it. The similarities and differences between the cylinder-seal image and the biblical text are equally telling.

Alongside its influences from Babylon, the vision described in Ezekiel 1 also reflects a transference to the heavenly realm of Israel's conception of divinity after the destruction of Jerusalem in 587 BCE. The texts from Jerusalem that are thought to date from the monarchical period have virtually nothing to say about "heaven" in connection with God's dwelling place (see especially Isaiah 6:1–11). Evidently, "pre-exile conceptions of God's dwelling place in Jerusalem did not entertain any thought of an explicit localization of the throne of God in the cosmic realm of heaven."[28] Such a conception only arose in the wake of the religious and historical transformations that took place following the loss of the First Temple. These changes modified the close connection between God and his place of worship— albeit in various different ways and with differing emphases. Hereafter,

God's dwelling place is in heaven and thus removed from political and military upheavals (see, for example, 1 Kings 8:30–39, 44–45; Psalm 2:4).[29] Even so, some of these texts are at pains to emphasize that even heaven is not large enough to contain God:

> But will God really dwell on earth? The heavens, even the highest heaven, cannot contain you. How much less this temple I have built! (1 Kings 8:27)

The Emergence of Judaism and Monotheism

Historically, the most significant consequence of the destruction of Jerusalem and the deportation of large numbers of Judeans to Babylon was the emergence of Judaism.[30] This process has left its mark throughout the Bible. The question of when Judaism was founded is a matter of dispute, however, and cannot be answered either unequivocally or with absolute historical accuracy. "Judaism" has never existed as a single, monolithic entity, and so determining when it began depends upon what one means by the term. The earliest position sets the starting point as Moses, and the latest as the destruction of Jerusalem by the Romans in 70 CE.[31] Neither of these positions is tenable. But at least these two points establish the bounds of the period within which Judaism gradually evolved from the religion of ancient Israel and Judah.[32] In any event, the emergence of Judaism was a process that had neither a clear beginning nor a definite end. It embraces many different developments and manifests itself in myriad forms.[33] In English-speaking countries, this has given rise to the rather unattractive, if factually accurate, expression "Judaisms."[34]

The term "Judaism" derives from the Greek *ioudaismos*. The earliest evidence for its use comes from the Hellenistic period, when it was coined as an antonym to "Hellenism." It is used in a particularly eloquent way in the book of 2 Maccabees, as for example in this passage from 2:19–21:

> Jason of Cyrene has recorded in five volumes the story of Judas Maccabeus and his brothers . . . who fought bravely and enthusiastically to defend Judaism. Our forces were few in number, but they plundered the entire country and routed the heathen forces.[35]

Here, the term "Judaism" denotes a theologically defined quality whose main purpose is to distinguish a specific group from the opposing camp. This aspect of social delimitation is also on display in 2 Maccabees 8:1:

> Judas Maccabeus and his friends went secretly from village to village until they had gathered a force of about 6,000 Jewish men who had remained faithful to their religion.

According to this account, people did not become adherents of "Judaism" by virtue of their heredity or place of residence, but as the result of a conscious decision. In substance, though, the entity denoted by the term "Judaism"—a distinct faith independent of all state structures, which defines itself through specific confessional content and a particular genealogical cohesion—is much older, dating back to the period of the Babylonian Exile. The biblical scholar Julius Wellhausen expressed this in terms that would today be regarded as politically incorrect but were in keeping with the modes of thought of his age: "The Jewish Church arose when the Jewish state declined."[36] But what existed prior to this? To quote Wellhausen again: "The Israelite religion worked its way up from paganism only very gradually; indeed, that process forms the subject matter of its history."[37] Modern historians of religion would object strongly to the disparaging category of "paganism" and the evolutionary metaphor of "working one's way up." Linear schemata of evolution or decadence are inappropriate when discussing developments in religious history. But leaving aside for a moment these problematic categories and terminologies, contemporary biblical scholarship is still inclined to consider Wellhausen's depiction of the course of Israel and Judah's religious history as a perfectly valid one—as evidenced by inscriptions and religious archeological finds from the monarchical period in addition to literary and historical reconstruction of the biblical texts. Indeed, over the past thirty years, the picture of the prevailing religion (or religions) of the monarchical period in ancient Israel and Judah that has emerged has been thoroughly well documented and confirms the essential features of Wellhausen's hypothesis.[38] Fertility and benediction icons, protective emblems, symbols of gods and goddesses, and grave goods all provide clear evidence, though we must guard against positing a simple dichotomy between a "polytheistic" religion of Israel and Judah during the monarchical period and a "monotheistic" religion of later Judaism.[39] The religious history of Israel did not unfold as a two-stage process; it witnessed a number of different developments that ran in parallel with one another, and in which we can identify both discontinuities and continuities.

The Hebrew Bible contains several reminders of the pre-monotheistic past of the religion of Israel and Judah. These cannot be reconstructed as fragments of literature preserved from the monarchical period; instead, they are contained within polytheistic language games that point to that period.[40] For instance, Deuteronomy 32:8–9 appears to contain a reflection on the multiplicity of religions that existed among the peoples of the region:

> When the Most High gave the nations their inheritance,[41] when he divided all mankind, he set up boundaries for the peoples according to the number of the sons of Israel [other versions: "the sons of God"]. For YHWH's portion is his people, Jacob his allotted inheritance.

Although the biblical text uses the phrasing "sons of Israel" instead of "sons of God," the version using "God" is confirmed both by one of the Dead Sea Scrolls fragments (4QDeut^j) and by the Septuagint. The current reading, with "sons of Israel," is almost certainly the result of an orthodox correction that was meant to erase the polytheistic undertones of the passage. In what was probably the original version, with "sons of God," the passage represents the position that God established the different peoples according to the number of minor deities, and that only the nation of Israel (expressed in the metonymic formulation "Jacob") is assigned directly to him as the highest God. Yet in religious-historical terms, the title "the Most High," which here refers to YHWH, evokes associations with the supreme god El, to whom this title was originally applied. This passage thus retains a gentle reminder of the fact that YHWH was not always seen as the supreme deity.

A similar text can be found in Psalm 82, which forms part of the so-called Elohistic Psalter (Psalms 42–82). In this section of the book of Psalms, the tetragrammaton YHWH has been replaced almost entirely by the Hebrew term *Elohim* ("God"); thus it is reasonable to assume that Psalm 82 originally made reference to YHWH. This text, too, has a monotheistic profile: YHWH is the only God, and the other gods must perish. It is played out within a conceptual world that is still polytheistic, however, in an imaginary courtroom scene in which YHWH, as the prosecutor, declares that the other gods are the sons of the "Most High":

> God [YHWH] stands in the divine assembly, in the midst of the
>   gods he holds judgment:
> "How long will you judge unjustly and favor the wicked? Selah.
> Do justice for the lowly and the orphaned, for the destitute and
>   needy provide equity. . . .
> I have spoken: 'You are gods and all of you sons of the Most High.'
> However: Like a human you will die and like the princes you will
>   fall."
> Arise, God [YHWH], judge the earth, for you have an inheritance
>   in all peoples. (Psalm 82:1–3, 5–8)[42]

Psalm 82 can no longer be dated to the pre-exile period, though it does appear to have retained some suggestions of early forms of Judaism. The psalm formulates its monotheistic program within the context of a polytheistic language game.

The emergence of Judaism in the time of the Babylonian Exile marked the beginning of a development within religious history that proved to be extraordinarily successful globally over the following twenty-five hundred years. Judaism and its daughter religions set the benchmark for what constituted a viable "religion." Judaism is the first "secondary religion" in world history, having evolved out of the "primary religion" of ancient Israel and Judah under diasporic conditions and subsequently been modified by Babylonian, Persian, and Hellenistic influences.[43] Primary religions include animisms, shamanisms, and religious systems that assign divine qualities to natural entities or events; secondary religions are based on specific kinds of information that are the object of particular beliefs. Christianity and Islam join company with Judaism as secondary religions. They, too, interpret reality with the support of sacred texts that proved decisive in shaping their interpretation of reality.

The Second Temple and Its Literature

Contrary to the view that prevailed within classical biblical scholarship of the nineteenth and twentieth centuries, it is now widely accepted that the

Second Temple period was the most important for the formation of biblical literature. The Second Temple was built in 515 BCE in the face of resistance not only from Samaria, but also from the people of Judah itself (see Haggai 1:2–11). Its dimensions were probably similar to those of the First Temple.[44] We have no idea what the First or Second Temple in Jerusalem really looked like, however, since the information in the Bible is not architecturally reliable.[45] In a sociological sense, the Second Temple would have had a similar makeup to the First. Priests and scribes were active there. Their role would have included the transmission of significant religious texts. The traditional priestly caste at the temple, the Zadokites, appear to have been somewhat eclipsed in the post-exile period. This caste traced its origins back to Zadok, the legendary high priest under King David. The Levites, formerly a highly influential group that was responsible for overseeing worship at local shrines, also declined in importance and seem to have become a kind of *clerus minor,* or lower clergy, at the Second Temple.[46] By contrast, the priestly caste of the Aaronites, who regarded Moses's brother as their founding father, gained considerably in importance after the Babylonian Exile. This may have had something to do with the deportations to Babylon. There, the Jewish priesthood developed its own self-identity and deliberately set itself apart in genealogical terms from the traditional groups who staffed the temple in Jerusalem. In their view, Aaron, as the brother of Moses, commanded greater authority than Zadok.

Because of the straitened economic and social circumstances in Jerusalem under Persian rule, some commentators have doubted whether many texts of what later became the Bible could possibly have been composed in this period.[47] In truth, most literary activity at this time would probably have been focused on revising existing texts. In terms of their content, however, the texts in question were of enormous importance. Monotheism, the covenant, and the law are theological characteristics of ancient Judaism whose role as key elements of a distinctive Jewish identity did not emerge until the Babylonian Exile period.[48] And yet their literary anchoring within the Hebrew Bible makes it almost impossible to read the texts without constantly calling to mind these characteristics—notwithstanding the fact that substantial sections of the Hebrew Bible predate the exile period.

The theological history of the Second Temple period is characterized by an antagonism between theocracy and eschatology, as the theologian Otto Plöger once neatly summarized this conflict.[49] "Theocratic" views saw the political, social, and religious situation of Judaism during the period of Persian rule as part of God's plan of salvation for the world and his chosen people. By contrast, "eschatological" views opposed foreign rule and the diasporic existence of Israel and anticipated a fundamental change in the future: God would intervene once more in history to restore his people to the conditions of the monarchical period. This binary contrast has often been criticized, but we should not misconstrue these as simple "either–or" categories within which the post-exile literature can be neatly pigeonholed. Instead, they should be regarded as two poles to which individual texts or scriptures have a greater or lesser proximity.

Whereas the overwhelming response in ancient Israel to the Assyrian and Babylonian occupying powers was one of outright rejection and subversion, in the case of the theocratic strand of post-exile literature, the attitude was quite the opposite. The reason for this is that the Persians, unlike the earlier imperial powers, pursued comparatively tolerant policies toward the peoples they conquered, granting them a large measure of linguistic, religious, legal, and cultural autonomy.[50] This was no doubt born of sheer necessity, given the vast extent of the Persian Empire, rather than the result of any (pre-) humanistic considerations.

"Theocratic" Concepts: The Priestly Source and the Books of Chronicles

The Persian imperial ideology of a pacified multiethnic state, in which each constituent province retained its own cultural and religious identity, was enunciated, for example, in Darius I's inscription at Mount Behistun (ca. 519 BCE).[51] As an Aramaic version discovered by archaeologists on the Nile island of Elephantine demonstrates, this inscription was also in circulation as a school text. It was taken up and assimilated in a positive way above all in biblical texts of the Persian period relating to matters of ritual observance, notably in the Priestly Source in the Pentateuch and in the books of Chronicles.[52]

These texts assume that the redemptive objective of YHWH's history with Israel and the world at large has been achieved in the form of Persian hegemony and the religious tolerance toward Judaism that came with it. To put it in a nutshell, they depict a state of "realized eschatology."[53] Of course, this objective still needed to be fully realized in a number of ways, but the turning point toward salvation had basically been reached. This position ultimately amounted to Jewish acceptance of official Persian imperial ideology.

In the Priestly Source this image of a peacefully ordered world, inspired by the era of Persian dominion, can be seen in the so-called Table of Nations in Genesis 10, which describes the repeopling of the world after the Great Flood. It contains a refrain that outlines the ordering of the world according to languages, clans, and tribes:

> The sons of Japheth . . . spread out into their territories by their clans within their nations, each with its own language. . . . These are the sons of Ham by their clans and languages, in their territories and nations. . . . These are the sons of Shem by their clans and languages, in their territories and nations. (Genesis 10:2, 5, 20, 31)

The Priestly Source's quietist stance and its theocratic conception of order are also apparent in the programmatic text of Genesis 9. After the flood, God causes a rainbow to appear in the clouds. But the simple Hebrew word for "bow" that is used here can also, as in English, signify a weapon of war. The image of the (rain)bow in the clouds thus hints that God renounces the use of force against his creation and, instead, guarantees it permanent existence (Genesis 9:14–15). Hence, for the Priestly Source, God himself declared such violence a closed chapter back in the mists of time, after the flood that wiped out virtually all life on earth. God's capacity to turn against living creatures on earth is interpreted as a prehistoric, now obsolete trait of his character:

> Then God said to Noah: "The end of all flesh has come up before me, for the earth is full of their wickedness. Therefore, I will eradicate them from the earth." (Genesis 6:13)[54]

This harsh proclamation of the "end" that has arrived is not an invention of the Priestly Source, but is taken from prophecies of the day of judgment:

> "What do you see, Amos?" he [YHWH] asked. "A basket of ripe fruit," I answered. Then YHWH said to me, "The time is ripe for my people Israel; I will spare them no longer." (Amos 8:2)

Son of man, this is what the lord YHWH says to the land of Israel: "The end! The end has come upon the four corners of the land! The end is now upon you. . . ." (Ezekiel 7:2–3)

The Priestly Source thus picks up the pre- and post-exilic prophecy of the day of judgment, but places it in a setting of ancient prehistory: yes, it admits, God did once resolve to put an "end" to the world, but that lies in the past, not the future.

Theologically, the message of the Priestly Source is likewise geared toward Israel. Just as the covenant with Noah in Genesis 9 guarantees the permanent survival of the earth, so the pact with Abraham expressed in Genesis 17 ensures Israel's continuing proximity to God. No conditions are attached in either case. For the Priestly Source, the "covenant" is a unilateral promise of redemption on YHWH's part. It is still possible for individuals to lapse from this covenant (for example, if they refuse to undergo circumcision), but not for Abraham's descendants taken as a whole.

In addition, the Priestly Source (or at least a significant portion of it) is responsible for the introduction of the Pentateuch into Genesis 1–11. This has the effect of placing the national and religious tradition of Israel and Judah in a universal context, both temporally and spatially. The historical explanation for this is that the Priestly Source is presumed to have been written during the early period of Persian rule. The desire to place a particular tradition in a global context is perfectly reasonable, given the exiled situation of its creators.

In the Chronicles (the two books of Chronicles were counted as a single book in antiquity), David and Solomon, in their capacity as initiators and builders of the temple, can be seen as the "prehistoric" models for Cyrus and Darius. Cyrus facilitated the rebuilding of the temple through his edict, while Darius ordered its actual construction. In the Chronicles, David and Solomon are almost entirely divested of their political functions and are presented instead primarily as the instigators of the temple cult.[55] This is also why the Chronicles devote by far the greater part of their account to the reigns of David (1 Chronicles 11–29) and Solomon (2 Chronicles 1–9) and why, in their treatment of history, they make no mention whatsoever of the northern kingdom. The north had nothing to do with the temple in Jerusalem, and as a result its political history was irrelevant. In the theology of the Chronicles the northern tribes remain part of Israel, as they always had been; the Chronicles are open to the possibility that the north might one day realign itself with the temple in Jerusalem.

In sections of the books of Jeremiah and Isaiah added by redactors, the striking descriptions of the foreign rulers as venerators—indeed, even as chosen ones—of the biblical God also form part of this theocratic view of the world. Thus, the Babylonian king of kings Nebuchadnezzar (who, lest we forget, destroyed Jerusalem and its temple) is described in Jeremiah 25:9, 27:6, and 43:10 as God's "servant," while his Persian counterpart Cyrus is addressed as "my shepherd" in Isaiah 44:28. Mention should also be made here of the stories of Daniel in Daniel 1–6, each of which concludes with the foreign ruler praising the God of Israel. These positions can only be understood historically against the background of the era of Persian rule, in which the idea developed that God might also make use of foreign kings in his dominion over the earth. This "theocratic" concept presupposes a decoupling of the religion of ancient Israel from a conceptual framework that was wedded to its own state and royal house and its universalizing expansion—something that only became a reality from the Persian period onward.

"Eschatological" Concepts: Prophetic and Deuteronomic Texts

During the Persian period the "eschatological" position was expressed primarily in the prophetic literature and within the so-called school of Deuteronomism. Deuteronomism refers to an intellectual movement that adhered to the theological principles of the Deuteronomic Code but sought to further develop them.[56] Its texts are couched in the language of Deuteronomy and share its fundamental convictions—that God enjoins his people to follow his laws, and if they do so their well-being is assured, while if they do not, misfortune will follow. The Deuteronomic position maintains that, with no kingdom and no country of its own anymore, Israel nevertheless remains bound by the law to which it once committed itself.

This position is evident in the updating of Deuteronomy itself and of the Former Prophets (Joshua to Kings), as well as in the book of Jeremiah. The tradition of the prophet Jeremiah, which arose immediately before and during the period of Jerusalem's destruction, lent itself especially well to speculation, in the form of literary disquisitions on the reasons for and the continuation of the judgment:

> From the time your ancestors left Egypt until now, day after day, again and again I sent you my servants the prophets. But they did not listen to me or pay attention. They were stiff-necked and did more evil than their ancestors. When you tell them all this, they will not listen to you; when you call to them, they will not answer. (Jeremiah 7:25–27)

The history of Israel and Judah is presented as a history of disobedience, which lasted until the time of Jeremiah and—this is undoubtedly how the text above is to be understood—also to the time of the readers of the book that bears his name. It is certainly true that Deuteronomic texts from the era of exile and the Persian period often augment the Deuteronomic view of history by providing prospects of salvation, which envisage Israel's return from exile, God's mercy on the day of judgment, and sometimes even the Second Coming.[57] Yet such events, even those that have already taken place, do not bring with them ultimate redemption. The severity of God's judgment has certainly been tempered somewhat by such factors as the building of the temple, the qualified degree of autonomy the Jewish people have attained, and the return of sections of the populace to Israel and Judah. Yet the only act that would bring about decisive change—God's intervention in history—was still widely anticipated.

In the view of these Deuteronomic theologians, the inverse conclusion was also perfectly admissible: not only does disobedience bring misfortune with it, but also, because salvation has failed to materialize, it must be that Israel is still failing to comply with God's will, just as it always has. For the history of post-exile theology, it is significant that by this time the conviction that human beings can through their own efforts heed God's voice and do his will seems to have steadily faded.[58] Instead, a different view was increasingly gaining ground—that humanity is no longer master in its own house. As a result, prophetic texts of the Persian period present visions that contemplate the emergence of a new kind of person. Regarding the promise of a new covenant, Jeremiah 31:33–34 anticipates that the law will be inscribed into the hearts of the people of Israel, so that they will no longer need to teach each other:

"This is the covenant I will make with the people of Israel after that time," declares YHWH. "I will put my law in their minds and write it on their hearts. I will be their God, and they will be my people. No longer will they teach their neighbor, or say to one another, 'Know YHWH,' because they will all know me, from the least of them to the greatest," declares YHWH. "For I will forgive their wickedness and will remember their sins no more." (Jeremiah 31:33–34)

This passage sets itself in opposition to the conviction underlying the *Shema Yisrael* (Deuteronomy 6:4–9)—that the law needs to be constantly called to mind and passed on:

These commandments that I give you today are to be on your hearts. Impress them on your children. Talk about them when you sit at home and when you walk along the road, when you lie down and when you get up. (Deuteronomy 6:6–7)

The internalization of the law ultimately renders the written Torah and the process of reciprocal teaching among people redundant. We should therefore hardly be surprised that Jeremiah 31:31–34 has been the subject of virtually no exegesis within Judaism, where the Torah and the teaching of the Torah have been considered indispensable.[59]

Alongside this idea, there is the even more far-reaching notion that God will not simply replenish the contents of the human heart but will actually replace the old heart with an entirely new one:

I will give you a new heart and put a new spirit in you; I will remove from you your heart of stone and give you a heart of flesh. And I will put my spirit in you and move you to follow my decrees and be careful to keep my laws. (Ezekiel 36:26–27)

For the book of Ezekiel, the implanting of new content in the heart does not go far enough. Instead, a heart transplant is required; only a new heart will be able to become the seat of the divine spirit within humans.[60]

In addition to anticipating the emergence of a new breed of humanity, prophetic literature of the exile and post-exile period also raised the prospect of a restoration of the royal House of David.[61] For these scriptures it was inconceivable that a theologically legitimate, meaningful, and fulfilled life might be possible under foreign rule. As long as Israel was not united under a new scion of the House of David or even a new David—a *David redivivus*—it was still threatened by God's judgment.

Delayed Redemption

In the early period of the Second Temple, the theocratic positions appeared to be self-evidently true, based on real-world experience. God's redemption was being realized in contemporary political developments. Yet with the passage of time, assessment of the empirical evidence began to change even within theocratic circles. The increasingly parlous state that Israel and Judah found themselves in, despite the building of the Second Temple, was now interpreted as a postponement of the expected redemption. Economic conditions were extremely depressed, to judge from the precarious circumstances described in Nehemiah 5. The population of Jerusalem and the whole of Judah again dwindled to a negligible level. The texts that are customarily referred to as the Trito-Isaiah (Isaiah 56–66; from the Latin root *trito-*, meaning "third") make clear reference to this problem. Except for the somewhat older core of the book in Isaiah 60–62, they can probably be dated to the fourth or third centuries BCE.[62] The salvation that was promised in the Deutero-Isaiah section (Isaiah 40–55) did not occur in the way it had been outlined. As a result of their firsthand experience of shortages, hardship, and injustice, the authors of the Trito-Isaiah inquired after the reasons; they identified these impediments to salvation as based in improper conduct by God's chosen people in both the religious and the social spheres. The warnings and laments found in these chapters are the result of this conclusion: Israel must repent and deal with these shortcomings—otherwise, the redemption promised by God cannot be realized. The Trito-Isaiah, contrary to what earlier scholars claimed, does not have its origins in a previous oral proclamation by an independent prophet. These chapters should instead be seen as the product of a scribal tradition of prophecy that never existed in any other form than texts for a book.[63] This scribal character is exemplified both by the radically different theological profile of Isaiah 56–66 when compared with Isaiah 40–55, and also by the new guise in which Isaiah 40:3 reappears in Isaiah 57:14:

A voice of one calling: "In the wilderness prepare the way for YHWH; make straight in the desert a highway for our God." (Isaiah 40:3)

And it will be said: "Build up, build up, prepare the road! Remove the obstacles out of the way of my people." (Isaiah 57:14)

In Isaiah 40:3, there is a call for a processional way to be laid out for God, so that he might return to Zion (Jerusalem) and reenter his sanctuary there. Isaiah 57:14 picks up this call but reinterprets it ethically: the social and religious failings among the people must first be eliminated if salvation is to be realized.

The position taken in Isaiah 56–59 did not, however, prove to be a sustainable solution to the problem of delayed redemption. The texts in Isaiah 63–66 transform the warnings and laments of Isaiah 56–59. The advent of the salvation that the people have been yearning for no longer depends upon an ever-expanding set of conditions, but is instead restricted to one group within Israel, the "devout." Followers from other groups may, however, attach themselves to this group. This signals a renunciation of the idea of God's chosen people. The closing texts of the book of Isaiah (chapters 65 and 66) foresee that salvation will be granted only to the just, while sinners will be subject to judgment (Isaiah 65:1–15; compare Isaiah 57:20–21).

In the history of theology, this step marks a dramatic break. It rescinded the notion of the chosen people "Israel" as a recipient of salvation—a concept that went largely unchallenged during the pre-Hellenistic period—and paved the way for an individualization of the Jewish religion. This change manifested itself first in the growth of so-called apocalypticism: salvation henceforth depended upon the behavior and destiny of the individual. This tendency subsequently gained in strength, especially in the wake of the destruction of Jerusalem in 70 CE, and it also had a decisive influence on Christianity. Christianity's message of salvation is likewise not aimed at any particular ethnic, social, or political grouping but at each and every person.

The Formation of the Torah under Persian Rule

One process must be recognized as among the most important stages in the development of a collection of authoritative scriptures during the Persian period. This is the formation of the Torah ("Law") as a self-contained body of text that was seen as normative within contemporary Judaism. This process meant that, for the first time in the intellectual history of the ancient Near East, a body of legislation was established as a significant entity independent of any royal authority.[64] Normative authority customarily resided in the person of the king; laws provided him with assistance in reaching his judgments, but they were not binding. The Torah of the Persian period was the first legal text of the Levant to claim binding force for itself.

In a literary sense, the Torah is an extremely heterogeneous entity. In its current form, its composite character is easy to discern.[65] For one thing, it does not possess a self-contained storyline. Reading on from the book of Deuteronomy (the last book of the Torah) to the book of Joshua, one finds the continuation of the story of Israel's founding that is recounted in the Torah. This story then continues on to the books of Kings. The break indicated by the separation of the Torah from the longer narrative that extends from Genesis to 2 Kings is evidently a secondary one, splitting texts that originally belonged together.[66] The section of narrative from Genesis to Deuteronomy was segregated as the Torah because all the legal stipulations are found there, above all within the biography of Moses, which runs from Exodus to Deuteronomy. In other words, the Torah comprises that part of the biblical history of Israel that is marked by the giving of the law and the lead-up to it.[67]

Second, the Torah gathers together a variety of textual materials that clearly do not belong together. The narrative and legal passages, for example, appear to come from different sources. The laws were almost certainly incorporated into the narrative flow over time. In addition, the two major traditional sections, comprising on the one hand the history of the forefathers in Genesis 12–50 and on the other the Exodus story, were joined together in a secondary operation. One indication of this is that the story of the forefathers does not lead on seamlessly to the Exodus narrative. Quite the opposite, in fact: the account of the forefathers first has to be curtailed narratively, so to speak, in Exodus 1:6–8 before the Exodus story can begin. Furthermore, the Exodus narrative does not depend on the story of the forefathers for its background.[68] This is demonstrated by the formula used to refer to Israel in other texts of the later Hebrew Bible or Old Testament: "Israel out of Egypt."[69] Also, those parts of the so-called prehistory in Genesis 1–11 that do not form part of the Priestly Source display a certain autonomy, which might indicate that they once formed a narrative in their own right.[70] In the formation of the Torah, then, we are dealing with two fundamental processes that happened at different times and each comprised a number of different stages: the literary linking of the materials in Genesis to Deuteronomy, and the separation of the Torah from the seamless narrative running from the book of Genesis to 2 Kings.[71]

Various observations and considerations lead us to conclude that the Torah assumed a comparatively fixed form during the Persian period. First, a Greek translation began to appear in the mid-third century BCE.[72] This translation displays similarities with the Zenon Papyri and fragmentary texts of Demetrius of Scepsis.[73] The differences between the Hebrew and the Greek Torah are relatively minor (the Greek text diverges from the Hebrew only in certain passages in Exodus 35–40).[74] So it is fair to assume that the body of text contained within the Torah was essentially complete even in the pre-Hellenistic period.

In addition, references to the Torah in both books of Chronicles, as well as in the books of Ezra (Ezra 7:10) and Nehemiah (Nehemiah 9:3), show that the law comprised a fully developed corpus.[75] Emphasis is often placed upon its being the "Torah of YHWH," indicating that the Torah was perceived even at this stage as the law of God.

Finally, we may cite the fact that no significant reflections on the collapse of the Persian Empire are found in the Torah. In the books of the prophets, it was this event that generated the notion of a comprehensive cosmic Last Judgment (see, for example, Isaiah 34:2–4). For the Torah, the first act of creation is the only one, and the permanence of heaven and earth is such that they can be called (in Deuteronomy 30) as eternal witnesses against Israel.[76]

Yet why and how did the Torah become a complete, closed entity?[77] Its formation must be viewed in the context of the legal organization of the Persian Empire, which had no central body of imperial law that applied to all subject peoples. Instead, the vassal nations were allowed to live in decentralized fashion according to their own legal systems, albeit systems that had to be sanctioned by the Persian authorities. A wide variety of edicts and regulations attest to the process by which the Persian central power authorized local norms.[78] In the case of the Torah, this process can only be inferred from several pieces of evidence, and in biblical research as a whole, the thesis that such a process was involved in the Torah's creation at all is not uncontested.

Yet an external impetus offers the most plausible historical explanation for the formation of the Torah, with its numerous disparate elements.

Moreover, criticism of the thesis of Persian imperial authorization of the Torah often rests on the misconception that the Persians compiled a central register of all local legislation. This was certainly not the case, and the thesis does not assume that it was. What needs to be acknowledged is simply that the Torah attained the status of imperial law by virtue of being recognized and sanctioned by the Persian central authorities.[79]

A strong indication that the Persians did authorize compilation of the Torah can be found in the letter of accreditation that the Persian king Artaxerxes is reputed to have sent to the scribe Ezra in Jerusalem (Ezra 7:12–26). At the king's behest, Ezra brings "the law of the God of Heaven" to Jerusalem. This is a reference to the laws of the Torah. At the end of the letter, the following decree is issued:

> Whoever does not obey the law of your God and the law of the king must surely be punished by death, banishment, confiscation of property, or imprisonment. (Ezra 7:26)

The dual formulation "the law of your God and the law of the king" is very striking. Up to this point in Ezra 7, there had only been mention of the law of Ezra's God, the "God of Heaven." Moreover, the Persian Empire had no centralized imperial law to which the expression "the law of the king" might refer. The simplest interpretation of this dual phrase is to understand "the law of your God" and "the law of the king" as both referring to the law of the Torah. In this interpretation, that law is named once from a Jewish perspective ("the law of your God") and once from a Persian point of view ("the law of your king"). According to this reading, the terminology reflects the status of the Torah as the local law of the Jews, which has been authorized by the Persians.

The theological alignment of non-Torah texts with this core tradition went hand in hand with the establishment of the Torah as an authoritative text. This development is particularly clear in the books of the prophets. Some of them have undergone a recognizable reworking, the effect of which is to present each prophet as a preacher of the Torah. This is especially apparent in Jeremiah, and to a lesser extent in Amos.[80] It is no coincidence that Jeremiah and Amos are both prophets who rose to prominence during the demise of the northern and southern kingdoms and were therefore particularly significant for the formation of tradition. The central theological patterns of interpretation were embedded in these books, and the book of Jeremiah, which was perceived as bearing witness to the destruction of Jerusalem, expanded to become the longest book of the entire Bible (based on the number of words).

Although the Torah appears to have been formed as an authoritative text, its actual significance in ancient Jerusalem must be qualified. To start with, the archeological finds from the Jewish colony on Elephantine—an island in the Nile that was the site of a Jewish military settlement—indicate that Judaism in Egypt at the time of Persian dominion over the Levant was by no means universally obedient to the Torah.[81] There is no evidence of a Torah among the papyrus finds from this period, nor have any biblical texts come to light there. This might be interpreted as pure chance, in view of the syncretism that was prevalent on Elephantine—many other gods besides YHWH were worshipped there. That is not very likely, however. Another telling piece of evidence is that the Jews on the Nile had their own temple, a clear breach of the laws set down in the Torah, which declare only a single shrine, the one in Jerusalem, to be legitimate (Deuteronomy 12:13–19).

Although there are no sources for the period of the Babylonian diaspora of Judaism, it is not out of the question that there, too, strict adherence to the Torah did not constitute the highest standard of religious and cultural life. As in the case of Elephantine, this hypothesis is strengthened by the (admittedly vague) indications that the Jews in Babylon had their own temple.[82]

In addition, one finds in the prophetic texts of the Persian and Hellenistic periods statements that directly contradict the Torah. For instance, in Isaiah 56:3–7 it is stated that eunuchs and foreigners may join the community of YHWH. This is an unequivocal revision of the so-called community law in Deuteronomy 23:1–7, which expressly bans precisely those two groups.[83] Similarly, in Isaiah 65:17–25 a promise is made that there will be a new heaven and a new earth. The Torah says nothing about this, and would not countenance it. According to the Torah, once heaven and earth have been created, they will endure for all time. Indeed, in Deuteronomy 30:19, 31:28, and 32:1, the fact that heaven and earth are called to bear witness against Israel presupposes their everlasting nature.

From these considerations, we can see that the Torah's claim to authority was asserted gradually over time. In the former kingdom of Israel, the first indication that a group in that region was adhering wholeheartedly to the provisions of the Torah and faithfully following its instructions comes in the Dead Sea Scrolls, which date from the second century BCE. After the destruction of the Second Temple by the Romans in 70 CE the Torah attained complete authority within Rabbinic Judaism, primarily because, of all the various groups within ancient Judaism in Israel, it was the Pharisees who survived and continued the rabbinical strain of the faith after 70 CE.

Inner-biblical Exegesis

One of the most important findings of modern biblical scholarship is that the Bible consists of text and commentary rolled into one.[84] Many stories, psalms, proverbs, and prophetic utterances no doubt first existed in oral form. Even the very first time these texts were committed to writing, they were subject to a process of interpretation, since the choice and arrangement of words necessarily altered the original oral material. No sooner had the texts become available in written form than they appear to have become the subject of inner-biblical exegesis (interpretation of biblical texts within the Bible itself). This process played a centrally important role in the creation of the Bible. It shows that, even from a comparatively early stage, many of the texts were regarded as so significant that they were susceptible to and in need of interpretation. The process of inner-biblical exegesis ensured that the texts in question would survive for such a long time. If they had not been actively handed down in writing and updated so as to be relevant to new situations, they would soon have been forgotten and lost. Biblical texts owe their transmission and continued existence across centuries solely to this process of ascribing to them meanings that transcend their immediate historical significance. This has ensured that they have outlasted antiquity, the Middle Ages and, one might even contend, the modern period.

Inner-biblical exegesis is especially prevalent in texts that have been understood as the expression of the divine will or plan, such as the laws of the Pentateuch.[85] The primary reason is that, as we have already seen, over the course of its literary and historical evolution, the legislative material of the Pentateuch came to be interpreted as the law of God. In accordance with ancient Near Eastern custom, the oldest legal rulings within the Covenant Code were formulated in the third person and were regarded as the king's law. Not until Deuteronomy did the idea arise of proclaiming God as a legal authority and interpreting the law as divine law.[86] An important result flowed from this: once the law had been endowed with a divine quality, it could no longer be easily changed. Only through inner-biblical exegesis was it possible to update such a law and give it new form.[87] The need for scribal exegesis of a law was a direct consequence of its having been proclaimed as divine in origin.[88]

A similar situation to that of the legal tradition also pertained in the books of the prophets. Here, too, pronouncements to which divine authority had been imputed needed to be updated, supplemented, or corrected over time. Evidently, techniques deriving from the legal tradition were also used in prophecy.[89] A prophet's word was regarded as open to fulfillment, and it could even be fulfilled several times in succession. These events could then be recorded in updates to the prophecy. A virtual "chain of updates" can be found, for instance, in Jeremiah 23:1-6. It begins with a judgment in 23:1-2, which is couched in terms of a prophetic pronouncement and ends with a formulaic attribution as a divine dictum. It contains a judgment directed against the kings of Judah ("shepherds"), who are guilty of having allowed their people to become scattered:

> "Woe to the shepherds who are destroying and scattering the sheep of my pasture!" declares YHWH. Therefore this is what YHWH, the God of Israel, says to the shepherds who tend my people: "Because you have scattered my flock and driven them away and have not bestowed care on them, I will bestow punishment on you for the evil you have done," declares YHWH. (Jeremiah 23:1-2)

This text is followed by a passage (Jeremiah 23:3-4) which is clearly written by another hand, for here it is not kings who have "driven away" their people but God himself. This passage makes it abundantly clear that the deportation from Judah was not an error but part of God's plan. This plan includes the subsequent gathering-in of the diaspora:

> "I myself will gather the remnant of my flock out of all the countries where I have driven them and will bring them back to their pasture, where they will be fruitful and increase in number. I will place shepherds

over them who will tend them, and they will no longer be afraid or ter-
rified, nor will any be missing," declares YHWH. (Jeremiah 23:3–4)

The verses in Jeremiah 23:5–6 once more contrast with what preceded them.
They specify that the new shepherd whom God will appoint to tend his people
will be from the House of David:

> "See, the days are coming," says YHWH, "when I will awaken for David
> a righteous branch; he will rule as king and rule wisely, and practice jus-
> tice and righteousness in the land. In his days, Judah will be helped,
> and Israel will dwell in safety. And this is his name that one will give to
> him: 'YHWH is our righteousness!'" (Jeremiah 23:5–6)[90]

This sequence of updates reflects the way the book of Jeremiah processes the
basic pronouncement made in Jeremiah 23:1–2, which over time came to be
seen as requiring updating. Jeremiah 23:3–4 had to counter the misconception that God had had nothing to do with the scattering of Judah among the
peoples of the earth, while Jeremiah 23:5–6 was born of the need to recruit
the future kings of the region from the lineage of David. These updates
are not interpretations, in a narrow sense, of the text that precedes them,
since they do not expatiate upon potential alternative meanings. Rather,
they formulate new perspectives that transcend the content of the earlier
pronouncement.

In the case of Jeremiah 23:1–6, each text takes its cue directly from the previous one. Yet there are also numerous examples from the later Bible in
which the initial and the updated passage are very far apart from one another
in literary terms. The promise of a new heaven and a new earth in Isaiah
65:17–25, for example, is formulated as returning to the contrast between the
"old" and "new" exodus in Isaiah 43:16–21 ("forget the former things"). It also
signals that, in the new situation of Isaiah 65 (part of the Trito-Isaiah section), as compared with that of Isaiah 43 (in the Deutero-Isaiah section), it is
no longer enough to simply reformulate the story of Israel's salvation. The
order of creation as such must—in contrast with the one presented in Genesis 1 ("In the beginning God created the heavens and the earth")—be re-
made anew:[91]

This is what YHWH says—he who made a way through the sea, a path through the mighty waters, who drew out the chariots and horses, the army and reinforcements together, . . . "Forget the former things; do not dwell on the past. See, I am doing a new thing! Now it springs up; do you not perceive it?" (Isaiah 43:16–19)

For thus says the Lord YHWH: "Look, my servants will eat, you will be hungry! See, my servants will drink, you will be thirsty! See, my servants will be joyful, you will be disgraced! For see, I am creating a new heaven and a new earth; one will no longer think on the former things, and no one will remember them any longer." (Isaiah 65:13, 17)[92]

Inner-biblical exegeses can, however, diverge widely from one another not only in a literary sense but also in terms of their content. For example, the prophetic position of Isaiah 65–66, together with its further developments in apocalyptic literature (see Chapter 4), are the subject of a spirited contradiction in the Wisdom literature. The book of Ecclesiastes (Qohelet) rejects the far-reaching hopes for a future eschatological intervention by God in world history. In contrast to the expectations of a "new heaven" and a "new earth" raised in the book of Isaiah, Ecclesiastes emphasizes that there is "nothing new":

What has been will be again, what has been done will be done again; there is nothing new under the sun. Is there anything of which one can say, "Look! This is something new"? It was here already, long ago; it was here before our time. No one remembers the former generations, and even those yet to come will not be remembered by those who follow them. (Ecclesiastes 1:9–11)

The Bible's inner network of exegesis interconnects its texts in a complex manner and, in this way, it handles theological questions in a historically and factually nuanced way. This finding is problematic for a fundamentalist reading of the Bible. But in fact, these nuances might ultimately explain how the Bible was able to become established worldwide as a normative text. A certain complexity within authoritative texts is a vital precondition for audiences to be able to accept them as relevant over long periods of time.

A New View of Humanity

The literary history of biblical texts composed after the period of exile shows evidence of a remarkable change in views about humanity. In the ancient Near East, the king wielded absolute authority. Monarchs constituted their own class of humanity, distinct from either free or enslaved people. The king was accountable to the gods, whereas to his subjects he was the supreme legislative and judicial authority. In dispensing justice and framing laws the king was, of course, obliged to comply with cosmic principles, but in the way he actually applied those principles he was a law unto himself. As a result, he was also the main focal point for the creation of tradition, which in large part concerned the institution of the royal court. This situation was similar in the ancient kingdoms of Israel and Judah, but the end of monarchical rule would bring about a fundamental change in this social arrangement.[93]

Having said that, the intellectual groundwork for this transformation was laid in Judah even as the monarchical period was drawing to a close. The first version of Deuteronomy saw the emergence of the idea not only of divine laws, but also of God as a lawgiver.[94] Judah was a vassal state of Assyria at that time (ca. 640 BCE), and King Josiah ascended the throne at the age of eight. The ultimate source of authority shifted from the monarchical to the spiritual realm. With the end of royal rule in Israel and Judah, the monarchical class disappeared and there arose in its place—for the first time in the ancient Near East—a system of thought based upon the immediate experience of God. This can be seen most clearly in the account of creation in Genesis 1, in which the first people created differ not according to their social standing but solely by gender, and man and woman alike are made in God's image (Genesis 1:26–28, 5:1, 9:6). Thereby, at least functionally, they are accorded the dignity of kings.[95]

In the wake of this major anthropological shift, a new conception of people as individuals became widespread. The monarch was no longer considered the only fully realized human being—that is, a person capable of making responsible decisions, experiencing deep emotions, and being the object of divine attention. This formerly privileged position was now accorded to each and every individual.

At the same time, an increasingly profound skepticism seems to have set in concerning whether individuals could ever have complete control over their own decisions. Within the prevailing mindset of the monarchical period, whose guiding principle was that the individual was subject to "external control," the question of an individual's autonomy had not played any major role, since all important decisions were made by the king.[96] But in the context of a post-monarchical society, the basic anthropological problem—that individuals cannot always rely on their "internal control"—was widely recognized from a comparatively early stage. This problem was deemed so fundamentally important that the biblical prehistory recounted in Genesis specifically addressed the question of the cognitive faculty in humans (Genesis 2–3, 6:5–8, 8:20–22). In Genesis 2–3, for example, although human beings are endowed with the capacity to distinguish between good and evil, the price they pay for this capacity is the loss of Paradise. The seat of all human thought and design, namely the "heart," is also described in Genesis 8:21 as being "evil from childhood."

These developments were of far-reaching importance for the emerging normative function of scripture. With the disappearance of what had once been the absolute control of the king, and the simultaneous awareness of the fundamental limitations of people's capacity for cognition and judgment, the increasingly authoritative scriptures took on even more of a binding character. Human beings' observance of sacred texts thus compensated for their defective "internal control."

The Book of Job

Within the literature of Judaism from the period of Persian rule, the book of Job is something of a special case.[97] This book is the most extensive coherent piece of fiction within the Bible. At the same time, of all the books of the Bible, it is the most unambiguously designed as a text exploring theological problems. Indeed, it might even be called a "thought experiment." Not even traditional rabbinical literature considers Job to have been a historical figure. The book of Job portrays its protagonist as a vehicle for addressing theological questions rather than as a real-life person: Job is God-fearing and righteous beyond all measure, and at the same time he is "the greatest man among all the people of the East" (Job 1:3). What are we to make of God's divinity in light of the catastrophes that can befall even someone like the righteous Job?

The book of Job was in all likelihood written around one or two centuries after the destruction of Jerusalem in 587 BCE.[98] However, the catastrophes it depicts, which ruin its protagonist to the point where he is left naked and destitute, clearly allude to these historical events. For instance, among the marauding hordes who steal Job's belongings and slaughter his servants are the "Chaldeans" (Job 1:17), that is, the Neo-Babylonians. Although the setting of the book evokes the time of the Patriarchs, and its location in the land of Uz is situated outside the bounds of Judah, Job 1:17 cross-fades this scene with the real historical situation of Jerusalem in 587 BCE and causes Job to experience on an individual level the fate that befell Judah as a whole. Job's homeland of Uz is usually considered as lying within the realm of Edom (compare Genesis 36:28), but "Uz" may be a fictitious name meaning something like "mystery."[99] In any event, the intention of setting the story in Uz is to suggest that Job's fate and his reflection upon it are both of wider human relevance.

The main plot line of the book of Job reveals itself through its structure, which consists of a framework comprising a prologue (chapters 1–2), an epilogue (42:7–27), and a dialogue section (3:1–42:6). The dialogue section can be further subdivided into a discussion between Job and his three friends (3–28), Job's monologue (29–31), the speeches of Elihu and Job's talk with a fourth friend (32–37), two speeches by God (38–41), and, finally, Job's response (42:1–6). The theological point of the book of Job derives from the tense interplay between the three basic sections of the work. The prologue expounds the problems of the protagonist but already provides readers with an answer to the question of why Job must suffer so much: he has become the subject of a divine test. The dialogues with the friends cover almost the entire gamut of possible explanations for Job's suffering. Perhaps he has unwittingly sinned after all, or perhaps he must suffer because he is, like all humans, fundamentally guilty, or perhaps he is to be led toward a particular insight. Job himself bridles at all these explanations, and readers know that he is right. Job's sufferings are rooted neither in the fact that he has actually transgressed against God nor in the fact that he, as a human being, can never be righteous in the sight of God. Even the idea that this is some educational measure by God must be ruled out. The cause of Job's suffering resides solely in the heavenly test that God and Satan are imposing upon him.

Because of the way the prologue and dialogues are arranged, the prologue preemptively critiques the friends' explanations. But the arrangement also, and probably more importantly, has a bearing on the speeches delivered by God (38:1–40:2 and 40:6–41:26), which follow the dialogues. These speeches provide only indirect answers to the problems expounded in the prologue. God's description of the well-regulated processes that occur within nature and the animal kingdom, as well as the motif of chaotic struggle presented in the examples of the hippopotamus (Behemoth) and the crocodile (Leviathan), represent a theology of ordered design governing the world. Though the sufferings of Job are not named in this exposition, it serves to place them within a wider interpretative context. To be sure, Job is suffering, but Job is not the world. Job's life is dysfunctional, but the world continues to function. And while Job finds himself in a state of chaos, the world as a whole is nonetheless sustained and directed by God. And yet, this state of order is contradicted by the prologue. The sufferings of Job do not fit into the order of the world, not even an order that is invisible and fluid. They are the consequence of a cruel test. In his reply to Job, God does not say a single word about the events outlined in the prologue.

But on another level, this represents a continuation of the same theme that was evident in the dialogues. The prologue criticizes not only the theology expounded by Job's friends, but also the revelation by God. From the perspective of the prologue, God is not accessible either through human or divine expositions. How, then, are we to talk about God? One possible answer that the book of Job provides for its readers may be inferred from God's statement to Eliphaz and his friends: "My anger burns toward you and your friends because you have not spoken correctly to me, as my servant Job has" (42:7).[100] Tellingly, the Hebrew text at this point is phrased in terms of speaking *to* God rather than *about* God. Thus, the book of Job emphatically rejects the idea of speculating about God; at the same time, it affirms ways of addressing, or even accusing, God that have been transformed by the personal experience of suffering. The fact that Job, in his troubles, turns to God to lament, and indeed even to accuse, is explicitly legitimized by Job 42:7. The book of Job thus lays out the fundamental intellectual inaccessibility of God to humans, though this state of affairs can be partially remedied by existential lament.

Interestingly, the book of Job ends with God himself restoring to Job all of the property that he has lost, twice over (42:10–12). God is thus behaving in accordance with the Torah, which stipulates that stolen property must be restored in double measure (Exodus 22:3–6). Implicitly, then, God is shown as just, even though he is not bound by his own laws.

In terms of the making of the Bible, the book of Job is particularly remarkable in that, for long stretches, it criticizes classical or established positions of biblical theology.[101] It sets its face against prophecy and the Deuteronomic literature, which assert that misfortune should be interpreted as divine punishment for human shortcomings. In contrast, the book of Job demonstrates that divine action can be gratuitously destructive. It also stands in opposition to the theology of the Psalms and the priestly literature, which maintain that salvation is ever present and is bestowed by God on his faithful followers. The case of Job makes it plain that God does not commit himself to automatically providing help and salvation to those who worship him. God's freedom trumps his attachment to humankind.

In the book of Job, then, key theological positions of biblical literature are expounded simultaneously with their antitheses. Although this makes the Bible more theologically ambiguous, it also renders it more interesting and viable in the long term.

It is hard to imagine who might have written such a theologically heterodox text as the book of Job. Some scholars have speculated that it may have originated outside the social context within which religious texts at the Second Temple in Jerusalem were customarily composed. However, the high degree of scribal erudition it displays makes this unlikely.[102] It is far more probable that the book of Job was created within the priestly milieu in Jerusalem. In that light, it provides emphatic proof of how diverse an environment this must have been. Job is of enormous importance for the writing of the later Bible because its inclusion signified that substantive criticism of eminent theological positions in biblical literature had gained entry to the biblical canon. By incorporating the book of Job, the Bible firmly presented itself as a discursive theological work.

4

Scripture in Judaism

The End of the Persian Empire and the Rise of Hellenism

The campaign of conquest waged by Alexander the Great brought to an end the reign of the Persians in the eastern Mediterranean region. This campaign, which lasted from 334 to 324 BCE, led Alexander and his army from their homeland in Macedonia first to Asia Minor and Egypt, then on to the Near and Middle East, and finally as far as India.[1] One important consequence of these wide-ranging conquests was that the Greek language, along with Greek religion, architecture, philosophy, and literature, permeated the Mediterranean region and the Near East. This development, which profoundly influenced Judaism and was a prerequisite for the emergence of Christianity, is known as Hellenism, a term coined by the nineteenth-century German historian Johann Gustav Droysen in 1836.[2] Admittedly, even before Alexander, the Greeks played a significant role in the ancient Near East.[3] But through the spread of their civilization as far as the Indus River and the resulting influence on local traditions in the regions that came under Greek control, the culture of the peoples who inhabited those regions was impacted to an unprecedented extent. This impact affected both Judaism and emerging Christianity.

Greek civilization influenced Judaism in so many ways that the faith during this period is referred to as "Hellenistic Judaism."[4] The relevant developments began in the third century BCE and lasted until the first century CE. The emergence of Rabbinic Judaism, as a reaction both to the destruction of Jerusalem and the temple and to the rise of Christianity, marked the start of a new phase in the history of the Jewish religion. Over time, Greek influences even became apparent within Rabbinic Judaism.

The extent to which Judaism became Hellenized varied in different parts of the Mediterranean region. There was greater openness to Greek culture in the Diaspora, especially in the cosmopolitan city of Alexandria, than in Israel and Judah. Yet deliberate "Hellenization programs" were carried out even in Alexandria.[5] Certain texts from the Hellenistic period—notably the books of Daniel and Maccabees—give the impression that Greek culture was shunned by the majority of Jews, but this reflects only one strand of Judaism, the "orthodox," anti-Hellenistic strand, which subsequently became dominant.[6] But in fact, Hellenism was widely accepted, as is evident from the fact that fierce controversies broke out within Palestinian Judaism between those who supported and those who opposed a blending of Jewish and Hellenistic cultures.

One important testament to the influence of Greek culture on Judaism was the translation of the Torah (and thereafter the remaining books of the Hebrew Bible) into Greek. This made the authoritative texts of Judaism accessible to Greek-speaking Jewish and non-Jewish communities alike. At the same time, it represented a significant development for the interpretation of the Scriptures, since their translation into Greek meant that they were now open to examination and exegesis by Greek intellectuals. Additionally, the Greek language itself was enhanced by this translation from Hebrew or Aramaic into Greek, which introduced a considerable number of additional meanings to Greek terms and phrases. These new coinages of Greek terms and grammatical constructions then went on to affect the composition of later Jewish texts written in Greek.

The combining of Jewish tradition with Greek thought is most apparent in translations and in Jewish texts originally composed in Greek—for example, the works of Ben Sira (Jesus ben Sirach) and of Pseudo-Phocylides, and the book of Wisdom (Wisdom of Solomon). The clearest evidence comes in the pithy formulations found in Sirach 24:23 and Baruch 4:1, where the Torah and wisdom are equated with each other: the Jewish Torah, it is claimed, is nothing other than wisdom encapsulated in written form. So tightly are these two traditions intertwined that anyone who engages with the Torah is essentially also dealing with Greek philosophy. This goes hand in hand with the claim that the Torah, although its substance constitutes wisdom, is nevertheless more than this since it derives from the one God, the creator and lord of the world.

Apocalyptic Literature and Ecclesiastes

The period from the third century BCE onward was characterized not only by Hellenism but also by the rise of so-called apocalypticism.[7] The apocalyptic way of viewing history—particularly the history of salvation—takes its name from the book of Revelation, whose title in early manuscripts is "Apocalypse of John." ("Apocalypse" here means "revelation" or "disclosure.") The influence of apocalypticism grew steadily throughout the Mediterranean region and survived in Judaism until the end of the first century CE, and in Christianity until around the fifth century CE. Yet its roots within religious history remain shrouded in mystery. Until the mid-twentieth century, the book of Daniel (especially chapters 7–12), which was completed in the period when the Maccabees were fighting against the Hellenistic rule of the Seleucids (168–167 BCE), was regarded as the earliest apocalyptic text of Judaism. However, the discovery of the Dead Sea Scrolls at Qumran clearly demonstrated that the pseudepigraphic books of Enoch, on the evidence of the manuscript alone, date back to a time before the Maccabean Revolt. Thus, as far as we can tell from the extant literature, the origins of Jewish apocalypticism lie in the books of Enoch.[8] Enoch is a portmanteau work comprising a number of different, originally self-contained, writings, some of which existed as separate books in Qumran. The oldest part is 1 Enoch 72–82, which is called the Astronomical Book.[9] It was therefore almost certainly specialist sacerdotal knowledge that underlay the cosmological and historical speculations of apocalypticism. Mesopotamian and perhaps even Persian influences may have played a part, though scholars have sometimes overstated such influences.

A number of historical events that took place several centuries apart (from the late fourth century BCE to the first century CE), but were equally significant in their effect on Judaism and its interpretation of history, played major roles in the emergence of apocalyptic literature. These were the collapse of the Persian Empire as a result of Alexander the Great's campaign, the desecration of the temple in Jerusalem by the Hellenistic ruler Antiochus IV in 164 BCE, and the destruction of the Second Temple by the Romans in 70 CE.[10] The first of these events was most significant for the initial phase of apocalypticism, the second gave rise to the visions that are recounted in the latter part of the book of Daniel (Daniel 7–12), and the third formed the background to the apocalyptic literature of the first century CE, such as 4 Ezra (also called 2 Esdras, or the Jewish Apocalypse of Ezra) and the Syrian book of Baruch.

Apocalyptic literature deals with the fundamental theological questions that arise when experiences of oppression, foreign domination, and dispersal radically challenge people's faith in divine justice: Where is God? Has he concealed himself? Has he shunned his people? Apocalyptic texts provide specific answers to these questions, composed by a visionary to whom the entire span of world history right up to its conclusion has been revealed. This history is an all-embracing divine plan whose ultimate objective is that sinners are punished and the righteous rewarded. The end of earthly history is often accompanied by the destruction of the world by cosmic forces, which apocalyptic texts describe in dramatic, sometimes even violent, terms. Despite—or perhaps precisely because of—the unsettling nature of such texts, the reader must always keep in mind that they represent a specific form of salvation history whose aim is to resolve the tension between negative experiences in the present day and a belief in God's power and justice.

The destruction of the Second Temple in 70 CE presented a special challenge regarding the issue of God's power. After all, in the eyes of Jews, the temple was the central site of the immanence of God in the physical world; thus its destruction required an unprecedented theological coping strategy. This is found in condensed form in 4 Ezra and the second book of Baruch, both of which were written toward the end of the first century CE. These works develop the idea of a "two eons" doctrine, which maintains that from the very outset, God created not one but two worlds (eons). The first eon is characterized by a continual withdrawal of God's will for salvation, which thus heads inexorably toward a final judgment. In this final reckoning, only the devout and those who have stayed faithful to the law will be spared. In the coming, second, eon the faithful will be granted a new, eternal life.

With its accounts of visions, apocalyptic literature draws upon the prophetic tradition (see, for example, Amos 7–9; Isaiah 6; Ezekiel 1–3, 11, 37, and 40–48; and Zechariah 1–6) and presents its findings as revelatory knowledge, not as the result of human reflection. In actuality, though, each apocalyptic text presents the theological stance of its writer, which he has arrived at through a combination of tradition and experience.[11] A characteristic trait of most Jewish and Christian apocalypses (the book of Revelation is an exception) is that the vision is put in the mouth of a prominent person from the history of ancient Israel (Enoch, Daniel, Moses, Ezra, Abraham, or Baruch). God has revealed to these figures the course of history, which each of them surveys right up to its endpoint from their respective fictitious historical locations. The book of Daniel, for example, was written in the first half of the second century BCE, during the reign of the Seleucid ruler Antiochus IV, yet it shifts its narrated time back to the period of the Babylonian Exile of the Israelites in the sixth century BCE.

This apocalyptic perspective on history also gave rise to opposing positions. The book of Ecclesiastes (Qohelet in the Hebrew Bible) sets itself up in opposition to the escapist stance of apocalypticism. It most probably dates from the end of the third century BCE, and its introductory verse runs thus: "The words of the Preacher [*qohelet*], son of David, king in Jerusalem." As a result, the text has often been attributed to Solomon (indeed, in German the book is sometimes called *Prediger Salomo,* or "Solomon the Preacher"). The Hebrew word *qohelet* is a made-up word meaning something like "a person who convenes an assembly," or "preacher." The configuration of the book as a collection of sayings is reminiscent of the rhetorical form of the diatribes in Greek popular philosophy. As for its content, Ecclesiastes is often thought to have an affinity with ancient skepticism, as well as Stoicism and Epicureanism. Undoubtedly there are some factual points of contact, which can most likely be traced back to cultural connections, but the stance of the book of Ecclesiastes differs at many points from that of the Ancient Greek philosophy of skepticism. A central tenet of skepticism, for example, is that knowledge as such is impossible to attain, and one should therefore refrain from making conclusive judgments about God and the world. Ecclesiastes, too, stresses the strict limitations of human knowledge, but it draws a very different conclusion. It presents the narrowness of human knowledge as the basic keystone of its practical philosophy. Although people may not be capable of knowing the world, they can still enjoy eating, drinking, and a general *joie de vivre* as gifts that God has given to humanity:

> He has made everything beautiful in its time. He has also set eternity in the human heart; yet no one can fathom what God has done from beginning to end. I know that there is nothing better for people than to

be happy and to do good while they live. That each of them may eat and drink, and find satisfaction in all their toil—this is the gift of God. (Ecclesiastes 3:11-13)

In this passage, Ecclesiastes extols the basic elements of life as set out, for example, in the prehistory of the Torah in Genesis 1-11.[12] At the same time, it dismisses all eschatological perspectives, in particular by taking issue with contemporary prophecy and apocalypticism; as Ecclesiastes 1:9 states, there is "nothing new under the sun."[13] Humanity is therefore exhorted to take this world as is. We cannot comprehend its order, but we can rejoice in its great bounties.

Prophetic Focus on the Torah, and the Nevi'im

Hellenism and apocalypticism form the two key intellectual foci of the later period in the making of the Hebrew Bible. But above and beyond these ideas, its books continued to be updated and given new points of emphasis. This was achieved through the work of scribes, an endeavor that was guided primarily by internal developments within Judaism.

The Torah had taken firm shape even before the rise of Hellenism, but a number of additions and revisions were undertaken during the Hellenistic period.[14] One example is the mention of ships from "Chittim" (Cyprus) in Numbers 24:24, an allusion to the Ancient Greeks most likely prompted by the conquests of Alexander the Great in the East.[15] Changes were also introduced to the chronological system of global history as outlined in the Torah. These alterations now dated the exodus of the Israelites from Egypt to the year 2666 from the creation of the world.[16] Given that four thousand years was considered an era, this would result in that era coming to an end during the Maccabean Revolt.

The Torah, however, had by this time assumed the status of a binding directive from God and so was becoming the core of the authoritative scriptures of Judaism. Within Judaism and then Christianity, the process of creating binding bodies of scripture, beginning with the recognition of the Torah as a normative text, can thus be seen as a canonical process.[17] But we should bear in mind that the term "canon" was associated in ancient Judaism neither with the Torah itself nor with other important texts. It is difficult to speak in terms of a definitive completion of the "canon" because both ancient Judaism and early Christianity took those texts that were seen as binding primarily as instructions and life guides, and updated and interpreted them accordingly. In addition, the distinction between texts that were binding and those that were more peripheral varied between regions and among different forms of both religions.

Within Judaism, the Torah was increasingly seen as a normative entity to be used as a guide for the community's self-understanding and for how its followers should lead their lives.[18] And yet scholars believe that in the Persian and Hellenistic periods it still largely remained a text for the elites. There are no reliable sources from an earlier period than those found at Qumran to prove that its precepts were actually followed. We have already mentioned the Jewish community on the Nile island of Elephantine, which in all likelihood neither possessed a written Torah nor was strictly monotheistic (see Chapter 3).[19] The books of Enoch, which form part of the canon of the Ethiopian church but originated in ancient Judaism, speak to the existence of a non-Mosaic Judaism that looked to the person of Enoch rather than Moses as a leading authority figure.[20] Likewise, the importance of the book of Esther in the Judaism of the Persian diaspora suggests that this community was also somewhat detached from the Torah. At no point in the entire book of Esther are Moses or the Torah explicitly named or even hinted at as guiding principles.[21]

At this stage the textual content of the Torah was not sacrosanct either. The "canonical formula" (in which God forbids adding to or taking away from the text), which appears at two places in the Torah (Deuteronomy 4:2 and 12:32), should primarily be interpreted as indicating not that the Torah was an unmodifiable, fixed text but rather that it was a theologically complete set of instructions from God to his people to live their lives in the manner set forth in Deuteronomy.[22] Even in the biblical manuscripts found at Qumran, it is evident that minor variations in orthography and vocabulary were still entirely possible.

The vital importance of the Torah to biblical literature is reflected in the fact that scriptures from the third and second centuries BCE other than the Torah tend to regard it as a theological code of practice. In its concluding verse, the Torah declares itself to be the prophecy of Moses, which ranks above all later prophecies: "Since then, no prophet has risen in Israel like

Moses, whom YHWH knew face to face" (Deuteronomy 34:10).[23] On the one hand, the Torah derives its authority from prophecy—after all, Moses was a prophet—but, on the other, it sets itself above prophecy by reminding its readers that Moses was the prophet par excellence against whom all subsequent prophets must be measured and found wanting. The effect is not merely to exalt the figure of Moses; it also has momentous theological implications. We might expect prophetic literature to proclaim, say, the re-creation of heaven and earth (Isaiah 65:17–25). But for the Torah, heaven and earth, once having been created by God, are not transient entities. As a result, they can be invoked by Moses as eternal witnesses in the matter of Israel's obligations to God (Deuteronomy 30:19, 31:28; see also 32:1).

Following the formation of the Torah, the prophets were increasingly seen as the means by which it was applied and interpreted—in other words, as preachers of the Mosaic Law. This manifests itself most clearly in the development of the canonical section of Nevi'im (Prophets), which comprises not just the classic prophetic books, from Isaiah to Malachi, but also the historical books, from Joshua to 2 Kings, which come between the Torah and the book of Isaiah. The books of Joshua, Judges, Samuel, and Kings are counted as part of the "prophets" in order to ensure the continuity between Moses, the first of all prophets, and the classical prophets, who in literary terms begin with the book of Isaiah.

Thus, at various points in the books of Joshua to Kings, as well as in Malachi 3:22, references are made to the "Torah of Moses" or some similar phrase (see Daniel 9:11).[24] This phrase invokes the Torah in fixed written form, extending from Genesis to Deuteronomy, which should now be taken (or should have been taken) as the yardstick of behavior for monarchs and ordinary people alike. Historically, of course, this is an anachronism, since the Torah, at least in its final form, is actually far younger than the phase of Israelite history portrayed in the books from Joshua to Kings. In the Bible, though, the Torah is portrayed as having been given to Moses and henceforth possessing authoritative force.

At the time they were written, the books from Joshua to Kings and from Isaiah to Malachi were presumably considered to be every bit as normative as the Torah, which was itself still evolving. Yet once the Torah was complete, the books from Joshua through Malachi were reappraised theologically. Of particular importance in this regard is the insertion made in

Joshua 1:7 and 9 and Malachi 3:22–24 (Hebrew Bible; Malachi 4:4–6 in Christian Bibles) concerning the entire Nevi'im section of the canon (i.e., Joshua through Malachi), which shows the Nevi'im to be subordinate to the Torah while at the same time presenting it to readers as an interpretation of the Torah:

> Only be strong and very determined, to keep the Torah that my servant Moses commanded. . . . This book of the Torah shall not depart from your mouth, and you shall meditate on it day and night. . . . Remember the word that Moses, the servant of YHWH, commanded you: YHWH, your God, will give you rest and give you this land. (Joshua 1:7–8, 13)[25]

> Remember the Torah of Moses, my servant, to whom I commanded statutes and ordinances at Horeb for all Israel. (Malachi 3:22; 4:4 in English-language Bibles)[26]

The allusion in the first chapter of the Nevi'im to its last chapter and, conversely, the reference in the last chapter to the first, make it clear that on the interpretive level of these passages, the entire body of text from Joshua to Kings is subordinated to the Torah as its ruling principle.

In the course of the formation of the Nevi'im as the part of the Bible that follows the Torah, it also appears that the book of Malachi was the first element of Zechariah (in which it surely originated) to be isolated as a text in its own right.[27] It was only in this way that the number of minor prophets reached twelve, and the three major prophets (Isaiah, Jeremiah, and Ezekiel) and twelve minor prophets thereby come to form something of an analogous grouping to the three patriarchs (Abraham, Isaac, and Jacob) and the twelve sons of Jacob, the progenitors of the twelve tribes of Israel. This configuration creates a parallel between the prophecy section of the Bible and the Torah. There are several indications that the book of Malachi was originally not a book in its own right. To begin with, an identically worded formula appears both in the introductory verse of Malachi and in Zechariah 9:1 and 12:1. Second, there are many textual points of contact, such as the direct quotation of Zechariah 1:3 in Malachi 3:7 (Hebrew Bible). And finally, there is the fact that the name "Malachi" is attested nowhere else in the Bible, nor on any inscriptions. It seems to be an artificial name taken from Malachi

3:1, meaning "my messenger." This coinage may well be an allusion to the promise made at the end of the book that the prophet Elijah will return (Malachi 3:22–24; Malachi 4:4–6 in English-language Bibles). This reference back to Elijah, who according to 2 Kings 2:11–12 did not die but was swept up to heaven in a whirlwind, was most likely intended to signal that prophecy as a contemporary phenomenon had reached an end, and that a prophet with a direct line to God would arise on only one more occasion, with the return of Elijah.

The idea of an end of prophecy also appears in the rabbinical literature.[28] The passages in question define prophets as only those individuals who proclaim their message orally. From the very beginning of the prophetic tradition, however, there existed a body of prophet-scribes who interpreted and updated the texts they were given to copy. In classical biblical criticism of the nineteenth and twentieth centuries, they were often referred to disparagingly as "amenders."[29] In actuality, though, some of the most innovative texts of prophetic literature can be traced back to them. Furthermore, the fact that they wrote their updates into existing books of the prophets indicates that they regarded their own amendments as prophetic.

This form of scribal prophecy continued right up to the end of the literary production work on the Hebrew Bible. During the Hellenistic period, it was most apparent in the closing passages of the book of Isaiah and the Book of the Twelve.[30] It was responsible, for example, for devising the apocalyptic scenarios in Isaiah 65–66 and Zechariah 9–14, which deal with the Last Judgment of YHWH on the peoples of the earth and the separation of the righteous from the sinful.[31] These texts reflect, among other things, the political turmoil of the third century BCE. The Ptolemaic dynasty, the ruling elite that gained control of Egypt after the death of Alexander the Great, found itself in constant conflict with the Seleucids, who ruled over the Mesopotamian region of Alexander's former empire.[32] Israel was caught between these warring powers along with the rest of the Levant, and it was particularly badly affected by this volatile geopolitical situation. It is therefore hardly surprising that thoughts of God turning his face away from world history and of an impending, all-encompassing final judgment become widespread in this period. In Israel, people increasingly lost faith in the restoration of an earthly theocracy of the kind they believed they had experienced under the Persians. The world had lost any discernible sense of order, and people sought guidance above all in time-honored traditions.

At the beginning of the second century BCE, however, scribal work on the books of the prophets also came to a halt. We can deduce that these books were assembled into a collection before the Maccabean Revolt from the fact that the book of Daniel, which deals extensively with the events of the religious crisis in the time of the Maccabees, was no longer included in the prophetic canon, despite being an inherently prophetic book.[33] Why did the books of the prophets draw to a close at this time? This process may be connected to the policies of Antiochus III, who ordered that the Jews, who were accustomed to the Persian idea of central sanctioning of local norms, should be settled in cities "under their own paternal laws."[34] The phrase "their own paternal laws" undoubtedly refers primarily to the Torah, though the works of the prophets, compiled together in the form of the Nevi'im, were at the same time regarded as its definitive exegesis.

The end of prophecy led to the rise of a separate literature of commentary, as exemplified above all by the Pesharim, the commentaries on the prophets that were discovered at Qumran (discussed later in this chapter). At the same time, the holy scriptures of Judaism were divided into "the Law and the Prophets," a phrase that subsequently reappears in the New Testament. Important evidence for this comes from the prologue to the Greek translation of the book of Sirach (or Ecclesiasticus). This is thought to date from about 132 BCE and was written by the grandson of Jesus ben Sirach:[35]

In the Law and in the Prophets as well as in the others [writings] that follow them, many great [teachings] have been given to us, for which Israel deserves praise for instruction and wisdom. . . . And so my grandfather Jesus, who had devoted much effort to the reading of the Law, the Prophets, and the other books of our ancestors and acquired considerable proficiency with these writings, felt himself led to write something about instruction and wisdom, so that those who love learning might also become familiar with it and make even greater progress in living according to the Law. . . . Not only this [work], but even the Law, the Prophets, and the rest of the writings differ considerably when read in the original language. When I, in the thirty-eighth year of the reign of Euergetes [i.e., Ptolemy VIII Euergetes II, 132 BCE] came to Egypt and remained here during the rest of his reign, I found many opportunities for instruction. I therefore considered it necessary that I, too, should devote some diligence and labor to translating this book. During this entire time, often into the night, I applied [all my] knowledge to complete and also to publish this book for all those [Israelites] living abroad who desire to learn and to conduct their lives according to the Law.[36]

This prologue indicates that, for the grandson of Jesus ben Sirach, the authoritative scriptures of Israel consisted of two parts: the Law and the Prophets. In this scheme of things, the Law is accorded a special authority among the books of the Bible, as the repeated and emphatic references to living one's life in accordance with the Law show. By contrast, the "other books" that are mentioned represent an open-ended and general category that in principle could be further developed.[37]

The phrase "the Law, the Prophets, and the rest of the writings" in the prologue should not, therefore, be interpreted as referring to the three-part Jewish Bible, which emerged only at a later date, but rather in the context of the use of these texts within the book of Sirach itself. Other texts may also be cited in this regard. For instance, the phrase "the Law and the Prophets" appears in 2 Maccabees 15:9 and again in 4 Maccabees 18:10 (the second book of Maccabees is thought to have been written in around 100 BCE, and the fourth book in around 100 CE).[38] These passages thus become a kind of formulaic shorthand, which is also found in the scrolls from Qumran and in the New Testament, for referring to the normative texts of Judaism.[39] We will return to this subject presently. But the key thing to note at this point is that Judaism customarily referred back to the core of its authoritative texts with the set phrase "the Law and the Prophets." This denoted a body of scriptures whose authority resided not least in its being interpreted, commented upon, and updated. That was achieved in part by means of the texts that are known today as the "Rewritten Bible."

The Rewritten Bible

During the standardization process of biblical texts in the late Persian and Hellenistic periods, a new literary form arose that put down firm roots in the later biblical canon, exemplified in the books of Chronicles. This form involves scriptures belonging to the "Rewritten Bible" genre, in which existing texts were retold from a new perspective.[40] The works of the Rewritten Bible do not graft their own theological position onto existing scriptures, but rather recount the events in question afresh. One reason for this may have been that the Torah and the Prophets were already seen as so authoritative that it was no longer possible to make any extensive changes to them. In addition, these new works were so powerful that they could not simply be used to rework existing texts.

The Books of Chronicles, Ezra, and Nehemiah

An early example of this form of retelling and revising of pre-existing texts can be found in the books of Chronicles, which were probably written in the third century BCE.[41] Because these books themselves went on to become part of the Jewish Bible and the Christian Old Testament, we are dealing here with a case of internal biblical exegesis. The books of Chronicles revisit the material of Genesis through 2 Kings, retelling it from a different viewpoint. The focus is shifted onto the story of Judah, as well as onto the temple in Jerusalem and the form of worship that was practiced there. This "new edition" firmly embedded the practice of re-narrating already existing books. In a certain sense, this phenomenon is comparable to the multiple retellings of the story of Jesus in the New Testament. The Gospels of Matthew and Luke are "new editions" of the Gospel of Mark, while the Gospel of John, with its strong emphasis on the concept of Jesus as the Word made Flesh, sets itself apart from, or even above, the three other gospels. The juxtaposition of four gospels in the New Testament resulted from updating or providing greater theological profundity to existing stories of Jesus, a situation analogous to that of the Rewritten Bible.[42]

That the books of Chronicles represent a new edition of the narrative books of Genesis through 2 Kings is primarily evident from their almost identical content: both recount the history of Israel from the first humans to the Babylonian Exile. The second book of Kings ends with the pardoning of King Jehoiachin in Babylon, while the second book of Chronicles concludes with the edict of the Persian ruler Cyrus the Great, which holds out the prospect of the return of the deported Jews and the building of the temple in Jerusalem. At the same time, it is clear that the books of Chronicles are seeking to give a new interpretation to the original story. The most obvious difference is in the basic structure of Chronicles: the period before King Saul is summarized in a genealogy (1 Chronicles 1–9) and, after the episode involving Saul (1 Chronicles 10), a great deal of attention is devoted to the reigns of David (1 Chronicles 11–29) and Solomon (2 Chronicles 1–9), which receive an idealized depiction. In the Chronicles, it is not the forefathers, the Exodus, the occupation of Canaan, or any other era in the history of Israel's salvation that constitutes the decisive chapter in the foundation of Israel, but instead the reign of David and Solomon. The "genealogical preamble" of 1 Chronicles 1–9 serves only as an introduction to this key period. The books of Chronicles shift the key moment of Israel's foundation to the beginning of the monarchical period. As the progenitors of the temple cult, David and Solomon are at the same time the founding fathers of Israel. They are also shown as having counterparts in the Persian kings Cyrus and Darius. In the same way that David laid the groundwork for the construction of the First Temple, Cyrus issued an edict ordering the building of the Second Temple. And just as the First Temple was actually built under Solomon, so the Second was erected during the reign of Darius.

The books of Chronicles thus present a conception of Israel's origin that has a decidedly autochthonous flavor, in that they closely link the period of the combined monarchy to that of the forefathers. Although they do not entirely skip over the Exodus and the entry into Canaan, these episodes are in the background. Moses appears in Chronicles not as the leader of the Exodus but as Israel's lawgiver, and the Exodus itself is only mentioned six times.[43] In the direct transposition of 1 Kings 8:21 to 2 Chronicles 6:11, it is left out altogether: YHWH's covenant, which in Kings is described as being made with the ancestors when he led them out of the land of Egypt, is described in the parallel passage in Chronicles simply as one made with the Israelites:

> I have provided a place there for the ark, in which is the covenant of YHWH that he made with our ancestors when he brought them out of Egypt. (1 Kings 8:21)

> There I have placed the ark, in which is the covenant of YHWH that he made with the people of Israel. (2 Chronicles 6:11)

The emphasis placed on the era of David and Solomon in Chronicles goes hand in hand with a new political perspective that presents an idealized

Israel formed around the twelve tribes and embraces both the northern and southern kingdoms. One noticeable feature is that Chronicles entirely passes over the history of the northern kingdom of Israel, which was regarded as religiously illegitimate. All the same, it is evident that the "Israel" of Chronicles describes more than just Judah. Judah and Jerusalem are clearly regarded as the center of the new realm, but there is a definite urge to connect this center with the north—the domain of the Samaritans—so as to reinstate "Israel" as a single, complete religious entity.

For the books of Chronicles, there is no amassing of guilt over a period of time. Instead, each generation is directly answerable to God and directly punished should it ever show any sign of apostasy. This individualized theology of guilt reflects a priestly underpinning: the ritual of atonement operated on the premise that individuals bear personal responsibility for their faults. The Chronicles presents this idea, though, not in moral terms but in terms of the history of theology: catastrophes are associated with guilt, while eras of prosperity testify to righteous and devout behavior. This is especially evident in the way King Manasseh of Judah is portrayed (2 Chronicles 33). Manasseh reigned for fifty-five years in Jerusalem, so he must have been a devout man; this contrasts with his negative portrayal in 2 Kings 21. In the same way, the Babylonian Exile is ascribed to the guilt of the last king of Judah, Zedekiah, and his generation (2 Chronicles 36:11–14).

Closely related to the books of Chronicles are the books of Ezra and Nehemiah, which in ancient times formed a single book. The division into two books did not occur until sometime in the early Middle Ages. These books originate from the same circle of scribes as the books of Chronicles but are most likely somewhat older, and were only linked with the Chronicles later, through the literary device of repeating the proclamation made by Cyrus concerning the return of the Jews from exile in 2 Chronicles 36:22–23 and Ezra 1:1–3. The books of Ezra and Nehemiah together report on the restoration taking place within Judah and, in the process, intertwine the activities of the priests Ezra and Nehemiah—who supervised the rebuilding of Jerusalem—in a rather idiosyncratic way. The account of the Jews' return and the building of the temple in Ezra 1–6 is followed by a section describing Ezra's work in Jerusalem (Ezra 7–10), while Nehemiah 1–7 recounts the measures undertaken by Nehemiah, and Nehemiah 8–10 then returns to Ezra and his proclamation of the law. Finally, in Nehemiah 11–13 we are given news of a further decree by Nehemiah. The composition of these two books was clearly an attempt to suggest that the two figures were active at the same time, although historically this may not have been the case. Nehemiah appears to have been a historical figure, but this is not so obviously true of Ezra. Irrespective of where one stands on this matter, the fact remains that the presumption in the book of Ezra is that the reconstruction of the city walls of Jerusalem instigated by Nehemiah had already been substantially completed. In all likelihood, then, Nehemiah was active in Judah before Ezra. Yet Ezra is traditionally placed first because he took precedence as a priest.

Prophecy plays a special role in the books of Ezra and Nehemiah. Ezra 1–6 describes the rebuilding of the temple as requiring prophetic support to succeed, and the restoration is implicitly depicted as the fulfillment of prophetic promises of salvation (see, for example, Isaiah 60:7, 9, and 13 and Ezra 7:27). The theological thinking behind this appears to be a desire to create a positive counterpart to historical prophecy. In the latter, disobeying the Law and shunning the advice of prophets customarily incurs harsh judgment. Ezra and Nehemiah demonstrate, conversely, that observing the Law and heeding the pronouncements of the contemporary prophets Haggai and Zechariah guarantee the prosperity of everyone in Judah (see Ezra 5:1 and 6:14).

The assemblage consisting of Chronicles, Ezra, and Nehemiah, which has been referred to as an "opus of historical chronicling," thus represents a Rewritten Bible not only by virtue of its retelling of the story recounted in Genesis through 2 Kings, but also in following the prophetic tradition of the books Malachi through Isaiah.[44] These books are thus a striking example of the Rewritten Bible literature. They show that textual exegesis and the writing down of texts are closely interlinked and that textual exegesis can itself become an integral part of "Scripture," that is, the emerging Bible.

The Book of Jubilees

In addition to the "opus of historical chronicling" in Chronicles, Ezra, and Nehemiah, the literature of the Rewritten Bible also includes several early Jewish works that did not ultimately find a place in the Jewish and Christian Bibles.[45] One key example is the book of Jubilees, also known as the "Little Genesis" (*Leptogenesis*). This work was written in around the mid-second century BCE and has only survived in complete form in an Ethiopian translation. It contains a retelling of the narrative from Genesis 1 to Exodus 24 and emphasizes that parts of the Torah were already known to the forefathers and observed by them. The story is embedded within a narrative framework that depicts an angel recounting the tale to Moses on Mount Sinai. The primary significance of the book of Jubilees lies in its "Mosaicization" of the history of the forefathers and patriarchs of Israel. Customarily, Moses is not introduced in the theology of the Torah until the book of Exodus. The book of Jubilees solves the problem that the forefathers could not yet have known the Torah by introducing the narrative of the "Heavenly Tablets," which were shown to the forefathers and enabled them to live in accordance with the precepts of the Torah.

In addition to the book of Jubilees, the Genesis Apocryphon found at Qumran (1Q20) contains an embellished re-narration of parts of Genesis (see the next section, on the Dead Sea Scrolls).[46] The book of Enoch is likewise among the texts of the Rewritten Bible. Certain parts of Genesis are retold in this complex book (notably the story of the fallen angels, which is based on Genesis 6:1–4), while the history of Israel from the Great Flood to the period of the Maccabean Revolt is revealed to Enoch in dream visions. Finally, Enoch also contains an apocalyptic overview of history, in which the progress of the world to its final destruction is imparted to Enoch.

An early Jewish text known by the title *Liber Antiquitatum Biblicarum,* which has been preserved only in a Latin translation, also forms part of the Rewritten Bible literature. Written by an unknown author sometime in the first century CE, it recounts the biblical story from Adam to the death of King Saul in a distinctive way.[47] It expands upon several passages in the biblical texts, while summarizing others only very briefly or omitting them completely. A series of extensive speeches by leading figures from the history of Israel highlights the election of the Israelites as God's chosen people, who, it is claimed, will successfully endure situations of great peril because God keeps faith with Israel.

The Rewritten Bible literature, which includes a number of other texts besides the ones mentioned here, demonstrates that in Judaism of the Persian and Hellenistic-Roman periods, certain texts gained authority not least through being narrated in a novel way, and that they became seminal for the new, altered circumstances in the history of Israel or Judaism. This appropriation through re-narration represents an important step toward the emergence of the Jewish Bible. It was supplemented by the interpretation of Scripture that was conducted in the Pesharim and various philological and exegetic commentaries. This brings us to another important area of Jewish literature of the Hellenistic-Roman period: the Dead Sea Scrolls.

The Dead Sea Scrolls

The scrolls that were discovered between 1947 and 1956 in the Judean desert on the shores of the Dead Sea are of enormous significance for interpreting the scriptures that became the normative texts of Judaism. The scrolls, which were found in eleven caves near the ancient settlement of Qumran, provide important insights into these biblical texts. Archeologists found a total of over nine hundred manuscripts in the caves, including more than two hundred Bible texts.[48] Many of these text finds are extremely small fragments, but nine scrolls were almost completely preserved. All the books of the Bible, with the exception of the book of Esther, are represented in texts from Qumran.[49] The overwhelming majority of the manuscripts are in ancient Hebrew, but there are a few in Aramaic and Greek, some of which are translations of Hebrew texts. Additional scrolls, including biblical texts, have been found at various sites along the western shore of the Dead Sea—at Wadi Murabba'at, Naḥal Ḥever, and the fortress of Masada.

The question of how the texts relate to the nearby settlement of Qumran has been the subject of much scholarly discussion. Most relevant in this regard are those texts that relate to the life of a Jewish group who lived in the Qumran settlement, such as the scroll of the Community Rule, the Rule of the Congregation (1QSa, sometimes also rather unfortunately termed the Sectarian Rule), and the scroll of Thanksgiving Hymns (1QH).[50] Most scholars believe that inhabitants of the settlement were members of a group within ancient Judaism known as the Essenes. References to this group appear in the works of the historians Josephus, Philo, and Pliny the Elder.[51] Pliny explicitly states that the Essenes were reputed to live near the Dead Sea, and that the town of Engada (present-day Ein Gedi) was situated to the south of their settlements. This description fits with the geographical location of Qumran. However, these ancient historical sources offer conflicting information about the Essenes and other settlement dwellers, such as their attitude to communal ownership, keeping the Sabbath, and marriage. Josephus, who wrote the most extensive account of the Essenes, reports that they were well represented in every town of the region, cultivated a frugal and ascetic lifestyle, set little store by wealth, held property in common, and were extremely devout.[52] One group of Essenes, however, took a different view of marriage; they did not practice celibacy but instead lived in a conjugal community.[53] Philo also reports that the Essenes led an abstemious existence and foreswore private property, and that no Essene took a wife. This final claim is also made by Pliny; he attributed the fact that the community still existed to its welcoming of newcomers.

The Qumran texts include some that describe life within the family unit and others that describe an ascetic group living by strict rules. Descriptions of family life are found in fragments of ten scrolls of the Damascus Document, and in a version of the Community Rule that was found in Cave 1 (1Q28 = 1QS). The Rule of the Congregation (1Q28a = 1QSa), known from fragments of eleven manuscripts, focuses instead on life in an ascetic community. How can we explain the differences between these texts?

It has been suggested that two groups of Essenes lived in Qumran: a more strictly observant group known as the *yakhad*, and a less strict group, represented by the Damascus Document. The discovery of the graves of women at Qumran strengthens the belief that it was not inhabited exclusively by a male community that abided by strict rules of celibacy. The two groups may have inhabited the settlement or the surrounding caves at the same time or one after the other. The texts allow us to put together a religious profile of the Jews who dwelt in Qumran.

Some of the biblical texts found at Qumran were probably produced and used by the settlement's inhabitants, while others were imported from elsewhere. Some of the scrolls predate the earliest known settlement of Qumran, suggesting that they must have been imported. Most of the scrolls do come from the same period as the settlement, however, and so were presumably produced in Qumran itself. The settlement of Qumran was razed to the ground by the Romans in 68 CE. The scrolls escaped destruction, most likely because they had been hidden in the caves by the local inhabitants.

The Dead Sea Scrolls date from a period ranging from the third century BCE to the beginning of the first century CE. Their significance therefore resides first of all in the fact that the biblical manuscripts found here are about a thousand years older than any previously discovered Hebrew or Aramaic manuscripts of the Bible. Moreover, they clearly demonstrate that neither the content nor the form of the Bible was set in stone at this time.[54]

The fact that these manuscripts represent almost all of the books of the Bible indicates that those scriptures were considered authoritative texts. But a number of other texts were also found at Qumran that belong to the categories of Apocrypha and Pseudepigrapha of the Old Testament or to those texts designated as the Rewritten Bible. These include the book of Enoch and the book of Jubilees, several fragments of which were found, mostly in Aramaic.[55] Fragments of the books of Sirach and Tobit in Hebrew and Aramaic were also discovered, suggesting that these works were originally composed in either or both of those languages and subsequently translated into Greek. For instance, there are four fragments of the book of Tobit in Aramaic and one in Hebrew (4Q196–200). Hebrew fragments of the book of Sirach were discovered at both Qumran and Masada. This work was known only in Greek translation for many centuries, before the first Hebrew fragments were found in a synagogue in Cairo in the late nineteenth century. The finding of these texts is significant because it provides clear evidence that "biblical" texts co-existed alongside ones that were later downgraded to Apocrypha or Pseudepigrapha, not just within the religious and intellectual environment that produced the Septuagint but also in the Hebrew or Aramaic linguistic regions of Judaism of the Hellenistic-Roman period.

It is also noteworthy that psalter manuscripts from Qumran exhibit various different sequences of psalms and also occasionally include, in between individual psalms, pieces that were either hitherto unknown or that were known only from non-Hebrew text traditions. Some of them, for example, contain Psalm 151 from the Septuagint, in its original Hebrew version.[56] Another connection to the Septuagint involves fragments of a shorter version of the book of Jeremiah, which was also previously known only in Greek translation in the Septuagint. The Greek book of Jeremiah is around one-seventh shorter than the one in the Hebrew Bible and may represent a more original version. A number of texts from Qumran that update or interpret the books of Genesis, Jeremiah, Ezekiel, and Daniel belong to category of the Rewritten Bible. They reflect a vibrant tradition of interpreting the biblical books. As a result, updates of authoritative scriptures and Rewritten Bible texts merge and cannot be clearly distinguished from one another.

This brings us to another important finding to emerge from the Qumran texts. Besides the biblical and other texts just discussed, there were also many commentary-like texts that provide interpretations of the books of the Bible. These texts, called the Pesharim texts (found only at Qumran), offer interpretations of the books of the prophets (for example, Habbakuk, Isaiah, and Hosea) and the psalms.

Another interpretative text found at Qumran is the Genesis Apocryphon (1Q20). Only a few columns that are hard to decipher have survived from what was once clearly a far more extensive scroll, written in Aramaic. The text is an interpretive retelling of parts of Genesis that focuses on the figures of Lamech (the father of Noah and a descendant of Cain), Enoch, Noah, and Abraham and is narrated mostly in the first person. The narrative has affinities with other paraphrases of Genesis, such as the books of Enoch and Jubilees.

Some of the Torah texts from Qumran display distinctive features. A number of them were composed in a special script called Paleo-Hebrew, which was common in the pre-exile period but was later supplanted by Hebrew square script.[57] Its use in some of the Torah scrolls from Qumran would have given them a noticeably antiquated feel, which may be related to their special status. No scrolls containing the complete Torah have yet been discovered at Qumran, though several have been found that contain two books: Genesis and Exodus, Exodus and Leviticus, and Leviticus and Numbers. One scroll from Wadi Murabba'at includes fragments of three books: Genesis, Exodus, and Numbers. It appears, then, that compilations of these books, and possibly even of the entire Torah, did exist at that time. A reference to the "book of Moses" occurs in the manuscript 4QMMT^d (= 4Q397) C 10, which may point to a compilation of all five books of the Torah in a single scroll. In this context, it is noteworthy that the texts often refer to "Moses" as a person who taught the Torah. The Torah, which is firmly associated with Moses either as its author or its teacher (hence the use of "Moses" as a metonym for the Torah), is presented here primarily as a living directive from God, which is to be taught, interpreted, and of course also followed.

One further peculiarity of the texts from Qumran is displayed by the fragments 4Q158 and 4Q364–367, which are often referred to as the Reworked Pentateuch. These texts exhibit idiosyncratic forms, order their material in a specific way, and contain supplements to the familiar Torah texts, such as various additions to the laws.[58] If we proceed from the assumption that the Torah was already regarded as authoritative by this stage, it is remarkable that it continued to be receptive to interpretative additions and edits. One might ask, however, whether these fragments should be seen as reworkings of an existing Torah text or as independent editions of the text in their own right. It remains to be determined whether these texts form part of the Rewritten Bible (representing autonomous editions of older texts) or whether they are to be counted as literature of commentary or interpretation—or indeed, whether these categories are even appropriate for describing them.

Of the Dead Sea texts composed in Greek, one that is of special interest is a scroll found in Nahal Hever containing the Greek text of the book of the Twelve Prophets. This scroll is believed to date from the first century BCE (or possibly the first century CE) and thus may be among the oldest surviving Greek Bible texts. Greek fragments of the books of the Torah as well as other books of the Bible such as Isaiah, Ezekiel, and the Psalms were found at Qumran.[59] Aramaic translations of books of the Bible (the Targumim) also came to light there, in the form of fragments of the books of Leviticus and Job.

The Qumran texts make repeated reference to the history of Israel, naming Moses and the prophets as the people who relayed God's authoritative decrees to the Israelites.[60] Moses began this process by writing down the Law that God confided to him. The prophets then disseminated the commandments to the people of Israel, who can thus be called God's "servants" or his "anointed ones." The texts also refer to the Torah (the five books of Moses) and the Nevi'im (the books of the prophets). The enactment of God's will through his agents Moses and the prophets, as well as the scriptures that they wrote on his behalf, are therefore seen as binding.

A very important passage concerning the naming of groups of authoritative scriptures is found in fragment 4QMMT C 10: "to you we have [written] that you must understand the book of Moses [and] the book[s of the pr]ophets and Davi[d . . .] [the annals of] each generation."[61] Alongside the prologue to the book of Sirach in Greek (discussed earlier in the chapter), this is one of the earliest known lists of groups of authoritative Jewish texts. It presupposes that the Torah was a completed corpus of law by then and that the books of the prophets had already been assembled into a group. What is not so clear, however, is what "David" and the "annals of each generation" refer to. Some commentators have speculated that "David" is a metonymic allusion to the Psalms, since David was considered to be their author. The gap could then be filled in as "Davi[d's Psalms]."[62] This might even be interpreted as a reference to the tripartite structure of the Jewish Bible, with "David" standing for the entire third part, the Ketuvim. But it is equally possible that David is being counted among the prophets; in that case, the Psalms would be considered as one of the books of the prophets. This would result in the following reading: "the books of the prophets and of David." One argument in favor of this reading is that the Qumran texts portray David as a prophetically inspired author—in much the same way as in the New Testament—and so the Psalms would have been interpreted accordingly.[63] Finally, David might simply refer to the individual, whose exemplary nature is alluded to elsewhere in the same text. The "annals" presumably refers to the books of Chronicles.

On the basis of this analysis, then, it does not appear that this passage from 4QMMT is referring to three or even four distinct groups of texts within the Jewish Bible. Rather, it places alongside Moses and the Prophets a number of other texts that were also regarded as prophetically inspired or that enjoyed widespread authority. Yet the aim in doing so was not to create a "canon" of biblical literature. This conclusion accords with other findings from this period, in which, apart from the Torah and to some extent the Prophets, no fixed groupings of texts had yet been formed, let alone any clear-cut "canon" of works. The formulation in 4QMMT should be viewed in a similar way to that in the prologue of the book of Sirach: the prophetic books and various other texts enjoyed a certain authority along with the Torah of Moses, which was seen as binding.

The findings from Qumran are of great significance for understanding how certain texts or groups of texts became authorized within Judaism of the Hellenistic-Roman period. At the time when the New Testament was beginning to take shape, the Torah and the Nevi'im were already considered authoritative collections. A number of other texts, such as the Psalms, the book of Job, the book of Proverbs, the Song of Solomon, and the book of Daniel, also carried great prestige. In addition, the finds from Qumran reveal an extensive literature of exegesis, in which texts were interpreted for their own age or with regard to what they said about the End of Days—that is, as revelations pointing beyond themselves. This same way of dealing with the scriptures of Israel occurs in the New Testament. There, too, they are taken as prophetic utterances that convey the Word of God, with relevance for both the contemporary world and the future.

The Qumran texts also reveal that the extent and the textual form of these writings was still in a state of flux, as they include several different versions and retellings of the Torah. There was not yet a self-contained, authoritative body of texts. Rather, a body of texts, such as the books of Jubilees and Enoch and versions of some biblical books, were regarded as binding for the Jewish community; but the forms those texts took looked very different from the later Jewish Bible. At the same time, these writings give us insight into the history of those books that did not become part of the Hebrew, Greek, or Latin Bibles.

Thanks to its inclusion in the Old Testament of the Ethiopian Church, the Enoch literature has been preserved down the centuries. The Aramaic Enoch texts, which in Qumran had not yet been assembled into a book, allow us a glimpse into an independent apocalyptic world of thought that is far removed from a form of Judaism based on the Torah. The book of the Watchers (1 Enoch 1–36), for example, expands upon the biblical episode of the marriage between the sons of God and the daughters of humans that is recounted in Genesis 6:1–4 and uses it as a springboard to describe the illicit revelation of heavenly secrets to humanity.[64] The authors' choice of Enoch as the pre-Mosaic bearer of revelations contributed to casting a veil of doubt over the literature that was compiled under his name and preventing it from being assimilated into Rabbinic Judaism.

The so-called Temple Scroll (11Q19–21), which probably originates from before the settlement of Qumran and is, at almost 8 meters, the largest of the Dead Sea Scrolls, contains instructions for how to build a temple. It takes into account the provisions outlined in the Priestly Source (Exodus 25–29 and 35–40) and the book of Ezekiel (Ezekiel 40–48). The Temple Scroll's text has not been preserved in its entirety, but on the basis of the borrowings from Exodus 34:10–16, in conjunction with Deuteronomy 7:25–26, we can clearly recognize that it relates to the giving of the Law to Moses before the entry into Canaan. Yet the Temple Scroll cannot be interpreted unequivocally as the (fictional) documentation of a further revelation that took place on Mount Sinai. It merges the revelation on Mount Sinai from the book of Exodus with the one on the Jordan River from Deuteronomy, arranges the respective laws thematically, and formulates them as a direct address by God. It is possible that the Temple Scroll was meant to be seen as outdoing the Torah, which would explain why it never became part of the tradition of classical Judaism.

The Creation of the Septuagint

The Septuagint is a translation of the Hebrew Torah—the five books of Moses—into Greek.[65] The term "Septuagint" (Greek for "seventy") refers to the rounded-down number of people, supposedly seventy-two, who, according to legend, claimed authorship of this translation (some sources do actually cite seventy translators). Later, the name "Septuagint" was extended to apply to other biblical texts in Greek translation as well as to Jewish scriptures originally written in Greek. In the Christian tradition, the Septuagint denotes the Greek Old Testament.[66]

The Letter of Aristeas

The beginnings of the Septuagint are closely associated with the Greek-speaking Jewish community of Alexandria in Egypt. It was there, on the island of Pharos, that the project to translate the Hebrew Bible was carried out, during the reign of King Ptolemy II Philadelphus (282–246 BCE). This makes the Septuagint the oldest translation of biblical texts into another language. The *Letter of Aristeas,* which was probably written in the second half of the second century BCE, gives an account of how the translation came about.[67] According to this source, the initiative came from the head of the Great Library of Alexandria, Demetrius of Phalerum, who suggested to the ruler that he should commission a Greek version of the Jewish body of laws. The king agreed and approached the high priest in Jerusalem to put the idea into action. The high priest duly dispatched to Alexandria seventy-two scholars, six from each of the twelve tribes of Israel, to carry out the work of translation. On their arrival, the scribes were received by the king in person. Aristeas's account does not dwell on the actual business of the translation itself; the final part of the letter simply states that it was completed within seventy-two days and that the translation was henceforth immutable. Most of the letter is taken up with the description of a banquet that lasted for seven days, during which the king disputed with the Jewish translators about the correct way to live. In the course of this debate, Jewish norms of behavior are portrayed as the highest form of ethical teaching. In his concluding remarks, the king avows that this doctrine has been of great benefit to him in his rule.[68] The writer of the *Letter of Aristeas* is primarily concerned not with divulging how the Torah was translated into Greek but with highlighting the importance of Jewish wisdom and ethics, which he claims are actually superior to Greek philosophy.

The Hellenistic Jewish historian Aristobulus of Alexandria, likewise writing in the second century BCE, also tells the story of the creation of the Septuagint.[69] Later, the legend of the translation as told in the *Letter of Aristeas* was further embellished by the Jewish scholar Philo, another resident of the city. According to Philo, although the translators worked in isolation from one another, they all came up with perfectly identical translations.[70] The historian Flavius Josephus, together with various Christian authors such as Justin, Irenaeus, Clement of Alexandria, and Tertullian, also knew the legend of the origin of the Septuagint as recounted in the *Letter of Aristeas*.[71] Over the course of time, the number of translators was reduced from seventy-two to seventy (in Josephus, Justin, Irenaeus, and Clement), and other modifications were made to the account.[72]

For a long time, scholars believed that the *Letter of Aristeas* had no historical value. The creation of the Septuagint came about not, they maintained, as the result of an edict of the Ptolemaic king, but in response to the requirements of the Jewish community in Alexandria. This city, founded in 331 BCE by Alexander the Great, was a major cultural, scientific, and religious metropolis, which boasted important scholarly institutions in the form of the Museion, a kind of center for intellectual endeavor, and the renowned Great Library.[73] All the important branches of contemporary learning flourished in Alexandria, including philosophy, philology, medicine, mathematics, and geography. The city was also an important center of religion.

A significant proportion of the population of Alexandria was Jewish. The Jews of the city were organized as an independent *politeuma* (commonwealth), which ensured them the right to self-determination in legal and religious matters. It is therefore plausible that the Jews of Alexandria commissioned a translation of the Torah into Greek, since they were presumably barely fluent in Hebrew, or perhaps did not speak it at all. They would not have been able to follow the reading of the Torah in synagogue services or use the text for private study.

Scholars have recently questioned, however, why all the ancient sources without exception agree that the project was the result of an external impetus and did not originate in the Jewish community of Alexandria. It is highly improbable that a tradition of this kind could have been based on pure invention. Why would Jewish authors have fabricated a Gentile initiative to translate their sacred texts if the Jews themselves had actually been responsible for it? A more likely explanation is that the creation of the Septuagint reflects the cultural and religious situation of contemporary Alexandria and its Jewish population. Unquestionably, the *Letter of Aristeas* and the Jewish and Christian sources that rely upon it have embellished the making of the Septuagint with a degree of myth and have molded it to serve their own purposes. All the same, this document may accurately describe the situation created or at least facilitated by the political authorities in Alexandria. The prominence of learning and culture, the highly advanced study of philology— especially in the exegesis of the works of Homer—and the religious conditions in the city constituted a special environment for the Jews who lived there. And Alexandria's political masters would have had a large hand in shaping this environment. It is this milieu that the *Letter of Aristeas* outlines when it tells the story of Demetrius of Phalerum, the president of the library, writing to King Ptolemy and informing him that, if the library's holdings were to be considered complete, the Jewish books of the law in an accurate Greek translation needed to be kept there, since they were a "philosophical and pure expression of the Law, by virtue of being God-given."[74]

Two factors may have acted together in the making of the Septuagint: on the one hand, the religious, cultural, and scholarly distinctiveness of Alexandria, which was fostered by the political and administrative elites of the city, and on the other, the concern of the Jewish community not just to utilize its traditions and scriptures in its own gatherings and in private study, but also to introduce them into the wider social and intellectual discourse of the city. In this scenario, it was the very particular circumstances prevailing in Alexandria that led to the Torah being translated into Greek. Since the time of Alexander the Great's campaigns of conquest, Greek had become the predominant language of the Mediterranean region. The significance of the Septuagint thus extends far beyond the context of Alexandria. A key factor contributing to the success of the Septuagint, as the *Letter of Aristeas* and Philo's account both stress, was that it was seen as the immutable, divinely inspired version of the Torah, in no way inferior to its Hebrew counterpart. It was duly held in high esteem in the Greek-speaking Jewish community. This did not change until, after the destruction of Jerusalem and the temple, Judaism reformed itself as Rabbinic Judaism and shifted its focus exclusively to texts written in Hebrew or Aramaic.

After the Torah, other texts were also translated into Greek—the history books, the Prophets, the Psalms, Wisdom literature like the book of Proverbs and the book of Job, and the Five Megillot (the "festival scrolls": Ruth, the Song of Solomon, Ecclesiastes [Qohelet], the book of Lamentations, and Esther). These were joined by other books that were written in Greek or had survived only in Greek translation, namely the deuterocanonical texts, or Apocrypha. Together, these books made up the Septuagint, which subsequently became the "Old Testament" of Greek Christian Bibles. Yet the cohesion of this content related primarily to its Greek linguistic form. As far as its scope was concerned, there remained in both Judaism and Christianity an awareness of the difference between the texts of Hebrew origin and those that were in Greek and were added later.

Jewish and Christian Revisions

Even after the creation of the Septuagint, Judaism continued to actively engage with Greek translations of biblical scripture. Some were revisions meant to align the Greek text more closely with the phraseology of the original Hebrew. A prime example is the *kaige* revision, so named because it consistently renders the Hebrew particle *gam* ("also") with the Greek *kaí ge* ("and indeed"). The Twelve Prophets Scroll, a Greek manuscript from Naḥal Ḥever, is one of these *kaige* revisions. Somewhat later, in the second century CE, more Greek translations were made which adhered more closely to the Hebrew text than the Septuagint does. These translations, which are called *recentiores* (because they are more recent), are principally associated with the Hellenistic Jewish scholars Aquila of Sinope, Symmachus, and Theodotion, about whom little else is known.[75] All of these translations—both the "original" Septuagint (also known as the "Old Greek") as well as its revisions and the later translations by Aquila and others—have only survived in fragmentary form. Complete Greek texts are only found in Christian Bible manuscripts from the fourth century onward.

With all of these versions in circulation, early Judaism knew the text of the Bible in various different guises. Besides the Hebrew version, there were a number of Greek versions as well as the paraphrastic Targumim. The Targumim, which are Aramaic versions of the Hebrew Bible, arose from the first century CE onward, initially in Palestinian Judaism and somewhat later in Babylonian Judaism. They are often of an interpretative nature, as can be seen in the manuscripts from Qumran relating to the books of Leviticus and Job. Because of their characteristic trait of not simply translating the text but also paraphrasing and embellishing it, the Targumim are not translations in the true sense of the word but rather renderings.[76]

The Hebrew text itself likewise existed in different forms. We see this in the manuscripts from Qumran, which diverge from the later, established Hebrew canon both in language and scope. They demonstrate that there was still no standardized text of the Old Testament at the beginning of the Common Era. Various versions of its books existed, each of them slightly different from the next. The diverse Greek translations were based on their myriad Hebrew models.

The Septuagint played an important role for emerging Christianity. The authors of the New Testament texts are given to quoting frequently from Greek translations of the books of the Bible, as are later Christian authors. On many occasions, their quotations precisely match the Septuagint manuscripts that have survived to the present day, though sometimes they diverge from them. It is not easy to determine which versions of Greek Bible texts early Christian authors would have consulted, for the very reason that the pre-Christian translations have only come down to us in fragments.

The early Christians engaged in their own way with the Greek Bible translations and their relationship to the Hebrew text. A particularly impressive example of such work is the so-called Hexapla ("sixfold"), which was written by the early Christian theologian Origen (ca.185–ca. 253) in around 230 CE in Caesarea Maritima. Consisting of a six-column chart, it aimed to provide a reliable version of the Bible text by comparing the Hebrew text (first column) and its transcription into Greek (second column) with the Greek translations by Aquila, Symmachus, and Theodotion (third, fourth, and sixth columns). In the fifth column, Origen himself revised the text of the Septuagint in light of the Hebrew text and the Greek translations. Even at this early stage, we encounter the problem that is intrinsically associated with the existence of a variety of different text forms and translations. When a person is confronted with different versions of the same text, the question inevitably arises of which should be given precedence—or, alternatively, whether one should use the various versions to create one's own text to try to more closely approximate the original Bible text. Scholarly research into the Bible and its history continues to wrestle with such questions to the present day.

Alongside the Christian revision by Origen, there were also several other Christian reworkings of the Septuagint. From the fourth century on, the Greek texts were incorporated into complete texts of the Bible in Greek. The oldest pieces of textual evidence for Greek Bibles containing both the Old and the New Testament are the Codex Sinaiticus, the Codex Vaticanus, and the Codex Alexandrinus. The edition of the Septuagint produced by Alfred Rahlfs, which was first published in 1935, is based on these codices. In the meantime, ongoing research has led not only to a revised edition of the Rahlfs text, but most importantly to a twenty-four-volume critical edition of the text, which was published between 1936 (1 Maccabees) and 2014 (2 Chronicles) by the Göttingen Septuaginta-Unternehmen, which is based at the Academy of Sciences in Göttingen.[77] The aim of this project is to create a text that is not just based on Christian codices of the fourth and fifth centuries but comes as close as possible to the original translations (the "Old Greek" texts).

The Septuagint played a key role both in Judaism during the Hellenistic-Roman period and in ancient Christianity. In the form of the Old Testament, it remained in force as an authoritative text for the Orthodox churches, while in the West it was supplanted by the Vulgate. An awareness of the Hebrew basis of biblical texts remained very much alive in both ancient Judaism and ancient Christianity. In the process of reconstituting Judaism after 70 CE, Rabbinic Judaism reverted to the Hebrew Bible. Christianity also (by analogy with some Jewish sources), included these twenty-two (or twenty-four) books in its Old Testament, which are sometimes explicitly enumerated.[78] The books in question are those that form the "canon" of the Hebrew Bible. In Judaism before 70 CE, however, as is clear from the finds at Qumran, other texts besides these also took on authoritative status. In a similar way, in Christianity the deuterocanonical or apocryphal texts were passed down as part of the Septuagint as well as the Vulgate. This demonstrates that the "canonical" texts always existed within the context of other texts and traditions. The concept of a canon, which is problematic for Judaism in any case, is in Christianity also embedded in a context related to the use of texts considered authoritative in liturgy and private study.

The Samaritans and the Samaritan Pentateuch

In order to trace the development of the Hebrew Bible, and in particular the Torah, during the Persian and Hellenistic periods, we also need to cast an eye on the Samaritans, a group in ancient Israel that was not part of Judaism but which saw itself as a significant entity in its own right.[79] This group can be traced back to the northern kingdom of Israel and takes its name from its association with the region around Samaria, the kingdom's former capital. The Samaritans recognized the Torah as a sacred text, but not the other books of the Hebrew Bible. They constituted a religious community that described itself as "Israelite." The Samaritans are still in existence today, albeit with only a few thousand members, in two communities—at Holon, near Tel Aviv, and on Mount Gerizim. They have their own high priests and synagogues and celebrate the Feast of the Passover (Pesach), in accordance with the precepts of the Torah, by sacrificing lambs. In antiquity, they were probably a far more powerful group, which may even have outnumbered the Judeans at times.[80] In the rabbinical literature, the Samaritans are referred to disparagingly as outsiders, the "Kutim."[81] This is an allusion to the Mesopotamian site of Kuta, mentioned in 2 Kings 17:24, which was believed to be the origin of the Assyrian portion of the Samaritan population.[82]

The negative attitude toward the Samaritans in the rabbinical tradition derives from the Bible's pejorative representation of them.[83] After the story of the demise of the kingdom of Israel (2 Kings 17:5–23), the next passage (2 Kings 17:24–41) recounts how, after the people of Israel were forced into exile in Assyria, the king of Assyria then proceeded to resettle sections of his own populace in the region of the former northern kingdom:

> The king of Assyria brought people from Babylon, Kuthah, Avva, Hamath and Sepharvaim and settled them in the towns of Samaria to replace the Israelites. They took over Samaria and lived in its towns. (2 Kings 17:24)

While the Bible conveys the impression that the entire populations of these two locations changed places in this operation, that is not what happened historically. It is certainly true that the Assyrians carried out deportations in both directions in an attempt to erase the religious and cultural identity of the people they had conquered. However, this exercise only ever affected part of the population.

From a Jewish perspective, the Bible portrays the religious situation in the region of the former northern kingdom as one of pronounced syncretism. It asserts that the people who came from Assyria continued to worship their own gods and idols while at the same time adopting the local cult of YHWH:

> Even while these people were worshipping YHWH, they were serving their idols. To this day their children and grandchildren continue to do as their ancestors did. (2 Kings 17:41)

What is described in 2 Kings 17:24–41 is the biblically distorted origin myth of the Samaritans. The Samaritans had been a distinct group with their own religious practices since the fifth century BCE. Archeological finds prove that a shrine dating from this period was situated on Mount Gerizim.[84] This shrine may have been erected by dissident groups of priests from Jerusalem with a Zadokite background who refused to accept the reformist policies enacted by Ezra and Nehemiah in the post-exile period.

The Samaritans thus found themselves in something of a competitive relationship with Jerusalem during the Persian and Hellenistic periods (see Ezra 4:1–5). A clean break with Judaism does not seems to have occurred until the second century BCE, after the Hasmonean ruler John Hyrcanus destroyed the temple on Mount Gerizim.[85]

The Samaritans recognize the Torah as Holy Scripture, though their tradition has assimilated this text in a slightly altered form. All the most important differences concern the explicit identification of Mount Gerizim as the exclusive site of worship chosen by God. For the Samaritans it is not Jerusalem but Gerizim, the "Mount of Blessing," that is the only legitimate shrine. They arrive at this conclusion through a revision of the Decalogue, which in the Samaritan Torah contains an extra commandment, following those listed in Exodus 20:17 and Deuteronomy 5:22, which instructs the Israelites to erect stelae of the Law and an altar on Mount Gerizim. This commandment combines together various elements from Exodus 13:11 and Deuteronomy 11:29, 27:2–3, 27:4–7, and 11:30. To ensure that the commandments in the Decalogue remain ten in number, the Samaritans excluded the customary preamble and began numbering the commandments from the one forbidding graven images and putting any gods before YHWH (customarily the Second Commandment). This left the tenth spot free for the Mount Gerizim commandment.[86] Another change is that the formulaic expression "the place YHWH will choose" in Deuteronomy (for example, Deuteronomy 12:14, 16:2) is rendered as having occurred in the past: "the place YHWH *has chosen*." This takes the focus away from Jerusalem, which is not mentioned in the Samaritan Pentateuch (or only indirectly, as "Salem" in Genesis 14:18, and as "Moriah" in Genesis 22:2), and redirects it to Gerizim. According to the wording of the Samaritan Pentateuch in Deuteronomy 27:4–5, this is the place where an altar to God should be erected:

> When you have crossed over the Jordan, then you shall erect these stones, as I have commanded you today, upon Mount Gerizim, and you shall plaster them with lime. And there you shall erect an altar to YHWH, your God, an altar of stones.[87]

Jewish manuscripts of the Pentateuch refer to "Mount Ebal" rather than "Mount Gerizim" in this passage. It is highly probable, however, that the wording of the Samaritan Pentateuch is the original one and that the replacement of "Mount Gerizim" by "Mount Ebal" was the product of anti-Samaritan polemics.[88] According to Deuteronomy 11:29 and 27:13, Mount Ebal is the mountain of curses. It is extremely unlikely that the building of an altar would have been envisaged at such a place in the original version of the text.

The shared respect for the Torah among both Samaritans and Jews—albeit with some specific textual differences—is a remarkable fact that requires an explanation.[89] Did Samaritans and Jewish theologians work on it together? To be sure, a paucity of relevant information means that the circumstances under which the Torah came into being will never be fully explained. In any event, however, the Torah clearly represents a conception of Israel that embraces both the north and the south. Although the northern kingdom vanished from the political stage in 722 BCE, it nonetheless remained an autonomous entity in cultural and religious terms that continued to regard itself, as it always had done, as "Israel." This name was appropriated by Judah in the south in the seventh century CE at the latest.[90] Important constituent parts of the Torah, like the story of Jacob, the Exodus story, and Deuteronomy, appear to have originated from northern traditions. This enabled the Samaritans to accept the Torah as an authoritative text for their community, and the Judeans could not disregard this origin. While much evidence argues in favor of the Torah having been largely composed in Judah, it does seem to have also intentionally incorporated elements that originally came from the north.[91] It was only because of this commonality that the Torah could become an authoritative text for both the Samaritans in the north and the Jews in the south.

Philo of Alexandria

The Jewish philosopher and scriptural exegete Philo was active in the first half of the first century in his home town of Alexandria.[92] He traveled to Rome in 40 CE as the head of a Jewish delegation that sought an audience with the Roman emperor Gaius Caligula to discuss the worsening position of the Jews in Alexandria and other parts of the Roman Empire. Philo wrote an account of this journey called *Legatio ad Gaium* ("On the Embassy to Gaius"). In this work he records the depravity of Caligula, who went so far as to demand that people venerate him as a god, and tells of the emperor's anti-Semitism and of the pogroms conducted against the Jews in Alexandria. The *Legatio ad Gaium* is among the last works Philo wrote.

Otherwise, we know little about Philo's life. The Jewish historian Flavius Josephus mentions Philo in his capacity as head of the legation, adding that he was held in high regard and was well versed in philosophy.[93] A similar assessment appears in the history of the early church that Eusebius wrote in the fourth century. Eusebius notes that Philo was a Hebrew by origin, but that his intellect and standing rivaled that of eminent non-Jewish scholars of Alexandria. Philo made a valuable contribution, Eusebius claims, to the study of the divine doctrines of his people, but was equally adept in philosophy, especially Platonic and Pythagorean teachings. Eusebius also refers to Philo's writings on Caligula's actions against the Jews and his mission to Rome.[94] These notes tally with what we know of Philo's extensive literary work, which has been largely preserved. As an Alexandrian Jew, his roots lay in the intellectual world of that metropolis. His works are just as steeped in philosophical tradition as they are in a thorough knowledge of philological methods of interpretation. Philo mentions Greek philosophers and poets such as Homer, Plato, and Xenophon and displays philological expertise, especially in his interpretation of Homer's works. He is totally unaware of Jesus Christ and the emerging faith of Christianity; his textual exegesis relates exclusively to the key books of the Jewish tradition.

Philo summarizes the texts of Judaism in his work *De vita contemplativa* ("On the Contemplative Life"). He says of the Jewish group known as the Therapeutae ("healers") that they would permit nothing to be brought into the houses where they conducted their studies in solitude except for "the laws and the prophecies and hymns [psalms] proclaimed by the Prophets, as well as other writings [or "things"] through which learning and piety are promoted and achieved" (§ 25).[95] This formulation—like that of the prologue to the Greek book of Sirach and the Qumran text 4QMMT—indicates that the corpora of the authoritative texts were fixed in their broad outlines by this stage. Yet we should not conclude that there was already a closed "canon" or an ironclad textual form to these scriptures.

As for the question of the emergence of a binding collection of texts for Judaism, Philo is primarily of interest because he dealt extensively with the exegesis of the Torah in several major commentary works. Philo occasionally quoted from other biblical works, but he never made them the subject of interpretation in a way that was comparable to his treatment of the Pentateuch. As his basis for commentary, Philo consistently used the Septuagint text of biblical scriptures, which he regarded as divinely inspired, like the Hebrew text, and hence to be interpreted literally. Because Philo himself, like many Jews in the diaspora, most likely did not speak Hebrew, he was not in a position to verify the Greek translation against the original or even to make corrections to it.

Philo's works of commentary treat the Torah as the most important part of the biblical scriptures. As a revelation from God, it contains philosophical and ethical teachings about understanding the world and human existence. These can be gleaned from the Torah by applying exegetical methods obtained from philology and philosophy.

The earliest of Philo's works is probably the *Allegorical Commentary*. It comprises twenty-one essays, in which Philo successively examines and interprets the texts of Genesis 2–41. Some of the essays are devoted to themes which Philo takes from the text of Genesis and expands into more broadly based disquisitions on fundamental questions of philosophy and ethics. For example, on the basis of the Bible's characterization of Abel and Cain (in that order!) as a "keeper of flocks of sheep" and a "tiller of the soil" respectively, he offers a wide-ranging exposition on the relationship between virtue and vice in the human soul.[96]

In the essay *On Husbandry,* Philo takes as his starting point the sentence, "Noah, a man of the soil, proceeded to plant a vineyard" (Genesis 9:20) and goes on to discuss the difference between the skilled farmer who is his own master (as represented by Noah) and the unskilled farm laborer who works for a wage (as represented by Cain). This leads him to reflect upon different human impulses, as symbolized by the image of the adept equestrian as opposed to the inexperienced rider. Skilled riders know how to control their instincts by applying good sense (*nous;* paragraph 73). Philo's allegory clearly owes much to the image of the human soul or psyche found in the works of Plato. Plato sees the soul as consisting of three parts: the charioteer (reason, *logistikon*), a horse of noble breed (moral impulses), and a horse that is wild and untamed (irrational passions).[97]

In the essay *On the Migration of Abraham,* Philo gives an interpretation of Genesis 12:1–6. The text concerns God's instruction to Abraham to leave his country, his people, and his father's household to move to a land that God will reveal to him, where he would found a great nation. It also recounts how Abraham followed this order. Philo interprets this text in terms of the six gifts that God bestows on humans: the ability to turn away from all mortal and earthly things and become aware of everlasting life; the capacity to live a virtuous life; the blessing to think the best and impart this to others; God's vow to "make your [Abraham's] name great" (Genesis 12:2), which Philo interprets as referring to people's ability to exhibit their goodness through good works; God's blessing of Abraham as proof that he is worthy of divine benediction; and, as the sixth and greatest gift, the beneficial effect of blessing on all aspects of the human soul, and by analogy that of a single righteous person on the whole of humankind.

Philo's *Allegorical Commentary* has survived almost complete, with only the commentaries on certain passages of the text of Genesis missing. There is some debate among scholars about whether the work originally began with an interpretation of chapter 1 of Genesis, which was subsequently lost.[98] The defining characteristic of this work is that Philo employs an interpretative method that was well known in Alexandria and was used especially in the exegesis of Homer's writings. At some points, Philo takes issue with other Jewish interpreters of the Torah over the correct understanding of biblical texts. In doing so, he sets great store by showing that the text in question includes no erroneous statements or other faults such as redundancies. Also, in his opinion the Bible contains no myths that should be read as symbolic tales and not interpreted literally. Rather, Philo stresses the literality of scripture, whose meaning is to be teased out through allegorical exegesis.

This point emerges particularly clearly in the treatise *On the Confusion of Tongues*. Here, Philo criticizes the view that the story of the construction of the Tower of Babel in Genesis 11:1–9 is a myth, like the one in Homer that recounts the attempt by the Aloads to pile up two mountains, Ossa and Pelion, on top of Mount Olympus and thus to ascend to heaven (the Aloads are the sons of Poseidon, or Aloeus, who were giants even as children). Philo develops an allegorical interpretation of the biblical text, to show that the meaning of the story is to be fathomed in another way. Interpretation, he contends, must search for a deeper meaning that transcends the literal sense of the text (paragraph 190). That meaning, in this case, is that any attempt to consolidate evil, or even to coerce goodness into the service of evil, cannot endure. God's actions are directed at preventing vices from working in concert with one another and in this way destroying their power over us. The meaning of biblical texts, then, is not plainly visible. As a general rule, Philo regards the external, literal meaning of words as merely the starting point for his reflections on the deeper philosophical and ethical sense of biblical scripture.

Thus, at the very beginning of the *Allegorical Commentary*, Philo emphasizes that the statement "And on the sixth day God finished the work that he had done" should not be regarded as a declaration of the time it took for God to create the world (Genesis 2:2 in the Septuagint; the Hebrew Bible text has "the seventh day" here). That kind of reading would be nonsensical, since time did not exist before the creation of the world; it had only come about as a result of the change from night to day. And this change, in turn, was the result of the rising and the setting of the sun, a heavenly body created by God. The world cannot therefore have been created at a particular time. Rather, time only came into being through the existence of the universe. As a result, Philo maintains, the number six does not stand for a number of days but instead represents the perfect number. He expands upon this idea by citing various speculations about the number six, including the movement of living creatures, who can move in six ways: forward and backward, up and down, right and left.[99]

In this way, Philo runs through the text of Genesis chapter by chapter, explaining it through allegorical interpretation. His intention is to emphasize its significance for the ethical and moral life of the Jews. So, for instance, the episode of the serpents in the desert, in which God inflicts venomous serpents on the people of Israel because they have sinned against him (Numbers 21:4–9), is designed to illustrate the curing of people from sinful passions. The serpents that are sent to bite the Israelites signal apostasy from God and punishment by death; healing can only be effected through another "serpent" that God orders Moses to erect on a pole. Anyone who looks at this bronze serpent after being bitten is cured (Numbers 21:9). The serpent on the pole stands for prudence, which only those who are loved by God possess. This is the reason, Philo claims, why the biblical text specifically phrases God's instruction as "Make yourself a serpent."[100]

On the basis of the statement in Genesis that God placed cherubim "facing the garden [of Eden]" (Genesis 3:24), Philo launches into an extensive disquisition on the term "facing" (Philo uses the Greek term *antikry* here, whereas the Septuagint translates the Hebrew with *apénanti*).[101] The expression can denote a hostile configuration but also something about which a judgment needs to be formed (such as when a judge "faces" the accused). But "facing" can also refer to the act of contemplating people or things and thereby familiarizing oneself with them (as, say, in the viewing of paintings). Philo concludes by clarifying these various options through examples that refer to ethical and moral forms of behavior.

Philo's method is designed to interpret the biblical text by bringing out the deeper meaning of messages, words, and phrases—especially those which might at first sight appear implausible, banal, or superfluous—through allegorical exegesis. The *Allegorical Commentary* presumes that readers will be familiar with the biblical texts and acquainted with the Greek translation. This is a work of commentary intended for an educated Jewish public in Alexandria, as is also reflected by the points of dispute with other Jewish exegetes. The allegorical interpretation clearly testifies to the authoritative status of the texts under discussion. For Philo, it is indisputable that the biblical texts are of foundational importance, even when this may not be obvious on first reading. Although the allegorical interpretation may sometimes depart from a literary reading of the biblical text, it does help corroborate its foundational importance for a philosophically educated readership.

Another of Philo's running commentaries on the Torah is known by its Latin title *Quaestiones et Solutiones* ("Questions and Solutions"). This work is known only from a few Greek fragments relating to the books of Genesis and Exodus, along with larger fragments in Armenian that relate to the same books. It is possible that this work of commentary originally covered the entire Pentateuch. The work is structured in a question-and answer format. Each question asks why a biblical phrase is formulated in a particular way, or wherein its deeper, universal meaning resides. These questions are then answered through an explanation of the relevant passage. Unlike in his *Allegorical Commentary*, Philo does not take issue with other exegetes here, but instead offers explanations on the meaning of the text along the lines of didactic schooling that was customary at the time. The work was evidently written for use in the educational establishments of Alexandria.

A third work of commentary by Philo is the *Expositio Legis* ("Exposition of the Law"). This is thought to be the most recent of Philo's three great commentaries. The work comprises an interpretation of the story of creation, descriptions of the lives of the three oldest sages of Israel (Abraham, Isaac, and Jacob, of which only the one on Abraham has survived), and portrayals of Joseph and Moses. These texts are of a biographical nature and show certain affinities to biographies by Greek and Roman writers, such as Plutarch's *Lives of the Noble Greeks and Romans*. Philo sees the patriarchs as embodiments of the unwritten laws and as symbols of the ways of virtue. Joseph, on the other hand, is the ideal "politician" who upholds his virtue in real-life situations of duress in Egypt. The account of Moses's life portrays him as the ideal lawgiver of the Israelites and as a prophet and philosopher. The legend of how the translation of the Torah into Greek came about is also incorporated into this depiction.[102] Philo defends Moses against accusations from non-Jewish quarters, in a way that exhibits connections with other apologias by Philo.[103]

Other writings that form part of the *Expositio Legis* are a treatise on the Decalogue and an explanation of special laws within Judaism. The latter is organized in such a way that the legislative regulations described in the

Pentateuch are attached to the commandments given in the Decalogue. This makes the Decalogue appear to be the key element of the Torah, as well as its organizing principle. It is also the basis of the distinction drawn between the commandments of the Decalogue as "general laws," and the remainder as "special laws." The *Expositio Legis* concludes with two treatises, *On the Virtues* and *On Rewards and Punishments,* in which Philo treats laws and topics that are not sufficiently covered in the preceding treatises.

The very structure of the *Expositio Legis* indicates that it is substantially different from Philo's other two works. Here, Philo does not engage in detailed philological exegesis of biblical scripture but elects instead to paraphrase it. His aim is to use his own synopses and retellings to present idealized biographies of the key figures of Jewish history and thus highlight the philosophical and ethical significance of Jewish laws. Unlike in the *Allegorical Commentary* and the *Quaestiones et Solutiones,* Philo's chief concern in the *Expositio Legis* is to explain to a non-Jewish readership the philosophical and ethical substance of the Jewish scriptures and their protagonists, and to defend them against criticisms. In this way it is similar to *Legatio ad Gaium* and another treatise, *Against Flaccus,* in which Philo also defends the Jewish people and their scriptures and traditions against hostile accusations and attacks from outside. Like *Legatio ad Gaium,* the *Expositio Legis* is aimed at a non-Jewish public, whereas *Against Flaccus*—an account of the anti-Semitic pogroms that erupted in Alexandria in 38 CE, fomented by the Roman governor of Egypt, Aulus Avilius Flaccus—is a work of consolation, directed at his co-religionists in the city.

Philo's significance for the process by which Jewish biblical texts became normative resides primarily in the fact that his thoroughgoing interpretation of the Pentateuch helped raise its profile as a key founding document of Judaism. In the intellectual milieu of Alexandria, where a preoccupation with classical authors such as Homer and Plato played a central role, Philo's commentaries promoted the idea of an authoritative body of texts for Judaism that were analogous to the seminal works of Greek history and scholarship. In particular, the *Allegorical Commentary* and the *Expositio Legis* were instrumental in ensuring that a particular, Greek, form of the Torah was recognized as normative. Alexandrian biblical exegesis, of which Philo was an outstanding exponent, thus worked toward establishing a "canon" of authoritative texts in a far more conspicuous way than was the case in the Palestinian region, as we have already observed in relation to the Qumran texts.

Ultimately, Philo must be seen as the true father of the genre of philological commentary on the books of the Bible. In comparison, the Pesharim from Qumran are of a markedly different nature. They are not philological and exegetical commentaries, but rather interpretations of biblical texts for their time. Philo interpreted biblical texts using the standard philological methods of his time but then conveyed them by means of philosophical and ethical ideas deriving from the intellectual world of Greece and Rome. In this way, he laid the groundwork for a form of textual exegesis that would be taken up and further developed by Origen—another scholar active in Alexandria, and subsequently in Caesarea—some two hundred years later.

5

Ancient Jewish Texts in Early Christianity

The Status of the Scriptures of Israel

Christianity arose from within Judaism and is firmly linked to its scriptures and traditions. Its beginnings lie in the life and work of Jesus of Nazareth and his ultimate fate. This is the subject of all the books of the New Testament, and other Christian texts associated with them. The anchoring of Christianity within Judaism, which eventually resulted in the emergence of the Christian Bible comprising the Old and New Testaments, thus has its historical starting point in the appearance of Jesus.[1]

Jesus grew up Jewish, in an environment where an attachment to Jewish life, its scriptures and rituals, was taken for granted. The people with whom he interacted were predominantly Jews. His disciples came from villages in Galilee, a region with a pronounced Jewish character, and it was among Jews that communities of his followers formed.[2] In early Christianity, however, the conviction soon arose that the Christian message was to be directed not just toward Jews but also toward the non-Jewish population. This was rooted in Jesus's own initiatives, such as his open-minded interpretation of Jewish purity laws, his solicitude for outcasts on the margins of society, and his claim that simply being part of the fellowship that he founded was the decisive prerequisite for attaining God's salvation. At the same time, many members of the Jewish community in Jerusalem, in particular Jews from the Diaspora, were beginning to take a critical stance toward the temple's role as the central sanctuary of Judaism. Such growing discontent may have been further fueled by Jesus's critique of the institution of the temple in his public utterances.[3] Eventually, the conviction grew that believing in Jesus Christ nullified the boundary between Jews and Gentiles. These developments took place primarily within the two most important communities of early Christianity, one in Jerusalem and the other in Antioch, an ancient Greek city on the Orontes River (now Antakya, Turkey).[4] They set the course for Christianity's emergence, prompting as they did the formation of Christian communities comprising both Jews and Gentiles, and hence social and religious groupings of a kind that had never existed before. Immediately after his conversion to Christianity, Paul became a member of the community at Antioch and from there embarked on his first missionary journeys. Through Paul, the view that both Jews and Gentiles could be part of the Christian communion established itself as the guiding principle behind the mission to spread the Gospel to those groups.[5]

These momentous developments placed the scriptures of Israel in a new light. Belief in Jesus Christ also changed belief in the God of Israel. On the one hand, Christianity held fast to monotheism and expressed this by speaking of "One God," which was inspired by the Jewish confession of faith (*Shema Yisrael*) in Deuteronomy 6:4 ("Hear, O Israel: YHWH our God, YHWH is One").[6] Mark 12:29 quotes this confession verbatim from the Septuagint. The description of YHWH as the "true and living" God is also echoed in the New Testament.[7] On the other hand, belief in the God of Israel was reframed by faith in Jesus Christ. Christians proclaimed God as the one who acts for the benefit of humankind through Jesus Christ. Jesus Christ was thus placed alongside God, and the Christian faith became first a bipartite creed, and later a tripartite creed, declaring belief in God as three-in-one: the Father, the Son, and the Holy Spirit. Consequently, the scriptures of Israel also became the authoritative texts of Christianity, and the history of Israel became the history of the Christian Church. Non-Jews were expected to view it as their history as well, and to regard the scriptures of Israel as binding upon them. The development of the New Testament can only be understood from this angle.

The authoritative status of the scriptures of Israel in the New Testament is immediately apparent from the frequent references to "Scripture" or "the Scriptures."[8] The authors of the New Testament took it for granted that their audience would know that "Scripture" or "the Scriptures" always referred to the scriptures of Israel, and that these had binding force. This is not surprising, since early Christian authors were addressing a Jewish readership. Most texts of the New Testament and many other writings of early Christianity were also directed toward non-Jews, however. The story of Israel that is told in the biblical texts was emphasized in just the same way as it was for Jewish readers. For non-Jews, too, a belief in the God of Israel was an essential prerequisite for believing in Jesus Christ. The profound consequences of this idea for emerging Christianity can scarcely be overstated, since it meant that biblical texts hereafter formed the basis of the faith not just for Jews, but for all those who believed in Christ.

The scriptures of Israel whose authority was recognized in emerging Christianity included the Torah, the books of the prophets (this category encompasses both the historical books of the Former Prophets, from Joshua to 2 Kings, and books of the Latter Prophets, from Isaiah to Malachi) and writings that form part of the Wisdom literature, such as the Psalms, the book of Job, and the book of Proverbs. During the period of emergent Christianity, however, there was not yet a set canon of texts. Instead, there were scriptures and groups of scriptures whose authority was beyond question. It is these scriptures that Jesus and the early Christians invoked when expressing their faith in the One God and the authority of his decrees.

Quotations in Early Christian Texts

The description of the biblical texts as "the Law and the Prophets," which was widespread in Judaism of the Hellenistic and Roman periods, also occurs in the New Testament. It is found in the letters of Paul, the Gospels of Luke and Matthew, and also (on one occasion) in the Gospel of John.[9] Furthermore, a turn of phrase that is akin to that in the prologue of the book of Sirach and the Qumran manuscript 4QMMT appears in Luke 24:44: "Everything must be fulfilled that is written about me in the Law of Moses and in the Prophets and in Psalms."[10] The term "Psalms" (without an article) denotes other valid texts beyond the first two groupings; it does not stand for the third part of the Jewish Bible, any more than the prologue to the book of Sirach or the 4QMMT text referred to a tripartite structure. Rather, the author of the Gospel of Luke uses it as a catch-all term for texts that he considers to be of special importance. In the Acts of the Apostles, it is no coincidence that, in addition to citing the Torah and the Prophets, Luke makes reference on many occasions to psalms as works written by the prophet David that anticipate Christ or the Christian community and its situation.[11] The passage from Luke spells out the distinctive feature of biblical scriptures from the point of view of the Christian faith: the risen Jesus states that everything written *about him* in the Scriptures will come to pass.

By contrast, nowhere does the New Testament mention by name any texts written by Greek or Roman authors, though Paul does allude to such works in the Areopagus speech in Acts 17:22–31. There, Luke puts into the mouth of Paul a quotation concerning humankind's affinity with God: "We are his offspring" (Acts 17:28). This quotation, from the *Phainomena* of the Greek poet Aratos of Soloi (third century BCE), is prefaced with the unspecific attribution, "As some of your own poets have said."[12] The Paul of Acts, who is portrayed as delivering his sermon to a group of Greek philosophers in Athens, refers his audience to their own tradition in order to emphasize that Greek writers also bore witness to the faith in God professed by Jews and Christians.

A statement about rebuking those who fail to do good by spreading false teachings, which Paul attributes to "one of them [Cretans], their own prophet" (Titus 1:12), appears in the pseudepigraphic letter of "Paul" to his coworker "Titus" (both the sender and the addressee are fictitious): "Cretans are always liars, evil brutes, lazy gluttons" (Titus 1:12). The reference to Crete is explained by an allusion to Paul's having left Titus behind on the island (Titus 1:5). The "prophet" in question is most likely Epimenides, a Cretan priest and sage, who lived in the seventh to sixth centuries BCE. He is designated a "prophet" because his dictum about Cretans, who in the epistle to Titus are presented as archetypically heathen antagonists, is expressly said to be true (1:13).

Paul himself uses a phrase, "Bad company ruins good habits" (1 Corinthians 15:33), that is believed to have been first coined by Euripides, though he introduces it simply as a common saying. In the Acts of the Apostles, during his sermon in Miletus, Paul recalls a saying of Jesus: "It is more blessed to give than to receive" (Acts 20:35). This is remarkable, in that the author of the Acts of the Apostles also wrote the Gospel of Luke, where no such statement appears (indeed, it appears nowhere else). The closest analogy to this saying is in the work of the Greek historian Thucydides (fifth century BCE), who remarks that, unlike the custom prevailing in the Persian Empire, the rich and powerful in Thrace tended to "take rather than give" (2.97.4). Presumably Luke was also familiar with such a phrase, which was either his own reformulation of an ethical maxim ("It is better to give than to receive") or a saying that was already in widespread circulation in that form.[13] He then puts the phrase into Paul's mouth as a quotation from Jesus. Finally, it is worth considering the phrase "to kick against the goads." It appears, once again, in the Acts of the Apostles (26:14), but may be traced back to the Greek poet Pindar, and circulated as a saying among Christians and others.[14]

This is the sum total of references by New Testament authors to Greek poets or to pagan Greek turns of phrase. By contrast, the scriptures of Israel are fundamental to key aspects of the Christian faith—Christ's ministry on earth, his suffering and death, and his resurrection and ascent to heaven—and are quoted frequently, sometimes at great length. "Scripture" as a binding, authoritative testimony is present in the form of moral precepts and prophetic witness, but its exact extent and wording had not as yet been firmly fixed.

The overriding significance which Christianity assigns to the scriptures of Israel is all the more remarkable because New Testament authors often direct their words toward a non-Jewish audience, explicitly addressed as "Gentiles."[15] The scriptures of Israel were clearly meant to apply to Gentile members of Christian communities as well as to Jews. Because the story of Christ can only be elucidated on the basis of these scriptures, a belief in Jesus Christ requires that a person believe in the God of Israel as the one true, living God. Therefore, unlike Jews, who already believed in YHWH, Gentiles had to convert to belief in this God if they were to become members of the Christian faith. For instance, Paul stresses the uniqueness of the God of Israel in his First Letter to the Thessalonians, when he praises his Gentile audience for having "turned to God from idols to serve the living and true God" (1 Thessalonians 1:9). Likewise, in his Letter to the Romans, Paul talks about the one God of the Jews and the Gentiles (Romans 3:29–30).

Generally speaking, the biblical scriptures were characterized in early Christianity as prophetically inspired testimony. Thus, in Romans 1:2, Paul speaks of God having promised the Gospel beforehand "through his prophets in the Holy Scriptures." This is not meant to signify any particular prophets or scriptures. Rather, Paul is characterizing the Scriptures in their entirety as prophetic testimony pointing forward to the Gospel of Jesus Christ. Similarly, the Letter to the Hebrews claims that in ancient times God "spoke to our ancestors through the prophets," but now, in the last days, he has spoken to us through his son (Hebrews 1:1–2). Here too, the biblical scriptures are invoked as prophetic testimony, forming an earlier counterpart to God's communication with humankind through Jesus Christ. At the same time, this mode of communication takes on a new quality as the final and definitive Word of God.

Early Christians were certainly aware of the practice of reading the Scriptures aloud during synagogue services, and they made reference to this in several different ways. Luke, for example, recounts an episode in which Jesus reads from a scroll containing the book of Isaiah in the synagogue at Nazareth (Luke 4:16–21). And in the Acts of the Apostles, Paul and Barnabas reportedly attend a synagogue service in Antioch of Pisidia, where Paul addresses the congregation "after the reading from the Law and the Prophets" (Acts 13:15–16). In the Second Letter to the Corinthians (3:14–15), Paul alludes to the fact that "Moses" is read in the synagogue. Regardless of whether these events actually happened as described, early Christians apparently made productive use of synagogue services in their descriptions of the proclamation of Jesus and the Christian message.

It is often said that a word from Scripture (or the Scriptures in general) was fulfilled in events that occurred during the life of Jesus Christ.[16] In keeping with this, quotations from Scripture are used to interpret Jesus's ministry on earth, his death, his resurrection, and his exaltation to sit at God's right hand. The story of Israel can therefore be presented in such a way as to suggest that it finds its continuation in the story of Jesus Christ and the community of his followers.

In this way, early Christianity participated in the process of interpretation that was an integral feature of the scriptures of Israel. Previous chapters have shown that biblical texts were subject to an ongoing process of updating and commentary throughout the history of Israel and Judaism, so that they could be appropriated again and again, as the circumstances of Judaism changed. The same exegetical traditions are also encountered in the New Testament. The synoptic overview of the history of Israel in Stephen's speech to the Sanhedrin in Acts 7:1–53, for example, stands in the tradition of other such summaries in Israelite and Jewish texts. The purpose of these texts was to interpret the history of Israel from new perspectives, making readers aware of how that history formed the background to their current situation.[17] Stephen's speech, along with various texts of Paul—for instance, Galatians 4:21–31, 1 Corinthians 10, and 2 Corinthians 3—contain some of the same specific exegetical traditions of the scriptures of Israel that are found in Jewish texts.

Jewish and Christian exegeses of the authoritative texts of Israel are thus closely intertwined. This necessarily raises the question of why Christian and Jewish perspectives on the scriptures of Israel ultimately ended up competing with one another, and why a dual-track history of interpretation of these scriptures later evolved (see Chapters 7 and 8).

Certain scriptures come to the fore in early Christianity. The three books most frequently quoted from are Isaiah, the Psalms, and Deuteronomy—in other words, those same texts that are often cited and interpreted in the Qumran scrolls. Reference is also sometimes made to the prophets Jeremiah, Hosea, and Joel.[18] Quotations are chosen on the basis of how readily they can be pressed into service to illustrate the ministry of Jesus or the Christian message. Thus, for example, a scriptural passage from Psalm 110:1 (Psalm 109:1 in the Septuagint) is applied to the exaltation of Jesus to sit at God's right hand:

The Lord says to my lord: "Sit at my right hand until I make your enemies a footstool for your feet."

This verse often reappears in the New Testament as a quotation or allusion, with the wording being influenced by a phrase taken from Psalm 8:6 ("You put everything under their feet"), so that it then reads, ". . . until I put your enemies under your feet."[19] This combination of two quotations from Psalms, which originated before the New Testament writings were composed and is already presupposed in Paul and Mark, reveals that this is a biblical reference that was used in Christianity from a very early date to present the exaltation of Jesus as an act of God. Another hybrid quotation occurs at the beginning of the Gospel of Mark. Here, the appearance of John the Baptist is interpreted by means of a quotation from Malachi 3:1 and Exodus 23:20: "I will send my messenger ahead of you, who will prepare your way." The quotation appears elsewhere in the Gospels of Matthew (11:10) and Luke (7:27), also in reference to John the Baptist, whom God sent ahead of Jesus as a "forerunner." This is another early example of the New Testament appropriating an Old Testament quotation in order to embed the ministry of Jesus within a history of scriptural tradition. The original quotation refers to the return of Elijah, dispatched to earth by God to announce his own coming on the day of judgment. Its reuse in the New Testament presents John the Baptist as the returned Elijah, sent to prepare the way for Jesus.[20]

The overwhelming majority of biblical references in the New Testament are taken from the Torah, the Prophets, and the Writings (Ketuvim)—that is, those collections that later became the "Old Testament," or the Jewish Bible. There are also occasional references to texts that were later designated "apocryphal" or "pseudepigraphic." Take, for example, the direct quotation from the book of Enoch in verses 14–15 of the Letter of Jude. The author of Jude clearly knew the book of Enoch and regarded it as an authoritative text. The First Letter of Peter (3:19) contains the idea of Jesus's proclamation to the imprisoned spirits of the dead, for which the book of Enoch provides an analogy. Finally, the Letter of Barnabas also quotes from the book of Enoch, which is cited as "Scripture" (Barnabas 16:5; see also 4:3). The book of Enoch, whose importance in ancient Judaism is primarily attested by fragments found in Qumran, thus also enjoyed recognition within early Christian circles.

Additionally, there are a handful of references to the book of Sirach: Mark 10:19 refers to Sirach 4:1; 1 Corinthians 9:10 to Sirach 6:19; 2 Timothy 2:19 to Sirach 17:26; and James 1:19 to Sirach 5:11. These are not explicit quotations, however. Rather, common phrases from early Jewish language or themes from the tradition of moral exhortation within Judaism found their way into both the book of Sirach and early Christian writings.

A particular passage from Paul's Letter to the Romans (1:18–32) reveals several points of contact with the Jewish book the Wisdom of Solomon. Here, too, we do not need to presume that Paul knew this writing itself, although the thematic connections are striking. Paul argues that human beings perceived God from his creation of the world and thus had no excuse not to worship him as the creator. By contrast, Wisdom 13:1–9 maintains that people were not able to deduce the existence of the creator from the creation. However, they are only to be mildly rebuked because they can easily be led astray (verse 6). But verses 8 and 9 then go on to state that they are not to be excused, for if they were capable of investigating the world, then they should have recognized its creator.

Finally, in 1 Corinthians 2:9, with the words "as it is written . . . ," Paul introduces a quotation that does not appear in any of the texts that are generally counted among the authoritative scriptures of either Judaism or Christianity:

> . . . as it is written: What no eye has seen and no ear has heard and no person has conceived in their heart, God has prepared for those who love him.[21]

It is possible that this quotation may be based on Isaiah 64:4:

> Since ancient times no one has heard, no ear has perceived, no eye has seen any God besides you, who acts on behalf of those who wait for him.

But Paul does not quote this passage verbatim, using instead a formulation that apparently comes from a Jewish text that has not survived.[22] The closest correspondence is to be found in the *Liber Antiquitatum Biblicarum* 26:13. While this text is thought to have been written at a later date than the letters of Paul, the quotation is undoubtedly quite independent of Paul. Besides, it also appears in a number of Christian texts that are neither part of the New Testament nor directly dependent upon Paul.[23] This example provides further proof that in early Christianity, quotations could be taken from texts that were not later included in the Jewish or Christian Bibles, and that we would be wrong to think that emerging Christianity drew upon a strictly defined stock of authoritative scriptures or even a "canon" of works. Rather, the authorization process itself led to certain texts—particularly the Torah and to some extent also the works of prophecy and other books—being more widely recognized within Judaism, while other texts only attained partial authoritative status within certain strains of Judaism.

Aramaic, Hebrew, and Greek

In what language did early Christians read, quote from, and interpret the Bible? Jesus and his immediate successors are thought to have spoken Aramaic, the vernacular of the region around Galilee in the first century. In the New Testament we find a number of Aramaic expressions, such as the divine appellation *Abba* ("Father"), *Rabbi* or *Rabbouni* ("teacher") as a form of address for Jesus, *Pascha* ("Passover"), *Amen*, *Barjona* ("son of Jonah"), and

Barjesus ("son of Jesus"), along with exhortations such as *Talitha koum!* ("Little girl, arise!") and *Ephphata!* ("Be opened!").[24] The invocation *Maranatha!* ("Come, O Lord!) in 1 Corinthians 16:22 also derives from Aramaic, as do various other expressions like *bar enosh* ("son of man").[25] In contrast, very few Hebrew expressions appear in the New Testament. Sometimes the Aramaic expressions were translated into Greek by the New Testament authors.[26] As for the early writings about Jesus, we may assume that they existed at least in part in Aramaic and were subsequently translated into Greek. These developments took place before the completion of the New Testament scriptures. Greek-speaking Jews who had joined the Christian community in Jerusalem were largely responsible.[27] These individuals played a key role in forming the early Christian faith tradition and in rendering early Christian concepts and traditions into Greek.

There is a good deal of evidence to suggest that biblical texts were read in Hebrew in Galilee and Judea, even though Greek translations already existed. The documents from Qumran indicate that Hebrew continued to be used for biblical and other texts in the early Jewish period. Also, other early Jewish writings such as the books of Sirach and Tobit, the first book of Maccabees, the book of Jubilees, and the Psalms of Solomon were written in either Hebrew or Aramaic. In many instances, however, only very few fragments of the original manuscripts of these works have survived—or nothing at all— and complete versions exist only in Greek. The spread of the Greek language from the second century onward, then, did not supplant the use of Hebrew and Aramaic in Judaism. Even so, the Greek language was widely used by the time the New Testament came into being. Jews in the Diaspora—that is, in regions outside of Galilee and Judea—spoke and wrote Greek, and numerous texts were translated into Greek or written in Greek in the first place. As a result, there are many examples of the influence of Hebrew and Aramaic on Greek terms.[28] This situation also holds true for the use of biblical texts in emerging Christianity.

While the Hebrew and Aramaic texts of the evolving Jewish Bible were successively translated into Greek from the third century BCE on, the texts of the New Testament, in common with many Jewish texts, were written in Greek. It is reasonable to assume, then, that the authors of the New Testament would have used Greek translations when they quoted from the scriptures of Israel or employed them in their own writings. And indeed, most of the time that is the case. And yet some quotations do diverge from their formulation in the Septuagint. It could be that the New Testament authors altered the quotations to make them fit the context in which they were using them. But it is also possible that they were quoting from Greek texts that have not survived. Finally, especially in the case of short quotations, they may have been quoting from memory. Some quotations correspond more closely to the Hebrew than the Greek text, even though they are quoted in Greek. Perhaps the author knew the Hebrew text and tried to match his Greek rendition to that text—presuming, that is, that he could himself speak Hebrew. Such an assumption is plausible in the case of the author of the Gospel of Matthew, but highly unlikely for the authors of the Gospel of Luke or the Letter to the Hebrews.

Some authors of early Christian texts evidently lived and wrote in a milieu that was heavily influenced by Greek language and culture, while others were in locations where people adhered to Jewish traditions and the principal language was either Hebrew or Aramaic. The authors of the older New Testament texts were either themselves Jews or lived in close communication with Jewish communities and were familiar with the Jewish scriptures.

It is only later texts, such as the Second Letter of Peter and the Pastoral Letters (1 and 2 Timothy and Titus), that are written by authors who did not come from a Jewish background and who lived at a greater remove from the Jewish language and Jewish thought. A growing influence of non-Jewish concepts and traditions becomes apparent in other writings of the late first and the second century CE, such as the First and Second Letters of Clement and the Letters of Ignatius and Barnabas. This trend could even give rise to a polemical comparison of the "Old Covenant" and "New Covenant" (as in the Letter of Barnabas), implying a parting of ways between "Jews" and "Christians." This prompts the question of how to square an appeal to the scriptures of Israel with the rise of a community that professed the Christian faith and was no longer part of Judaism. We will return to this question in Chapter 6.

Jesus's View of the Scriptures of Israel

Jesus's ministry formed the historical starting point for the rise of the Christian faith and influenced the form it subsequently took. The Gospels of the

New Testament present this ministry in the light of convictions that formed within Christianity following Jesus's resurrection. The Gospels as a whole bear witness to Jesus's resurrection and exaltation; Matthew and Luke also assert that his birth was effected by the Holy Spirit, and the Gospel of John even speaks of the pre-existence of Jesus and credits him with a divine nature, as expressed in the phrase "and the Word [*Logos*] was God" (John 1:1), that is, of divine essence. The question of the "historical Jesus" has to take this character of the Gospels into account. When considering the meaning of the scriptures of Israel within early Christianity, we must always bear in mind the distinction between the image of Jesus that evolved after his resurrection and the historical basis of Jesus's attitude toward the scriptures and traditions of Israel.

The characteristic features of Jesus's ministry may be gleaned above all from the first three gospels of the New Testament, the Gospels according to Matthew, Mark, and Luke. These works are often called the Synoptic Gospels because, with their very similar structure and subject matter, they can easily be placed alongside one another and their content compared. By contrast, the Gospel of John paints quite a different picture of Jesus. Here, Jesus is the divine "Word" from on high, whom God reveals in the world, and who is one with God (John 10:30: "I and the Father are one"). The Jesus of John's gospel speaks about himself and his ministry in a totally different way than in the Synoptic Gospels. Right up to the events of the Passion, he retains sovereignty over his path and fate. He refers to his provenance from on high, which will eventually lead him back to the Father. His death is thus described as his exaltation and glorification. Even before the events of the Passion, he prepares his disciples for the period after his ministry in long farewell speeches (John 14–16). The Gospel of John often quite explicitly highlights this theological reflection on Jesus's life and work. Thus, a group simply identified as "we" affirms having seen the glory of the Word made flesh (1:14: "The Word became flesh and made his dwelling among us. We have seen his glory"), and within the narration, attention is drawn to the fact that the disciples did not recognize the true meaning of his ministry until after his resurrection (2:22, 12:16).

Some scholars have wondered whether the "apocryphal" gospels, those that were not included in the New Testament, might also contain historical information about Jesus (further discussed in Chapter 6). This discussion has focused in particular on the Gospel of Thomas, which contains a number of sayings and parables of Jesus that are the same as or similar to versions in the New Testament gospels. Other noncanonical texts, such as the Gospel of Peter, the Egerton Papyrus, and the so-called Jewish-Christian Gospels, may contain early traditions relating to Jesus. These texts all come from a later period than the New Testament gospels, however, and already form part of the history of their reception, even though from a literary standpoint they do not necessarily depend directly on them. Moreover, these texts do not contain any additional information on the historical, social, and religious environment of the ministry of Jesus that substantially broadens or changes the picture presented in the New Testament gospels. They reflect the ministry of Jesus in the context of later stages of Christianity, say, from the second half of the second century, and often display only rudimentary knowledge of Jewish traditions and scriptures at the time of Jesus. The apocryphal gospels thus offer insights primarily into the later history of ancient Christianity.

The geographical and temporal setting of the Synoptic Gospels includes the Galilee and the adjacent regions as well as Judea and Jerusalem in the first decades of the first century. At that time, Galilee had a pronounced Jewish character, while Jerusalem was the political and religious center of the whole of Judaism.[29] The Gospels underline the Jewish context of Jesus's upbringing by describing his Jewish family background, his circumcision when he was eight days old (Luke 2:21), and his travels to Jerusalem to celebrate Jewish feast days.[30]

No reliable historical information is available about the childhood and youth of Jesus. The stories of his birth in Matthew and Luke (including the birth in Bethlehem) have a mythical quality, while the episode concerning the twelve-year-old Jesus in the temple at Jerusalem (Luke 2:41–52) is a literary composition by the author of the gospel. These stories, which are designed to demonstrate Jesus's special nature through the extraordinary circumstances of his birth and his exceptional, precocious wisdom as a child, were subsequently taken up by the apocryphal Infancy Gospels and embellished with additional episodes.[31] The only fact that is historically certain is that Jesus grew up as a Galilean Jew. He would most likely have been raised and educated within the family home, as was customary for Jewish children. Aramaic was probably his native language, but he may also have known Hebrew and Greek.

Judea and Galilee in the Time of Jesus

Sidon

ITUREA

Damascus

PHOENICIA

SYRIA

Tyre

Caesarea Philippi

BATANEA

Mediterranean Sea

Gishala

Lake Hula (Merom)

GAULANITIS

Ptolemais

GALILEE

Rafana

Jodapata

Arbela

Capernaum

Sea of Galilee

Sepphoris

Tiberias

Dion

Nazareth

Yarmuk

Gadara

Dor

Scythopolis

DECAPOLIS

Caesarea Maritima

Jordan

Pella

Plain of Sharon

SAMARIA

Sebaste (Samaria)

Gerasa

Shechem

Jabbok

Joppe (Jaffa)

PEREA

Lydda

Bethhoron

Jamnia

Jericho

Philadelphia (Amman)

Ashdod

Jerusalem

Qumran

JUDEA

Bethania

Bethlehem

N

Gaza

Hebron

S

Arnon

IDUMEA

Masada

Dead Sea

NABATEAN KINGDOM

Negev Desert

0 10 20 30 km

☐ Under Roman administration
☐ Tetrarchy of Herod Antipas
☐ Tetrarchy of Herod Philip II
☐ Decapolis

The scriptures of Israel played an important part in the public ministry of Jesus. Alongside the Torah, it is very likely that he was also familiar with the works of the prophets and the Psalms. Time and again, Jesus makes reference to the Jewish scriptures and uses them as the basis for his arguments. Several of the gospels tell of Jesus visiting synagogues and expounding his teachings there.[32] In his gospel, Luke sketches out a programmatic scene portraying the beginning of Jesus's public ministry. In a synagogue in Nazareth, Jesus reads aloud from a scroll containing the book of the prophet Isaiah:

The spirit of the Lord is upon me, for he has anointed me; he has sent me to preach the good news to the poor; to preach liberation to the imprisoned; and to the blind, that they shall see again; to liberate the oppressed; to preach the year of jubilee of the Lord. (Luke 4:17–19)[33]

It is unlikely that this scene took place in the manner described; it is probably a literary invention in which Luke presents certain basic characteristics of the first public phase of Jesus's life. This is corroborated by the fact that this passage combines two quotations from the book of Isaiah (61:1–2 and 58:6). Jesus could not therefore have found "*the place* where it is written" in Isaiah. This quotation from Scripture is intended, rather, to show Jesus's ministry as inspired by the spirit of the Lord and to characterize its substance through the features mentioned in Isaiah. This is why it shows Jesus concluding his reading from the scroll by announcing that the word of this scripture has been fulfilled "today" in the hearing of the audience (Luke 4:21).

This episode clearly shows that in early Christianity, Jesus's ministry was interpreted in the context of the scriptures of Israel. This accords with Jesus's understanding of himself as God's representative and of his ministry as the beginning of God's reign on earth.

Another telling passage is the one in which Jesus responds to emissaries sent by John the Baptist to ask Jesus if he is "the one who is to come":

Go and declare to John what you have seen and heard: the blind see, the lame walk, the lepers are cleansed and the deaf hear, the dead are resurrected, to the poor good news is preached. And blessed is the one who takes no offense at me. (Luke 7:22; Matthew 11:5–6)[34]

Admittedly, this passage does not quote directly from Scripture. However, the listing of what the messengers see and hear makes it seem as though Jesus is fulfilling the prophetic promises of healing and salvation that God will perform at the end of time. Certain passages from the book of Isaiah, in which such promises are formulated, provide the backdrop to this.[35] A similar combination of elements also appears in a fragment found at Qumran:[36]

(12) he will heal the badly wounded, and will make the dead live, he will proclaim good news to the poor,
  (13) and [. . .] . . . [. . .] he will lead the [. . .] . . . and enrich the hungry.
[. . .] and all [. . .]

In this text, which is often given the title "Messianic Apocalypse," God's acts of salvation on the day of judgment are described as prophetic promises. Line 1 of the fragment also refers to "God's anointed one" (or "anointed ones"; it is unclear whether the form is singular or plural). Precisely whom this is meant to denote is unclear. It is rather unlikely that this is a reference to the Anointed One ("Messiah") from the House of David who is prophesied to appear—and with whom Jesus is frequently identified in the New Testament—since in the Jewish tradition, no such acts of the kind described in the fragment are expected of that figure. What is clear, in any event, both in the prophetic texts from the book of Isaiah and in the Qumran fragment, is that these expectations focus on God and his acts of salvation, since the "he" here does not refer to the Anointed One. By contrast, in Jesus's answer to John the Baptist, the ministry of Jesus is described as one that will bring the prophetic promises of salvation to fruition. In other words, God's actions have been "delegated" to Jesus.

The Synoptic Gospels contain many accounts of disputes between Jesus and his adversaries—the Pharisees, Sadducees, and scribes, as well as the Sanhedrin (the supreme Jewish legislative council) in Jerusalem. One prominent issue concerns the question of what is the greatest commandment, which a scribe poses to Jesus. Jesus responds by citing the *Shema Yisrael,* the exhortation to love God, the one Lord, with all one's heart and soul and mind and strength (Deuteronomy 6:4–5), and adds to this the commandment to love one's neighbor as oneself, from Leviticus 19:18 (Mark 12:28–31; see also

Matthew 22:36–39). This double commandment of love in Christianity is a combination of two injunctions; it does not occur directly in Jewish texts but does have analogies there. This episode shows that Jesus and his Jewish opponents, who wanted to provoke him by posing this question, were in agreement that there is only one God of Israel, who is attested in the Scriptures. Luke reinforces this point when he recounts how an "expert in the law" himself responded to Jesus's counter-question, "What is written in the Law?" by quoting the double commandment of love (10:25–27).

In other disputes with the Pharisees and Sadducees, the points at issue are the meaning of the purity laws in Judaism, keeping the Sabbath, divorce, and resurrection. The biblical passages behind these questions generally come from the Torah, whose interpretation is a bone of contention between Jesus and his opponents. Thus, the Sabbath controversies turn upon the question of whether people are permitted to pick some heads of grain from the fields on the Sabbath (Mark 2:23–27), and whether acts of healing may be performed on the Sabbath (Mark 3:1–6, Luke 13:10–17, 14:1–6). The arguments concerning the purity laws include the question of whether a person is defiled by eating without first washing the hands (Mark 7:1–21, paralleling Matthew 15:1–20). In the disputes about divorce and resurrection, the Pharisees or Sadducees challenge Jesus to state his position on a particular quotation from the Torah (Mark 10:2–9, paralleling Matthew 19:3–9, 12:18–27). In the first case, the rigorous proscription of divorce is the point at issue. Jesus upholds this position, though the provision in the Torah that a man can write his wife a certificate of divorce and dismiss her countermands this. In the second instance, the Sadducees, who do not believe in resurrection, try to set a trap for Jesus by applying a *reductio ad absurdum* argument to this question (Luke 20:27–38).

On all of these topics, Jesus acted in the context of contemporary debates within Judaism about how to read and interpret the Torah. A range of positions existed on the question of keeping the Sabbath and matters of divorce and resurrection. Jesus interpreted the Torah both as an expression of God's will and as a practical "handbook" addressing people's basic needs. In the light of this, he countered the Pharisees' reference to the certificate of divorce that Moses had prescribed for dismissing a woman from a marriage (Deuteronomy 24:1–4) by pointing to the order of creation: God created people as men and women, and hence man and woman were of one flesh; therefore, what God had joined, no man should separate. Moses allowed divorce, he explained, only because people were so hard-hearted. In Jesus's understanding of Scripture, the order of creation trumps the order that was subsequently issued by Moses.

Once again, the issue is not whether this dispute between Jesus and the Pharisees ever took place in the manner described. The fact that Jesus's response amalgamates two passages from Scripture—the creation of humans from Genesis 1:27 and the joining of man and woman as "one flesh" from Genesis 2:24—suggests that this passage is a literary conceit. Nevertheless, the episode clearly conveys the idea that Jesus's primary concern in his disputes with Jewish groups was to interpret the will of God as laid down in Scripture in such a way that it benefited humankind and made for a spiritually fulfilled life.

In interpreting the Sabbath commandment, Jesus responded to a rigid interpretation of the law that placed restrictions on the saving of lives on the Sabbath, and in the case of animals completely forbade it, with a more open-minded reading.[37] Given that some less strict Jewish traditions allowed animals to be helped on the Sabbath, then, Jesus said, how much more permissible was it that humans should also be healed (Luke 13:10–17, 14:1–6). Jesus gets right to the heart of the matter when he cures a woman who has been ill for eighteen years; even in such non-emergency cases, curing people is more important than observing the Sabbath rest.

In the episode concerning eating with unwashed hands, Jesus interprets the purity laws from an ethical standpoint: it is not what people ingest that makes them unclean, but rather what emanates from them, namely, evil thoughts, murder, adultery, fornication, and so on (Mark 7, Matthew 15). Mark interprets this teaching as annulling the distinction between clean and unclean (Mark 7:19), whereas for Matthew the ethical dimension of purity is the most important consideration.

The Gospels often polemically distort the standpoints of certain Jewish groups—above all the Pharisees and the Sadducees, along with the "scribes" who form part of the same milieu. It seems reasonable to assume that these groups, too, were concerned to reach an adequate understanding of Scripture and to make it relevant. The Pharisees, in particular, were renowned as skillful interpreters of the Torah, yet it is precisely they who are often deliberately misrepresented, for example, through the accusation that they do not practice what they preach and that their piety is merely for show (Matthew 23:2–7). This portrayal is intended to succinctly characterize them as archetypes of negative behavior.

One final attribute of Jesus's attitude toward the scriptures of Israel is the assured, authoritative way in which he interprets them. This is indicative of his lofty claim to be the person through whose ministry God's Will will be enacted. A prime example of this position can be seen in Jesus's statement that the Son of Man is Lord even of the Sabbath (Mark 2:28). This attitude toward the Torah is also found in condensed form in the "six antitheses" of the Sermon on the Mount. This passage is undoubtedly a creation of the writer of the Gospel of Matthew rather than a sermon that Jesus actually preached. It is based, however, on older traditions and may be viewed as encapsulating Jesus's attitude to the Jewish scriptures, especially the Torah. The section in question is introduced in Matthew 5:17–20 with a general statement of Jesus's attitude to the Law and the Prophets:

> Do not think that I have come in order to abolish the Law and the Prophets; I have come not to abolish but to fulfill.[38]

The formulation "Do not think . . ." is meant to forestall any potential misunderstanding. Jesus's appearance on earth is in accordance with the Scriptures, even when he proceeds to interpret them in unexpected ways. At the same time, this introductory verse makes it clear that what follows should not be construed as anything other than the fulfillment of what is written in the Law and the Prophets.

The Jesus of Matthew's gospel then highlights by example the key features of a form of righteousness that surpasses what the scribes and the Pharisees preach. Each separate element begins with a salutation to those listening to the sermon that refers to the ancients: "You have heard that it was said. . . ."[39] A quotation from scripture follows, which Jesus counters by saying, "But I tell you. . . ." He then proceeds to interpret the biblical passage by intensifying it, correcting it, or fundamentally criticizing it. Jesus thus fulfills the Law and the Prophets by bringing out the true meaning of God's commandments. A consistent application of the injunction "You shall not kill," for example, is meant to rid the world of all anger and affront. Likewise, the injunction against adultery prohibits a man from even casting a lustful look at a woman.

The commandment not to bear false witness is now intensified into an injunction not to swear oaths of any kind. As for the requirement to take an eye for eye and a tooth for tooth, this is now countermanded by an instruction to refrain from exacting revenge and to love one's enemy. The section ends with the injunction, "Be perfect, therefore, as your heavenly Father is perfect" (Matthew 5:48).

The six antitheses of the Sermon on the Mount neatly sum up Jesus's relationship with the Torah in particular and the scriptures of Israel in general. They have often been interpreted as an attempt by Jesus to outdo the Torah and establish his own authority above it. According to this interpretation, Jesus's "Messianic claim" is no longer to be explained from within Judaism, but must be viewed as something new and exceptional, and his belief in the importance of his own person and his public ministry goes beyond Judaism.[40]

More recent interpretations, however, have emphasized that Jesus's ministry is to be understood as operating within Judaism and that his attitude to the scriptures of Israel can be explained within the context of Jewish intellectual discourse at the time. There can be no question that Jesus, through his public ministry, posed a very serious challenge. The terminology used to explain this challenge has, however, changed. Today, talk of Jesus "breaking from," "abandoning," or "outdoing" the Jewish religion is regarded as an inadequate model for describing his position with regard to the scriptures of Israel and the Judaic traditions of his time. Even the opposition of Jesus and Judaism is questionable, for Judaism at that time was extremely diverse, with a multitude of different tendencies and beliefs. The ministry of Jesus must be explained within the parameters of this pluralistic Judaism, taking into account that, like that of other Jewish exegetes and groups, its aim was to highlight the will of God as laid down in the scriptures of Israel. This is apparent in the passage we examined from the Sermon on the Mount in two ways. First, the introduction to the section in question is expressly geared toward "fulfilling" the Law and the Prophets. Second, Jesus's criticism is not leveled at the biblical passages themselves, but at what his listeners have "heard"—in other words, at existing interpretations of the scriptures. And it is to counter those interpretations that he offers a different take on the commandments.

This critical reading of the Sermon on the Mount contends that in appraising the scriptures of Israel, Jesus was taking issue with other Jewish viewpoints on how to interpret the Torah and the Prophets—viewpoints that he clearly regarded as inadequate. He was focused on interpreting those commandments in a way that offered practical guidelines for everyday life and emphasized an ethos of shared humanity.

The Gospels interpret the ministry of Jesus with the help of prophetic biblical passages concerning God's acts of salvation at the end of days, and they also relate his passion to the Jewish scriptures.[41] In this way, they place his ministry and fate under the auspices of God's actions as recorded in the Scriptures. This interpretation of Jesus's path through this earthly life, until he ascends to heaven and sits at God's right hand, is evident throughout the Synoptic Gospels. The scriptures of Israel are also fundamental to the Gospel of John, although it refers back to them in a distinct way. In John, the Scriptures are cited as an attestation of Jesus, which only becomes apparent if one does not construe them in a literal way but rather recognizes Jesus as the one who reveals God's glory in the universe. Thus, Jesus is the one about whom Moses and the Prophets wrote (1:45), to whom the Scriptures bear witness (5:39), and through whose agency the Scriptures will be fulfilled (13:8, 17:12, 19:24, 28, and 36). However, the Scriptures can also be misunderstood if one tries to contrast Jesus's earthly origin with his role as the divine revelator (7:41–42).

It is especially in Matthew's gospel that Jesus's earthly way is presented as the fulfillment of the scriptures of Israel. Matthew repeatedly indicates that certain events had to happen in precisely the way they did in order to fulfill what was written in the Scriptures or was proclaimed by the Prophets (mostly Isaiah). Thus, even the birth of Jesus is placed in the context of a prophetic foretelling of a virgin who will become pregnant and call her son "Emmanuel" (Matthew 1:22–23). In similar fashion, his birth in Bethlehem, the flight to Egypt, Herod's slaughter of the innocents, Jesus's move from Nazareth to Capernaum at the start of his ministry, the appearance of John the Baptist, Jesus's acts of healing, his rejection within Israel, and the events of the Passion are all related to the scriptures of Israel.[42] Some passages even refer quite directly to the fulfillment of righteousness (3:15), the Law and the Prophets (5:17), and the Scriptures (26:56). This conveys a key feature of Jesus's ministry: his conception of himself as the one through whom God's redemption, as prefigured in the scriptures of Israel, will be enacted for the benefit of his people.

Christological Interpretation of Scripture

Christian Communities in Jerusalem and Antioch

The Christian interpretation of the scriptures of Israel takes its starting point from a belief in the divine legitimization of Jesus's ministry. As we discussed in the previous section, this was made clear in the Gospels on the basis of the interpretation of his earthly ministry. Other texts also contain affirmations and characteristic turns of phrase that early Christians used after Jesus's resurrection to voice beliefs that are fundamentally important for the Christian faith as a whole and hence also for its perspective on the meaning of the scriptures of Israel. These beliefs predate the texts of the New Testament and go back to the very earliest days of Christian communities. The communities in Jerusalem and Antioch are especially important in this regard.[43] A Christian community with the circle of twelve disciples formed by Jesus as its nucleus grew up in Jerusalem after the events of the Passion.[44] Peter and later James, the brother of Jesus, commanded special authority. Other Jews joined this community, including those whose native language was Greek and who were familiar with Hellenistic culture. Some of them had most likely come from abroad and settled in Jerusalem. These Greek-speaking Christians of Jewish origin played a key part in the development of early Christian traditions, in terms of both content and language. In the Acts of the Apostles (6:1), Luke refers to such Christians as "Hellenists," as opposed to "Hebrews"— Jewish converts to Christianity whose mother tongue was Aramaic. The Hellenists were instrumental in developing the idea of God acting through Jesus Christ and were also responsible for translating Aramaic texts into Greek.[45]

The missionary activities that emanated from Jerusalem very soon led to the founding of a second important Christian community in Antioch.[46] According to the Acts of the Apostles, the Christian message was proclaimed there not just to Jews but also to Gentiles (Greeks) (Acts 11:19–20). The result was the emergence of a Christian community of former Jews and Gentiles, a blend that was highly significant for its later development. There was a need to clarify what meaning Jewish traditions and rituals had within Christianity, a process that also affected the interpretation of the Jewish scriptures.

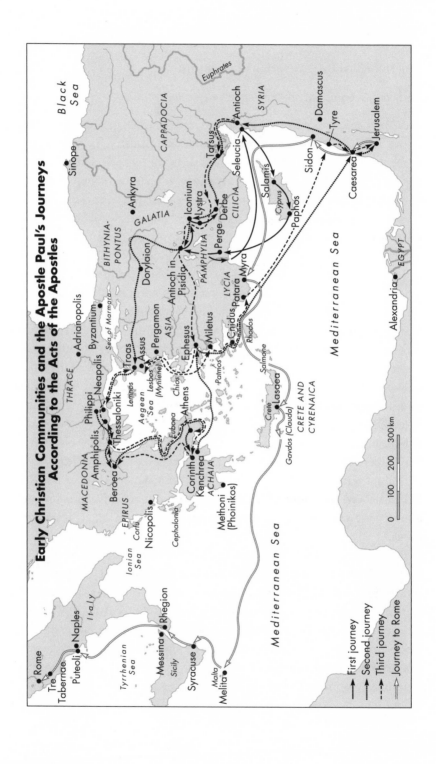

Early Christian Communities and the Apostle Paul's Journeys According to the Acts of the Apostles

Black Sea

Euphrates

Sinope

CAPPADOCIA

SYRIA

Antioch

Damascus

Ankyra

Tarsus

Seleucia

Tyre

Jerusalem

GALATIA

Iconium

CILICIA

Sidon

Caesarea

BITHYNIA-PONTUS

Lystra

Derbe

Salamis

Dorylaion

Perge

Cyprus

Paphos

Antioch in Pisidia

PAMPHYLIA

Byzantium

LYCIA

Adrianopolis

Sea of Marmara

Pergamon

ASIA

Patara

Myra

THRACE

Troas

Assus

Miletus

Cnidus

Rhodos

Philippi

Neapolis

Lemnos

Lesbos (Mytilene)

Ephesus

Amphipolis

MACEDONIA

Thessaloniki

Aegean Sea

Chios

Patmos

Salmone

Beroea

Euboea

EPIRUS

Nicopolis

Athens

Corinth

Kenchrea

ACHAIA

Crete

Lasaea

Corfu

Ionian Sea

Cephalonia

Gavdos (Clauda)

CRETE AND CYRENAICA

Mediterranean Sea

Methoni (Phoinikos)

Mediterranean Sea

Alexandria

EGYPT

Rome

Tre Tabernae

Puteoli

Naples

Italy

Rhegion

Messina

Sicily

Syracuse

Tyrrhenian Sea

Malta Melita

0   100   200   300 km

→ First journey

⋯▶ Second journey

--▶ Third journey

⇨ Journey to Rome

After his conversion, Paul became a member of the community at Antioch.[47] His religious thought evolved there, and he made a significant contribution to the formation of the community's theology. The Antioch community also engaged in missionary work. According to the Acts of the Apostles, Barnabas and Saul (Paul) were sent from Antioch to Cyprus, Barnabas's homeland. From there, they extended their missionary work to several regions in Asia Minor.[48]

The early Christian tradition that developed in Jerusalem and Antioch is mentioned at many points in the letters of Paul, but it left its mark on other New Testament texts as well. It forms an important basis for interpreting the ministry of Jesus Christ, or God's actions through Christ, against the background of the scriptures of Israel.[49]

The Tenets of the Christian Faith and the Scriptures

The starting point of the Christian faith is the affirmation of Jesus's resurrection from the dead:[50]

> If you confess with your mouth, "Jesus is Lord," and believe in your heart that God raised him from the dead, you will be saved. (Romans 10:9)

> You seek Jesus, the Nazarene, the crucified one. He has been resurrected; he is not here. (Mark 16:6; compare Matthew 28:5–6)

The creed of the resurrection is based on the conviction that God has dominion over death and can bring the dead back to life.[51] The beginnings of this belief within the Jewish faith can be found in the books of Daniel (12:1–3) and Enoch (see, for example, 102–103). It was developed further in later Jewish texts, in both the apocalyptic and wisdom traditions.[52] This belief focuses on the idea that righteous people and martyrs do not remain dead, but that God grants them eternal life. Sinners, on the other hand, will be punished on the day of judgment. The belief in God's sovereignty over death is thus based on faith in his universal power of creation, and it is related to the dispensation of justice at the end of time, when God will bring an end to all injustice.

That this conviction lies behind the affirmation of Jesus's resurrection is clearly evident in Paul, for instance, when he describes Abraham's faith in Romans 4:17–18:

> He believed in God, who makes the dead live and calls the nonexistent into existence. He believed, hoping against hope, that he would become the father of many nations.[53]

A few verses later, Paul relates Abraham's faith—which is based on God's promise that he will have a son by his wife Sarah, in spite of his advanced age and the fact that she is barren—to the Christian faith. For the Scriptures do not simply discuss Abraham's faith in order to make it clear that it counts to his credit as a sign of his righteousness, "but also for our sake, to whom it should be credited, who believe in him who resurrected Jesus, our Lord, from the dead" (Romans 4:24).[54]

Thus, faith in Jesus Christ's resurrection from the dead is rooted in the belief expressed in the Scriptures that the God of Abraham, Isaac, and Jacob is a God of the living, not of the dead (Mark 12:26–27). This is underlined by another early declaration of faith:

> I have passed on to you at the beginning what I had received: that Christ died for our sins according to the Scriptures, and that he was buried, and that he was resurrected on the third day according to the Scriptures, and that he appeared to Cephas, and then to the Twelve. (1 Corinthians 15:3–5)[55]

This text is a very early summary of some important tenets of faith: Christ died for our sins, was raised from the dead, and appeared to Cephas ("Peter" in Aramaic) and the entire group of twelve disciples. Paul identifies the disciples here as the principal authorities for Christ's resurrection. This is at odds with the evangelists Mark, Matthew, and John, in whose gospels women are the first to witness the risen Christ.

It is stated twice in 1 Corinthians that Christ's death, resurrection, and appearance to the apostles took place "according to the Scriptures," but there is no reference to any specific passages. It is stressed, instead, that these events taken as a whole are in complete conformity with what the scriptures of

Israel presaged. Similarly, it is stated in Luke 24:44 that everything that was written about Jesus in the Laws, the Prophets, and the Psalms must come to pass. Immediately before this, the risen Christ had already made an announcement to the two disciples he met on the road to Emmaus:

> "Did not the Christ have to suffer and enter into his glory?" And he began with Moses and all the Prophets and interpreted from all the Scriptures for them that which referred to him. (Luke 24:26–27)[56]

Belief in the Resurrection conveys a particular view of God's actions. God is described as the one "who raised Jesus from the dead."[57] This attribute of God is analogous with descriptions of God in the scriptures of Israel, such as that he is the one "who made heaven and earth" (Psalm 146:6), and the one "who brought you [Israel] out of Egypt" (Leviticus 19:36). Jewish texts also characterize God as "he who revives the dead."[58] To these characteristics, the Christian religion adds another, decisive one—that God gave evidence of the power of his actions through Jesus by raising him from the dead. The resurrection of the dead that will take place at the Last Judgment has already begun, and it is guaranteed that those who follow Jesus Christ will one day themselves be resurrected.[59]

In the Pentecostal sermon of Peter in the second chapter of the Acts of the Apostles, Christ's resurrection is explained through an interpretation of Psalm 15:8–11 from the Septuagint (Psalm 16 in the Hebrew text):[60]

> I saw the Lord before me always; because he is at my right hand, I will not waver. Therefore, my heart was joyful and my tongue exulted, also my flesh will dwell in hope. For you will not give my soul over to Hades, nor will you allow your holy one to see decay. You have made known to me the ways of life; you will fill me with joy before your face.

Peter subsequently explains that David, the author of the Psalms, cannot be talking about himself, since, as was well known, he died, and his grave is still "here in our midst" (that is, in Jerusalem). Rather, as a prophet, David was referring to a descendant of his who would one day sit on his throne. Looking ahead, David therefore spoke of the resurrection of the Anointed One (Christ). It was this person, namely Jesus, whom God had raised from the dead and exalted to sit at his right hand. In addition, Peter cites Psalm 109:1 from the Septuagint (Acts 2:35–36), a passage that was frequently looked to as scriptural evidence for the exaltation of Jesus Christ.

The declaration of faith from 1 Corinthians 15:3–5 also places the death of Christ in the context of the scriptures of Israel. The New Testament frequently states that Christ died for the sins of humankind, and in so doing paved the way for a new relationship between God and humans.[61] This conviction casts the scriptures of Israel in a new light. An important statement on this score may be found in Paul's letters:

> God designated Jesus Christ as the place of grace through faith in his blood, as the manifestation of his righteousness, for the release from previously committed sins. (Romans 3:25)[62]

The expression "place of grace" (*hilastêrion* in Greek) appears in the Septuagint at a prominent place in Leviticus 16 (see also Hebrews 9:5). There, it denotes the lid of the Ark of the Covenant, on which the high priest would customarily sprinkle the blood of a sacrificed animal on Yom Kippur, the Day of Atonement. He did this in order to cleanse the Holy of Holies, which had been defiled by the sins of the people. The lid of the ark was the place where God showed his grace to Israel through the medium of the high priest. In Romans 3:25, Paul is presumably using an existing tradition in stating that God designated Jesus Christ as this "place of grace." The phrase "in his blood" demonstrates unequivocally that henceforth the cleansing of sins will be effected through the death of Jesus Christ. And the formulation "through faith" shows that it is belief in Jesus Christ that will bring about this purification. Christ's crucifixion by the Romans in Jerusalem is interpreted in a highly creative and theologically thoughtful way: it is seen as an act through which God himself has intervened for the benefit of humans and absolved them of their sins.

The Letter to the Hebrews picks up this interpretation of the death of Jesus and elaborates upon it.[63] This is the only New Testament text to use the term "high priest" for Jesus and thus lays the foundation for an interpretation of his death as an event through which sin is removed from the world "once and for all" (9:26). The letter also gives a detailed account of proceedings on the Day of Atonement and relates the high priest of Israel to Jesus, although Jesus is a priest of a very different kind. In an ingenious interpretation of Genesis

14:17–20, the author of Hebrews explains that Jesus did not descend from the tribe of Levi like the high priests of Israel, but from the priest Melchizedek. Because Melchizedek had no genealogy and was "without beginning of days or end of life," he resembled the Son of God and remained a priest forever (Hebrews 7:1–3).

Jesus is thus described as a priest "in the order of Melchizedek" (Hebrews 5:6, 7:7, including a quotation from Psalm 109:4 in the Septuagint version). As such, he is the "high priest of a new covenant," as Hebrews 8 explains by quoting a passage concerning the promise of a new covenant from Jeremiah (38:31–34 in the Septuagint version; 31:31–34 in the Hebrew Bible). The essence of this new covenant is that the high priest no longer enters the earthly Holy of Holies every year on the Day of Atonement in order to offer up sacrifices for his own and the people's sins, but that the heavenly sanctuary itself is purified by Christ's self-sacrifice. The Letter to the Hebrews uses the model of a "true" heavenly tabernacle and its earthly counterpart. Through the cleansing of the heavenly sanctuary, the sins of humankind are removed for all time, meaning that there will be no need for any annual sacrifices in future.

Another interpretation of the death of Jesus relates to Isaiah 53, which is written from the perspective of a group loosely identified as "we."[64] It recounts how an innocent and defenseless servant of God carried the burden of "our" sin and that "we" were healed through his wounds. Evidently, the people of Israel are speaking here about God's Chosen One, who, for their salvation, bears the burden of their sins. The wording of the Septuagint is significantly different from the Hebrew text, especially concerning the significance of the servant's fate.[65] Verses 8 to 10 of the Hebrew text read as follows:

> From affliction and judgment, he was picked out. But his fate—who is concerned about it? For he is cut off from the land of the living; because of the transgression of my people he was stricken. And he was given a grave with the godless and the rich when he died, even though he had not committed any violence, and there was no deception in his mouth. But the Lord desired to strike him with disease.[66]

In the Septuagint the same passage reads:

> In his humiliation his judgment was taken away. Who will describe his generation? Because his life is being taken from the earth, he was led to

death on account of the acts of lawlessness of my people. And I will give
the wicked for his burial and the rich for his death, because he committed no lawlessness, nor was deceit found in his mouth. And the
Lord desires to cleanse him from his blow.[67]

The Septuagint focuses not on presenting and explaining the servant's fate,
but instead on his salvation through purification and his removal from the
earth.

This text's presentation of an innocent servant suffering in lieu of others
and his preservation by God made it an obvious choice when interpreting
the suffering and death of Jesus.[68] This link may be made in a concise, formulaic manner, as in Paul's letters. For example, when considering the fate
of Christ in Romans 4:25, Paul harks back to Isaiah 53:12:

He was given for our transgressions and raised for our justification.[69]

Alternatively, a direct analogy may be drawn between the innocent suffering
of the servant and that of Jesus, as in Acts 8:32–33. This passage cites Isaiah
53:7–8 in the Septuagint version, which stresses the helpless suffering of the
servant, who in his humiliation was deprived of justice; he was "led like a
sheep to the slaughter, and as a lamb before its shearer is silent, so he did not
open his mouth."

Isaiah 53 is quoted extensively in the First Letter of Peter. Peter 2:21–24
refers to several passages from Isaiah about the servant of God who committed no sin and uttered no deceitful words (1 Peter 2:22; Isaiah 53:9), who
bore our sins (1 Peter 2:24; Isaiah 53:4), and by whose wounds we were healed
(1 Peter 2:24; Isaiah 53:5).

From these examples, we can see that early Christianity drew extensively
upon the scriptures of Israel to interpret the suffering and death of Jesus
Christ. The presentation of this event as a ritual, sacrificial act and as an instance of suffering and death in place of others both find their antecedents
in Old Testament scripture. By relating them to Jesus's death through crucifixion they gain a new meaning, in becoming revelatory of the fate of Christ.

Another key element of early Christian statements about Jesus Christ is
the claim that he has an exclusive relationship with God, that he manifests
God's providence in the world, and that he imparts God's salvation to hu-

manity. By extension, it is said that he was with God even before the creation of the world and that God created the world through him (John 1:3; Colossians 1:16–17; Hebrews 1:2).[70] This unique closeness of God and Jesus Christ coalesced into professions of faith that name God and Jesus Christ in the same breath:

> For us there is one God, the father, from whom everything is, and for whom we exist, and one Lord Jesus Christ, through whom everything is, and we through him. (1 Corinthians 8:6)[71]

In this declaration, which is one of the earliest Christian credos and is cited by Paul, a profession of faith in the one God who is common to both Christianity and Judaism is combined with a profession of faith in the one Lord Jesus Christ. In the process, Paul expands upon Deuteronomy 6:4, which talks of the God of Israel as the only Lord. The prepositions that Paul uses make it clear that God and Jesus Christ are still distinct from each other: God is the creator *from* whom all things came (God's characterization here as "the father" is also connected with his power of creation), whereas Jesus Christ is the one *through* whom God acts. And both are related to "us," an objective pronoun doubtless intended to denote believers in Jesus Christ. God and Jesus Christ are distinguished from one another yet closely interlinked. God's work of salvation is performed through Jesus Christ, and only through believing in Jesus can a person attain God's redemption.

This credo gives Jesus Christ the same position which in Jewish texts is taken by wisdom, the Torah, or the Word. In Proverbs 8:22–31, wisdom is designated as a pre-existing entity, which was already with God before all the other works of creation and stood constantly at God's side (or as an adjunct to him) when he made heaven and earth. In Sirach 24:3–9, wisdom is described as the first work of creation, which seeks a place on earth and eventually finds it in Israel. Wisdom is equated with the Torah, which God gave to Israel. Finally, in the book of Wisdom—the most recent text of the Wisdom literature, which was written in Greek at the beginning of the first century CE—wisdom is likewise granted a special role within creation (9:9). It is described as the "brightness that shines forth from eternal light" and the "perfect image" of God's goodness (7:26). The terms "brightness" or "radiance" and "image" are used in relation to Jesus Christ in the New Testament to characterize his relationship to God (Hebrews 1:3; 2 Corinthians 4:4, Colossians 1:15). The term "Logos" (Word) can also be used this way. Philo of Alexandria calls the Logos the "image of God" (*On the Special Laws* 1.81), and talks about the conceptual world, made before the creation of the sensorily perceptible world, as the "Word of God" (*On the Creation of the Cosmos* 25). The term "Logos" is also used at the beginning of John's gospel to describe the entity through which God created the world. In John, the Word is identified with the person of Jesus Christ. In the person of Christ, the divine Word became a human being, in whom God's glory may be apprehended (John 1:14: "The Word became flesh and made his dwelling among us. We have seen his glory").

The beginnings of the Christian faith are thus marked by certain basic beliefs about how God operates through the agency of Jesus Christ. In the New Testament, these beliefs come into play to varying degrees. For example, the pre-existence of Jesus Christ—that is, his state of being with God before the creation of the world—is a concept that appears explicitly in a handful of texts, is implicit in some, and in yet others may not even exist in the background. The same can be said of the idea of the exaltation of Jesus to sit at the right hand of God or the interpretation of his death. Different declarations can be found in the New Testament on these topics as well, indicating that the authors called upon different traditions when setting out their ideas of the life and work of Jesus Christ and portraying his relationship with God. All the same, it is clear that even at the earliest stage in the history of Christianity there was firm conviction of Jesus Christ's unique significance as an instrument of God's salvation. This belief developed on the basis of the scriptures of Israel and at the same time signified a new attitude toward those texts.

Assimilation of the Scriptures of Israel

In the Christian community that evolved in Antioch, a strong conviction arose that membership in the Christian communion overrode the distinction between Jews and Gentiles (see, for example, Galatians 3:28, 1 Corinthians 7:19). This community was the source of important missionary initiatives, including those of Paul, who set off from Antioch on journeys to Asia Minor and Greece.[72] On these missions, he founded communities in the Greek cities of Philippi, Thessaloniki, and Corinth, as well as in Galatia (a region in north-central Anatolia). He later addressed letters to members of these congregations. His Letter to the Romans occupies a special position, for in this case Paul was not writing to a community that he had established, but was instead introducing himself to the Christian community in Rome, which he intended to visit later. The Letter to the Romans is also something of a special case because it is the last letter Paul wrote. He never managed to realize his plan of visiting the Roman Christians and traveling from there to Spain (Romans 15:24, 28). He was arrested in Jerusalem, transferred to Caesarea, and finally taken in captivity to Rome (Acts 21–28). There, at the beginning of the 60s CE, he was put to death. The Letter to the Romans can therefore be read retrospectively as Paul's last will and testament, though Paul himself certainly did not intend it as such.[73] In it, he looks back on his missionary activity in the eastern Roman Empire and reflects on what the Gospel means for the individual believer, for the community of the faithful, and for the inhabitants of Israel who did not follow Christ ("For I am not ashamed of the gospel, because it is the power of God that brings salvation to everyone who believes: first to the Jew, then to the Gentile" [Romans 1:16]).

In his letters, Paul directs his message for the most part toward non-Jewish believers in Christ. He often addresses them directly as "Gentiles" (in the sense of "non-Jews") and admonishes them to live their lives in accordance with faith in God and Jesus Christ. There was no doubt for Paul that Gentiles who embraced a belief in Jesus Christ must also believe in the God of Israel. The credo from 1 Corinthians 8:6, where the one God and the one Lord, Jesus Christ, are mentioned in the same breath, makes this abundantly clear. Alongside this passage we might also cite 1 Thessalonians 1:9–10, in which Paul praises the Thessalonians for having "turned to God from idols to serve the living and true God, and to wait for his Son from heaven, whom he raised from the dead—Jesus, who rescues us from the coming wrath." The fact that Paul is addressing his words to Gentiles is also reflected in his frequent reminders to his readers to abstain from "fornication" and "idolatry." Jews would not have needed to be reminded to shun such things. Later letters, such as the Letter to the Ephesians and 1 Peter, are also aimed at non-Jewish addressees. In them, interpretations of the scriptures of Israel are always offered in the conviction that the gospel of Jesus Christ is to be preached not only to Jews but also to Gentiles.

An instructive example of this is a quotation that, according to the account in Acts of the Apostles, was cited by Jesus's brother James at the Apostolic Council held in Jerusalem in around 50 CE. At this meeting, representatives of the communities in Jerusalem and Antioch wrestled with the question of whether Gentiles who had converted to Christianity should also be required to integrate into Judaism by being circumcised. According to Paul and Luke, who reported on this event in Galatians 2 and Acts 15, respectively, this proposition was rejected. Luke, however, relates that the council reached an accord whereby Gentiles were obliged to follow the rules outlined in Leviticus 17 and 18, which applied to foreigners living in Israel. These rules required them to "abstain from food polluted by idols, from sexual immorality, from the meat of strangled animals and from blood" (Acts 15:20; compare Acts 21:25). James emphasizes that these rules also applied to Gentiles by quoting the "words of the prophets":

> . . . as it is written, "Afterward I will turn back and again build David's decayed hut and rebuild its ruins so that the remnants of the people and all Gentiles over whom my name is called will seek [it], declares the Lord, who does this, which was known from eternity." (Acts 15:16–18)[74]

Most of this quotation comes from Amos 9:11–12 (though the beginning has some similarities to Jeremiah 12:15 and the end to Isaiah 45:21).[75] The quotation is taken from the version of Amos in the Septuagint, however, not from the Hebrew text of Amos. This is of particular importance, since the second part of the Septuagint version quoted in Acts is quite different from the second part of the Hebrew text of Amos:

> . . . so that they may take possession of what is left of Edom and all the nations over whom my name was called out. Declaration of YHWH, who does this. (Amos 9:12)[76]

Whereas the Hebrew text speaks of the capture of Edom and Israel's dominion over the Gentiles, in the Septuagint the rebuilding of David's fallen tent (or shelter) is begun with the intention that all peoples should seek it out, in other words that they should turn to the God of Israel. Only in this version does the Amos quotation make any sense when uttered by James. Thus, in Acts, Luke has James cite the Septuagint version at the council in order to corroborate his view that the Gentiles should embrace both Christianity and the God of Israel.

Further significant references to the scriptures of Israel occur in other speeches in the Acts of the Apostles. For instance, the Pentecostal speech of Peter in Acts 2 includes a quotation from Joel 3:1–5 proclaiming the outpouring of the Spirit of the Lord during the events of Pentecost in Jerusalem. And the speech delivered by Stephen in Acts 7 provides an overview of key moments in the history of Israel: God's calling of Abraham, Joseph's sojourn in Egypt and the arrival of his brothers and his father Jacob, God revealing himself to Moses and the Exodus of the Israelites from Egypt, Israel's rejection of Moses as a prophet and the making of the golden calf as an idol, the transporting of the "tent of the congregation" (the tabernacle) from the desert to the Promised Land, David's pitching of the tent to house the Ark of the Covenant, and finally the building of the First Temple by Solomon. Stephen presents the temple construction as a presumptuous act, because "the Most High does not live in houses made by human hands" (Acts 7:48). His address ends with a denunciation of his audience—the high priest and the Supreme Council of Jerusalem (the Sanhedrin). He accuses them of resisting the Holy Spirit, of acting just as their ancestors had done by persecuting and killing prophets who proclaim the coming of the Righteous One (Jesus), and of disobeying the Law of God.

This speech, which Luke probably reworked from an older text, summarizes the history of Israel from a critical perspective. It emphasizes that the most important parts of this history took place outside the land of Israel; that the Israelites spurned and killed all the prophets that God sent to them, beginning with Moses; that they turned away from God and began worshipping idols; and that they ultimately believed they should venerate God in a temple built of stone. The address amounts to a stinging criticism of the authorities in Jerusalem from within Judaism, contending that the history of Israel is tied neither to the country nor to the temple. Rather, God is lord over all the world and so can be worshipped anywhere.

Another remarkable appropriation of the history of Israel from a Christian standpoint can be seen in the letters of Paul. In 1 Corinthians 10:1–13, he explains that the Israelites, while crossing the Red Sea during the parting of the waters, had been "baptized into Moses in the cloud and in the sea"

(1 Corinthians 10:2), and that in the desert they had consumed "spiritual food" and "spiritual drink" (verses 3 and 4; a reference to manna from heaven and water from the rock). And yet despite this, says Paul, some of them had become idolaters, committed sexual immoralities, and been "scattered in the wilderness" by God. This should serve as a warning to the Christian community to treat God's gifts with due reverence. (The gifts Paul is alluding to are the "spiritual food" and "spiritual drink" of the Christian communal meal.) In this way, the occurrences in the Sinai Desert became "exemplars" (*typoi*) and the events surrounding them "exemplary" (*typikôs*) because they foreshadowed the experiences of the Christian community (1 Corinthians 10:6–11).

Paul's intention in this text is to warn the community in Corinth not to take part in other (pagan) cultic meals alongside the Lord's Supper. In verse 21, he contrasts the "Lord's table" with the "table of demons." What is remarkable here is that Paul is reclaiming the history of Israel for the Christian community in Corinth, which to a large extent consisted of non-Jews. They too, according to Paul, were involved in the history of Israel, with its "spiritual food" and "spiritual drink," and should understand the meal of the Christian communion in this context.

One important dimension in the way the scriptures of Israel were interpreted concerns the relationship between the Christian faithful and Israel. The first text to consider here is the third chapter of Paul's Second Letter to the Corinthians. In it, Paul contrasts Moses's ministry of the "old covenant" with his own ministry of the "new covenant." The ministry of the old covenant possessed its own glory, but not like that of the new covenant, which is a ministry of the spirit rather than the letter. In extending this comparison, Paul recalls an episode from Exodus 34, which narrates how Moses's face became so radiant when he spoke with God on Mount Sinai that the Israelites were afraid to look at him when he descended the mountain carrying the tablets of the Law. After Moses had spoken with his people he placed a veil over his face, which he only removed again when he entered the tent of the congregation (tabernacle) and was once more in the presence of the Lord.

This episode has been the subject of many interpretations within Judaism, for example in the works of Philo of Alexandria and the Pseudo-Philo, and subsequently in the rabbinical tradition. Paul's interpretation is that, in covering his face with a veil, Moses prevented the Israelites from witnessing the end of the old covenant of the letter. Instead, their minds were made dull and obstinate, and to this day, Paul claims, the same veil remains when the old covenant is read out. Only when Israel turns to the Lord, that is to Christ, will the veil be lifted.

Paul draws a stark contrast between the old and the new covenants, portraying the old covenant as a ministry of the letter, which "kills," while the new covenant is one of "the Spirit that gives life." Correspondingly, the old covenant is "transitory," whereas the new one is everlasting. This antithesis sounds like a blueprint for Christian anti-Judaism, although of course that was not Paul's intention. Two matters should be borne in mind here. First, Paul found himself in a polemical conflict with competing missionaries, who evidently challenged his right to preach as an apostle of Christ in Corinth, and who boasted of their Jewish heritage (see 2 Corinthians 11:22). Second, Paul was himself a Jew and developed his Christian faith based on the scriptures of Israel. In such a situation it was only natural that he should seek to distinguish himself from rival missionaries, who contested Paul's conviction that faith in Jesus Christ erased the boundaries between Jews and Gentiles and that it was therefore not necessary to integrate Gentiles into Judaism before they became Christians. Paul linked Christianity with the Scriptures in a different way than either his rivals or the author of the Gospel of Matthew. Nevertheless, Paul's belief in Christ developed from a belief in the God of Israel, and the experience of seeing a considerable number of Jewish people close their minds to the Christian gospel grieved him. This is clear in two passages from the Letter to the Romans.

In the fourth chapter of the Letter to the Romans, Paul addresses the question of Abraham's faith. He chooses this issue because the connection between faith and righteousness is of central importance to him. The Torah contains a sentence precisely relating to this issue: "Abraham believed in the Lord, and he credited it to him as righteousness" (Genesis 15:6). Paul had already discussed this sentence and the connection between Abraham's faith and Christianity in the Letter to the Galatians (Galatians 3:6–39). In the Letter to the Romans he devotes the whole of the fourth chapter to interpreting this sentence, which, he argues, depicts Abraham as the father of all believers, circumcised and uncircumcised alike. Paul makes use of the fact that Genesis mentions Abraham's faith, which God counted as evidence of his righteousness (Genesis 15), before referring to circumcision (Genesis 17).

Therefore, for Paul, Abraham's faith is a "faith of uncircumcision" because it was neither justified by "works" nor premised upon his being circumcised. And so, Paul maintains, the faith of Abraham can serve as a model for the Christian faith, which is also "credited as righteousness" without having to justify itself through works. This faith binds Jewish and non-Jewish people together into a community of those who believe in God as the one "who raised Jesus our Lord from the dead" (Romans 4:24). Therefore, the faith that is presented in Scripture as being "credited as righteousness" without "works" brings into the story of God and Abraham those people who are not part of the nation of Israel but who nevertheless belong to the wider community of the faithful.

The question raised by this analysis, which troubled Paul greatly, was what would become of those people of Israel who closed their minds to the Christian faith. In Romans 9–11, he undertakes an intensive critique of the scriptures of Israel in an attempt to demonstrate that the only way of attaining salvation is to believe in Christ. In this respect, there is no difference between Jews and Gentiles (Romans 10:12; compare 3:22). And yet at the same time, God appointed the Jews as his chosen people, a status that remains unchanged; so even those Jews who do not believe in Christ will also be saved. In order to reconcile these two contradictory beliefs, Paul explains that Scripture itself testifies to a split within Israel and to the salvation of only a "remnant." God is thus free, Paul claims, to choose to spare a portion of Israel while preventing the other portion from gaining any insight into the salvation that is guaranteed through Christ—in other words, to make them "obstinate." Admittedly, at this point, Paul has still not provided an answer to the question of how the obstinate portion will be saved. He begins by using the analogy of the olive tree, whose branches can be reinserted into the tree after they have been broken off (Romans 11:17–24). In the same way, the portion of Israel that refuses to believe in Christ can be reintegrated into God's story of redemption. Paul cannot explain, however, why this part of Israel was rendered "obstinate" by God or how they will ultimately be saved. Indeed, he states that this is a "mystery" (*mystêrion*, 11:25) concealed within God's plan. Some Jews were made obstinate, Paul claims, in order that the Gentiles could be included. This obstinacy (rendered in some translations as "hardening" or "blindness") is a strictly time-limited phenomenon, which will last only "until the full number of the Gentiles has come in"—that is, have been attracted to the Christian faith. At that point, "all Israel will be saved" (11:25–26). Paul is expressing his certainty that the division of Israel into one portion that believes in Christ (to which he and other Jews who follow the Christian faith belong) and another that does not will be healed.

This healing will be brought about by God himself, as Paul demonstrates with a quotation combining passages from Isaiah 59:20–21 and 27:9:

> The savior will come from Zion; he will remove godlessness from Jacob, and this is my covenant with them, when I remove their sins. (Romans 11:26–27)[77]

The "savior from Zion" is God, whose acts of redemption are frequently described in the scriptures of Israel as emanating "from Zion."[78] God's agency will end the current division in Israel, creating the conditions for the salvation of all Israel. Paul develops this belief through an intensive analysis of the scriptures of Israel. Time and again in Romans 9–11 he cites passages of Old Testament scripture—from the Torah, the Prophets, and the Psalms— in order to make it clear that the history of Israel, which progresses from division, to restoration of unity, and finally to salvation, is actually mapped out. These texts, according to Paul, are valid for both portions of Israel and, as he argued in Romans 4, also for those believers who are not Israelites.

In the New Testament texts under discussion here, the scriptures of Israel are related in a number of different ways to God's actions through Jesus Christ and the history of Christian communities. Quotations that speak of God as the "Lord" can even be applied to Jesus Christ as the "Lord." For instance, in 2 Corinthians 3, Paul relates Exodus 34:34 ("Whenever he [Moses] entered the Lord's presence to speak with him, he removed the veil") to converting to Christianity. When Paul alludes to this passage by saying, "Whenever he [Moses] turns to the Lord, the veil is taken away," he is using "Moses" as a metonym for the part of Israel that does not yet believe in Christ. For Paul, unlike in Exodus, the term "Lord" denotes Jesus Christ.

In Romans 10:13, Paul describes a quotation from Joel 2:32 (in the Hebrew Bible, Joel 3:5)—"Everyone who calls on the name of the Lord will be saved"— as invoking the name of Jesus Christ.[79] In Joel, of course, it denoted an appeal to God. Likewise, in 1 Corinthians 1:31 and 2 Corinthians 10:17, in reference to Jesus Christ, Paul uses a turn of phrase ("Let the one who boasts boast in the Lord") that recalls Jeremiah 9:23. And in 1 Corinthians 10:26, Paul quotes Psalm 23:1 from the Septuagint: "The earth is the Lord's, and everything in it." Once again, it is clear from the context that the "Lord" to whom Paul refers is Jesus Christ. Finally, at the end of a paean of praise to Christ (the Philippian hymn) in Paul's Letter to the Philippians 2:6–11, we find the statement:

> . . . at the name of Jesus every knee should bow, in heaven and on earth and under the earth, and every tongue acknowledge that Jesus Christ is Lord, to the glory of God the Father.

This wording derives from Isaiah 45:23 in the Septuagint version: "Before me every knee will bow; by me every tongue will swear." The Philippian hymn relates God's words in Isaiah to the exalted Lord Jesus Christ, to whom God has given a name above all other names.

All these passages show that early Christians assimilated the scriptures of Israel in the belief that speaking of God in such a way accentuated not only God's salvation of Jesus Christ, but also his salvation of humankind through Christ.

From today's perspective, we might question whether this use of the scriptures of Israel did them full justice or whether it was an act of "Christian appropriation." After all, the original texts made no mention at all of Jesus, nor can they truly be characterized as prefiguring his coming. But to raise such an objection would be to misjudge the way in which both Judaism and Christianity interpreted these texts. In the history of Israel and Judaism, these scriptures had attained the status of binding testimonies to God's agency in the world. They were not merely "historical" reports informing people about the past history of Israel, but rather the living Word of God imparting moral precepts for the present day and foretelling the future. The key question was how to make these texts relevant at any given time. In this respect, there is no difference between the Jewish and Christian reception of these scriptures. In the texts from Qumran and the works of Philo we see that Jewish groups and individual exegetes crafted interpretations for their own societies. The Christian interpretation of these texts had its beginnings in Judaism. Central to a Christian reading was the conviction that God's grace is conveyed through the ministry of Jesus Christ and that faith in Christ leads to salvation. This is the key difference between the Jewish and Christian perspectives on these scriptures.

The Jewish and Christian interpretations of the scriptures of Israel constitute two distinct routes by which those texts were made to yield content that corroborated each faith's view of the actions of the God of Israel. These routes continued in the scriptural exegeses undertaken by the authors of the New Testament, and they have frequently overlapped and influenced one another. It is through this process that the scriptures of Israel came to form the "Old Testament" for Christianity, while they became the Jewish Bible for Judaism.

6

The Formation of the Christian Bible

Jews and Christians—A Parting of the Ways?

Along with the fundamental scriptures of Judaism, a number of other texts
came into being that also achieved authoritative status within early Christianity. These texts reflect certain important developments. The preservation
and handing down of stories and writings concerning the life of Jesus led to
the creation of the Gospels. Christianity spread throughout Asia Minor and
Greece thanks to the missionary work of Paul and other itinerant preachers.
In connection with Jewish synagogue congregations, Christian communities began to emerge in the various provinces of the Roman Empire, as
distinct offshoots of either Jewish or Gentile society. These communities developed their own structures of organization and governance, forms of worship, rituals, and creeds.[1] Not least, a Christian ethic also evolved.

The formation of the "New Testament," which took its place alongside the
scriptures of Israel (now distinguished as the "Old Testament") as a collection of the authoritative texts of Christianity, must be considered in light of
these developments. The New Testament is made up of those scriptures that,
following a long process of differentiation and demarcation, became firmly
established as authoritative for all Christians, irrespective of any doctrinal
differences between denominations. They also served as a way of separating
"orthodox" from "heretical" beliefs—a practice that did not, however, remain
uncontested.

During this process, the canonical texts of Judaism took on a new role as
foretelling the life of Jesus or of God's actions through him. The emergence
of the Christian Bible can only be understood in the context of these two developments: the appropriation and re-interpretation of the scriptures of Israel, and the emergence of Christianity's own traditions and texts.

The texts of the New Testament were neither integrated into the—as yet incomplete—third canonical section of the evolving Jewish Bible (the Ketuvim, or Writings) nor appended to the Jewish Bible as a fourth element of the canon. Instead, a bipartite canon came into existence, the two parts of which carry equal weight and stand side by side, yet are also in tension with each other. This canon is regarded as a single entity: *one* Holy Scripture comprising *two* testaments. From the late second century on, these were referred to as the "Old Testament" and the "New Testament." One of the central endeavors of Christian theology ever since its inception has been to define the relationship between these two testaments. The beginnings of this endeavor lie in antiquity, where it prompted sometimes heated and polemical arguments.

Several factors explain the emergence of a two-part Christian Bible. First, the writing of the New Testament texts in Greek may well have created a certain distance from the Hebrew or Aramaic Jewish texts. Furthermore, not only the "Law and the Prophets" but also the Ketuvim, which was in the process of completion, already comprised their own discrete collections. The situation was not conducive to the expansion of existing collections through the addition of scriptures of a totally different nature. But above all, it was the wholly original view of God and his actions through Jesus Christ that led Christians to create a scriptural collection of their own.[2] This development occurred concurrently with the formation of a separate community, which made free use of the texts and traditions of Judaism while interpreting them from its own standpoint. This naturally presented Judaism with a major challenge.

These developments took place during a period that was already extremely tense due to long-running political conflicts and military clashes. Especially momentous events took place over the course of the Jewish–Roman War of 66–74 CE. This conflict, which ended with the capture of the Jewish fortress of Masada near the Dead Sea in 74, also brought about the destruction of Jerusalem and the Second Temple in the year 70.[3] In 115–117 a major uprising broke out within the Jewish diaspora in North Africa (Egypt and Cyrenaica). This revolt also spread to Cyprus and Mesopotamia and was eventually crushed by the Romans with much bloodshed. The war of 132–135, which was sparked by the Bar Kochba rebellion, ended with the widespread destruction of villages and towns throughout Palestine and the transformation of

Jerusalem into a Roman settlement called Colonia Aelia Capitolina.[4] These defeats seriously weakened the organizational structure and the culture of Judaism in both Palestine and the Diaspora. A phase of reconstruction within Judaism ensued in the second and third centuries, precisely the same period when the conflict with emergent Christianity began to loom larger. The main focus of Rabbinic Judaism, which evolved in parallel with Christianity and centered on a number of locations in Galilee, was to provide interpretations of the Torah (Laws).[5] These exegeses were assembled in various different works—the Mishnah, the Midrashim, and the Jerusalem (or Palestinian) Talmud. This same period also witnessed sometimes heated disputes between Christians and Jews over the legitimacy of Christianity's invocation of the scriptures of Israel.[6]

The Emergence of Distinct Christian Communities

Jesus's ministry provided an important impetus to the growth of Christian communities. Jesus believed he had been tasked by God with establishing his dominion on earth. As God's representative, he saw himself as acting in his name among the people of Israel. His ministry involved healing the sick, forgiving sin, proclaiming the coming kingdom of God, and encouraging people to become his followers and to build communities dedicated to living according to God's will. Jesus's claim to autonomous, divine authority, evident in his self-assured interpretation of the scriptures of Israel, prompted early Christians to regard the life and work of Jesus as being on a par with the scriptures of Israel themselves, and even to take his ministry as the yardstick for interpreting them. Closely linked with this was the conviction of Jesus's followers that their community formed the nucleus of a resurgent Israel. Anyone who believed in Jesus Christ also proclaimed the One God of Israel and believed that he had raised Christ from the dead (see, for example, Romans 10:9). In the words of Paul, Christians affirmed their faith in One God, the Father, and in "one Lord, Jesus Christ" (1 Corinthians 8:6).

Early Christians were adamant that Jesus's coming did not merely signal the appearance of a "prophet" or an "anointed one" in Israel—though these and other epithets were applied to Jesus in his time.[7] Instead, they saw the coming of Jesus as an event of decisive, overwhelming significance. Such certainty gave rise to Christianity's self-image as a community of believers certain that they had been chosen, vindicated, and sanctified by God. So epochal and urgent was God's intervention through Jesus Christ that the Letter to the Hebrews (1:2) describes it as having occurred "in these last days." Similarly, the outpouring of God's Spirit will happen "in the last days" (Acts 2:17), and the new covenant sealed with God "in Christ" would, Christians believed, rid the world of sin once and for all (Hebrews 8–10).

Christians soon came to believe that God's agency through Jesus Christ effaced all differences between Jews and Gentiles, enslaved and free people, and men and women.[8] In order to become a Christian, all one needed to do was proclaim the God of Israel as the only God and have oneself baptized into the Christian communion. Peter and Paul played a key role in these developments, which were closely associated with the community at Antioch. From the Acts of the Apostles and the Letter to the Galatians, it is evident that Peter was actively involved in early Christian missions originating from Jerusalem and was instrumental in establishing a Christian community of Jews and Gentiles in Antioch. The conditions that were brokered for the Antioch community and enshrined in the Apostolic Decree, which were based on provisions set out in Leviticus 17–18, required Gentiles to abide by a series of minimum standards for co-existence with Jews (Acts 15:20–28, 20:28). They had to abstain from the consumption of blood and the meat of animals that had been strangled or sacrificed to false gods, as well as from acts of sexual immorality. Even though the Apostolic Decree's scope and duration were limited, it laid the groundwork for the formation of communities of Jews and Gentiles elsewhere.

Just as Christianity is rooted in the scriptures and traditions of Israel and Judaism, so Rabbinic Judaism arose out of conflict with emerging Christianity.[9] The Jewish and Christian Bibles thus evolved under conditions of reciprocal influence and dissociation, a development that has sometimes been called a "parting of the ways."[10] Yet this model has recently been subject to reappraisal. Critics point out that the image of two "ways" that supposedly "parted" simplifies the processes that actually occurred and is based on a mistaken conception of Judaism and Christianity as monolithic entities. These communities were in fact both extremely diverse groups, which formed connections with one another in a host of different ways. To compound the problem, its critics contend, this model is a Christian one that evinces an apologetic tendency to justify Christianity's use of Jewish texts.[11] Moreover, any talk of a "parting of the ways" highlights differences at the expense of commonalities.[12]

Scholars studying specific cases have shown that the designations "Jew" and "Christian" were far from unambiguous in the early days of Christianity and Rabbinic Judaism.[13] They had different connotations depending on the standpoint of the person or people using them. For example, they could be terms of self-identification for people to distinguish themselves from others, or labels applied by outsiders in a positive, neutral, or polemical way, or even metaphorical terms to describe particular religious behaviors. In the case of Greek and Roman authors, it is not always clear whether they are referring to Jews or Christians.[14] A simplistic antithesis of "Jews" and "Christians" cannot do justice to the complex religious and social conditions in antiquity. This is shown, for example, by the Jewish-Christian Gospels—scriptures from the second century, like the Gospel of the Hebrews and the Gospel of the Ebionites, that are quoted by Origen and other ancient Christian theologians. These gospels depict followers of Jesus who saw no contradiction between continuing to cultivate a Jewish lifestyle and observe Jewish laws, and professing a faith in Christ.

In the New Testament, it is above all the Gospel of Matthew that maps out Jesus's integration into the history of Israel by identifying him as the fulfillment of the Law and the Prophets (Matthew 5:17). This approach is characteristic of early Christianity, which was strongly oriented toward Jewish traditions and saw them as a governing framework for those who believed in Jesus.[15]

Christian Updating of Jewish Scriptures

Early Christians handed down, translated, and in some cases updated Jewish texts that, in the absence of such treatment, would most likely have been lost to posterity. The writings of Philo of Alexandria and Flavius Josephus, for example, were transmitted only by Christians. The same is true of Jewish scriptures like the book of Enoch and the book of Jubilees. Christians were also responsible for translating the fourth book of Ezra, a Jewish apocalyptic text from the late first century, into several Near Eastern languages as well as Latin. In its Latin version, it was associated with two Christian writings from the second or third century that are known today as 5 Ezra and 6 Ezra.

Christians reinterpreted the Jewish apocalyptic book 4 Ezra by identifying the "Messiah" mentioned in this text with Jesus and by combining it with two Christian texts consisting of prophetic speeches of Ezra and a vision of the Son of God on Mount Zion. In this form, 4 Ezra was incorporated into the Vulgate in the sixteenth century, while other translations of it into Ethiopian, Syriac, Arabic, and Armenian became part of the Christian tradition without the addition of 5 Ezra and 6 Ezra. The biblical figure of Ezra was thus integrated into Christianity as a prophet and visionary.

Another example is the Ascension of Isaiah. Like the book of Enoch and the book of Jubilees, the complete text of this work exists only in a translation into the Ethiopian liturgical language Ge'ez. The Ascension of Isaiah is a Christian text, most likely from the second century, which combines several different traditions. The first part (chapters 1–5) narrates the martyrdom of the prophet Isaiah and includes a vision of the descent and ascent of Christ as witnessed by the prophet. The second part (chapters 6–11) recounts Isaiah's ascent into heaven, where he sees the descent and ascent of Christ. The text interprets the fate of the prophet Isaiah from a Christian perspective, in order to claim this key figure of Israel's past for the history of Christianity.

It is also unquestionably the case that communities professing a belief in Jesus Christ came to regard themselves from very early on as distinct from Jewish communities. Even as early as 54–55 CE, Paul distinguishes "the believers" from Jews and Gentiles and says of himself, "To the Jews I became like a Jew. . . . To those under the law I became like one under the law. . . . To those not having the law I became like one not having the law" (1 Corinthians 9:20–21).[16] Christian authors of the second and third centuries occasionally described their co-religionists as people who "worship God in a new, third way," as a "third race" (*tríton génos*), or even as a "new race."[17] In this way, Christianity set itself apart both from the Jewish faith and from the Greek and Roman veneration of multiple deities. The new faith apparently needed to carve out its position on many sides. This is unsurprising, given that Christianity was from the very outset a missionary religion that proclaimed a belief in the one God of Israel and the gospel of Jesus Christ. Given this tendency, it is remarkable that the scriptures and traditions of Judaism continued to form an indispensable part of the Christian faith.

This distinction between Jews and Christians affected both social and religious life. It manifested itself in different ways at different places and led to a variety of expressions of the relationship between Jews and Christians. The Gospel of John provides telling testimony. On three occasions this work uses the term *aposynágôgos,* which roughly means "expelled from the synagogue" (John 9:22, 12:42, 16:2). Because no other instances of it occur elsewhere, this word must have been coined by the writer of the gospel himself. It reflects a situation in which followers of Jesus and a synagogue congregation were confronting each other. Apparently, in the town or region the writer is referring to, adherents of Christianity were no longer tolerated in synagogues and were even expressly barred from them. Some scholars have suggested that there is a direct connection between this situation and the way in which the Jewish prayer known as the *Amidah,* or *Shemoneh Esreh* ("eighteen"), was amended. After 70 CE, when the Second Temple in Jerusalem was destroyed, an ironic "blessing on the apostates" (*Birkat Haminim*) was added to the *Amidah.* To all intents and purposes, this new "blessing" amounted to a curse on those who had broken away from Judaism. It is unlikely, however, that there is any direct connection between the *Amidah* and the Gospel of John or its use of the term *aposynágôgos.* In the gospel, the expression reflects a history of conflict between Jews and Christians that had already been in existence for some time.[18] The *Birkat Haminim* simply forms part of that history.

"Jews" and "Christians"

The first time the terms "Christianity" and "Judaism" are used in strict opposition to one another is in the writings of Ignatius of Antioch.[19] Ignatius evidently thought it necessary to emphasize Christianity's autonomy from Judaism, since this was by no means self-evident. The communities to which Ignatius was addressing his letters appear to have included many people who saw no contradiction between believing in Christ and following a Jewish way of life.

Similarly, the Letter of Barnabas, which was written ca. 130—around the same time as the Letters of Ignatius—posits a radical contrast between God's covenant with Israel and his covenant with the Christians. In Barnabas's view, Israel did not prove itself worthy of the covenant, so Moses smashed the tablets of the Law "in order that the covenant of the beloved Jesus might be sealed upon our hearts."[20] The writer relies extensively on Scripture, which he relates exclusively to Christ and Christians. This letter, which was included in the Codex Sinaiticus—widely regarded as the earliest extant Christian Bible—represents an extreme position concerning the relationship between Jews and Christians. The Letter of Barnabas is thought to have been composed in Alexandria, a region that saw brutal suppression of Jewish uprisings by the Roman authorities in the early second century. The author of the letter was at pains to distance himself from the Jews and make it clear that the Christians were a separate community, one that Moses and the prophets were addressing in their scriptures and within which the covenant of the Lord held sway, unlike in Judaism.

The works of the Christian teacher and apologist Justin Martyr, who was active in Rome around the middle of the second century, also clearly distinguish the two religious communities. Justin's writings are of special importance for the genesis of the Christian Bible. Justin was a Gentile philosopher influenced by Platonism who, after his conversion to Christianity, made an intensive study of the role Jewish scriptures played in the Christian faith. In his defense of Christianity, the *First Apology,* which he addressed to the Roman emperor Antoninus Pius, as well as in a (presumably fictitious) dialogue with a Jew named Trypho, Justin provided exhaustive expositions of how the texts of the Septuagint (he uses this term for the Greek Old Testament) had a bearing on the contemporary situation of Jews and Christians.[21] These texts, he claimed, prefigured Christ, and their true meaning could only be grasped if they were interpreted from a position of belief in Christ.

One passage in Justin's *First Apology* (chapter 47) relates Old Testament prophecies to his own time. He begins by quoting the following message from Isaiah 64:10–12:

> Zion is deserted, Jerusalem has become like a desert, accursed. The house, our sanctuary, and the glory that our fathers praised was burned down with fire, and all of its magnificence collapsed. And with all of this you remained restrained, Lord, you remained silent and humbled us greatly.[22]

This is followed by another quotation about the obliteration of Jerusalem and the fact that no Jew will be able to live there anymore. Justin relates this

situation to the Romans' destruction of Jerusalem and the ban on Jews setting foot in the city, which was imposed in the aftermath of the Bar Kochba
rebellion of 132–135.

In the following chapter (48), a passage from Isaiah 35:5–6 is interpreted
as a prophecy of the coming of Christ, his healing of the sick, and his raising
of the dead:

> When he appears the lame will leap like deer, and clear will speak the
> tongue of the deaf; the blind will see again, lepers will be cleansed, the
> dead will rise and walk around.

The death of Jesus, Justin claims, is alluded to in another prophecy by Isaiah,
which speaks of a "righteous man" who perished without anyone taking it to
heart.

Justin points out in chapter 49 that "the same Isaiah" predicted that the
Gentiles would worship Christ but that the Jews would not recognize him
when he came:

> I became manifest to those who did not ask for me; I was found by those
> who did not seek me. I said: "Behold, here am I" to a nation that did not
> call on my name. I held out my hands to an obstinate and rebellious
> people, to those who walk in a way that is not good but follow their
> sins—a people who provoke me to my very face. (compare Isaiah 65:1–3)

According to Justin, the Jews not only failed to recognize Jesus but even went
so far as to mistreat him, even though their own prophets had foretold his
coming, and they had been waiting for the Messiah. By contrast, thanks to
the message spread from Jerusalem by the apostles, the Gentiles abandoned
their worship of false gods and devoted themselves to the one unbegotten
God through Christ.

In his *Dialogue with Trypho,* a long doctrinal conversation with a Jewish
interlocutor about how a person may truly know God, Justin returns repeatedly to the differing Jewish and Christian views of the scriptures of Israel.
Using the form of a Platonic dialogue, Justin explains why the scriptures
of Israel can only be properly understood if they are read as a prophecy of
the coming of Jesus Christ. The discussion concerning Jesus's birth from

the Virgin Mary is a striking example of his critical analysis of Jewish objections.

In chapter 43, Justin broaches the mystery of Christ's birth and relates it to a prophecy by Isaiah about a virgin who will become pregnant and bear a son whose name will be Emmanuel (Isaiah 7:14). This passage was already cited in the Gospel of Matthew as foretelling Jesus's birth to a virgin (Matthew 1:22–23). The Christian doctrine of Christ's virgin birth had attracted opposition and criticism from both Gentile and Jewish quarters. Justin's account addresses this opposition. He takes to task the Jewish contention that the passage in Isaiah does not refer to a "virgin" but to a "young woman" and that it was an allusion to King Hezekiah (or Ezekias) rather than to the future coming of Christ. The reading "young woman" is not attested in Greek manuscripts but does appear in the Hebrew text of Isaiah 7:14, and, according to Irenaeus, the Jewish Bible translators Theodotion and Aquila also translated the phrase in this way.[23] The Septuagint, however, uses the word "virgin," which also underpins the statements in the Gospels of Matthew and Luke that the birth of Jesus came about through the power of the Holy Spirit.[24]

In the dialogue, Justin tells Trypho that he will provide proof that this passage in Isaiah relates to the Christ whom Christians proclaim as Lord ("I shall endeavor to discuss shortly this point in opposition to you, and to show that reference is made to Him who is acknowledged by us as Christ"[25]). And indeed, he returns to this topic later and explains at length that Scripture itself points forward to a new covenant and refers to the promised son of the House of David (chapters 66–68, 84). He also says that the "sign" that God will send by means of the birth of a son to a virgin refers to the "first-begotten of all creation," who will not, like everyone else, be conceived through sexual intercourse. And so, Justin claims, the passage from Isaiah can only be properly understood if it is taken as a prophetic foretelling of Christ. A key issue for Justin is the reliability of the translation into Greek of the Bible text— which, as he emphasizes, was done by Jewish scholars.[26]

These examples show once more that faith in Christ was closely bound up with the scriptures of Israel, and that ancient theologians struggled to determine the relationship between the two. The relationship between "Christianity" and "Judaism" therefore needs to be defined in a nuanced way.[27] Much evidence suggests that the lines of demarcation that formed between the two faiths were far less clear and unequivocal than the writings of early

Christian theologians might suggest. When they insist upon a clear demarcation between "Judaism" and "Christianity" and state that a belief in Christ is wholly incompatible with a Jewish way of life, it reveals that these ideas were not taken for granted in the everyday lives of many early Christians. Gentiles who had converted to Christianity and hence to a belief in the God of Israel may have believed they had an obligation to adopt a Jewish lifestyle—while Christians of Jewish origin may have believed themselves justified in continuing to practice Jewish rites. It is by no means clear whether Jewish converts to the Christian faith regarded themselves as "Christian Jews" or as "Jewish Christians," or whether they considered the labels "Jew" and "Christian" contradictory or complementary descriptions of how they saw themselves and their religious observance. We may fairly presume that attitudes varied from region to region, from one community to another, and from one individual to another. There were Jews who became Christians and yet continued to hold to purity laws, keep the Sabbath, and circumcise their sons. Greeks and Romans who felt drawn to Judaism and its religious customs clung to these practices after they had converted to Christianity. Other "Gentiles" who had nothing to do with Judaism gravitated toward the Christian faith while continuing to attend pagan temples and sacrificial feasts. Jews who renounced their Jewish way of life after conversion to Christianity lived alongside Gentiles in communities where the same rules applied to everyone without exception. Elsewhere, Jews and Gentiles agreed to observe certain Jewish rites—for example, refusing to eat meat that had been sacrificed to Greek or Roman deities or any animals that had not been slaughtered in accordance with Jewish practice, and not engaging in sex outside of marriage. At the same time, though, Gentiles were not expected to comply fully with every last aspect of Jewish law.[28] To describe the relationship between Jews and Christians as a "parting of the ways" does not do justice to this diversity. It would be more fitting to use the metaphor of a house with many rooms, some of which were connected to one another, or, following Paul, the image of a tree with a common root and different branches (see Romans 11:17–24).

The Literary World of Early Christianity

The texts that acquired authoritative status in Christianity and were placed alongside the "Old Testament" came into existence within a variety of different religious and social contexts. And yet these texts represent just part of the entire literary production of early Christianity. The creation of the New Testament must therefore be examined as part of a much broader spectrum.

The Twenty-seven Scriptures of the New Testament

The New Testament gathers together texts that became authoritative for Christianity, in their capacity as testimony to the life and ministry of Jesus and the apostles. These texts were written in the period from around 50 to 150 CE, beginning with the letters of Paul, which were composed from about 50 to 56 and are the earliest of all the Christian scriptures, and ending with the Second Letter of Peter, which dates from the middle of the second century and is the most recent of the texts to find its way into the New Testament. The New Testament includes twenty-seven texts: the Gospels according to Matthew, Mark, Luke, and John, the Acts of the Apostles, thirteen letters that have come down to us under the name of Paul, two letters of Peter, three under the name of John, one letter each of James and Jude (the brothers of Jesus), and finally the Letter to the Hebrews and the book of Revelation.[29]

Discussions about the authority of the Scriptures suggest that other selections of texts might have been possible. Only two gospels might have been incorporated into the New Testament, or the Second and Third Letters of John or the Letter to the Hebrews might have been omitted. Conversely, the Gospel of Peter, the First Letter of Clement, and the *Didache* (also called Lord's Teaching through the Twelve Apostles to the Nations) could have been integrated into the New Testament. There is no simple explanation why these twenty-seven texts in particular form the corpus of the New Testament from the fourth century onward. Some of the processes that led to this selection can be easily traced, whereas in other cases the process remains unclear. Chance occurrences and vested interests that have nothing to do with the content of the texts may sometimes have played a role.

The scriptures that eventually came to form the New Testament were in most instances written as individual texts, but in one case as a two-part work (the Gospel of Luke and the Acts of the Apostles) and in another as a corpus of three letters that were compiled as pseudepigraphic letters of Paul in around 120 CE (the Pastoral Letters, including two letters to Timothy and one to Titus). In some cases, multiple texts are the work of the same author but were written separately and relate to different situations. This is the case with Paul's letters and also with the Second and Third Letters of John.[30]

The first step on the way to the New Testament was the creation of smaller groupings of texts, which were subsequently joined together. This process began with the assembling of Paul's letters into collections toward the end of the first century.[31] These collections are made up both of letters that Paul himself wrote and of ones that were written later in his name and apply the lessons of his life and work to contemporary situations. For instance, the Letter to the Hebrews, which was neither written by Paul nor attributed to him (it is the work of an anonymous author), still found its way into the New Testament as an integral part of Paul's letters. Likewise, the Gospels according to Mark, Matthew, and Luke are closely related in literary terms, whereas the Gospel of John builds upon these three earlier gospels and paints a very different picture of Jesus. Nonetheless, these texts were assembled into the collection of the four gospels over the course of the second century.

The collection of the seven Catholic Letters was added somewhat later. This term, which was first used by Eusebius, refers to the letters of Peter (2) and John (3), along with those of James and Jude.[32] The name conveys the idea that these are "general" (in Greek, *kathólikai*) letters directed toward the church as a whole, unlike the letters of Paul, which are addressed to individual congregations. Some of the Catholic Letters are composed in the form of encyclicals to Christian communities in a particular region of the Roman Empire, such as the First Letter of Peter, which addresses Christians in various provinces of Asia Minor. The Letter of James is directed to "the twelve tribes scattered among the nations [*diasporá*]"—evidently meaning to embrace the whole of Christianity. Others of the Catholic Letters, in spite of their name, do address a specific community (2 John) or an individual person (3 John) and were only later understood as addressing all Christians and placed among the "general letters."

The letters of Paul were written during his missions abroad and treat situations and problems arising during those journeys. Later letters written in Paul's name then carried his message forward and updated his theology for changed circumstances. Ascribing these later works to Paul was less an act of deception than an attempt to give the new letters the same authority as the originals.

Working on the basis of existing traditions and the belief in Jesus Christ as the risen and exalted Son of God, the Synoptic Gospels of Mark, Matthew, and Luke paint a picture of the life and ministry of Jesus. Although these traditions have certain affinities to the letters of the New Testament, the driving force behind them was different from that which inspired the Johannine writings.

The Acts of the Apostles represents a special case among the scriptures of the New Testament. It carries forward the story in the Gospel according to Luke, recounting the events that took place from the ascension of Christ up to the arrival of Paul in Rome. Its theme is the spreading of the Christian message first by the twelve apostles, then by the Hellenists (the Greek translators of the Hebrew Bible), and finally by Paul. Its principal focus is on Paul and his missionary work; the second part of the book gives an account of his journeys and teachings. The Acts of the Apostles and the pseudepigraphic Pauline letters all form part of the reception of Paul's writings within the New Testament.

Although the Gospel of Luke and the Acts of the Apostles were written by the same author and display close linguistic and thematic similarities, they do not appear as a connected, two-part work in any New Testament manuscript or list of the Christian canon. The two books were apparently published separately, and the Acts of the Apostles was only included among the authoritative Christian writings after the Gospel of Luke had already become part of the collection of the four gospels. In the New Testament, the Acts of the Apostles is placed either before the non-Pauline letters (that is, the Catholic Letters) or between the gospels and the letters of Paul. The latter arrangement is the one that is found in most modern editions of the Bible. In this location, the book acts as a bridge from the story of Jesus to the letters of Paul.

The book of Revelation occupies its own unique position. It stands at the end of the New Testament and hence also of the Christian Bible as a whole. In some codices it is followed by writings that are not part of the New Testament, such as the Letter of Barnabas and the Shepherd of Hermas, or the Letters of Clement. The book of Revelation ties in with the apocalyptic literature of Judaism, reprising it from a Christian perspective. Apocalyptic passages are also found in the Old Testament, for example in the book of Daniel and in certain chapters of the book of Isaiah. There are several other

Jewish apocalyptic texts that stand outside the biblical canon, such as the book of Enoch, the fourth book of Ezra, the Apocalypse of Baruch, and the Apocalypse of Abraham. The apocalyptic literature of Judaism, which forms the literary and theological context of the book of Revelation, is thus considerably more extensive than it might appear from the biblical scriptures.

In a series of five successive visions, the book of Revelation, or Apocalypse of John, portrays the destruction of the existing world and its replacement by "a new heaven and a new earth" (Revelation 21:1). Lost in reverie, the seer John, who identifies himself by name at the beginning and end of the book (Revelation 1:1, 4, 9; 22:8), finds himself standing before the throne of God. There he sees a slaughtered lamb that is the only being worthy of opening the scroll with the seven seals; after the seals are opened, the events of the end time take their course. These are recounted in successive visions of seven seals, seven trumpets, and seven bowls, which are interrupted in chapters 12–14 by an account of a war in heaven that ends in victory over Satan, his fall to earth, two beasts on earth that blaspheme God and wage war against his chosen people, and finally the triumph of the Lamb, which stands atop Mount Zion in the company of the 144,000 elect of God. According to Revelation, the end of time is marked by the destruction of Babylon, which stands here for Rome. This event will be followed, the vision claims, by a thousand-year reign of peace under the Messiah and ultimately complete triumph over Satan.

Revelation aligns itself with the risen Christ, who has already achieved victory over Satan. The forces opposed to God that are still active on earth—again, a reference to the Roman Empire and its institutions—wage war against the elect of God and the Lamb, but are ultimately vanquished. Like the First Letter of Peter, the book of Revelation takes as its premise a crisis situation for Christianity. It urges believers to hold fast to the faith and, in light of the victory that has already been secured over godlessness and evil, to refuse to bow down to the godless power (presumably an allusion to the cult of the Roman emperor). Unlike the First Letter of Peter, which urges the faithful to suffer the hostility of a Gentile society for being Christians, Revelation stresses the incompatibility between believing in God and Jesus Christ and abiding by the parameters set by godless forces.

The book of Revelation contains seven letters (the "missives") addressed to communities in Asia Minor. including Ephesus, Smyrna, and Pergamum.

The missives call upon the addressees to hold firm until the end of time, when God's chosen ones will be granted salvation.

Noncanonical Texts

Several early Christian writings that were not included in the New Testament were compiled into separate collections in the modern era—the Apostolic Fathers and the Apocrypha. Other noncanonical texts include various liturgical writings and church constitutions, philosophical treatises of ancient Christian theologians, and catechisms. Some of these works were written at the same time as the New Testament scriptures, that is, in the century between 50 and 150 CE. Others date from the period when the New Testament canon was taking shape. This process began as early as the end of the first century, with the gathering together of the letters of Paul, and came to a provisional close by the mid-fourth century—"provisional" because not all Christian churches share the same biblical canon and also because the church never issued an official edict identifying the scriptures that composed the "Old Testament" and "New Testament." There was simply a de facto recognition of which ones were included. Some of the texts written during this period relate in various ways to the scriptures that found their way into the New Testament: they either pick up and expand upon the themes in those scriptures, engage critically with them, or set themselves up in direct competition. The story of how the New Testament came into being is therefore a tale of disputes between different doctrines, groups, and tendencies and the writings in which they expounded their views. This may be illustrated by considering the kinds of texts that belonged to the literary world of early Christianity but were only assembled into collections at a much later date than the New Testament.

In 1672, the Catholic theologian Jean-Baptiste Cotelier compiled the writings of Barnabas, Clement, Hermas, Ignatius, and Polycarp, supposed followers of the apostles, along with several other texts, into a collection which he entitled *SS. Patrum qui temporibus apostolicis floruerunt* ("Works of the Apostolic Fathers who flourished at the time of the apostles").[33] This corpus was later expanded to include other writings: the *Didache,* the Fragments of Papias of Hierapolis, the Apology of Quadratus, and the Letter to Diognetus. The texts of the "Apostolic Fathers" were written between the end of the first century and the end of the second. The older works (the First Letter of Clement, the *Didache*, and the Letters of Ignatius) come from the same period as the later scriptures of the New Testament (the Acts of the Apostles, Revelation, the First Letter of Peter, the Pastoral Letters, the Letter of Jude, and the Second Letter of Peter). Until Cotelier assembled them, these texts had never been gathered together within a single collection. They were individual works created quite independently of one another, and throughout antiquity and the Middle Ages they were not thought to belong together. For the most part, they expand on scriptures that did find a place in the New Testament.[34]

The *Didache* is thought to build upon the Gospel of Matthew, while also reflecting other early Christian traditions. This text, which was written toward the end of the first century, represents the oldest extant Christian community rule. It is a collection of guidelines concerning ethics, baptism, prayer and the communion, treatment of itinerant prophets and teachers, the gathering of congregations to celebrate the "Lord's Day" (Sunday), and the election of bishops and deacons. It concludes with a warning to the faithful to be vigilant, since the coming of the "Lord" might be surprisingly close at hand.

The First Letter of Clement was written in Rome and is addressed to the Christians of Corinth. It takes as its starting point Paul's First Letter to the Corinthians but also relates to Jesus traditions and possibly the Letter to the Hebrews as well as the Septuagint. It exhorts Corinthians to change the way they live and follow the precepts of the Christian faith. The Letters of Ignatius were written while Ignatius was being taken as a prisoner from Antioch, the city where he had been bishop, to Rome, where he would be executed, sometime between 98 and 117 CE. They are addressed to various communities in western Asia Minor (Ephesus, Smyrna, and Tralles, among others) and stress the unity of Christian congregations under the leadership of their bishops, elders, and deacons, as well as the importance of the Eucharist conducted by a bishop as a unifying symbol of the congregation. Ignatius is also intent on finding theological justifications for his path to martyrdom and defending himself against criticism. He is familiar with the letters of Paul and other early Christian works, including those that are associated with the Gospels (especially the Gospel of John). His letters give an idea of the formal church structures and institutions that were starting to emerge in the middle of the second century.

Some of the texts in the "Apostolic Fathers," especially the Shepherd of Hermas, were highly regarded in early Christianity. It was by no means a foregone conclusion that they would ultimately not be included among the "canonical" scriptures. The boundaries of the canon were fluid for quite some time, as is evident in the configuration of early Bible codices. The Codex Sinaiticus, for example, includes the Letter of Barnabas and the Shepherd of Hermas, while the Codex Alexandrinus contains the First and Second Letters of Clement. The fragmentary Codex Vaticanus breaks off midway through the Letter to the Hebrews; thus, it is unknown whether this manuscript originally contained even more scriptures than those that in a narrow sense form part of the New Testament.

The "Apocrypha of the New Testament" was first compiled in 1703 by the philologist and theologian Johann Albert Fabricius. Unlike the use of "apocryphal" in the works of ancient theologians, Fabricius was not using the term, which literally means "hidden," in the pejorative sense of "falsified" or "heretical."[35] It was simply meant to denote those literary testimonies of early Christianity that had not become canonical; in other words, had not been included within the New Testament. Since Fabricius published his edition, many other works have become known that are now counted among the Apocrypha.[36] The discovery of a large number of papyri at Oxyrhynchus in Upper Egypt starting in the late nineteenth century was extremely important in this respect. This archeological find included both biblical texts and extra-canonical sayings and stories of Jesus. Thirteen papyrus codices of Coptic texts incorporating a great diversity of Christian and non-Christian writings came to light at Nag Hammadi (also in Upper Egypt) in 1945.[37] Among the Christian texts found there were the Gospel of Thomas and the Gospel of Philip, along with other gospels, philosophical and mythological treatises, apocalypses, and more.[38] Many of these texts were translated from Greek to Coptic in the fourth and fifth centuries, though the actual works themselves date from the second or third centuries.

Some earlier fragments—from, say, the second or third centuries—exist of texts that are only known in full from manuscripts dating from later centuries (and often in translation).[39] This is the case with the Gospel of Thomas, for example. Before the discovery of the Nag Hammadi codices, fragmentary Greek papyri had been found in Oxyrhynchus that were subsequently identified as part of the Gospel of Thomas. Two Greek fragments from the third century exist of the Gospel of Mary, which is further attested by an incomplete Coptic manuscript of the fifth century. Although this text was not found at Nag Hammadi, it has a number of features in common with writings from there. Early Christian theologians sometimes refer to apocryphal texts such as the gospels of Thomas, Peter, the Hebrews, and the Ebionites.

Many of the apocryphal texts are similar in literary genre to texts that were later included in the New Testament; they include gospels, letters, stories of the apostles, and apocalypses. It would be inaccurate, however, to speak of an "apocryphal New Testament," given that the texts in question were only gathered together and identified as "apocryphal" texts at a significantly later date.[40]

Only some of the apocryphal texts promulgate "heretical" doctrines. Most fall within the same spectrum of teaching upon which the texts of the New Testament are based. The failure of certain texts to become canonical may have been due to their later date of composition or to their use by groups at the margins of Christian congregations, or simply to the fact that they were not sufficiently well known or widespread.

The apocryphal texts, as a result, cannot be reduced to a single common denominator by describing them as, say, "falsified" or "secret" writings. They include some texts that expound doctrines concerning the origin of the world and humankind and the significance of Jesus Christ that deviate from New Testament texts, and texts that paint a legendary picture of the life and childhood of Christ or his crucifixion, as well as writings that recount miraculous deeds of the apostles or incorporate additional traditions from the period of early Christianity. The diversity of early Christian texts reflects the sheer breadth of views on the content and the meaning of the Christian faith that arose within the various different strands of Christianity.

The Jesus Tradition and the Gospels

Paul and the Canonical Gospels

Jesus embarked on his public ministry with the claim that his deeds would establish the kingdom of God on earth and convey God's salvation to humankind. This self-consciousness of Jesus, which has sometimes been described as a "Messianic claim," was perpetuated by his followers after his death on the Cross.[41] Against this background, Jesus's teaching and ministry were passed down in early Christianity and interpreted under new circumstances.[42]

Jesus did not leave behind any writings, but instead set out his teachings by word of mouth in different situations—when teaching his disciples or talking to crowds of people, in disputations with his adversaries, at table fellowships, and so on. Stories of the ministry and teachings of Jesus continued to be passed down orally for several decades. From around 70 CE onward, that is, about forty years after Jesus's death, the "Jesus tradition" was put into writing in the form of the Gospels. In oral transmission, this tradition was translated from Aramaic, in which most of it had first been told, into Greek (see Chapter 5).[43] The transmission process not only shaped the content of the tradition but formed it into parables, stories of healing, and other short anecdotes culminating in a pointed saying or action of Jesus.

Traces of the Jesus tradition can be identified in the letters of Paul. At two points in his First Letter to the Corinthians, he talks about a "word of the Lord" (1 Corinthians 7:10–11, 9:14). The first instance relates to the proscription against divorce, and the second to the practice of providing support for itinerant missionaries. These topics are also treated in the Gospels.[44] Paul refers to the corresponding instructions of the "Lord," that is the exalted Jesus. He does not quote the words of Jesus that appear in the Gospels, but instead paraphrases them. The situation is different in the case of Jesus's Last Supper. Here, Paul acknowledges a tradition that has already been established and which also appears in the Gospels:

The Lord Jesus, on the night that he was handed over, took bread and gave thanks, broke it, and said: "This is my body for you. Do this in remembrance of me!" In the same way, also the cup after the meal and said: "This cup is the new covenant in my blood. Do this, as often as you drink [it] in remembrance of me!" (1 Corinthians 11:23–25)[45]

Paul introduces this passage with the words: "For I received from the Lord what I also passed on to you." The terms "received" and "passed on" reveal that Paul is describing a practice in which he is well versed, since these are technical terms for the transmission of traditions. This shows that the narrative of Jesus's Last Supper as a partaking of his body and blood—of his life and death—is one of the earliest traditions of Christianity. It creates an important link between the letters of Paul and the Synoptic Gospels, in which it also appears.[46]

In historical terms, it cannot be established beyond doubt that Jesus used these or similar words at the Last Supper with his disciples in Jerusalem. All the same, this event on the eve of his crucifixion was already being narrated at a very early stage. The emphasis is on the meaning of this meal for the community that has gathered in the name of Jesus Christ. The gestures of breaking and passing around the bread and drinking wine from the same cup by all participants are expressly related to the life and death of Jesus. The broken bread symbolizes his body—that is, his earthly existence—and the wine symbolizes his spilt blood—that is, his death, which is already looming at the Last Supper. The crucified and risen Jesus Christ is called to mind, and those who partake in the meal share in the redemptive power of his life and death.

In 1 Corinthians 15:3, Paul introduces another tradition in exactly the same way as that of the Last Supper: Christ's death for our sins, his burial and resurrection, and his post-resurrection appearances to his disciples: "For what I received I passed on to you at the first: that Christ died for our sins."[47] This similar treatment indicates that both traditions were of equal importance to Paul. When referring to the ministry of the earthly Jesus, he always speaks of the "Lord" or the "Lord Jesus," which shifts the focus onto the resurrection and exaltation of the earthly Jesus, for it is in light of these events that he is called "Lord." The ministry of the earthly Jesus is only significant to Paul because he is looked upon by Christians as the exalted "Lord."[48]

No other direct traces of the Jesus tradition can be identified in the letters of Paul.[49] Yet some issues treated by Paul are linked to traditions that the authors of the Gospels pick up. These include the observance of the purity laws, the commandment not to seek revenge and to love one's enemy, and the exhortation to be vigilant lest Jesus return unexpectedly to judge humankind.[50] All these themes appear in Paul's letters without being explicitly labeled as part of the Jesus tradition, whereas in the Synoptic Gospels they are presented as the teachings of Jesus. This suggests that it was principally traditions of an ethical or advisory kind that were in circulation in early Christianity. In the Gospels, these are usually presented as the teachings of Jesus, but are sometimes cited without such an attribution. Similar themes appear in other texts without being specifically ascribed to Jesus, for example, in the Letter of James and the First Letter of Peter, as well as in the *Didache*.

The authors of the Synoptic Gospels gathered the traditions of the ministry and crucifixion of Jesus, edited their content and language, and integrated them into their own accounts. The oldest of these accounts is the Gospel according to Mark, which was written in around 70 CE. It was composed during the Jewish–Roman War of 66–74, presumably not long after the destruction of Jerusalem in the year 70. Jesus is portrayed as the Son of God imbued with the Holy Spirit, whose communions, acts of healing, and other demonstrations of power all bear witness to God's omnipotence. He also calls men to be his disciples and so establishes his own community. While God's kingdom is ever present, it is still hidden and will only be revealed by God in the future, at the second coming of Jesus as the Son of God to judge humankind. The relationship between the present state of concealment and a future revelation is illustrated by the parable of the sower in Mark 4:3–34, which Jesus describes as "the secret of the kingdom of God" (4:11). In view of the concealed nature of the kingdom of God, which leads to doubts over whether his reign on earth really began with the coming of Jesus, Jesus urges his disciples to continue to follow him, even if that means following the "way of the cross"—that is, suffering from persecution. Eternal life is ensured only by following Jesus and turning toward the kingdom of God that began with his ministry (Mark 8:34–9:1).

Great historical and theological significance attaches to the composition of Mark's gospel. Its account of Jesus's life, which begins with John the Baptist and ends with the Resurrection, is a literary form that later writers of accounts of the life of Jesus also adopted. Mark uses the Greek term *euangélion,* meaning "good news," or "glad tidings," to characterize the events surrounding Jesus Christ.[51] The English equivalent of this term, "gospel," combines words meaning "good" and "message." The writers of the other gospels do not use this term.[52] Only in the second century did *euangélion* become the standard literary designation for writings that recount the ministry and fate of Jesus. The first work to do so is that of Justin Martyr, who uses the plural term "*euangélia*" ("gospels"). Later this designation was also adopted by the writers of the apocryphal gospels.

With its narrative characterized as a "gospel," the Gospel of Mark assigns a special importance to Jesus's ministry on earth. Jesus is not just the risen and exalted Lord but is at the same time a man who acted with God's authority in Galilee and the surrounding regions, who founded his own community of followers, and whose activity led to his crucifixion by the Romans.

The Gospel according to Mark thus establishes the theological connection between the life of Jesus and his resurrection, exaltation, and return at the end of time.

The authors of the Gospels of Matthew and Luke use the Gospel of Mark as the basis of their accounts. They also tap into other traditions that were available to them in written form, at least in part. Both of these gospels were composed sometime between 80 and 100 CE. In addition to the Gospel of Mark, whose structure they follow for large sections, the Gospels of Matthew and Luke also build on other traditions, some of which correspond very closely to one another, even linguistically. In the nineteenth century, this feature gave rise to the hypothesis that Matthew and Luke used a second source besides the Gospel of Mark.[53] This supposed source, which is usually abbreviated as Q in the research literature (standing for the German word *Quelle,* "source") is not preserved in ancient manuscripts or mentioned by ancient writers, so its existence cannot be proved. All the same, there is a very plausible argument for such a source. Assuming that Matthew and Luke used the Gospel of Mark independently of each another, it is hard to explain the close accord between them when they convey material that does not derive from Mark's gospel unless they both drew on another common source. Because this source can only be determined on the basis of common material in Matthew and Luke that is *not* found in Mark, its precise extent and literary profile can only be guessed at.[54] Having said that, Q is generally assumed to have contained sayings of Jesus—hence its alternative designation as the "logia" source (*logia* means "sayings").

The Gospel of Matthew paints a distinctive picture of Jesus that differs from the one presented in the Gospel of Mark.[55] Jesus is portrayed as the Messiah of Israel, whose ministry is firmly rooted in the Jewish scriptures and traditions and can only be properly understood against this background. Consequently, this gospel repeatedly stresses that events in the story of Jesus occurred in a certain way "in order to fulfill what was spoken through the prophets" (or a similar phrase), followed by a quotation from Scripture.[56]

At the very start of the Gospel of Matthew, Jesus is integrated into God's history with Israel by means of a genealogy, being referred to as the "Son of David" and the "Son of Abraham." These two epithets yoke together a lineage that focuses on Israel (through the promise of a future ruler from the House of David) with a lineage that is universal (hinting at the promise God made to Abraham, that he would become the father of all nations). Unlike Mark, Matthew sees the ministry of Jesus as faithful to the Torah and even as the fulfillment of the Law and the Prophets. Indeed, he firmly refutes any idea that Jesus may have come to abolish the Law and the Prophets (5:17–18).

The evolution of the Church of Jesus Christ from the fellowship of the disciples convened by Jesus plays an important role in the Gospel of Matthew. Matthew's gospel is the only one in the New Testament to use the term "church," or "community" (*ekklêsía*). The church (community) is founded on the fellowship of the disciples, and in particular on Peter. He is the one whom Jesus singles out, stating that he will build his church (community) on Peter as the "rock" (*pétra;* 16:18). Peter is the disciple who displays faith and doubt in equal measure; he makes a special effort to emulate Jesus, but repeatedly fails to do so.[57] The Gospel of Matthew provides strict rules for interaction between members of the congregation. In Matthew 18, care of the "little ones" (denoting not just children, but needy members of the community in general) and mutual forgiveness are cited as crucial modes of behavior. The rule requiring forgiveness of sins was instituted by Jesus himself, who intended it to be put into practice by his community.

Finally, a crucial theme treated in the Gospel of Matthew is the relationship between the emerging Christian church (community) and the Jewish people. Matthew reveals a tension in Jesus's ministry between an "exclusive" viewpoint, focusing on Israel alone, and an "inclusive" one, embracing all nations. The former is expressed in the mission of Jesus and his disciples to Israel. In Matthew 10:5–6, Jesus expressly instructs the disciples not to "go among the Gentiles or enter any town of the Samaritans" but only to go "to the lost sheep of Israel." And in 15:24, Jesus tells a Canaanite woman, "I was sent only to the lost sheep of Israel." Standing in sharp contrast is the "great commission" at the end of the gospel, in which the risen Jesus dispatches his disciples to "go and make disciples of all nations" by baptizing them and instructing them in his teachings (28:19–20). This picks up on the previous designation in Matthew of Jesus as "son of Abraham."

The Gospel of Luke paints its own unique picture of the life and ministry of Jesus. Jesus is proclaimed the "Son of the Most High" who will sit on the throne of David (1:32). Through Jesus's coming, Luke says, God has prepared salvation for all nations, bringing enlightenment to the Gentiles and glory to the chosen people of Israel (2:30–32). Here, too, Jesus directs his ministry

primarily toward Israel and describes it as the fulfillment of prophetic promises (4:18–19). The special emphasis in Luke is on ethical behavior in accordance with the will of God. The evangelist stresses the importance of a responsible attitude toward earthly possessions and highlights the fact that God
has brought redemption to his people through Jesus. The gospel ends with
Jesus first appearing to his disciples after his resurrection and then ascending
to heaven. At the beginning of the Acts of the Apostles there is another encounter between the risen Christ and his disciples, which lasts for forty days.
During that time, Jesus instructs his disciples about the coming kingdom of
God. The gathering is again terminated by Jesus's ascent to heaven, an event
that will be matched by his second coming at the end of time.

The story of Pentecost in the Acts of the Apostles sets in motion the prop-
agation of the Christian message. The principal agents in this spread of Christianity are the twelve apostles, the Hellenists, and Paul. A key aspect of their
mission is to announce that the emerging church is firmly rooted in the history of Israel and represents a continuation of that history, even though the
message of Christ is often spurned by the Jews but accepted by the Gentiles.
This is why Paul, at the end of the Acts of the Apostles, is reported as saying
that God has hardened the hearts of the Jews and made them incapable of
realizing that he enacts his will through Jesus Christ. The Gentiles, on the
other hand, will heed this message (Acts 28:25–28).

A quite different image of Jesus emerges from the Gospel of John. Here,
Jesus is depicted as the Word of God that became flesh, who has revealed
God's presence in the world and who leads those who believe in him to eternal
life. The Jesus of John's gospel speaks about himself figuratively as the "bread
of life," the "light of the world," the "good shepherd," and the "true vine."
His acts of healing and other mighty deeds are interpreted as signs that show
him to be a revelator who has come into the world. The Gospel of John portrays Jesus's path as a downward trajectory from the higher divine realm
into the cosmos, which is matched by an upward movement when Jesus returns to the Father. Accordingly, John uses terms like "lifting up," "leaving,"
"going away," and even "glorification" to describe Jesus's death.[58] Likewise,
the Crucifixion is interpreted as Jesus's exaltation, that is, as the start of his
journey to the divine realm.

The "farewell discourses" (13:31–16:33) have a special significance in the
Gospel of John. They are introduced through a new situation—Jesus alone

with his disciples over a meal—and are followed by a long prayer to the Father (13:1–30 and 17:1–26, respectively). John places special emphasis on the circumstances that will ensue after the departure of Jesus: the disciples will remain in the world while not being part of the world, and Jesus will send the Paraclete (Holy Spirit) as a "mediator," "advocate," or "comforter" to guide his disciples in the ways of truth. In this way, John's gospel underlines more emphatically than the Synoptic Gospels that it is looking back at Christ's ministry in full knowledge of his resurrection and is reflecting upon the significance of his time on earth for the faithful.

The history of the Jesus tradition from its beginnings to the writing of the four gospels that were subsequently incorporated into the New Testament shows that the life and ministry of Jesus—including the Crucifixion, the Resurrection, the appearances of the risen Christ to his disciples, and his exaltation—were a major impetus to the creation of scriptures for Christianity that would parallel those of Judaism. Jesus's ministry was seen as the transmission of God's redemption, as the start of the foundation of God's kingdom, and as the fulfillment of the Laws and the Prophets. He was called the Son of God and the Anointed One (the literal meaning of "Christ"), whose authority and legitimation by God remained in force even in the face of his death on the Cross.

Jesus Traditions outside the New Testament and the Apocryphal Gospels

Words of Jesus appear not only in the New Testament writings, but also in other early Christian texts and additions to the New Testament gospels. Thus, we can observe that in early Christian writings, over time, words of Jesus as "words of the Lord" acquired their own authority alongside the authoritative Jewish scriptures. This process is already in evidence in the *Didache*, which was written at the end of the first century and quotes the words of Jesus from the "gospel of our Lord" or "his gospel."[59] The Second Letter of Clement, which was composed in the mid-second century, also quotes a "word of the Lord" from "the gospel" (8:5). At another point, the letter's author quotes from Isaiah 54:1 and immediately thereafter, with the introductory phrase "another scripture says," cites the words of Jesus: "I have not come to call the righteous, but sinners" (Mark 2:17; compare Matthew 9:13; Luke 5:32). In a similar vein, the Letter of Barnabas introduces the saying "Many are called, but few are chosen" from Matthew 22:14 with the formulation "as it is written" (Barnabas 4:14).

This extension of "words of the Lord" is first encountered in the transmission of the Synoptic Gospels themselves. Thus, in the Codex Bezae, a Bible manuscript from the fifth century, a supplementary episode, or "agraphon" (a saying of Jesus not found in the New Testament gospels), is appended to Jesus's dispute with the Pharisees about his disciples picking heads of grain on the Sabbath. Jesus sees a man working on the Sabbath and says to him, "Man, if you know what you are doing, you are blessed. But if you do not know then you are cursed and a transgressor of the Law." This is a remarkable extension of the topic just treated in the preceding episode. Another story that was incorporated into the textual tradition of the New Testament is the one concerning Jesus and the adulteress in John 7:53–8:11. This also appears in the Codex Bezae and in many later manuscripts.[60]

Writings about Jesus, or "words of the Lord," are also found in some texts of the Apostolic Fathers.[61] The author of the First Letter of Clement, which was written toward the end of the first century, urges his readers to heed the "words of the Lord Jesus," through which Christ taught clemency and forbearance. There follows a series of words of the Lord that touch upon events in the Synoptic Gospels, especially the Sermon on the Mount in Matthew (Matthew 5–7) and the Sermon on the Plain (Luke 6:20–49). Another reference to "words of our Lord Jesus" appears in 1 Clement 47:7–8. Here, Jesus utters a cry of anguish, which has a number of analogies in the Synoptic Gospels. Similarly, in the Letter of Polycarp there is a reference to one of the Lord's teachings: "Do not judge or you too will be judged" (2:3). Other connections to material in the Synoptic Gospels are also found in the *Didache* and the Letter of Barnabas.

Finally, Jesus traditions have also been preserved in fragmentary form on papyri.[62] The Egerton Papyrus 2 (as well as the Cologne Papyrus 255—a text that is thought to have been written toward the end of the second century) contains various scenes from the ministry of Jesus, including a version of the episode from Mark 1:40–44 in which he cures a man with leprosy, as well as Jesus's disputations with Jewish elders and legal scholars. The papyrus evidently once contained a story of Jesus similar to those that were included in the New Testament. Because no more than a few fragments have survived, however, we can only draw very limited conclusions on this score.

Papyrus Oxrhynchus 840, a small fragment from a miniature codex on vellum (its designation as a "papyrus" is therefore somewhat misleading), has a total of forty-five lines written on both sides.[63] They describe an encounter on Temple Square in Jerusalem between Jesus and a Jewish high priest of the Pharisees named Levi. At the heart of their conversation is a disagreement on the question of purification. The background to this episode may have been a controversy concerning Christian baptism as a cleansing ritual carried out with water, versus a "spiritual" baptism in "waters of eternal life." If this interpretation is correct, this fragment may reflect a clash within Christianity between opposing conceptions of baptism, and possibly of the sacraments in general. The high priest would represent a position that is being criticized by the author of the text in an internal Christian controversy. By extension, this dispute may also have been fueled by differing views on how Christian traditions related to Jewish ones. One indication in this direction is that in the dispute, the high priest contends that the ritual cleansing must be performed by descending into a pool of water by one set of steps and exiting by another, and finally by putting on white clothes—a clear allusion to the Christian baptismal rite.

Many other papyri containing Jesus traditions have also survived, though in many cases their fragmentary state of preservation does not allow us to make detailed observations about them. These fragments do, however, show that the Jesus tradition was far more extensive than just the four gospels that were included in the New Testament might suggest. It is frequently possible to identify points of contact with those gospels, but sometimes the noncanonical writings about Jesus follow their own path. As a result, a great diversity of references to the person of Jesus and his ministry becomes apparent. From the second to the fourth centuries, this corpus of Jesus traditions was distilled down into the four gospels of the New Testament, which for the Christian church became the definitive portrayal of the life and death of Jesus.

Explicit mentions of noncanonical, "apocryphal," gospels occur in the writings of ancient theologians from the late second century on. These commentators display a range of attitudes to these gospels. Although they quote from them, they treat them as distinct from the four canonical gospels, and while some writers judge them, on closer inspection, as unsuitable for the Christian community, others reject them outright and decry them as "heretical."

The works of certain early Christian theologians, such as Clement of Alexandria, Origen, Jerome, and Eusebius, mention a "Gospel according to the Hebrews" and a "Gospel according to the Egyptians." In addition, Epiphanius of Salamis (fourth century) quotes from a gospel used by the Jewish-Christian sect of the Ebionites. All that is known nowadays of these texts, which are often collectively referred to as the "Jewish-Christian Gospels," are the quotations cited by these authors. No manuscripts have survived.[64] Clement of Alexandria makes the following intriguing remark in a note: "We did not find this saying in the four gospels that have come down to us, but in the 'Gospel according to the Egyptians.'"[65] The note refers to a quotation in which Jesus responds thus to Salome's inquiry about when salvation will come: "When you have trodden upon the garment of shame and when the two become one, the male with the female, neither male nor female." Analogous statements to this saying appear in other apocryphal gospels, such as those of Thomas and Philip. It refers to a notion expressed in early Christian writings (as well as by Philo) that human beings were originally a single entity combining both male and female, a state that was lost when they entered the world. This Platonic idea was open to interpretation by Christians as meaning that with the coming of Jesus Christ, knowledge of how the original completeness of humankind might be regained also came into the world. This idea resurfaced in various different forms in Christian writings of the late second, third, and fourth centuries and clearly forms the background to the saying quoted from the Gospel according to the Egyptians.

An example of rejection of an apocryphal text after close scrutiny occurs in a letter that Bishop Serapion of Alexandria wrote to the Christian community of Rhossos on the Mediterranean coast of Syria in around 180. The letter has come down to us through Eusebius:

> For we, brethren, receive both Peter and the other apostles as Christ; but we reject intelligently the writings falsely ascribed to them, knowing that such were not handed down to us. When I visited you I supposed that all of you held the true faith, and as I had not read the Gospel which they put forward under the name of Peter, I said, If this is the only thing which occasions dispute among you, let it be read. But now having learned, from what has been told me, that their mind was involved in

some heresy, I will hasten to come to you again. Therefore, brethren, expect me shortly. But you will learn, brethren, from what has been written to you, that we perceived the nature of the heresy of Marcianus, and that, not understanding what he was saying, he contradicted himself. For having obtained this Gospel from others who had studied it diligently, namely, from the successors of those who first used it, whom we call Docetæ (for most of their opinions are connected with the teaching of that school) we have been able to read it through, and we find many things in accordance with the true doctrine of the Savior, but some things that deviate from it, which we have pointed out for you farther on. (Eusebius, *Church History* 6.12.3–6)[66]

This letter, which, according to Eusebius, came from a treatise by Serapion with the title "On the So-Called Gospel of Peter," demonstrates in the first instance that early Christian communities were reading texts with the title "Gospel" other than the four gospels of the New Testament. These were texts of a very diverse nature, whose only common feature was that they contained writings about Jesus.

Serapion's letter is the earliest reference to a gospel bearing the name of Peter.[67] In 1886–1887, a codex containing four texts in Greek was discovered in the grave of a monk in the Upper Egyptian settlement of Akhmîm. One of these texts was probably a fragmentary gospel. Because its author refers to himself twice in the first person as the narrator, and on the second occasion adds that his name is "Simon Peter," the work was identified as the (or at least a) Gospel of Peter. The fragment that has survived dates from the sixth or seventh century, and so is a later transcript. However, there is at least one other Greek fragment from a much earlier period (late second or early third century). Together with the letter of Serapion, this fragment suggests that the Gospel of Peter was composed sometime in the second century. The subject matter of this gospel is a version of the events of the Passion presented from a specific perspective. It runs from Pontius Pilate's interrogation of Jesus to the disciples' return to Galilee after the Crucifixion. It is no longer possible to determine the extent of the complete, original text—for instance, whether a description of Jesus's ministry preceded the Passion account. The Gospel of Peter's narration of the events of the Passion places particular emphasis on the Jews' hostility toward Jesus and his disciples, reflecting a growing alienation and enmity between Jews and Christians that can be discerned on various occasions throughout the second century.

Among the Nag Hammadi codices found in 1945 was an almost complete manuscript in Coptic of the Gospel of Thomas, a work rejected by ancient Christian theologians (Figure 37).[68] As with the Gospel of Peter, several Greek fragments of this gospel dating from the end of the second or the beginning of the third century are also extant. These were discovered even earlier than the Coptic manuscript from Nag Hammadi, but at the time they were found, in the late nineteenth century at Oxyrhynchus, they were not identified as part of the Gospel of Thomas because of the simple fact that its text was not yet known.[69]

The Gospel of Thomas contains a wealth of sayings and parables, each of which is introduced by the phrase "Jesus says" or "Jesus said."[70] There are also some short sections of narrative text. Yet in comparison with the gospels of the New Testament, the proportion of narrative material is drastically reduced. It is confined to a handful of allusions to places and people relating to the life of Jesus, plus a few references to Jewish traditions.

Thomas's gospel contains many analogies to the Synoptic Gospels, but it conveys a highly individual image of Jesus. The purpose of the sayings and parables is to characterize Jesus as the revealer of "hidden words," the correct understanding of which leads a person to eternal life ("Whoever finds the meaning of these words will not taste death"). It is addressed to those who come from the "kingdom of the Father" and are worthy of returning there. By contrast, the "world" is described as a "corpse," a place that is not the true home of those who belong to the Father. As a result, the gospel states, one should shun the world, love one's brother, and not hanker after worldly possessions. Those to whom Jesus addresses his words are called "individuals" or "chosen ones." They are called upon to heed what he says and so fulfill their destiny and return to the Father.

Another of the apocryphal gospels is the Gospel of Mary.[71] All that has survived of this work are a few pages in Coptic in a codex from the fifth century that includes three other texts. This codex is known as the Berolinensis Gnosticus because it forms part of the papyrus collection held at the Egyptian Museum of Berlin. The Gospel of Mary appears on pages 7–10 and 15–19 of the codex; pages 1–6 and 11–14 are missing. Two Greek fragments of this

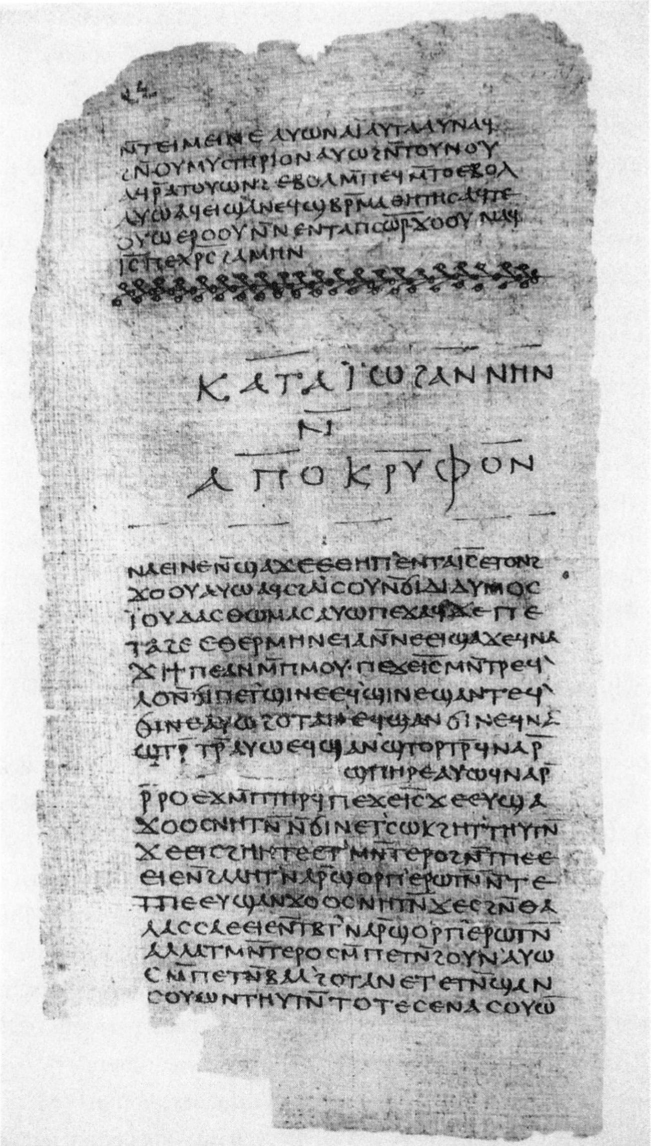

Figure 37. Page from a Nag Hammadi codex showing the beginning of the Gospel of Thomas.

gospel (Papyrus Oxyrhynchus 3525 and Papyrus Rylands 463) have also been preserved. These enable us to date the text to the second century.

The Gospel of Mary (the name refers to Mary Magdalene) tells of a meeting of Jesus with his female and male followers after his resurrection. The surviving text begins at the end of a question posed to Jesus by the disciples, which is believed to be, "Will matter then be utterly destroyed or not?" The answer given by the "Savior," as Jesus is often referred to here, is that all things that currently exist will dissolve and return to their origins. After Jesus has concluded his discussion with his followers and departed, Mary reveals to the disciples a vision in which Jesus told her about the ascent of the soul, which must triumph over hostile forces. After this, an argument about the meaning of this vision breaks out between Peter, Andrew, Levi, and Mary, with Peter and Andrew taking an adversarial position toward Mary. Finally, they all disperse to preach the gospel.

The Gospel of Mary thus contains the teaching of the risen Christ about the ascent of the soul to a higher plane after death. It is one of several scriptures that link the teachings of Jesus with philosophical questions about the origins of humankind and its way to salvation. It may also point to different strands within early Christianity, here represented by the disciples (in particular, Peter) on the one hand and Mary on the other.

An apocryphal gospel of a quite different kind is the Protevangelium (or Proto-Gospel) of James.[72] This text, from the second century, exists in more than 140 Greek manuscripts as well as numerous translations into a variety of languages, mostly Middle Eastern. This speaks to the popularity of this scripture in the Eastern churches. The first part of the Protevangelium gives a long account of Mary, the mother of Jesus, who was born to her parents Joachim and Anna after they had been childless for many years, and who grew up in a prosperous Jewish household. The second part tells of the birth of Jesus and the fact that Mary's virginity remained intact even after this birth. Here the Protevangelium avails itself of the descriptions of Jesus's birth found in the gospels of Matthew and Luke, even quoting certain passages verbatim. It concludes with the story of the audience of the Magi with King Herod and Herod's attempt to have the newborn king of the Jews slain (see Matthew 2:1–18). Both Jesus and John the Baptist, however, are saved from Herod's persecution. In an epilogue, James, the brother of Jesus, announces himself as the author of the work.

The Protevangelium of James had a lasting influence on the reception and interpretation of the birth of Jesus and the events surrounding it, as well as the veneration of Mary, including Marian feast days, in ancient Christianity. This text was the first to mention Mary's parents, and, in addition to emphasizing Mary's continuing virginity, it recounts that Jesus was born in a cave (there is no mention of the manger that appears in Luke's gospel). The text was incorporated into later works called Infancy Gospels and embellished with further traditions. Pictorial representations of the birth and childhood of Jesus have also been heavily influenced by the Protevangelium. Scenes from this work appear, for example, in early mosaics, such as those in the basilica of Santa Maria Maggiore in Rome (ca. 432–440), alongside others from the canonical gospels.

The Protevangelium's firm focus on Mary's virginity suggests that it was written in circumstances where Christianity found itself exposed to polemical assaults on this tradition. Its adoption of traditions concerning Herod's persecution may also reflect a situation of hostility toward Christianity. At the same time, the Protevangelium integrates the birth of Mary and Jesus into the history of Israel and emphasizes the Jewish milieu of Jesus's family.

In spite of its popularity, the Protevangelium was spurned by early Christian theologians. The primary reason for this was that it tapped into a different tradition concerning the siblings of Jesus than the one generally accepted by Western theologians. According to the Protevangelium, Jesus's siblings were the children of Joseph from a former marriage, whereas the common view in the West (as stated most notably by Jerome) was that those who were called the brothers and sisters of Jesus were the children of Mary's sister (another Mary), and so were his cousins. As a result of this rejection, the Protevangelium remained unknown for a long time in the West and was not brought back into circulation there until the sixteenth century, when the French scholar Guillaume Postel brought it back from a trip to the East and translated it into Latin. Postel was also responsible for giving it the title "Protevangelium" ("Pre-Gospel") because he considered it a preface to the Gospel of Mark. The work's original title was "The Birth of Mary," with the subtitle "Revelation of James."

Among the apocryphal gospels that were not included within the New Testament, then, we find: narrative accounts that have a different emphasis from those found in the gospels that did become part of the New Testament;

texts that interpret the ministry and teachings of Jesus as conveying true knowledge about humankind's origins and destiny; and mythologizing accounts that fill in "gaps" in the New Testament gospels, providing details, for instance, about Jesus's birth and childhood. In antiquity, the apocryphal gospels were passed down as individual scriptures, never as collections. The thirteen Nag Hammadi codices represent something of an exception, but these are hardly comparable with the canon of the New Testament. Rather, they are a compilation of very diverse texts that probably never formed the basis of a religious community.

It was by no means a foregone conclusion that from the broad spectrum of Jesus traditions and gospel texts that existed in early Christianity—and of which we have only been able to present a small selection here—it should have been the four gospels according to Matthew, Mark, Luke, and John that made it into the New Testament. It would have been equally possible for just one or two of them, or for other gospels entirely, to have become canonical scriptures. Another conceivable scenario would have been for a selection of Jesus's sayings or a compilation of various different traditions to have been incorporated into the Christian Bible as a single gospel.[73] The fact that there are *four* gospels in the New Testament is the result of developments during which precisely these four texts coalesced into a collection and became "canonical," whereas other gospels were rejected as "heretical" or "counterfeit."

The Evolution of the Group of Four Gospels

One reason why the church has precisely four gospels can be found articulated in the third book of Irenaeus's major work, *On the Refutation and Overthrow of the So-Called Gnosis* (usually referred to as *Against Heresies*), which he wrote in around 180.[74] In it, he takes issue with various "heresies," which in his view make assertions that misrepresent the Christian message as spread by Jesus and his apostles. Irenaeus subsumes these different doctrines under the umbrella term "gnosis" and posits a genealogical relationship among them.[75] These are in fact highly disparate Christian doctrines and tendencies that are not all connected to one another.

In refuting the "heresies," Irenaeus frequently invokes the testimony of Jesus and the apostles. This indicates that the basic outline of the New Testament had come together by this stage. Alongside the four gospels, Irenaeus was familiar with, and quotes from, the books of the later New Testament; he knew of the Acts of the Apostles, the letters of Paul, two letters of John, one letter of Peter, the Letter to the Hebrews and the Letter of James, and the book of Revelation. He also draws special attention to the link between the old and new covenants, which he says were both instituted by the same God.[76] He thus had at his disposal all the requirements needed to identify the "Old Testament" and the "New Testament" together as the basic documents underpinning the Christian faith. Nonetheless, a number of gray areas still remained at this stage, and the "Old Testament" and "New Testament" did not yet constitute physical volumes (let alone a single book) in which the books of the Bible were collected.

In referring to the Gospels, Irenaeus explains why the church has four gospels by first pointing to the four "zones of the world in which we live and four principal winds" (*Against Heresies* 3.11.7–9). What he calls the "fourfold gospel" thus symbolizes the spread of the church throughout the world. Irenaeus was writing this explanation at a time when, in spite of those four gospels being in widespread use among Christian communities, other gospels were in circulation as well, and various Christian doctrines existed that recognized only one of the four. In common with other Christian theologians of this period, Irenaeus was familiar with apocryphal gospels, which he distinguished from those regarded as authoritative by the church.

That the gospels are four in number is likewise an undisputed fact in the works of Clement of Alexandria and Origen. Both writers distinguish these gospels from others that in their view were not authoritative texts, or that they even considered heretical. This is clear from Clement's remark about the Gospel according to the Egyptians (quoted in the previous section), while in his homilies on the Gospel of Luke, Origen notes that the church possesses four gospels, whereas heresy has a great many.[77]

The writings of Eusebius of Caesarea contain an important note regarding the unity of the four gospels. Eusebius maintains that Clement of Alexandria, in his work *Hypotyposes,* stated the following about the sequence of the four gospels: The gospels with genealogies of Jesus (Matthew and Luke) were the first to be written. Mark then responded to requests by those who had heard Peter preach in Rome that his words should be recorded for posterity. Finally, John, acting on his insight that these gospels treated the human nature of Jesus, was guided by the Holy Spirit to compose a "spiritual gospel."[78]

A comparable declaration that the gospels are four in number appears in the Muratorian Fragment.[79] The document to which the fragment belonged is believed to have been written in Rome in around 200. The fragment, which lists the scriptures recognized by the church, gives an overview of their contents, and differentiates them from other, heretical works, was published in 1740 by the Italian scholar Ludovico Antonio Muratori. It takes the form of a (bad) Latin translation from Greek, thought to date from the fourth or fifth century. It is contained in a codex originally from the library of Bobbio Abbey and now held by the Ambrosian Library in Milan.

Alongside the four gospels, the Muratorian Fragment places the letters of Paul and various other scriptures on the church's approved list. The embryonic New Testament as a collection of diverse texts is identifiable from this list; at this stage, however, its exact configuration was not as certain as it would become by the fourth century.

The text of the fragment begins in the middle of a sentence that probably refers to the Gospel of Mark and then goes on to talk about the Gospel of Luke:

> . . . at which nevertheless he was present, and so he placed [them in his narrative]. The third book of the Gospel is that according to Luke. Luke, the well-known physician, after the ascension of Christ, when Paul had taken with him as one zealous for the law, composed it in his own name, according to [the general] belief.[80]

It is probable that the first, incomplete sentence of the fragment stated that Mark did not write his gospel from his own perspective, but instead on the basis of Peter's didactic sermons, "at which . . . he was present." After mentioning the Gospel of Luke, the fragment goes on to describe the Gospel of John. John, the writer claims, wrote down the revelations that were imparted to the apostles after three days of fasting. This statement establishes an awareness that there are differences between the gospels, but that these are irrelevant where the Christian faith is concerned, since the one Spirit informs all of them and sets out the key stages in Jesus's path—his birth, the Passion, his resurrection, his post-resurrection meeting with his disciples, and his first and second coming.

By the turn of the second to the third century, ancient Christian theologians were in agreement that the gospels were four in number. The fact that the Gospels of Matthew, Mark, Luke, and John possessed an internal cohesion had also been established—a vital precept given the clear differences between them—and was being put forward as a feature that distinguished them from other gospels. As we saw in Chapter 1, codices containing multiple gospels are documented from the third century, and one of these, Papyrus 45, even contains all four gospels and the Acts of the Apostles. On the other hand, no manuscript has yet come to light that contains a gospel that later became canonical alongside an apocryphal one. This strongly suggests that by the end of the second century the four gospels were already considered the definitive account of the life of Jesus. But the question still remains: Why these four gospels in particular?

The first thing to note is that these are the oldest of the gospels. They were written in the first century and were known to Christian authors of the second century. Although it cannot be proved incontrovertibly that Marcion and Justin, or the authors of the Second Letter of Clement and the Shepherd of Hermas, knew all four gospels, these authors do all refer to gospels that exist in writing. We cannot always say exactly which gospel or gospels were known to them. They cite sayings of Jesus or episodes from his life that might well derive from the Gospels of Matthew or Luke, though some are hybridized forms of the two. It is possible that they were quoting freely from memory and may sometimes have combined wording of the same episode from two gospels. In any event, written gospels must already have been so widespread that authors in various locations were able to consult or quote from them.

Certain observations apparently made by Papias, bishop of Hierapolis in Asia Minor in around 120, appear to bear out this supposition. No direct testimony by Papias exists, but Eusebius reports that he was the author of five books of "Exegeses of the Words of the Lord" (*Logiôn kyrakiôn exêgêsis*).[81] In these, according to Eusebius, Papias recounted that he asked those who had been personally acquainted with the apostles, including John the Presbyter, what the foundations of the faith were. John the Presbyter also furnished him with information on the creation of Matthew's and Mark's gospels. According to John, Mark had never seen Jesus, nor had he been one of his disciples. But in his capacity as an "interpreter of Peter," he had carefully written up Jesus's sermons from memory, albeit not in order. Matthew, on the other hand, said Papias, had collected Jesus's sermons in Hebrew, which people had then translated, each according to his ability. Eusebius further reports that Papias referred to the testimony provided in the First Letter of John and of Peter and also invoked the episode of a woman who was accused in Jesus's presence of having committed many sins. This latter incident, said Eusebius, was recounted in a text called the Gospel according to the Hebrews, a gospel that probably originated in the second century and is known from several quotations by early Christian authors.

To judge from Eusebius's comments, Papias must have been familiar with at least the Gospels of Mark and Matthew. Yet his observations are rather puzzling. It is not clear, for example, what his critical note about Mark not recording Peter's sermons "in the correct sequence" refers to. Some commentators have assumed that Papias was measuring Mark's gospel against the Gospel of John, which he may have gotten to know in Asia Minor.[82] In that case, he would have been familiar with three of the gospels that were later included in the New Testament. However, this is by no means certain, and Papias's remark may simply refer to the nature of Mark's gospel, which Papias did not consider a strictly chronological account of the ministry of Jesus. There is certainly no proof that Papias knew the Gospel of John.

The comment concerning the Gospel of Matthew is also remarkable. This gospel was definitely not originally written in Hebrew. It is unclear where Papias obtained such information or whether it was meant to convey something about the nature of Matthew's gospel, such as a particular closeness to Jewish texts and traditions. The remark was taken up by Irenaeus, who noted that Matthew "produced a Gospel for the Hebrews in their language." Finally, the note about Papias and the Gospel according to the Hebrews is also somewhat opaque. Eusebius's remark could be taken to mean that Papias knew something called a "Gospel according to the Hebrews" and took from it the episode about Jesus and the adulteress, which also appears as a late addition in the Gospel of John.[83] But it is also possible—and indeed even more likely—that Papias knew the episode of Jesus and the adulteress and it was Eusebius who expanded upon this by adding, ". . . which is found in the Gospel according to the Hebrews." In this case it would have been Eusebius himself who assigned the episode recounted by Papias (who most likely passed it on without ascribing it to a particular gospel) to the Gospel according to the

Hebrews. The fact that this episode was passed down elsewhere besides the Gospel of John is also attested by Didymus the Blind (fourth century). Didymus notes that the story is found "in certain gospels." Accordingly, the remark in Eusebius may be construed as putting readers on the track of finding the episode in the Gospel of the Hebrews. But we cannot deduce from this with any certainty that Papias knew that gospel.

Another reason why it is these four gospels that are recognized by the church is that they stand in a literary relationship to one another. Today it is widely believed that the authors of the Gospels of Matthew and Luke knew and used the Gospel of Mark, along with other common traditions that were available to them—at least in part—in written form. According to this viewpoint, these three gospels derive from a common tradition. The Gospel of John is based on its own set of traditions, but, at least at a later stage of transmission, it does display some knowledge of the Synoptic Gospels.[84] In its linguistic and textual configuration, the Gospel of John presents itself as an authoritative, "biblical" account of the importance of Jesus and of his relationship to God and his ministry in the world. Even the opening phrase, "In the beginning was the Word," echoes the opening of Genesis: "In the beginning, God created the heavens and the earth." It may also be an allusion to the first lines of the Gospel of Mark: "The beginning of the good news about Jesus the Messiah." The Gospel of John thus lays claim to presenting information about Jesus in the form of a mature, well-considered portrayal that effectively perfects other accounts in both literary and theological terms.

In the early second century a supplementary chapter (chapter 21) was appended to the Gospel of John. This added a codicil and a second conclusion to the original end of the text (20:30–31). The appendix recounts further post-resurrection appearances by Jesus; these no longer take place in Jerusalem but in Galilee. Scenes in which the disciples net a large haul of fish in the Sea of Galilee and in which they and Jesus have a meal together repurpose older traditions into stories of Jesus's appearance. In addition, a dialogue between Jesus and Peter emphasizes the latter's role as the "shepherd" to Jesus's "lambs." Peter, who appears in the Synoptic Gospels as the leading figure of the twelve apostles, thereby attains a special authority in the Gospel of John, as well. The preceding chapters of John's gospel referred to an unidentified "beloved disciple" who was the closest to Jesus. Also, at the end of chapter 21, it is the "disciple whom Jesus loved" who "testifies to these things" that have been recounted in the foregoing gospel. Now, in the supplement to chapter 21, Peter, as the "shepherd" of the flock, stands alongside the beloved disciple. In this way, the Gospel of John is marked out as the concluding testimony to the person of Jesus, his earthly ministry, and his role as the revelator of God in the world. At the same time, its connections to the Synoptic Gospels are strengthened, so that the Gospel of John appears as the consummation of the witness to Jesus's ministry on earth.

In the first half of the second century, a series of concluding episodes were also added to the Gospel of Mark. In two of the most important early Bible manuscripts, the Codex Sinaiticus and the Codex Vaticanus, as well as in a number of other translations, Mark's gospel ends with the women fleeing when they find Jesus's tomb empty, "for they were afraid" (Mark 16:8). Most Bible manuscripts contain the "longer," or "canonical," ending to the Gospel of Mark (16:9–20). This text was known to Irenaeus and Tatian of Adiabene and must therefore have been added to the gospel at an early date. There also exists a "shorter" ending to Mark, though it is only found in a Latin codex dating from the fourth or fifth century, the Codex Bobbiensis (now held by the Biblioteca Nazionale in Turin). Some manuscripts even pass down both endings, the shorter and the longer, in succession. Finally, a gospel manuscript from the fifth century, the Codex Washingtonianus, also transmits within the longer ending (between verses 14 and 15) an additional dialogue between the disciples and Jesus, called the "Freer logion" (after Charles Freer, who purchased the codex in Egypt in the early twentieth century). Jerome was already familiar with this expanded version.

Unlike in the case of John 21, the different endings to Mark's gospel have only a superficial linguistic and textual connection to the gospel itself. The shorter conclusion recounts that the women told everything that the angel at the tomb had commanded them to report to "those around Peter." The longer ending tells of several appearances by Jesus: to Mary Magdalene, to two of his disciples as they walked along a country road, and finally before the eleven disciples. Jesus tasks them with spreading the gospel to all creation and baptizing believers, and is then taken up to heaven. This conclusion links the Gospel of Mark with the accounts of Jesus's post-resurrection appearances in the other gospels.

The endings must have been added to the Gospel of Mark because without them it concludes in a somewhat puzzling way. It is ultimately a moot point whether the remark about the women being afraid really was the original ending, or whether the ending was lost, or indeed whether Mark's gospel, for whatever reason, ended as a fragment. In any event, as a result of both of these appended endings, the gospel concludes in a way that is compatible with the other gospels. In the longer ending, elements of the other gospels' conclusions—Jesus's appearances, his instruction to spread the faith, his ascension, and his mention of the disciples proclaiming the Word and of the Lord working with them—are all joined together in a totality that is found in none of the other gospels.

Both John 21 and the addition to Mark indicate that the literary and textual interconnections between the four gospels were strengthened at a very early stage. At the same time, the differences between them were played down. Nonetheless, each gospel retains its own individual character.

Another way of linking the four gospels closer together was to combine them into a single narrative. This strategy was adopted in the Diatessaron (*día tessárôn* means from or through four), a work of around 170 CE by the Syrian theologian Tatian, which was intended to supplant the four individual gospels. And that is indeed what happened in the Syrian church. Up to the fifth century, in this branch of Christianity the Diatessaron rather than the four gospels constituted the section of the New Testament recounting the ministry of Jesus.

This combining of the gospels into a single narrative remained an isolated instance; in the evolution of the New Testament, the juxtaposition of the four gospels prevailed. Setting them alongside each other accentuated their commonalities, one of which was their shared dissimilarity to other gospels that did not become part of the canon. In addition, the differences between them were diminished during the history of their exegesis and impact, not least because they were read, interpreted, and illustrated together as a unit.

From an early period, the four gospels were widely disseminated throughout Christian communities. Regardless of their differences, they were understood as bearing common witness to Christ's ministry. This is the sense of Irenaeus's phrase "fourfold gospel." The phrase is important for the evolution of the New Testament in two ways: first, it means that no other gospels have the same status as these four; and second, it emphasizes that the four gospels have the force of an authoritative testament to Jesus when read together, and that they should not be played off against one another.

The rejection of other gospels did not necessarily have to do with their content. Some early Christian theologians give the impression that they did not have a very deep knowledge of these works. The reasons for their repudiation are presumably many and varied. And yet despite this rejection, at least some of these gospels—especially the Infancy Gospels—have played an important role in the history of Christian devotion. Other gospels that were decried as heretical have disappeared altogether from the collective memory of Christianity. They only re-entered people's consciousness as a result of discoveries of texts and new text editions beginning in the last decades of the nineteenth century.

Marcion and the Letters of Paul

Alongside the Gospels, and independently of them, the second important section of the later New Testament also took shape. This section is called the Corpus Paulinum, a term denoting a collection of fourteen letters, thirteen of which carry the name of Paul. The fourteenth, the Letter to the Hebrews, is anonymous, but it was included in the letters of Paul and was incorporated into the New Testament alongside the others. Not all of the letters that bear Paul's name were actually written by him. Most scholars believe that only seven of the thirteen "letters of Paul" were authored by him: the Letter to the Romans, the two letters to the Corinthians, the Letter to the Galatians, the Letter to the Philippians, the First Letter to the Thessalonians, and the Letter to Philemon. The remaining six are judged to be pseudepigraphic writings. This distinction played no part in the emergence of collections of Paul's letters, however, and in all likelihood was not even known about at the time they came into being.

Almost all of the letters of Paul are addressed to Christian communities that he established. One letter is addressed to an individual (Philemon), while the Letter to the Romans, Paul's final letter, is written to Christian communities in Rome that Paul did not himself found. The letters are evidence of his missionary activity. They reinforce the link between Paul and his communities, address problems that have arisen in setting up the faith communities, develop an ethical way of living in accord with a belief in Jesus Christ, and reflect upon what God's revelation in the Gospels means for Israel and other nations.

The person and theology of Paul became highly influential in the regions where he conducted his mission—western Asia Minor, Greece, and Rome. This is evident from the fact that letters were written in his name that exploit his authority and update his theology. Prime examples of such works are the Pastoral Letters: the two letters to Timothy and the Letter to Titus. These letters are based on a twofold fiction, whereby "Paul" supposedly writes to his two fellow missionaries "Timothy" and "Titus," figures who were already familiar from his own letters and (in the case of Timothy) also from the Acts of the Apostles. These letters, however, were most likely not written until the first third of the second century. They treat questions relating to the organization of the communities—namely the roles of the bishop, elders, and deacons—and promulgate the Christian faith as a "heritage" to be nurtured and preserved.[85] The principal aim of these letters is to strengthen the Christian faith and reinforce the local church structure in Paul's mission area (Timothy is said to live in Ephesus, and Titus either on Crete or in Dalmatia). This is achieved through instructions issued by "Paul" to his colleagues. Paul is therefore the sole source of authority in the Pastoral Letters, which make no mention of other apostles.

The Letter to the Ephesians is also a pseudepigraphic letter of Paul. It was written at the turn of the first century and may not ever have been directed toward Ephesus, given that the title identifying the addressees ("To the Ephesians") is missing in many of the most significant manuscripts. It is categorized as one of Paul's "general" letters. It interprets Paul's theology as forming the basis for Christian communities comprising Jews and Gentiles and stresses that the church was built on the foundations of the apostles and the prophets, that Christ is its cornerstone, and that its community includes evangelists, shepherds, and teachers (Ephesians 2:20, 4:11). The church is the great abiding theme of the Letter to the Ephesians, which in consequence has also been called a "treatise on the church." The church is made up of two parts, the Gentiles and Israel; Christ has broken down the fence between them, with the result that the Gentiles, too, are now "fellow citizens with the saints and members of the household of God" (Ephesians 2:19).

The Pastoral Letters and the Letter to the Ephesians demonstrate how Paul's missionary activity and theology were picked up and profitably adapted for later circumstances. At the same time, the Paul of the New Testament must be distinguished from the historical Paul. The updating of his theology (alongside the letters mentioned, the Letter to the Colossians and 2

Thessalonians may be cited in this regard) and the appeal to his authority in establishing church organizational structures, but also the account of his conversion, his missionary journeys, and his detention and interrogation as recounted in the Acts of the Apostles, all form part of the authoritative testimony of Paul, and were treated as such in early Christianity.

References to the letters of Paul are also found elsewhere. The First Letter of Clement, the Second Letter of Peter, and the works of Ignatius and Polycarp, from the late first and second centuries, draw on the testimony of Paul and display a knowledge of several of his letters. It is not possible in every case to determine exactly which letters are being referred to. What is clear, though, is that Paul's testimony is by this stage beginning to be distilled down as a coherent corpus made up of multiple letters. This process would by no means have been self-evident, since the majority of Paul's letters were written to individual communities and sometimes treated very specific matters of contention between Paul and those communities. Notwithstanding this feature, from an early stage, Paul's statements were seen as fundamental in establishing the nature of the Christian message and the configuration of Christian communities. They were doubtless also intended as such by Paul himself.

By the mid-second century, many of Paul's letters were well known, at least in certain localities. It is evident that copies were made of them and disseminated to communities that were not the original intended recipients. It may be that a practice encouraged in the Letter to the Colossians played a part in this development: "After this letter has been read to you, see that it is also read in the church of the Laodiceans and that you in turn read the letter from Laodicea" (4:16).

Collections of Paul's letters appear prominently in the work of Marcion. Marcion was an early Christian teacher who came from Sinope in the region of Pontus on the Black Sea and was active in Rome in around 140.[86] He succeeded in attracting a large group of followers and founding communities of his own. For early Christian theologians, Marcion represented serious competition, since he was spreading his own teachings, which were at odds with those of the emerging Christian church. Marcion played a key role in the evolution of the collection of Paul's letters—and indeed of the New Testament as a whole—because he was actively engaged in compiling a written collection of the letters of Paul. He regarded these writings, together with a version of the Gospel of Luke, as the foundation of the Christian faith. Marcion's work therefore raised the question of the precise form in which Paul's letters should be read and interpreted.

Marcion also drew up a collection of Jesus traditions and apostolic testimonies, thereby anticipating to a great extent the shape of the later New Testament. He occupied a central place in the story of the evolution of the New Testament canon well into the twentieth century.[87]

Marcion's principal activity was as a philological and theological interpreter of the letters of Paul and the Gospels. This fact needs to be emphasized because for a long time he was seen as an arch-heretic who had set the Christian message against the Old Testament, repudiating the latter and so casting doubt on Christianity's roots in the history of Israel and Judaism.

Both of these contentions—that Marcion played a significant part in the emergence of the New Testament canon, and that he questioned the Jewish roots of Christianity—are not without foundation, but neither are they easy to substantiate, given that not a single text by Marcion has survived. A profile of his person and writings has to be pieced together from other sources. This task is methodologically challenging and calls for diligence and circumspection, because Marcion's views were fiercely opposed by early Christian theologians. Marcion must not be judged from the perspective of an already existing New Testament, any more than the strident attacks on him by early Christian theologians should be ascribed to a considered judgment of his aims and methods. Rather, Marcion's intentions must be understood against the background of circumstances prevailing around the mid-second century, when the key questions regarding the formation of Christian theology and of an authoritative collection of Christian scriptures were still open.

Marcion apparently had access to a collection of ten letters of Paul (excluding the Pastoral Letters), as well as the Gospel of Luke. Why this gospel in particular should have formed the basis of his reconstruction is no longer possible to determine. Through his philological work on these texts, he tried to restore their original form. He was convinced that the gospel proclaimed by Luke was incompatible with the law of the Old Testament. The message of Jesus that formed the basis of the gospel was not, he contended, the proclamation of the God of Israel. Instead, Jesus had proclaimed a different, higher deity, who was also the subject of the gospel proclaimed by Paul. Marcion believed that both the message of Jesus and the letters of Paul had been misconstrued from the outset. Jesus's disciples had, he maintained, interpreted his proclamation according to their understanding in light of the scriptures of Israel, and none of the apostles except Paul had properly understood the gospel. In consequence, both the message of Jesus and the gospel proclaimed by Paul had been misinterpreted and handed down in a corrupted form. Marcion's aim was to sweep away the falsifying textual emendations and additions and so uncover the original gospel of Jesus and its interpretation by Paul.

Marcion's approach to Jesus and Paul posed a direct challenge to other theologians of the second and third centuries. Their frequent and sustained assaults on his theology bear witness to the threat he posed. His most outspoken opponent was Tertullian, who devoted five books with the title *Adversus Marcionem* ("Against Marcion") to refuting his position. Both Tertullian and Irenaeus accused Marcion of treating Paul's testimony in isolation and playing it off against that of the other apostles. By contrast, they stressed the consistent testimony offered by all four gospels, Paul's integration into the fellowship of the apostles, and the fact that faith in Jesus Christ and faith in the God of Israel were indivisible.

Marcion played an important part in the formation of the New Testament and the Christian Bible as a whole because he compelled other Christian theologians to respond to the question of which texts the church should base its teachings upon, and to carefully consider how the scriptures it saw as authoritative fit together and cohered internally. And finally, Marcion's views also raised the question of how the Old and New Testaments related to each another.

Yet it was not Marcion who came up with the concept of a "New Testament."[88] The connection between the Jesus tradition and the apostolic testimonies is already found in Luke's two-part work (his gospel and the Acts of the Apostles).[89] What is more, leaving Marcion aside, by the first half of the second century the process of combining the gospels and the letters of Paul was already underway. Even without Marcion's input, a body of canonical scriptures would have emerged in contradistinction to other, apocryphal, writings and in conjunction with the formation of the Christian creed (the *regula fidei*).

The Muratorian Fragment also enumerates the letters of Paul. It begins by naming his letters to the Corinthians, Galatians, and Romans and then goes on to provide a more comprehensive list of Pauline letters. According to the fragment's author, Paul, like John before him (the John of the book of Revelation, that is), wrote to a total of seven communities—the Corinthians, the Ephesians, the Philippians, the Colossians, the Galatians, the Thessalonians, and the Romans. He then wrote a second time to the Corinthians and the Thessalonians. The Muratorian Fragment also names the letters to Philemon and Titus and the two letters to Timothy. It deems the letters to the Laodiceans and the Alexandrians to be counterfeit.

These references in the Muratorian Fragment reveal that several different variants of the sequence and number of Paul's authentic letters were in circulation. The first group of letters it cites is a chronological listing: Paul, it claims, wrote the letter to the Corinthians first, then the one to the Galatians, and finally the one to the Romans. The fragment also provides a brief thumbnail sketch of the letters' contents. The second listing is governed by the principle of the seven communities, which symbolize the church's presence throughout the entire known world. Apparently inspired by the seven letters that appear in the book of Revelation, it bases its list of Paul's letters on the number seven as the quintessential symbol of completeness, and in so doing expressly relates these two texts to one another.[90] Paul, the fragment suggests, followed the arrangement of his predecessor John; with their sets of seven writings, both directed their message toward the church worldwide.

The Muratorian Fragment thus gives us an interesting insight into the genesis of the New Testament canon. The four gospels, the Acts of the Apostles, and the letters of Paul are accepted scriptures of the church. The author of the fragment attributes the book of Revelation, or Apocalypse of John, to the writer of John's gospel—and then proceeds to mention the Revelations (Apocalypses) of John and Peter by name. Of these works, the writer of the fragment states that some people did not want the Apocalypse of Peter (a Christian apocalypse that was composed in the second century) to be read aloud in church. He then goes on to name a letter of Jude and two letters of John, which he once again identifies with the author of the Gospel of John. Intriguingly, he also mentions the Wisdom of Solomon among the New Testament writings. Of the Shepherd of Hermas, he claims that it is permissible to read this writing, though not publicly in church.

What these passages from the Muratorian Fragment demonstrate is that several gray areas existed regarding the extent of texts accepted by the church.

This is why its author feels a need at various points to justify the inclusion of particular texts. For instance, he is at pains to stress the unified testimony of the four gospels as well as the fact that the letters of Paul, while addressed to specific communities or individuals, were at the same time thought to apply to the whole church. To back up his assertions, the author puts forward his theory about the seven letters—though this sits uneasily with his earlier chronological listing of the letters and also fails to take account of the letters to Philemon, Timothy, and Titus. The Muratorian Fragment does not underpin its theory about the seven letters by pointing to the seven Catholic Letters, though this would have been an obvious analogy to draw. The only possible explanation for this omission is that the author of the Muratorian Fragment was still unaware of such a collection of letters, as distinct from those written by Paul. This would also explain why he only cites the letters of Jude and John and says nothing about the letters of Peter and James.

Another important document corroborating the existence of an early collection of Paul's letters is Papyrus 46 (see Chapter 1). This codex, which was written at around the same time as the Muratorian Fragment, was originally 104 pages long, of which 86 have survived. It is believed to have contained ten (or possibly eleven) letters of Paul.[91] They were evidently arranged according to their length, beginning with the Letter to the Romans. The Letter to the Hebrews, which is anonymous and about whose origins there was no clear consensus in early Christianity, occupied second place, so it must have been incorporated into the New Testament as part of the collection of Paul's letters. Yet for a long time, its inclusion in this collection—and hence in the emerging New Testament—was far from certain. The Muratorian Fragment does not name the Letter to the Hebrews, and a degree of uncertainty exists among other early Christian theologians over the authorship of this letter. Clement of Alexandria attributes it to Paul but notes that Luke translated it into Greek.[92] Tertullian claims that Paul's fellow missionary Barnabas wrote the letter, while Origen takes the view that, while the opinions expressed in the letter were certainly Paul's, the phraseology and style of writing show it to be the work of someone who has memorized the apostle's teachings.[93] Origen therefore concludes that it may well be counted as a Pauline letter, though God alone knows who actually wrote it.[94]

These remarks indicate that the Letter to the Hebrews was considered a foundational text of Christian theology by dint of its content. The letter's highly sophisticated interpretation—based on an intensive exegesis of the Septuagint—of Jesus Christ's trajectory from pre-existing Son of God to earthly High Priest was largely responsible for this assessment. Hebrews expounds the idea that Christ died to expiate humanity's sins for all time and that his death is therefore analogous to the sacrifices of Israel, which thereby reached their conclusion. Though the linguistic and conceptual world of Hebrews is unequivocally not that of Paul, it is possible to discern certain affinities here with Pauline theology. Moreover, the mention of Paul's fellow missionary Timothy at the end of the Letter to the Hebrews (13:23) creates a personal connection to Paul. Papyrus 46 provides evidence that Hebrews already formed part of the collection of Paul's letters by the early third century. However, it took until the fourth century for it to be fully integrated into the canon of New Testament scriptures.

The Formation of the New Testament Corpus

The collections of the four gospels and of the letters of Paul formed the basic core of the evolving New Testament. Each of these originally belonged to its own realm of tradition within Christianity, but before long they were connected to each other. Even so, for a long time the exact contours of the New Testament canon remained ill-defined. Around this body of authoritative scriptures, other "apostolic letters" besides those of Paul kept appearing, in particular letters by Peter and John and also by James and Jude. In the second century, though, these letters did not as yet constitute a body of work on a par with the Gospels and the letters of Paul. The Muratorian Fragment cites the letters of Jude and John by name, while Eusebius mentions that Papias referred to testimony provided in the first letters of John and Peter. Eusebius also notes that Origen was familiar with a widely recognized letter of Peter, though the authenticity of a second letter supposedly by the same author was in doubt. Likewise, according to Eusebius, John, the writer of the gospel and the book of Revelation, was also the author of a letter, though a second and third letter of John were not universally acknowledged as genuine. The Letters of James and Jude are mentioned in Eusebius, and the Muratorian Fragment contains a reference to the Letter of Jude.

The rubric "Catholic Letters," under which seven letters were ultimately incorporated into the New Testament (two letters of Peter and three of John, plus the letters of James and Jude), appears for the first time in Eusebius.[95] He remarks at one point that James, the brother of Jesus, whose story he has just recounted, was the author of the first of the Catholic Letters, but that it was widely held to be counterfeit. The Letter of Jude, Eusebius continues, also belongs to this group of letters. Both were read out publicly in most communities.[96] At another point, Eusebius notes that Clement, in his *Hypotyposes*, gives an account of the complete scripture (that is, the whole Bible), excluding the texts that were rejected: the Letter of Jude, the remaining Catholic Letters, the Letter of Barnabas, and the Apocalypse of Peter.[97] Cyril of Jerusalem, writing in the fourth century, names seven Catholic Letters, together with the four gospels, the Acts of the Apostles, and fourteen letters of Paul.[98]

Clearly, then, the corpus of the Catholic Letters did not evolve until later.[99] This is evident from the fact that Eusebius only counts one letter each of Peter and John among the canonical scriptures, while consigning the other five to the disputed texts.[100] There are a number of reasons why these five—the Second and Third Letters of John, the Second Letter of Peter, and the Letters of James and Jude—finally made it into the Bible. One such reason may well be the literary connections between individual letters. For instance, the two "small" letters of John (the second and third) share the same sender (the "Presbyter," or "elder"), the Second Letter of Peter presupposes the Letter of Jude and explicitly calls itself the "second letter" of Peter (2 Peter 3:1), and the Letter of Jude refers to James in its prologue and claims to have been written by his brother—that is, another brother of Jesus. These connections must have played a part in the compilation of these letters, acting as it were as mutual "bonds of attraction." In addition, there are of course many links between the all of the letters of John, as well as between the two letters of Peter.

Another reason why these letters coalesced into a unit may be that they were seven in number. As we have already seen from the Muratorian Fragment, the number seven was applied to the letters of the book of Revelation and to the letters of Paul (despite the latter not actually numbering seven). This suggests that the number seven was believed to symbolize completeness in the case of the Catholic Letters too, all the more so because that also implied that they were of significance for the church as a whole. The term "catholic," or general, is also to be understood in this sense, though it hardly does justice to the letters' content.

One final factor which may have influenced the inclusion of these letters in the New Testament was that they augmented the testimony of the Pauline letters—notwithstanding that they were all, without exception, pseudepigraphic writings. The attraction of this approach was that it made the apostles Paul, James, Peter, John (and also Jude) all appear as common witnesses to the Christian faith. There is a strong indication that the Catholic Letters really did perform this function, in that in the majority of New Testament manuscripts they were combined with the Acts of the Apostles, and together with this text formed a third group of scriptures alongside the Gospels and Paul's letters. The running order in these manuscripts can vary: the Gospels may be followed by the Acts of the Apostles and the Catholic Letters, and then the Pauline letters. But another sequence also sometimes appears: Gospels, Pauline letters, Acts of the Apostles plus Catholic Letters. The customary running order nowadays—Gospels, Acts, Pauline letters, Catholic Letters—is seldom found in antiquity and the Middle Ages. The only complete anomaly is in Lutheran Bibles, which separate the Letter to the Hebrews from the rest of the Pauline letters; because Luther considered Hebrews, James, Jude, and the book of Revelation to be "disputed books," he separated them off and placed them at the end of his New Testament in an appendix. Luther thus de facto dissolved the corpus of the Catholic Letters and created his own sequence of biblical books on the basis of their content.

The Christian Bible of Old and New Testaments

What, then, was the process by which individual texts or collections of texts coalesced into the "New Testament" and ultimately into the Christian Bible, comprising the Old and New Testaments? In early Christianity, there was no book containing the Gospels, the letters of Paul, and other writings that was circulated under the title "New Testament" and read in Christian communities—let alone any question of these texts already having been combined with those of the "Old Testament."

A typical Christian community of the second or third century may well have possessed a manuscript containing the Gospel of Matthew and the Gospel of Luke, another with a scripture entitled "The Birth of Mary" (the Protevangelium of James), the letters of Paul to the Romans, Corinthians, and Ephesians, a copy of the First Letters of Peter and John, a manuscript of the Acts of the Apostles, one of the *Didache,* and one of the Shepherd of Hermas. But in another community, the stock of scriptures might have looked very different. There, a Gospel of John and a Gospel of Peter may have been available, along with some of the letters of Paul, and the Apocalypses of John and Peter. So, to begin with, the "New Testament" was not a book, but rather a designation for those texts that bore authoritative witness to a faith in Jesus Christ. In answer to the question of exactly which texts those were, you would have received a variety of answers in the second century—all depending upon where you were and who you asked.

This situation was reflected in the scriptures' material appearance. The "Old Testament" and "New Testament" took the form of individual codices or scrolls containing, say, the Pentateuch, the book of Isaiah, one or two (or in some cases even all four) gospels, and ten or fourteen of the letters of Paul. Accordingly, "Old Testament" and "New Testament" were for a long time simply content-related labels for the scriptures of Israel and the testimony to the Christian faith before they became the names for the collections of the respective books. The principal reason that the four gospels, the letters of Paul, the Acts of the Apostles, the Catholic Letters, and the book of Revelation coalesced into the "New Testament" is that these texts were seen as providing definitive evidence of the ministry of Jesus and the apostles for the Christian faith.

Hence, a key element in the emergence of the New Testament was a clear conception of what constituted the essence of the Christian faith. This essence was encapsulated in the "rule of faith," which represented a yardstick or guiding principle according to which Christians should live their lives. It also determined how the authoritative scriptures of Christianity—the Old and New Testament alike—were to be interpreted. This "rule" is a topic that is frequently addressed by theologians of the second and early third centuries, such as Irenaeus, Clement of Alexandria, and Tertullian. (The Greek word for it is *kanôn,* and the Latin *regula;* it is often more narrowly defined as the "rule of truth," "rule of faith," or "church rule.") The rule is not a strictly formulated creed or specific dogmatic regulation, but rather summarizes the essential elements of the Christian faith, which can manifest themselves in a variety of ways.

The rule of faith was the criterion by which an orthodox Christian interpretation of biblical scripture was established and defended, in contrast to both Judaism, which invoked its own scriptures in its own way, and other

Christian positions. Even as relatively early a Christian theologian as Justin, who admittedly did not invoke any "rule of faith," developed a hermeneutic reading of the Old Testament from a Christian perspective. He remarks that "the prophets veiled what they said and did in parables and types" (*Dialogue with Trypho* 90.2). In this way, Justin claims, they concealed the truth of the words they spoke so that those who wished to discover it and learn from it would have to exert themselves to do so. The hermeneutic rule that scripture presents God's revelation in the form of riddles is also found in the work of Clement of Alexandria. According to Clement, this served the purpose of leading people toward a precise understanding of divine mysteries, which were not merely self-evident.[101]

In discussing the rule of faith as "an organic system or framework which constitutes the shape and the meaning of God's revelation," Irenaeus also defends an orthodox Christian reading of the scriptures of the old and new covenants against the gnostic exegeses of the Valentinians (disciples of the second-century theologian Valentinus, who were considered heretical).[102] In the passage of his work which treats this topic, *Against Heresies,* Irenaeus's principal concern is to show that the numerological speculations of his adversaries have no basis in Scripture.[103] Like Justin, Irenaeus notes that the prophets "spoke many things in parables and allegories and not in accordance with the actual wording." As regards his own interpretation of Scripture, Irenaeus appeals to the "rule of truth" and works this up into a doctrine concerning a proper understanding of Scripture. He is well aware that parables are ambiguous and admit of many different interpretations. Precisely because of this, he says, we must follow certain procedures in order to arrive at correct interpretations. The first requirement is to start with the clear, unambiguous passages of Scripture and proceed from there to solve the parables. Second, we must take the structure and the context of the text into account if we want to get to the truth. Irenaeus makes reference to the "parables of the Lord, the sayings of the prophets, and the words of the Apostles"—a direct appeal, in other words, to the testament of Jesus, the prophetic writings of the old covenant, and the testimony provided by the Acts of the Apostles and the letters. Third, we must observe the rule of truth if we are to recognize the Word of God in Scripture.[104]

Elsewhere—albeit without using the actual terms themselves—Irenaeus summarizes what he understands the substance of the rule of faith to be: belief in the one God, the Father Almighty, who made heaven and earth and the sea and all things that are in them; belief in the one Christ Jesus, the Son of God, who became incarnate for our salvation; and belief in the Holy Spirit, which proclaimed through the prophets the dispensations of God and the advent of Christ Jesus, our Lord. There follows a long disquisition on Jesus Christ, his birth, sufferings, resurrection, ascension to heaven, and return in the glory of the Father.[105]

This rule of faith, which was subsequently reformulated as the Apostolic Creed (as well as the Niceno-Constantinopolitan Creed), clearly states that the scriptures of Christianity are to be interpreted on the basis of faith in the one God, the creator of all things, who revealed himself in Jesus Christ and who acts in the world through his Spirit.[106] This rule therefore confers on the biblical scriptures, for all their differences, an internal consistency and distinguishes them from those texts that do not conform to this rule. At the same time, the rule of faith ensures the unity of the Old and New Testaments, inasmuch as the scriptures of the Old Testament are understood to be prophetic texts allusively prefiguring Christ. The characterization of these scriptures, already evident in the New Testament, as prophecy that has come true in the person of Jesus Christ thus becomes the hermeneutic basis of the connection between the Old and New Testaments.

The emergence of the New Testament and—in parallel with this—the rule of faith presupposes that the Christian church exists as an entity comprising a multitude of individual congregations at various different locations while simultaneously existing as a wider, overarching community. This idea finds eloquent expression in Irenaeus's phrase "fourfold gospel," symbolizing the church's global reach, and in the image of the seven communities in the Muratorian Fragment, a notion based on the seven supposed letters of both John and Paul.

Accordingly, the formation of the New Testament cannot be ascribed to the resolution of a church synod or a directive issued by a council of bishops. There were no such resolutions or directives. Listings of scriptures, which start to resemble the eventual complement of Christian Bibles only from the fourth century on, instead hark back to developments whose beginnings can be traced all the way back to the writing of the New Testament scriptures themselves. In light of this, the pronouncements of theologians and bishops of the second through the fourth centuries may be thought of as attempts to sharpen the dividing lines between accepted, canonical texts and rejected, apocryphal ones. These borderlines had been porous for quite some time and remained so even after the biblical canon began to take clearer shape. It becomes clear from both the codices of this period and the pronouncements of Christian theologians that this process resulted in the New and Old Testament together becoming the Christian Bible.[107]

Various factors thus combined to produce the particular configuration of the New Testament that became the authoritative standard in Christian churches:

- The Gospels and the Pauline letters laid claim to embodying the definitive form of the witness of Jesus and the Gospel of Jesus Christ.
- Early Christian theologians used these scriptures as testimonies to the origins of the Christian faith.
- In theological disputes with Judaism and with Christian doctrines that were seen as heretical, these scriptures were interpreted, updated, and formed into collections.
- The scriptures were used in public worship and private study.
- The witness of the apostles was augmented by additional apostolic letters and the Acts of the Apostles.
- Finally, the book of Revelation was accepted into the canon as a piece of early Christian apocalyptic literature.

During this process, there were for a long time no clearly defined borders between canonical and noncanonical texts. Thus, it was unclear whether certain texts, such as the Second and Third Letters of John, the Second Letter of Peter, and the Letter of James, should be incorporated into the New Testament. Texts like the Shepherd of Hermas, the *Didache,* and the Apocalypse of Peter, which were later rejected, circulated within the same environment as texts that were ultimately included in the canon. Although it was decried within Christianity as a heretical text, the Protevangelium of James was extremely popular and widely disseminated. The New Testament could therefore have taken quite a different form than it did—with fewer, more, or totally different texts than the ones which eventually made up the canon. The term "canon" only came to be applied to the authoritative texts of Christianity in the fourth century.

There are several reasons why "complete Bibles" containing the Old and New Testaments started to appear in the fourth century. Christianity's position changed radically at the start of that century, after the Roman state ceased its persecution of Christians and Roman emperors granted Christians religious freedom and even began to actively promote Christianity and made it the official religion of the empire.[108] It then became possible to produce large codices holding the text of the entire Christian Bible. Even in their external appearance, these codices differ fundamentally from those of the second and third centuries. They are elaborately crafted luxury volumes, with no expense or artistry spared in their production.[109] Their lavish appearance expressed not least the vested interest of the Roman state in promoting Christianity as a religion that would lend new cohesion to the empire.

These fourth- and fifth-century codices use the text of the Septuagint for the Old Testament (making them the oldest Christian manuscripts of the Old Testament). Since they additionally contain the Greek New Testament, they are Christian "complete Bibles" in Greek. Where the Old Testament is concerned, they reflect the extent of the Septuagint—in other words, they also include those books that were not originally written in Hebrew. Even so, ancient theologians were clearly aware of the difference in extent between the twenty-two or twenty-four books with a Hebrew origin and the wider inventory of texts found in the Septuagint (see Chapter 1). The boundaries between the narrower "Hebrew" and the wider "Greek" Old Testament canon were fluid, whereas the New Testament canon was firmly established from the fourth century on.

The canonical scriptures also display a fluid boundary where the noncanonical texts of ancient Christianity are concerned. As noted earlier, the Codex Sinaiticus contains the Letter of Barnabas and the Shepherd of Hermas at the end of the manuscript, after the scriptures of the New Testament, while the Codex Alexandrinus contains the Letters of Clement. Other noncanonical texts, like the Protevangelium of James, found widespread acceptance among Christians, though sometimes they were confined to certain regions. Some other texts vanished entirely, presumably because they were barely read anymore and so were no longer being copied and disseminated. The thirteen codices found at Nag Hammadi in 1945 gather together a large number of such writings, which were evidently used by Christian groups for a while but were then dropped from the stock of literature used in the mainstream Christian church after being judged heretical.

Even today, then, there is no hard-and-fast dividing line between canonical and noncanonical, or biblical and nonbiblical, texts—even though the printing of Bibles might give this impression. The canonical scriptures have thus, to borrow a very apposite phrase of Dieter Lührmann's, "*become* canonical," in the same way that at least some of the apocryphal texts first "*became* apocryphal" before being rejected by ancient theologians as counterfeit or heretical.[110] Noncanonical texts have always formed the literary environment of the canonical scriptures. In this capacity, they serve to highlight both the social and the theological contexts in which the distinctions between different groups of scriptures arose.

Although the impression has been created, since the invention of printing, that "the Bible" is a precisely defined body of scriptures, this impression is soon dispelled when one looks at how the Bible came into being. Perhaps the increasing use of texts in digital form will help us move away from the image of a defined corpus of scriptures set in stone and toward one that is more flexible.

7

The Jewish Bible, the Mishnah,
and the Talmud

The Completion of the Ketuvim

Within Judaism of the Hellenistic and Roman period, the phrase "the Law (Torah) and the Prophets," or, alternatively, "Moses and the Prophets," became firmly established as a designation of its authoritative texts. These two collections, the Torah and the Prophets, had by this stage become self-contained bodies of authoritative scripture. The second and fourth books of Maccabees, for example, use the phrase "Law and Prophets," and the Community Rule found among the Dead Sea Scrolls in Qumran contains this formulation: "as he [God] has ordained it through Moses and through all his servants, the Prophets" (1QS 1.3). The prologue to the book of Sirach lists "The Law, the Prophets, and the other writings." Finally, the Letter of Instruction, or Halakhic Letter—a reconstructed text from Qumran also known as 4QMMT ("Some Precepts of the Torah")—names other scriptures besides Moses and the Prophets: "that you must understand the book of Moses [and] the book[s of the pr]ophets and Davi[d . . .] [the annals of] each generation" (4QMMT C 10).

Emerging Christianity also adopted this terminology. In the New Testament, Paul (Romans 3:21), Matthew (7:12, 22:40), and John (1:45) all use the phrase "the Law and the Prophets." Likewise, the writings of Luke include the following references: "The Law and the Prophets were proclaimed until John"; "They [your brothers] have Moses and the Prophets"; "If they do not listen to Moses and the Prophets"; "And beginning with Moses and all the Prophets, he [Jesus] explained to them what was said in all the Scriptures concerning himself" (16:16, 16:29, 16:31; 24:27). In the Acts of the Apostles, we find, "from the Law of Moses and from the Prophets" (28:23). Luke adds mention of the Psalms on one occasion: "Everything must be fulfilled that is written about me in the Law of Moses and in the Prophets and in Psalms" (24:44).[1]

The "Psalms" referred to in Luke and in "Some Precepts of the Torah" are not regarded as a third group of authoritative scriptures, but rather as prophetic literature. We can conclude this from the fact that the Psalms are treated as prophetic texts in other writings from Qumran; and, similarly, Luke characterizes David, the author of the Psalms, as a prophet who foretells Christ's resurrection from the dead.[2] In the first century CE, then, the division of the scriptures of the Hebrew Bible into three distinct parts had not yet taken place.

Regardless of the fact that the two text corpora of the Law and the Prophets already existed, neither in Judaism nor in Christianity was the extent of these authoritative scriptures clearly defined. This is evident from the quotations mentioned in Chapter 5, and also from various allusions to certain texts that do not have their origins in the Law and the Prophets. For example, the Letter of Jude includes a quotation from Enoch, Paul (in 1 Corinthians 2:9) quotes a passage of scripture very similar to one in the early Jewish text *Liber Antiquitatum Biblicarum*, and a handful of allusions to the book of Sirach can be found in New Testament authors (see Chapter 5). Although the Law and the Prophets were the crucial scriptures for early Christian writers, this clearly did not preclude them from occasionally citing texts that would today be counted among the deuterocanonical, or apocryphal, scriptures of the Old Testament. The dividing line between the biblical writings of the Law and the Prophets and the peripheral writings around this core was fluid. Different groups within Judaism developed their own ideas of what should count as authoritative, "holy" texts. The Sadducees, for example, appear to have recognized only the Torah, while for the community or communities at Qumran, texts such as the book of Jubilees and the Enoch literature were just as valid as those scriptures that later came to form the Hebrew Bible.[3]

But how and when did the tripartite division of the Hebrew Bible into the Torah (Law), Nevi'im (Prophets), and Ketuvim (Writings) come about? The third of these collections seems to have evolved into an independent body of works during the course of the first century. The earliest signs occur toward the end of the century, in the writings of the historian Flavius Josephus and of Rabbi Gamaliel II.[4] Included in the Ketuvim are the books of Psalms, Job, Proverbs, the Five Megillot (Ruth, Song of Songs, Qohelet [Ecclesiastes], Lamentations, and Esther), Daniel, Ezra-Nehemiah, and the two books of Chronicles.

In the tradition of manuscript transmission within Judaism, the running order of the Ketuvim can vary quite considerably (based on evidence from medieval manuscripts). Such variation indicates that this section of the Tanakh was never subject to the same firm arrangement as the Torah or the Nevi'im. We can trace this back to the fact that the Ketuvim—unlike the Torah—does not have a coherent narrative line. And unlike the historical and prophetic books that make up the Nevi'im, the texts within this third group cover a variety of literary genres.

As the longest and most important book in the collection, Psalms represents the core of the Ketuvim. While it is true that the psalms might also be regarded as prophetic writings, when the three-part Hebrew Bible began to take shape, it appeared to make more sense to allocate them to the Ketuvim. The other writings that were assigned to this group were books of Wisdom literature, like Job and Proverbs, and texts from diverse literary genres that were linked to Jewish festivals (the Megillot) as well as some historical scriptures (Ezra, Nehemiah, and the books of Chronicles). The book of Daniel, which was written in the second century BCE and relates the story of Daniel at the court of King Nebuchadnezzar by means of a fictitious retrospective, is also counted as part of this collection. In the Christian Bible, however, it is part of the Prophets. With the emergence of the Ketuvim as a distinct group of scriptures, the bipartite division of the authoritative texts of Judaism—an arrangement that had been in place since the late first century—was superseded by a tripartite division.

In the overwhelming majority of early Hebrew Bible configurations that we know about, the book of Psalms opens the Ketuvim. Thus, in addition to the introductory role it plays in the Psalter, the First Psalm can also be read as setting the agenda for the Ketuvim:[5]

> Blessed is the one who does not walk in step with the wicked or stand in the way that sinners take or sit in the company of mockers, but whose delight is in the law of YHWH, and who meditates on his law day and night. That person is like a tree planted by streams of water, which yields

its fruit in season and whose leaf does not wither—whatever they do prospers. Not so the wicked! They are like chaff that the wind blows away. Therefore the wicked will not stand in the judgment, nor sinners in the assembly of the righteous. For YHWH watches over the way of the righteous, but the way of the wicked leads to destruction. (Psalm 1:1–6)

From the very beginning, Psalm 1 states that anyone who takes the Torah as their guide through life will thrive. It is probably with good reason that this psalm refers to the Torah as the "law of YHWH" (and not the law of Moses); this Torah no doubt includes other texts, besides the law of Moses, that are held to be manifestations of God's will. The structure of the Psalter that follows this introductory psalm is of special interest. By analogy with the Torah of Moses, it is subdivided into five books by the four doxologies that appear in Psalms 41:14, 72:18–19, 89:53, and 106:48. This structural affinity with the Torah lends the Psalter the force of law. Psalm 1 also picks up on the opening text of the Nevi'im (Joshua 1:8), where God makes the following pronouncement after the death of Moses:

Keep this book of the law always on your lips; meditate on it day and night, so that you may be careful to do everything written in it. Then you will be prosperous and successful.

This reference serves to transport the readers of Psalm 1 back to the situation Joshua found himself in immediately after Moses's death. The psalm thus scrolls back the history of Israel's salvation to a time before the Israelites' entry into Canaan—the point where Israel's history of misfortune commences, culminating in the Babylonian Exile—the effect being to lay open all possibilities to the individual once more. At the same time, Psalm 1 also makes every individual accountable. So *everyone,* not just prominent figures like Joshua and the kings of Israel, is tasked with observing the Torah, since the ultimate welfare of all depends on it. This focus on the Torah speaks to a proto-Pharisaic tendency within the Ketuvim, inasmuch as it requires strict observance of the law in every aspect of daily life.

Moreover, the fact that the beginning of the Ketuvim (Psalm 1) links to the beginning of the Nevi'im (Joshua 1) and not to the end suggests that the texts of the Ketuvim offer their own interpretation of the Torah alongside the testimony of the Prophets. Accordingly, the three-part Hebrew Bible is not structured in a linear manner, in the sense that the Torah, Nevi'im, and Ketuvim succeed one another. Rather, the Ketuvim has a direct relation to the Torah and thus refers back beyond the Nevi'im.[6]

This orientation of the Ketuvim to the Torah is indirectly corroborated by a second internal biblical reference within Psalm 1. The image of the tree beside streams of water is taken from Jeremiah 17:8:

> They will be like a tree planted by the water that sends out its roots by the stream.
>   It does not fear when heat comes; its leaves are always green. It has no worries in a year of drought and never fails to bear fruit.

The allusion to Jeremiah in Psalm 1 qualifies Jeremiah's prophecy of doom. Anyone who conducts their life in the manner recommended in Psalm 1, that is, through meditation and reflection on God's Torah day and night, need not fear the kind of judgment that Jeremiah heralded and suffered—or, to paraphrase Psalm 1 more accurately, such judgment will not happen to those who devote themselves to studying the Torah, whereas it definitely will happen to sinners.

The placement of the Psalms at the beginning of the Ketuvim is the most common arrangement, though occasionally the books of Chronicles are positioned first. In this configuration, these books, which tell of the founding of the temple cult under Kings David and Solomon, are construed as a historical introduction to the Psalms. In the Aleppo Codex (950 CE) and the Codex Leningradensis (1008 CE), however, the books of Chronicles stand at the end. In this arrangement, the Hebrew Bible concludes with the Edict of Cyrus, which allows the exiled Jews to return to their homeland and rebuild the temple, and with the momentous "Exodus" pronouncement:

> Any of his people among you may go up, and may YHWH their God be with them. (2 Chronicles 36:23)

Another variation in some manuscripts is to place the book of Ruth before Psalms. This has the advantage of forming a smooth transition between the end of Ruth, with its genealogy culminating in David, and the Psalms, authorship of which is traditionally ascribed to David:[7]

> This, then, is the family line of Perez: Perez was the father of Hezron, Hezron the father of Ram, Ram the father of Amminadab, Amminadab the father of Nahshon, Nahshon the father of Salmon, Salmon the father of Boaz, Boaz the father of Obed, Obed the father of Jesse, and Jesse the father of David. (Ruth 4:18–22)

Biblical scholars have put forward several theories to explain the formation of the Ketuvim. The most widely held view maintains that the Ketuvim became a "reservoir" of further authoritative texts after the completion of the Nevi'im collection. Another viewpoint holds that the Ketuvim was an instrument for preserving tradition during the upheavals of the Maccabean Revolt.[8] This theory, however, only works if one assumes an untenably early date for the completion of the canon, namely, sometime in the second century BCE. A third approach claims that the Ketuvim was an anthology of illustrative Jewish literary genres put together to counteract the mounting pressure of Hellenistic culture.[9] Finally, a fourth theory identifies a wish to differentiate Jewish scriptures from Christian New Testament scriptures as the prime mover behind the creation of the Ketuvim as a third corpus of texts alongside the Torah and the Prophets.[10] These various theories are not mutually exclusive, and they identify a number of factors that may have promoted the formation of the Ketuvim in different ways. In saying this, we should bear in mind that there are no clear textual criteria governing the inclusion or exclusion of this or that scripture from the Ketuvim.[11] On the question of a text's validity (its "canonicity"), the truly decisive factor was its liturgical usage, which frequently depended on established practices or even happenstance.

In fact, then, the closest analogy to the process by which the Ketuvim coalesced into a third body of scriptures in the Hebrew Bible is the emergence of the Catholic Letters in the New Testament (see Chapter 6). In the case of that collection, too, factors such as the use to which scriptures were put, literary similarities, and the natural affinity between certain texts—such as the letters of James and Jude, which were connected to each other by shared or related authorship—led to the formation of a third group of texts besides the collection of the four gospels and the Pauline letters as an integral part of the evolving New Testament.

There was much discussion in Judaism during the first and second centuries CE about which of the texts belonging to the Ketuvim "soiled the hands" (that is, had the status of "holy scriptures"). This peculiar turn of phrase has its origin in the idea that physical contact with any sacred object, such as during public recitation of a holy scripture, required a person to wash their hands afterwards.[12] The Qohelet and the Song of Songs, in particular, were the subjects of fierce debate as to whether they "soiled the hands." Most rabbis held that they did, with the result that these two books found their way into the Ketuvim.

There is no agreement between scholars on what finally led to the completion of the Ketuvim as a self-contained corpus of texts, and agreement on this matter will likely never be reached. The fact that the Ketuvim never presented a standardized picture in manuscript transmission and that it was not treated in Christian Bibles as a clearly circumscribed collection suggests that the corpus was always a loose assemblage of texts rather than a collection with a fixed content. The texts from Qumran indicate that the inventory of "biblical" books as a whole was not set in stone when the first century CE dawned.[13] In addition, one should consider the general process by which the Bible came into existence: there was never any formal resolution on which texts should or should not form part of the Ketuvim. Instead, over time particular texts acquired a certain authority and came to be used in public worship. And so, like the evolution of the New Testament, the completion of the Ketuvim was a process that was based not on any specific decisions but on gradual developments over a long time period, accompanied by a steady accretion of ritual practices.

The Formation of a Closed List of Books

Following the completion of the Ketuvim, first-century Jewish authors began to compile lists of the books that belonged in the Bible. This process necessarily entailed distinguishing between biblical and nonbiblical texts, but it did not mean that a particular wording of these books was established at this stage. Although different versions of the same Bible texts from Qumran are stable in overall content, they contain many minor textual differences, as well as a number of more significant ones. There are differences in spelling, some archaic words have been replaced by more current ones, and names are written in varied ways.

The subject of a closed list of biblical books is broached explicitly in the work of the Jewish historian Flavius Josephus and in the fourth book of Ezra, chapter 14. In his polemical tract *Contra Apionem* (*Against Apion*), which he wrote as a defense of Judaism, Josephus characterizes the Old Testament tradition as follows:

> For we do not possess a great multitude of books, disagreeing with and contradicting one another, but only 22 books, which contain the records of the entire timespan [of the history of Israel] and which are justly thought to be divine. And of these, five are writings of Moses, which contain his laws, and the traditions of the origin of mankind, up to Moses's death. This period was not far short of three thousand years. But as for the time from the death of Moses up to the reign of Artaxerxes, king of Persia, who reigned after Xerxes, the prophets, who came after Moses, wrote down what was done in their times, in thirteen books. The remaining four books contain hymns to God; and precepts for the conduct of human life. Although our history since Artaxerxes has been recorded in great detail, it is not deemed to wield the same authority as the history written by our forefathers, because there has not been an exact succession of prophets since that time. (*Against Apion* 1:8)

Josephus proceeds from the assumption that there is a fixed number of twenty-two books of the Bible, which correspond to the letters of the Hebrew alphabet and thus symbolize self-containment and completeness. This idea recurs in the writings of Christian theologians, who, regardless of their use of the Greek translation of the Hebrew Bible (the Septuagint), with its additional books, were well acquainted with the notion of twenty-two books of the "Old Testament" and the connection with the letters of the Hebrew alphabet (see Chapter 1).

Interestingly, Josephus's account levels its criticism primarily at the Greek tradition, which encompasses "a great multitude" of different books and thus in his view cannot be reliable. We may presume that Josephus was responding to an argument that the small number of authoritative books among the Jews precluded these works being a faithful account of the entire history of humankind. Josephus makes a virtue out of this necessity, putting forward the argument that the twenty-two books of the Jewish Bible were handed down from the prophets, a surefire guarantor in his eyes of their reliability.

The exact categorization of the books of the Bible is not fully clear from Josephus's account, however. In all probability, the thirteen books that follow the law of Moses comprise Job, Joshua, Judges (including Ruth), Samuel, Kings, Isaiah, Jeremiah (including Lamentations), Ezekiel, the twelve Minor Prophets (counted as one book), Daniel, Chronicles, Ezra-Nehemiah, and Esther. The "remaining four" books to which Josephus refers are most likely Psalms, Proverbs, Qohelet (Ecclesiastes), and the Song of Songs, though this is not absolutely certain.[14] Moreover, Josephus indicates that he subscribes to a theory of prophetic authorship when he mentions in the same breath the writing of the biblical books and the unbroken succession of prophets from Moses to the time of the Persian ruler Artaxerxes, whose reign, according to the evidence of the Bible, saw the appearance of Ezra and Nehemiah.[15]

The fourth book of Ezra, a Jewish apocalypse that was written toward the end of the first century but was passed down only in the Christian tradition, sketches out a model of the binding books of Judaism in its fourteenth and final chapter.[16] It is believed that 4 Ezra was originally written in Palestine in a Semitic language (Hebrew or Aramaic), but it has only survived in Latin and various translations into Middle Eastern languages.[17] It was composed approximately thirty years after the Romans razed Jerusalem in 70 CE. It discusses this experience only indirectly, by pointing back to the first destruction of the city and its temple by the Babylonians in 587 BCE. It also attempts to offer a theological interpretation of this event. The two catastrophes that hit Jerusalem are viewed together: for the author and his readers alike, a description of the first destruction of the city clearly alludes to what has recently taken place in Roman times. Chapter 14 describes the rewriting of the biblical and other books that the Babylonians burned when they sacked Jerusalem. Thanks to divine inspiration, Ezra was in a position to dictate these destroyed books to a circle of scholars:

> And the Most High gave understanding to those five men [the scribes to whom Ezra is dictating], and by turns they wrote what was dictated, in characters which they did not know. They sat forty days, and wrote

during the daytime, and ate their bread at night. As for me, I [Ezra] spoke in the daytime and was not silent at night. So during the forty days ninety-four books were written. And when the forty days were ended, the Most High spoke to me, saying "Make public the twenty-four books that you wrote first and let the worthy and the unworthy read them; but keep the seventy that were written last, in order to give them to the wise among your people. For in them are the springs of understanding, the fountains of wisdom and the river of knowledge." (4 Ezra 14:42–47)[18]

"The twenty-four books that you wrote first" are clearly identifiable as those of the Hebrew Bible. They are accessible to everyone, whereas the seventy remaining books, which are to be kept hidden, evidently comprise the deuterocanonical, or apocryphal, scriptures, including 4 Ezra itself.[19] These books are only available to the initiated, the "wise among your people," as they are not simple to understand and are aimed at an intellectual elite. Although Ezra's count of twenty-four books is at variance with the theologically loaded number of twenty-two given by Josephus, it may represent an older tradition.[20] It is far easier to imagine that the figure of twenty-four was rounded down to twenty-two to tally with the number of letters in the Hebrew alphabet than that the lower number was increased. Having said that, in the rabbinical tradition, the figure of twenty-four appears to have become the accepted norm; it is far better attested there than the figure of twenty-two.[21]

In all likelihood, the discrepancy between twenty-four and twenty-two did not derive from a genuine difference in the complement of books, but to the combining of Lamentations with the book of Jeremiah and Ruth with Judges. In 4 Ezra 14, as in Josephus, we also find the motif of prophetic authorship, this time thanks to Ezra's dictation.

Biblical scholars in the late nineteenth and early twentieth centuries commonly associated the idea of a canon found in Josephus and 4 Ezra with a supposed synod or council held in Jamnia (Jabneh or Yavne), at which this canon was allegedly decided upon (see Chapter 1). While it is true that Jamnia became an established center of Jewish scholarship after 70 CE, no such council was ever convened there, nor did any discussions take place in Jamnia about the nature of the Old Testament scriptures as a whole. The only historically documented theological debates in the city concerned the status of the book of Qohelet and the Song of Songs.[22]

We may still ask why the concept of a clearly delimited list of books arose at all toward the end of the first century. Although Josephus directs his criticism of "a great multitude of books" primarily at Greek literature, it may be no coincidence that the definition of what constituted the Jewish Bible came precisely at a time when Judaism found itself challenged by nascent Christianity, which was itself based on new texts that had been added to the traditional scriptures. For instance, in the Tosefta, a work of commentary on the Mishnah, we find the following passage in a tractate on hand-washing and impurity:

> The gospels [gilyonim] and the books of the heretics [minim] do not render the hands that touch them ritually unclean. The books of Ben Sirach and all books written thereafter likewise do not soil the hands. (Yadayim 2:13)

The books named here do not therefore exercise binding authority. Remarkably, the concept of heretics, a category that includes (Jewish-) Christians, arose at around the same time as independent collections of authoritative texts began to evolve in the Christian church.[23] The fact that this quotation mentions the books of Christianity in the same breath as the book of Sirach and other more recent books of Judaism shows that Rabbinic Judaism was concerned to dissociate itself not just from Christian literature but also from Jewish texts that did not possess the same venerable antiquity as the books of the Hebrew Bible.

The Talmud

The Judaic scholar Jacob Neusner has claimed that neither Judaism nor Christianity can truly be described as a "biblical religion," since both interpret their respective Bibles from an extra-biblical standpoint. Judaism does this via the "oral" Torah, which is found in Jewish traditional literature, and Christianity through affirming belief in Jesus as the Christ, an article of faith shaped by church tradition.[24] Informing this judgment about Judaism is the rabbinical view that Moses on Mount Sinai received not just the written Torah that is now enshrined in the Hebrew Bible but also an oral Torah that was never recorded in writing in biblical times.[25] The core of this oral tradition can be found in the Mishnah (literally, "repetition"). The Mishnah was transcribed in around 200 CE as a collection of oral doctrines dating back at least in part to the late Second Temple period.

Over the following centuries, the Mishnah was augmented by the Gemara, which contains rabbinical commentary and analysis in Aramaic of the Hebrew Mishnah. Together, they make up the Talmud, which has been passed down in a shorter Palestinian (or Jerusalem) version and a longer Babylonian version (Figure 38).[26] The Palestinian Talmud was completed in around 500, whereas the work of editing the Babylonian Talmud may have extended well into the Islamic period and was not completed until around 800.[27] Not least as a result of the influence of the Pharisaic-Rabbinic strain of Judaism after 70 CE, correct practice of the law came to be of primary importance in post-biblical Judaism.[28] Conversely, less attention was paid to defining a body of scriptures as the basis of doctrine. In other words, "orthopraxy," an emphasis on proper liturgical and ethical conduct, became more important than "orthodoxy," where the stress is on correct belief.

Although the Talmud clearly relates to the Bible, it can only be obliquely understood as an example of biblical exegesis. First and foremost, it is an interpretation of the Hebrew Bible at second or even third hand. The Gemara is a commentary on the Mishnah, and the Mishnah regards itself as a Torah in its own right—that is, as a transcription of the oral Torah from Mount Sinai, which took shape centuries after Moses:

> Moses received the Torah at Sinai and transmitted it to Joshua, Joshua to the elders, and the elders to the prophets, and the prophets to the men of the Great Assembly. (Pirkei Avot 1:1)

The Mishnah primarily offers "halakhic" material—legal discussions on the correct way to live—whereas in the Talmud as a whole there is a preponderance of "aggadic" text—nonlegalistic disquisitions of a didactic nature.[29]

The lack of any formal analogy to the Mishnah in other traditions is striking; no other work of literature displays the same form of discursive discussion of problems.[30] It appears to be completely sui generis, which makes it hard to place in a historical context.[31] A tractate of the Mishnah that deals with ethics, the Pirkei Avot ("Chapters of the Fathers"), provides a retrospective theological interpretation, but the Mishnah itself stakes no claim to

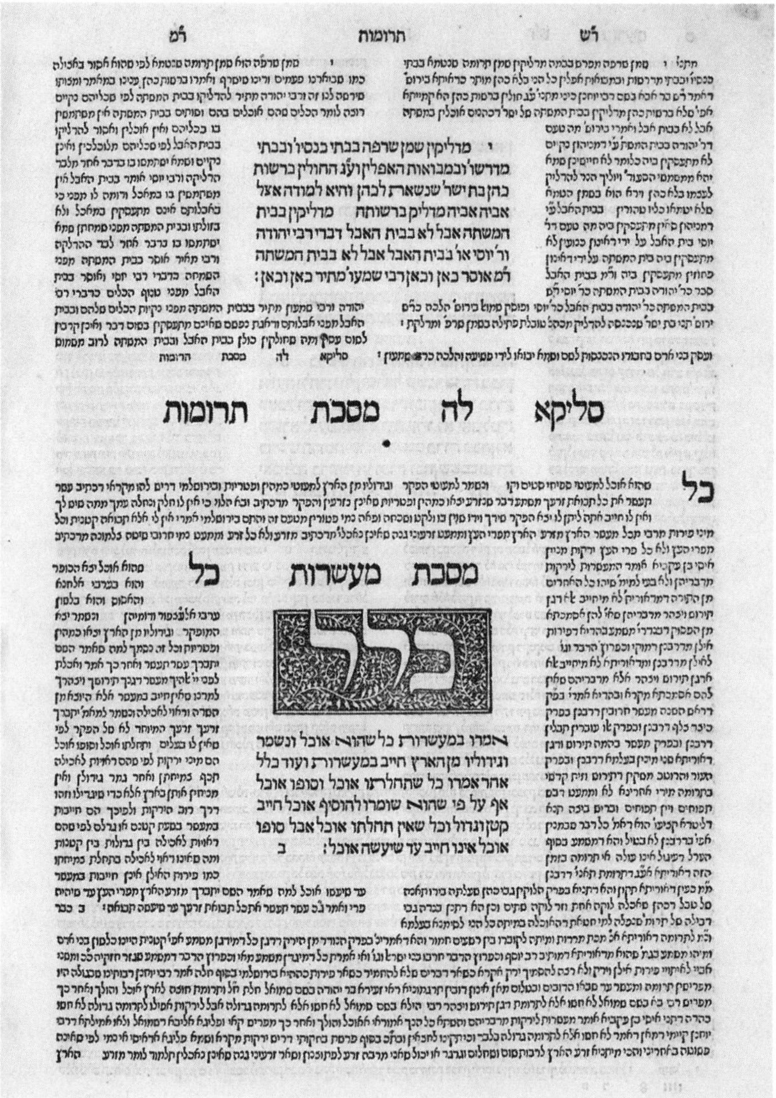

תרומות

מדליקין שמן שרפה בבתי כנסיו' ובבתי
מדרשו' ובמבואות האפלין וע"ג החולין ברשות
כהן בת ישר' שנשארת לכהן והיא למודה אצל
אביה אביה מדליק ברשותה מדליקין בבית
המשתה אבל לא בבית האבל דברי רבי יהודה
ור' יוסי או' בבית האבל אבל לא בבית המשתה
ר"מ אוסר כאן וכאן רבי שמעו' מתיר כאן וכאן:

סליקא לה מסכת תרומות

מסכת מעשרות

כלל אמרו במעשרות כל שהוא אוכל ונשמר
וגידוליו מן הארץ חייב במעשרות ועוד כלל
אחר אמרו כל שתחלתו אוכל וסופו אוכל
אף על פי שהוא שומרו להוסיף אוכל חייב
קטן וגדול וכל שאין תחלתו אוכל אבל סופו
אוכל אינו חייב עד שיעשה אוכל: ב

Figure 38. The Babylonian Talmud, printed by Daniel Bomberg in Venice in 1543–1544. This page shows the Seder Zera'im, the first order, or division, of the Mishnah.

great antiquity; rather, it presents itself as a discursive text containing the doctrinal opinions of a variety of rabbis, none of whom lived before the first century.[32]

A prime example of the Mishnah's unique line of theological reasoning can be seen in the opening lines of the Tractate Berakhot. Its subject is the rules governing prayers, and in particular the time of evening during which the prayer *Shema Yisrael* ("Hear, O Israel!") should be recited:

From what time should one recite *Shema* in the evening?

From the time when the priests enter to partake of their *terumah* [a harvest offering] until the end of the first watch. [This is the] statement of Rabbi Eliezer.

The Sages say: Until midnight.

Rabbi Gamliel says: Until dawn.

One time, Rabbi Gamliel's sons were returning very late from a wedding hall, and said to him: We still have not recited *Shema*.

He said to them: If the dawn has not yet arrived, you are obliged to recite *Shema*.

And not only with regard to the reciting of *Shema*, but rather wherever the Sages say "until midnight," the mitzvah [the religious duty of intoning the prayer] may be performed until dawn.

The burning of fat and limbs on the altar may be performed until morning dawns; and all burnt offerings that the Sages state may only be eaten until midnight by Torah law may be eaten until dawn. If so, why did the Sages say that they may only be eaten "until midnight"?

In order to keep the people far away from transgression.

This passage presents different doctrinal views on a subject without deciding in favor of one or another. Instead, it strives to make the difference understandable. Thus, the stricter view that the *Shema Yisrael* must be recited before midnight, rather than any time before dawn, is only meant to ensure that a person does not say the prayer too late.

Before long, it seems that the business of offering biblical exegeses in the Talmud became more important to classical Judaism than engaging with the Bible itself. Essentially, the Bible was read and interpreted in the light of this traditional literature. In Judaism, the tripartite Bible never achieved the same exclusive and normative status as the Christian Bible. The concept of a "canon" only became established within Judaism after the philologist David Ruhnken from Leiden University in the Netherlands used the term to refer to the writings of classical Greek authors in his 1768 work *Historia Critica Oratorum Graecorum*.

The creation of a body of independent traditional literature in late antiquity was of crucial importance for the further development of Judaism. It may well be that, as Christianity grew ever stronger and expanded, a desire to assert a clear religious identity prompted Judaism to develop the Mishnah and the Talmud. Seth Schwartz of Columbia University ventures the opinion that, without these external stimuli, Judaism might have merged with paganism by late antiquity and so not survived beyond the ancient world.[33] Whatever the case, distinguishing itself from Christianity became a decisive factor in the emergence of Rabbinic Judaism.[34]

A Split Diaspora?

In 2007 and 2008, the Israeli scholars Doron Mendels and Arye Edrei published two papers on what they called the "split Jewish diaspora."[35] Although their findings have not had widespread resonance in the critical literature due to a lack of supporting evidence, they nonetheless highlighted a significant problem. The authors put forward the view that, after the destruction of Jerusalem by the Romans in 70 CE, the eastern, Hebrew- and Aramaic-speaking Jewish diaspora and the western, Greek- and Latin-speaking one evolved in very distinct ways. Whereas in the East the traditions of the oral Torah were transcribed into the Mishnah and the Talmud, giving rise to hierarchically organized schools of Jewish scholarship, there was no sign in the West that these traditions were being maintained or even took root there in the first place. The Greek-speaking diaspora of Judaism, the authors claimed, initially had no access to the world of the Talmud. Instead, alongside the Hebrew Bible, it cultivated its own "deuterocanonical" scriptures, which had been preserved in the Septuagint.[36] Jewish life was thus more heavily influenced by biblical traditions in the West and by Talmudic traditions in the East. Only from the seventh century onward did the impact of rabbinical teaching make itself felt in the West as well, after it had been recorded in written form in the East.

This hypothesis of a "split diaspora" can neither be proved nor refuted. Especially in the case of western Judaism, there are no documents to indicate which scriptures were invoked, or even which were known, though it is highly probable that both the material availability of traditional Hebrew and Aramaic literature from the East and the linguistic capacity to read them were very limited.

Yet whatever attitude one adopts toward the idea of a split diaspora, there is no denying that from the Islamic period on, Judaism gradually developed a comparatively unified relationship to tradition. The Talmud assumed a central position in scriptural study in the West as well as in the East. Mendels and Edrei provide no explanation for this process. One may, however, conjecture that the widespread Christianization and Islamization of Europe, North Africa, and the Middle East put pressure on Judaism to cultivate a stronger collective identity. A stronger identity also came about as a result of the dissemination and acceptance of the Talmud in the western Mediterranean region. For all the many divergences between different strands, the result was that Judaism took on a relatively consistent form in the Middle Ages and the modern era.

Christians and Jews on Holy Scripture

In the first centuries CE, the dividing line between Judaism and Christianity developed very gradually. Jesus was a Jew, and early Christians formed a special group within a Judaism whose identity was so diverse at the start of the first century that Anglo-Saxon scholarship even talks in terms of "Judaisms."[37] Apocalyptic writings such as the Enoch literature were far removed from the key beliefs that underlay later Rabbinic or Classical Judaism. In this literature, the principal medium of divine revelation is not Moses but Enoch. Enoch was an obvious choice as a mouthpiece for these revelations since it is said of him that, after living for 365 years, he did not die but was taken away by God—in other words, he was transported to heaven (Genesis 5:21–24). Gabriele Boccaccini has suggested the term "Enochic Judaism" for this strain of Second Temple Judaism, since Enoch was evidently a higher authority than Moses for Jews at that time.[38]

With the destruction of the Second Temple in 70 CE, the diverse character of ancient Judaism was drastically diminished. Out of the many strands that had once existed, that of the Pharisees emerged as dominant and proceeded to develop into Rabbinic Judaism.

As Judaism and Christianity continued to evolve, in a process that was characterized by further instances of reciprocal demarcation and differentiation, a distinct antithesis crystallized from the second century on, which also expressed itself in very different attitudes toward biblical scriptures.[39] Judaism clearly had no interest in conceding any authority to the newly emerging Christian texts. Especially telling in this regard is the section of Yadayim 2:13 from the Tosefta quoted earlier, which categorizes the Gospels as nonauthoritative. Yet as a general rule it is striking how infrequently both Jewish and Christian attempts at demarcation refer to the question of the status of particular texts. Polemics regarding specific matters of content are much more common.

At some points in the Talmud, we find critiques of the figure of Jesus.[40] The Jerusalem Talmud, from the perspective of Rabbinic Judaism, is concerned with combating Christendom as a sect, whereas the Babylonian Talmud tends to attack the person of Jesus. Some passages in the Talmud can be interpreted as refutations of theological positions adopted by the monastic literature of Christianity.[41]

Conversely, there are a number of passages in the New Testament—notably in the Gospel of John—which project disputes of the second century between the two faiths back to the time of Jesus and in the process take an oppositional stance to Judaism.[42] In the centuries that followed, the patristic literature further developed this antithetical model.[43]

The key feature that separates the Jewish from the Christian tradition is the notion of an oral Torah. Only Judaism recognizes alongside the written law an oral Torah of God, which was imparted to Moses on Sinai and is now available in written form in the Mishnah. In all probability, it was the wish to emphasize this difference from Christianity that caused the Mishnah and the Talmud to be given precedence over the Bible in the religious practice of scriptural study.[44]

The relationship between Judaism and Christianity was not solely a polemical one, however. It is worth recalling that emerging Christianity, in its reception of the Hebrew Bible as the Old Testament, did not add a Christian gloss to it. This shows that the Old Testament, without requiring any theological reworking, could be understood on the basis of the hermeneutic principle that it pointed forward to Christ. In Christianity, the belief prevailed that God had revealed himself in a new way in Jesus Christ—in other words, that a personal revelatory experience stood at the center of the Christian faith, rather than a text that was fixed in extent and linguistic form. This may have been the reason why the Christian Bible never became a book with a clearly defined scope and a set linguistic form, such as happened with the Hebrew Bible in Rabbinic Judaism. Instead, the Bible was able to evolve into a variety of different forms within different Christian denominations. Although its core content remained stable, it was highly fluid at the peripheries. The text of the Bible as such was not, and is not, the most important factor, but rather how it is read and understood in any given setting.

8

The Book of Books

Translations and Their Dissemination

The Christian Bible is the most widely disseminated book in world literature.[1] In the form of the Old Testament, the books of the Jewish Bible became known within Christianity, too. According to current figures, Christianity is the largest religion by number of worshippers; it has around two and a half billion followers, or roughly a third of the world's population. By contrast, adherents of Judaism number only some 16 million. Most of the traditions of the Bible are also familiar within Islam, which has a following of around 1.7 billion people worldwide. The Qur'an borrowed and processed not just biblical stories, but also a whole range of apocryphal stories that do not appear in the Bible. It was sometimes very free in its interpretation and reworking of this material. Biblical figures such as Noah, Abraham, Isaac, Ishmael, Jacob, Joseph, Moses, David, Mary, John, and Jesus are mentioned and interpreted in a different way in the Qur'an. The Qur'an thus incorporates Jewish and Christian traditions of both a biblical and an extra-biblical kind.

From a global perspective, Christianity at present finds itself in a period of remarkable growth. It is attracting large numbers of new followers in East Asia, as well as in Africa and Latin America. Places where church membership is dwindling, such as Central Europe, are the exception rather than the rule.

By the early twenty-first century, some five billion copies of the Bible had been produced, most of them in the last one hundred years. According to the *Global Scripture Access Report,* Christian "complete Bibles"—that is, Bibles comprising both the Old and New Testaments—are available in no fewer than 674 languages.[2] The New Testament on its own has been translated into a further 1,515 languages, while individual biblical texts occur in another 1,135 languages. It is estimated that around 5.4 billion people, or 71 percent of the total world population, have access to the Bible in their mother tongue.

These figures indicate that the Christian Bible does not exist in any particular "sacred" language but that it can, as a matter of principle, be translated into any language without suffering a loss in its meaning.[3] Modern biblical studies as an academic discipline pays attention to the original languages the Bible was written in—Hebrew or Aramaic and Greek—not because these are regarded as "sacred" tongues but because philological and historical analysis is the best way to reveal the precise semantic content of biblical texts.

When considering the history of the Bible, however, it should be noted that the Council of Trent in 1546 decreed the Latin translation of the Bible, the Vulgate, to be the definitive text for use in the Roman Catholic Church. The council declared that the Vulgate was a "time-honored, general translation, tried and tested over many long centuries of ecclesiastical usage." This situation remains largely unchanged today, though use of the Bible and celebration of Mass in the vernacular steadily gained traction in the second half of the twentieth century following the liturgical reforms approved by the Second Vatican Council in 1962–1965. In Orthodox churches, Bible translations and celebration of the liturgy also exist in a variety of local languages, but the definitive form of the text of the Old Testament continues to be the Septuagint.

The situation is somewhat different in Judaism, though not fundamentally so.[4] In Jewish congregations throughout the world, Hebrew occupies a privileged position. The Torah is regarded as a direct record of the revelation of God's instructions to his people and is recited in Hebrew in synagogue services. But a translation commanded the same authority as the Hebrew original within Hellenistic Judaism, as noted in our discussion in Chapter 4 of the oldest rendering of the Torah into Greek and the accompanying myth of the genesis of the Septuagint in the *Letter of Aristeas*. The translation into Greek was traced back to a second revelation by God, as evidenced by the way Philo of Alexandria built upon this tradition in the aftermath of the *Letter of Aristeas*.[5] According to Philo, the seventy-two translators of the Torah worked in isolation from one another and yet, "as if guided by divine inspiration" or even "like prophets," each one produced exactly the same Greek text. From the thirteenth century on, further translations of the Hebrew Bible appeared in Yiddish and Ladino—the languages of Judaism in eastern Europe and on the Iberian Peninsula, respectively.

Within Judaism, however, the question of the Torah's translatability was not without controversy. On this subject, the Tractate Soferim of the Talmud, which is thought to come from the eighth century, notes:[6]

> [The Torah] may not be written in Hebrew characters [Paleo-Hebrew script] or in the Aramaic, Median, or Greek languages. Writing in any language or script may not be used for the lection [the statutory synagogue service], except in the case that it is in Assyrian [Hebrew square script].

Of course, the writer of this tractate knew about the existence of the Septuagint, which he strongly criticized:

> It once happened that five elders wrote the Torah for King Talmai [Ptolemy II Philadelphos] in Greek. That day was as ominous for Israel as the day on which the [golden] calf was made, since the Torah could not be accurately translated. (Soferim 1:7)

As things turned out, this opinion prevailed: throughout the history of Judaism, the Hebrew original of the Torah has always retained its preeminence.

The considerably greater openness to Bible translations in Christianity rests on the conviction that it is not the Bible per se that represents the central revelation of God, but rather his intervention in the history of Israel and his actions on earth through Jesus Christ. The Bible bears witness to this revelation of God as an experience that is interpreted and recorded in writing by humans. The message of the Bible must therefore constantly be highlighted afresh in every new historical situation. And one key aspect of this adaptability is the freedom to translate it into different languages.

Islam takes a fundamentally different view from Judaism and Christianity on this question of translating the holy scriptures. The Qur'an is considered a direct record of God's revelations to Muhammad and may therefore be recited only in the form in which they were originally conveyed, namely, in Arabic.[7]

Christian Bible Translations

The history of Christian translations of the Bible begins with the Septuagint, a Jewish translation of Hebrew scriptures into Greek, which arose within the context of diaspora Judaism and its intellectual and literary center in Alexandria (see Chapter 4). As the "Old Testament," the Septuagint became part of the Christian Bible, while Judaism created new Greek translations or revisions that adhered more closely to the original Hebrew text. These Jewish scriptures spurned rendering the name of God with the term *Kyrios* ("Lord"), which in a Christian context suggested an equivalence between the God of the Hebrew Bible and the "Lord" Jesus Christ. Not least in reaction to the Christian use of the Septuagint, Judaism took its cue directly from the Hebrew text of the Bible, which became the decisive shaping influence of this religion.

In the long term, Greek did not remain the lingua franca of the Mediterranean region. From the second century CE on, Christian communities in the western provinces of the Roman Empire no longer understood Greek, making it necessary to produce Latin translations of the Bible. These were later given the collective name of *Vetus Latina* ("old Latin [translations]"). They are subsidiary translations of the Septuagint, and consequently do not get closer to the original Hebrew texts than their Greek models.[8] All the same, they are highly informative about the beginnings of Latin Christianity and its theology.

At the instigation of Pope Damasus, the church father Jerome, who came from Dalmatia, subsequently created the Vulgate (literally, "vernacular") starting in 383. For the Old Testament, he went back to the original Hebrew texts.[9] Jerome was one of the few people in the Latin West who was versed in Hebrew and aware of the Hebrew origins of these texts.[10] Thanks to his revision, the Hebrew configuration of the text of the Bible, called the *Hebraica veritas* ("Hebrew truth"), came to exert an indirect influence on subsequent translations.

In the Christian Middle Ages, the Vulgate was considered the authoritative version of the Bible. It played an important role in that it secured the Latin tradition, over and against the biblical texts in their original languages, and it preserved the more extensive Old Testament of Greek and Latin tradition. The denominational controversies between the Roman Catholic Church and the churches of the Reformation are clearly in evidence here. Before the Council of Trent's definitive endorsement of the Vulgate, access to the Bible had primarily been through Greek and Hebrew texts and German translations from them: the Greek edition of the New Testament published by Desiderius Erasmus of Rotterdam in 1516, Martin Luther's translations (1522, 1534), and Huldrych Zwingli's Zurich Bible of 1531.

Even in antiquity, a number of translations into other languages existed alongside the Greek and Latin translations of the Bible. A translation into Syriac, the so-called Peshitta ("the simple one"), took shape starting in the second century.[11] It continues to be the standard version of the Bible in churches of the Syriac tradition to the present day. The Peshitta differs from Bible editions used in Western churches in the running order of the books of the Old Testament. For instance, the book of Job follows immediately after the Torah, since it is ostensibly set in a period that is close to that of the stories recounted in Genesis. Also, in the New Testament, in place of the four gospels the Peshitta uses the Diatessaron—the composite account of Jesus's life and ministry created from the Gospels by Tatian of Adiabene. Originally composed in Syriac, and translated into Greek, Latin, and Georgian, among other languages, the Diatessaron was very popular and was widely read for a long time. However, it did not remain in official church use in the Latin West or the Greek Eastern churches after the fifth century.

Beginning in the third to fourth centuries, Egyptian Christians produced a Coptic translation of the Bible, an endeavor that transformed this vernacular tongue into a literary language. This was followed somewhat later by Ethiopian translations of the Bible, the text of which is largely based on Greek versions. The Bibles of the Ethiopian church are among the most extensive in the whole of Christianity. Ethiopian Christians refer to them as the "eighty-one books." This collection includes scriptures such as the book of Jubilees and the books of Enoch, whose Hebrew or Aramaic versions remained unknown for a long time, until the discovery of the Dead Sea Scrolls brought to light fragments of the Semitic originals (see Chapter 4).

The expansion of Christianity throughout the Caucasus was followed by widespread dissemination of the Bible in this region. During the fifth century, it was translated from Syriac into Armenian and thence into Georgian.[12]

Gradually, Christianity also found its way into central, western, and northern Europe. Ulfilas, a Goth of Cappadocian Greek descent, prepared a Gothic Bible translation beginning in 340. Its Old Testament has only survived in very fragmentary form, and it is not certain whether Ulfilas translated all the books of the New Testament.[13] The first Bible translations in German appeared in the eighth century. The earliest complete German Bibles date from the fifteenth century, translated from the Vulgate for the most part. From the start of the sixteenth century, the invention of the printing press and the Reformation movements brought an enormous increase in the number of German Bibles. Luther's translations begin with the September Testament, a translation of the New Testament that Luther wrote while living incognito under Elector Frederick the Wise's protection at the Wartburg in Saxony in 1521–1522. The first complete Luther Bible appeared in 1534. The Zurich Bible was composed between 1524 and 1529 before being published as a complete Bible for the first time in 1531 by the Zurich printer Christoph Froschauer. These Bible translations broke the stranglehold of the Vulgate by translating directly from the Hebrew or Greek. Because few Christians knew Hebrew in the pre-Reformation Christian Middle Ages, Jewish teachers played a vital intermediate role in facilitating the translation of the Old Testament.[14]

Translations of the Bible into English begin with the Venerable Bede's translations of the Gospels in the eighth century. Until the Reformation, English translations relied upon the Latin text. The King James Version of the Bible became the standard text of the Anglican Church after 1611, and it was also widely used by English colonists in North America.[15]

In the ninth century, Cyril and Methodius, Byzantine Greek missionaries who evangelized the Slavs, created a translation of the Bible in Old Church Slavonic. This text was highly significant in promoting the further development of Slavonic languages and literature.[16] The first Bible in Russian appeared in 1499.

Although some Danish and Swedish translations appear to have been written prior to the Reformation, they have only survived in very fragmentary form. The first firm evidence of such Bibles comes during the Reformation, with a Swedish version of 1541 and a Danish one dating from 1550.

The first complete Bible translation in French, using Jerome's Vulgate as a source text, was produced by the humanist Johannes Faber Stapulensis (Jacques Lefèvre d'Étaples) in 1530. In 1535 Pierre Robert Olivetan, a cousin of John Calvin, produced a Bible for French Protestants that was based on Greek and Hebrew manuscript sources and was subsequently named for him. The Olivetan Bible formed the basis of the Geneva Bible of 1588, the standard translation used by Huguenots.

The Waldensians, members of a proto-Protestant movement based in Lyon and around the French-Italian border, were prime movers in early efforts to translate the Bible into Italian. None of their translations have survived, however. A translation of the Vulgate into Italian first appeared in Venice in 1471.

The first Spanish Bible translation was produced in Antwerp, in the Spanish Netherlands, in 1543. Bibles in Portuguese were first developed by Calvinist communities on the island of Java: 1681 saw the publication of a New Testament, followed in 1753 by a complete Bible.

With the worldwide spread of Christianity as a result of European colonialism and missionary movements, Bible translations began to appear in numerous vernacular languages of Asia, Africa, and America. In several instances, these Bibles represented the first written documents of the civilization in question, as for example in Massachusetts (1663), Madagascar (1835), Tahiti (1838), Botswana (1857), and Lesotho (1878). As a consequence, biblical thinking and concepts have been influential in shaping the written languages of these cultures, including their vocabulary, style, and grammar.

A Tree with Many Branches: The Bible in Judaism

The world of Jewish scripture resembles a tree that branches out farther and farther from its roots. From the roots of the Torah and other texts of the Hebrew Bible, it branched first via the Midrash and the Talmud and then on to the medieval and modern commentaries of Jewish traditional literature. Indeed, in Judaism, the Bible itself can be characterized as consisting simultaneously of text and commentary.[17] Biblical exegesis begins within the Bible; each new interpretation, whether from within or outside the Bible, refers back to the foregoing texts and carries on the process of their exegesis.[18] The Torah, as the factual and historical nucleus of the Hebrew Bible and the starting point of all subsequent interpretative literature, forms the foundation for this process.[19] Owing to a lack of source material, its use within Jewish worship in antiquity is far from simple to reconstruct. The public reading of texts from the Torah in Shabbat services is explicitly attested in the first century CE.[20]

In contrast to the books of the prophets, it was customary to recite the Torah from beginning to end week by week. In Palestine, this occurred in a three-year cycle, while in Babylon a one-year cycle became the norm (see the Tractate Megillah 29b in the Babylonian Talmud), which of course entailed correspondingly longer passages being read out on each Sabbath.[21]

Jewish tradition frequently allows later interpretations of Bible texts to supersede their original meaning. A well-known example of this can be found in a Midrash from the Babylonian Talmud, which explains how Moses is transported by God to the school of the famous Rabbi Akiva (second century CE), where he sits in on a lesson:

> But he [Moses] did not understand what they were saying and he was distressed. When they came to consider a certain matter the students asked Rabbi Akiva: "Master, from where do you know this?" and he said to them, "It is a law given to Moses at Sinai" and Moses was comforted. (Babylonian Talmud, Tractate Menachot 29b)

According to this Midrash, not even Moses was able to follow the rabbinical commentaries on the Torah. Nonetheless, this story emphasizes that Rabbi Akiva's interpretation is all part of God's plan, even though that interpretation remains beyond the grasp of the originator of the Torah, Moses himself. The passage continues:

> Rabbi Yehuda said in the name of the Rav: When Moses ascended on high to receive the Torah, he found the blessed Holy One, sitting and attaching little crowns to the letters. Moses said to him: "Master of the Universe, what is holding you back from giving the Torah?" (Menachot 29b)

"Little crowns" is a reference to the calligraphic embellishments of the Hebrew letters in the Torah scrolls, which are believed to have been placed there by God himself (Figure 39). God is waiting until these crowns are completed before he reveals the meaning of the Torah. God answered Moses's question as follows:

> There will be a man in the future, at the end of many generations, and Akiva the son of Joseph is his name. He will interpret multitudes of laws from just the tips of these crowns. (Menachot 29b)

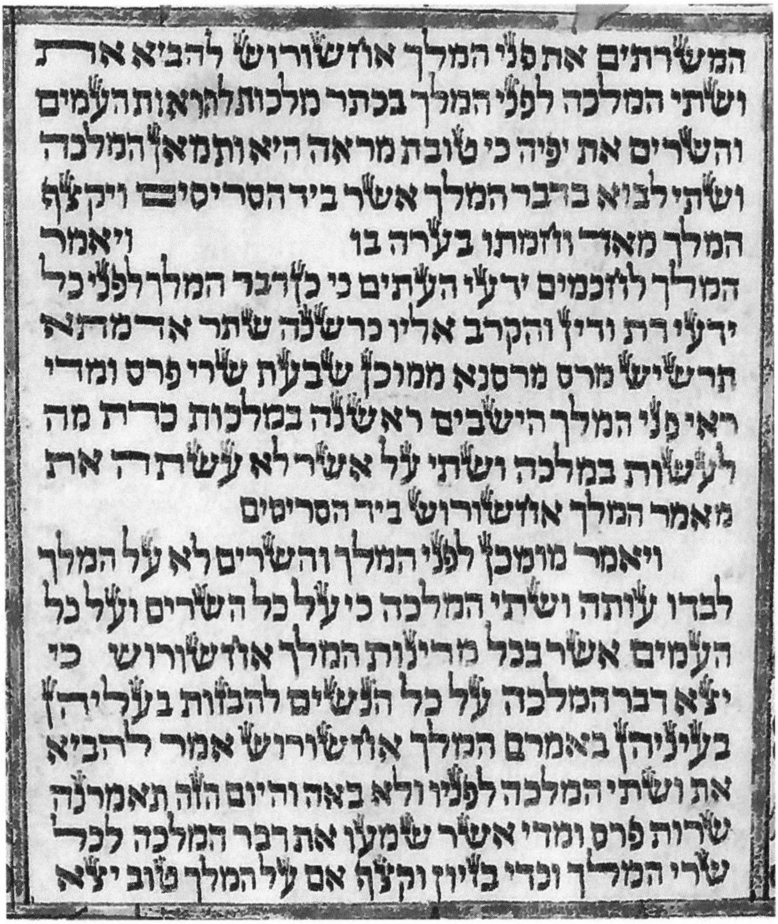

המשרתים את פני המלך אחשורוש להביא את
ושתי המלכה לפני המלך בכתר מלכות להראות העמים
והשרים את יפיה כי טובת מראה היא ותמאן המלכה
ושתי לבוא בדבר המלך אשר ביד הסריסים ויקצף
המלך מאד וחמתו בערה בו ויאמר
המלך לחכמים ידעי העתים כי כן דבר המלך לפני כל
ידעי דת ודין והקרב אליו כרשנא שתר אדמתא
תרשיש מרס מרסנא ממוכן שבעת שרי פרס ומדי
ראי פני המלך הישבים ראשנה במלכות כדת מה
לעשות במלכה ושתי על אשר לא עשתה את
מאמר המלך אחשורוש ביד הסריסים
ויאמר מומכן לפני המלך והשרים לא על המלך
לבדו עותה ושתי המלכה כי על כל השרים ועל כל
העמים אשר בכל מדינות המלך אחשורוש כי
יצא דבר המלכה על כל הנשים להבזות בעליהן
בעיניהן באמרם המלך אחשורוש אמר להביא
את ושתי המלכה לפניו ולא באה והיום הזה תאמרנה
שרות פרס ומדי אשר שמעו את דבר המלכה לכל
שרי המלך וכדי בזיון וקצף אם על המלך טוב יצא

Figure 39. Manuscript of the book of Esther with decorated letters, Baghdad, ca. 1850.

In other words, all God does himself is prepare the little diacritical marks in the Torah; their interpretation is up to the rabbis who will one day study and offer exegeses of the Torah. The Bible scholar Carl Ehrlich has said of this passage, "It could be argued that the rabbis placed their own tradition of interpretation before the written Torah."[22] This position is expressed in Rabbinic Judaism's contention that the exegetical literature is just as much a product of God as the Bible itself and likewise comes under the umbrella term "Torah":[23]

When God revealed himself at Sinai to give the Torah to Israel, he taught to Moses the following order: Bible, Mishnah, Talmud, and Aggadah, as it says: "God spoke all these words" (Exodus 20:1)—even what a student will ask his teacher, God [already] taught to Moses at this time. (Exodus Rabbah 47:1)

The Bible, Mishnah, Talmud, and Aggadah—all these scriptures come from God himself, and God recited them to Moses on Mount Sinai. So rabbinical literature, notwithstanding that it consists of a discussion between different schools of thought, actually sees itself as the Word of God. The internal polymorphism, indeed polyphony, of the rabbinical tradition is not at odds with its overall self-characterization as the Word of God. This idea, too, is expressed in the rabbinical literature:[24]

For three years the school [*beit,* literally "house"] of Shammai and the school of Hillel disagreed. The former maintained: The law [*halakhah*] is in accordance with our opinion, while the latter claimed: The law is in accordance with our opinion. Ultimately, a Divine Voice emerged and proclaimed: The opinion of both the former and the latter are the words of the living God. However, the law is in accordance with the opinion of Beit Hillel. (Babylonian Talmud, Tractate Eruvin 13b)

In the view of the rabbis, it is perfectly possible for contradictory opinions to equally reflect the will of God, which should not be thought of as uniform. Yet the aim of this rabbinical text is not to give free rein to unchecked pluralism. Decisions are required, but they do not necessarily divide neatly into right and wrong ones. Instead, they may simply represent more or less appropriate positions. In the case of the decision in favor of the school of Hillel, the following explanation is offered:

Since the opinion of both the former and the latter are the words of the living God, why were Beit Hillel privileged to have the *halakhah* established in accordance with their opinion? The reason is that they were agreeable and forbearing, showing restraint when affronted, and when they taught the *halakhah* they taught both their own statements and the statements of Beit Shammai. Indeed, when they formulated their teachings and cited a dispute, they cited the opinions of Beit Shammai before expressing their own. (Eruvin 13b)

Whereas the Christian reception of the Torah placed greater emphasis on its narrative passages, Jewish interpretations focused on its legal texts. Scholars refer to this as "halakhic" biblical exegesis. The main aim of the rabbinical interpretation of the 613 core laws of the Torah was to erect "a protective fence around the Torah" (Pirkei Avot 1.1). Mindful of this goal, exegesis was intended to formulate supplementary laws needed to prevent infringement of the core laws. Thus, the dietary proscription against cooking a goat kid in its mother's milk was broadened first to direct that dairy and meat products not be prepared together, second that different utensils should be used in their preparation, and third that a certain amount of time must elapse between the consumption of dairy products and meat.[25]

The narrative material in the Bible has also been interpreted in many different ways. A distinction is made between two principal methods of exegesis: *peshat* and *derash*.[26] *Peshat* ("simple" interpretation) refers to the literal meaning of the text, whereas *derash* ("inquiry") presents a detailed, homiletic interpretation. The dividing line between these two methods is frequently blurred. In the Middle Ages, under the influence of the esoteric Jewish school of thought known as Kabbalah, two further methods evolved: *remez* ("allusion") and *sod* ("secret"). *Remez* inquires into the allegorical sense of a text, while *sod* uncovers its deeper, mystical meaning. Elided together, the names of these four different methods form the acronym PaRDeS. The Hebrew word *pardes* means "orchard" or "garden," and mystical strains of Judaism saw the four levels of textual exegesis as affording a person a way into "paradise" (the English word is cognate with *pardes*, hence the alternative term Garden of Eden).[27]

Besides the Torah, the Five Megillot ("scrolls")—Song of Songs and the books of Ruth, Lamentations, Qohelet, and Esther—have a particular significance within Jewish worship.[28] The Song of Songs is associated with Passover (Pesach), Ruth with the Festival of Weeks (Shavuot), Lamentations with Tisha b'Av (the festival commemorating the destruction of Solomon's Temple on the ninth of Av in 587 BCE), Qohelet with the Feast of Tabernacles (Sukkot), and Esther with Purim. However, combining these five books into the Megillot and attaching them to particular festivals in the Jewish calendar can only be traced back to the medieval period. Each book is recited in its entirety on the appropriate occasion, and so these are some of the most familiar texts in Judaism. The prophetic literature is represented in worship by the Haftarot, a series of selections from the books of the Nevi'im (the Former and Latter Prophets, from Joshua to Malachi) that are recited in conjunction with passages from the Torah.[29]

The reverence with which the Bible is held in Judaism is revealed in a somewhat paradoxical form. Because the Bible plays such a central role, while also being open to reception, it has generated many readings and interpretations that have over time assumed a leading role in forming the religious character of Judaism. Of course, these interpretations always refer back to the original text, without which they cannot be understood; yet they act less like exegeses of the Bible than like holy writ of divine origin in their own right, with their own character and gravitas.

Academic, and in particular historical-critical, exegesis of the Bible has always had, and still has, a difficult time of it in Orthodox Judaism.[30] The philosopher Baruch Spinoza's founding of this discipline led to his ostracization from the Jewish community. In the late nineteenth century, the findings of biblical criticism associated above all with the name of the German Bible scholar Julius Wellhausen were denounced by his contemporary, Rabbi Solomon Schechter, the principal architect of American Conservative Judaism, with the slogan, "higher criticism—higher anti-Semitism."[31] In particular, Wellhausen's late dating of the Torah and his characterization of post-exile Judaism as a petty, legalistic institution led critics to accuse him of latent anti-Semitism.[32] In the final analysis, though, it was the underlying maxim of critical biblical scholarship, that the Bible should be treated and interpreted like any other piece of literature, that was mainly instrumental in creating a virtually unbridgeable chasm between historical-critical Bible studies and Orthodox Judaism's perception of the Bible, which at root could not countenance such a leveling.[33]

Nevertheless, in the nineteenth century, the Wissenschaft des Judentums (Scholarship of Judaism) movement in Germany succeeded in instigating critical investigation of Judaism's central religious and cultural traditions. This movement began with the founding of the Verein für Cultur und Wissenschaft der Juden (Jewish Cultural and Scientific Society) in Berlin in 1819, whose in-house publication, *Zeitschrift für die Wissenschaft des Judenthums*

(Journal of Judaic Studies), began publication in 1822. The movement acquired its own academic teaching establishment in 1854 with the founding of the Jewish Theological Seminary in Breslau (now Wrocław). This was followed by sister institutions in Berlin, Vienna, Budapest, and New York. Gradually, at least in the academic realm, a fundamental principle of openness was established, which accepted the sense and necessity of academic study of the Bible while at the same time disputing the existence of any intrinsic connection between biblical criticism and intellectual anti-Semitism.[34] When the Hebrew University of Jerusalem was founded in 1925, it was unthinkable for it to have a Bible Studies Department where the Bible would become the subject of research and teaching like any other form of literature. It was not until the 1950s that Bible Studies was admitted as a discipline to this institution. This department went on to flourish over the ensuing decades.

The Bible in Western Churches

The different denominations of Christianity have all developed their own individual approaches to the Bible. Where language traditions are concerned, the Eastern and Western churches differ primarily in the preeminence of Greek in the Orthodox churches and Latin in the churches of the Roman West. In addition, specific ways of approaching the Bible also evolved.

In the Western church, a mode of thinking known as the *via moderna,* or nominalism, emerged in the late Middle Ages. According to this mode, human knowledge derived from experience, and things were named on the basis of that experience, rather than knowledge being derived from an essence that is inherent within things and precedes human thought. This debate concerning the nature of human knowledge, its preconditions, and its relationship to reality, also called the problem of universals, which played an extremely important role in medieval philosophy, signaled the emancipation of human reason from the notion that things have a preexisting intrinsic meaning. The issue would resurface in the Reformation, with regard to the question of how one viewed the Bible.

The individual's relation with the Bible was of central importance to the Reformation movements of the sixteenth century. This is evident from the fact that the translation of the Bible produced in Wittenberg by Martin Luther and his collaborators and the Zurich Bible of Huldrych Zwingli and his circle both had theological agendas attached to them. Luther and Zwingli both saw a reappraisal of the Bible as the decisive step toward a root-and-branch renewal of the church. Late medieval nominalism effectively laid the groundwork for the reformers' appeal to biblical scripture as a counter to the tradition of the established church.[35] Earlier religious reform movements such as those of the Waldensians and the Cathars, along with preachers like Jan Hus and John Wycliffe, who were important forerunners of Protestantism, had also made a point of appealing to the evidence of Scripture. Although there is no direct line of descent from these movements and individuals to the Protestant Reformation, the sixteenth-century reformers believed that they were upholding the tradition of these schools of thought and their critical view of the institution of the church. As a result, later commentators came to identify them as "pre-Reformation movements" and to see within them the germ of developments that in the sixteenth century were to lead to the division of the Western Church into the Roman Catholic Church and the churches of the Reformation.

The sixteenth-century Reformation—or more precisely Reformations, plural, since the movement encompassed a multitude of initiatives in various European countries—can to all intents and purposes be described as the start of a wholly new approach to the Bible and its interpretation. Whereas in Bible interpretation of the Middle Ages the stress was on the concordance between the biblical text and the church's teachings, the authority of the Bible was now presented as being at odds with church tradition. The significance of the Bible in Christian theology and the Christian confession was considerably strengthened not only by translations into the vernacular, but also by hymn compositions, catechisms, and prayers. This firm focus on the Bible as the center of theology and faith was expressed in pithy turns of phrase that became the "brand essence" of the Reformation. These include Luther's demand that Scripture should be seen as the sole infallible source of authority for Christians (*sola scriptura regnare*) and the phrase describing Holy Scripture as the only "judge, rule, and standard," which was included in the 1577 Lutheran statement of faith known as the Formula of Concord (this is more resonant in the alliterative German original: *Richter, Regel, und Richtschnur*).[36]

It therefore comes as no surprise that a whole new intensity in reading and studying the Bible emerged from the Reformation. This feature characterizes the churches of the Reformation to the present day and marks a clear difference from both the Orthodox and the Roman Catholic traditions. The Bible plays a central part in Protestant worship and its culture of preaching, in official church statements, and in community life. The Bible translations of Martin Luther and his collaborators form the bedrock of the Lutheran tradition—an impressive testament to his theology and his highly individual, forceful use of language, which has been described as a "rhetoric of the heart."[37] The reformer's prime concern was to produce a Bible text that truly engaged people and brought the message of the Scriptures home to them. The Luther Bible has undergone a number of revisions starting in the late nineteenth century, with the latest edition appearing in 2017. The editors' constant aim has been to retain the particular character of Luther's language and theology. In the Calvinist tradition, much the same can be said of the Zurich Bible, which is characterized by philological exactitude and linguistic precision. The Zurich Bible has also seen several revisions, the latest of which was completed in 2007.

Major biblical texts have been set to music by such composers as Heinrich Schütz (*The Nativity*), Johann Sebastian Bach (*Christmas Oratorio, St. Matthew Passion,* and *St. John Passion,* as well as many of his cantatas), and Felix Mendelssohn (the oratorios *St. Paul,* from the Acts of the Apostles, and *Elijah,* from 1 and 2 Kings). These are impressive theological and musical interpretations of texts from Luther's Bible, which helped this rendition become enshrined as *the* definitive text of the Bible in parts of Europe strongly influenced by Lutheranism.

Another integral part of this intense engagement with the Bible in the late fifteenth and sixteenth centuries was the rediscovery of the manuscripts of biblical texts in the original Greek and Hebrew. This development was stimulated by the invention of the printing press and the educational ideals of Renaissance humanism, which saw a revival of interest in the works of Greek and Roman classical antiquity. Two editions in their original languages, one of the complete Bible and another of the New Testament, appeared in the early sixteenth century. These are the Complutensian Polyglot Bible (whose name derives from the Spanish city of Complutum, now Alcalá de Henares) and an edition of the Greek New Testament (the *Novum Instrumentum omne*) by Erasmus of Rotterdam (Figure 40).

The Polyglot was a luxury edition commissioned and largely financed by Cardinal Francisco Jiménez de Cisneros. The cardinal had founded the

Figure 40. The Complutensian Polyglot Bible (1514–1517), showing Genesis 21:28–22:3.

University of Alcalá in 1499, as an institution for promoting the study of ancient texts in the spirit of humanism. In order to produce the Polyglot, a complete Bible in five volumes, the translator acquired numerous manuscripts in the original Hebrew and Greek. The end of the fifth volume, and a supplementary sixth volume, contain lexicographical addenda as aids to deciphering the Bible texts. The first four volumes are devoted to the Old Testament, which is printed in three columns—Hebrew on the outside, the Greek Septuagint on the inside, and the Latin Vulgate in the middle. This was a visual reminder of the central position of the Latin text, a consideration explicitly noted in the preface. In the books of the Pentateuch, an ancient Aramaic text of the Torah (the Targum Onkelos) and its Latin translation appear at the bottom of each page, together with the Peshitta (the Syriac translation) in Hebrew transcription. The fifth volume contains the New Testament with the Greek text and the Latin translation from the Vulgate. This volume was the first to be finished, in 1514, but was held back until the lengthy work on the Old Testament was complete and the whole Bible could be published together. At the same time, Erasmus was working on an edition of the Greek New Testament, on the basis of a number of medieval manuscripts dating from the twelfth to the fifteenth centuries.[38] Erasmus placed the Greek text in the left-hand column, but deliberately chose to place in the right-hand column not Jerome's Vulgate translation, which was widely seen as the authorized form, but his own Latin translation (Figure 41). This was his way of emphasizing the need for a new translation of the New Testament on the basis of the Greek text.

Because of the delay in publishing the Complutensian Polyglot, Erasmus was able to publish his edition of the New Testament slightly earlier, in 1516. A second edition appeared in 1519. The Complutensian Polyglot finally appeared in 1517, in a print run of some 600 copies, but most of these were lost in a shipwreck en route to Italy. Erasmus managed to obtain an exclusive four-year publishing privilege from Pope Leo X and the Holy Roman emperor, Maximilian I, in 1516. As a result, the surviving copies of the Polyglot did not come into circulation until 1520. Although Erasmus's *Novum Instrumentum omne* was only based on a handful of not very old manuscripts and was somewhat inferior in scholarly status to the New Testament of the Complutensian Polyglot, it remained the definitive Greek text of the New Testament right up to the nineteenth century. It became the first work to which

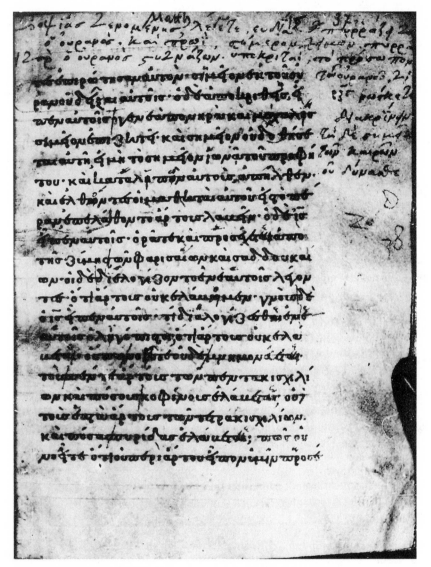

Figure 41. One of the twelfth-century source manuscripts used by Erasmus in creating his edition of the Greek New Testament. Shown here is the text of Matthew 16:1–11, with Erasmus's emendations in the margin.

the term *textus receptus* ("received text," that is, the universally accepted text of a literary work) was applied. Luther based the translation of the New Testament that he wrote at the Wartburg in 1522 on the second edition of Erasmus's *Novum Instrumentum,* as well as on the Vulgate. Not until the nineteenth century was it supplanted by new critical editions of the Greek New Testament based on many more and better manuscripts than those available to Erasmus. These editions were necessitated not least by new text discoveries, including Constantin von Tischendorf's spectacular find of the Codex Sinaiticus in St. Catherine's Monastery at the foot of Mount Sinai in 1844.[39]

Over the decades that followed, textual criticism on the Bible was further expanded by the use of philological and historical methods. The modern period owes its intellectual origins and its dynamism not least to biblical criticism and the supplanting of church doctrine by reason as the bedrock of knowledge. This led to a search for a "religion of reason," as expounded most famously in the work of the eighteenth-century German Enlightenment playwright and philosopher Gotthold Ephraim Lessing. Scholars increasingly began to investigate the historical contexts in which biblical scriptures were created, and raised the question of the historical Jesus for the first time. The eighteenth-century German philosopher Hermann Samuel Reimarus was the first to draw a distinction between the accounts offered in the New Testament and the actual ministry of Jesus and to identify a degree of contradiction between the two. Lessing published Reimarus's writings posthumously, and for his own part argued for distinguishing between the "religion of Christ" and the "Christian religion"—that is, between the religion that Christ himself recognized and practiced as a human being, and the religion that makes Christ a divine object of veneration. Lessing also called for a religion based on reason, against traditional ecclesiastical formulations of faith.

The work of Lessing and other Enlightenment thinkers helped advance the conviction that the Bible was susceptible to exactly the same methods of interpretation as all other literature and, what is more, that the statements made in biblical texts were to be measured against the yardstick of critical reason.[40] For many intellectuals of that period, this signaled a rejection of the doctrine of inspiration, which held that biblical texts were divinely inspired and on that ground to be distinguished from all other literature. For example, in his groundbreaking work of 1771–1775, *Abhandlung von freier Untersuchung des Canon* (Treatise on a Free Enquiry into the Canon), Johann Salomo Semler treated the Bible as a document written by human beings, which was by no means devoid of errors.[41] A clear distinction should therefore be drawn between Holy Scripture and the Word of God, Semler claimed. Although the Bible contained the Word of God, it was not to be simply equated with it. The first effect of this new way of looking at the Bible was to dissolve the unity of the Old and New Testaments as well as the boundaries of the biblical canon.[42] Historical-critical biblical scholarship thus lent new urgency to the question of how the Old and New Testaments related to each other as well as to the question of how canonical and noncanonical works might be differentiated.

This process of "demystifying" the Bible, shifting it from an inviolable sacred document to a collection of writings open to critical reading, took place over a long period. Differing views on the status of the Bible can still be found today. There are a number of communities, both Jewish and Christian, that continue to regard the Bible as infallible—even on nonreligious topics—and such an attitude is not entirely absent from the academic sphere.[43]

Far into the twentieth century, the Catholic Church either remained aloof from historical criticism of the Bible or rejected it outright.[44] The decisive steps toward greater openness were taken with the publication of the papal encyclical *Divino afflante spiritu* in 1943, and especially with the reforms instituted by the Second Vatican Council.[45] Historical-critical research into biblical texts then developed within Catholicism, too, which has had an enduring and beneficial influence on biblical studies as a discipline.[46] While the period since then has largely seen a convergence of Protestant and Catholic interpretations, and a great deal of cooperation between the denominations, a certain reserve toward historical-critical biblical scholarship is still discernible within the realm of Roman Catholic dogma.[47] A recent example of this is the trilogy of works on Jesus of Nazareth by Joseph Ratzinger, which also appeared under his papal name of Benedict XVI.[48]

The development of historical biblical criticism has fundamentally changed both Christian, and to a certain extent also Jewish, theology.[49] The German theologian Ernst Troeltsch summed up this change succinctly:

> The historical method also took hold of theology, at first in a somewhat timid and fragmentary manner with all kinds of provisos and reservations, but then ever more energetically and comprehensively, until it achieved here what it had achieved elsewhere—namely, a fundamental shift in people's mindset and the way they looked at a subject.[50]

Once it had been acknowledged that the cosmological, anthropological, and ethical ideas contained in the Bible were conditioned by the era that gave rise to them, this made it possible, indeed imperative, to regard its viewpoint not as valid for all time but as historically determined. The worldview of the Bible now came to be seen as a reflection of its time, namely antiquity. This also opened the way for a dialogue with other academic disciplines, especially the natural sciences. Henceforth, questions about the origins of humanity or how the universe was formed were open to discussion regardless of how much they might conflict with what was presented in the Bible. Biblical texts were now seen as having been created in a variety of environments with different intellectual horizons. In sum, they were underlain by cultural, religious, and ethical principles very different from those which prevailed in Europe and the United States in the nineteenth and twentieth centuries. It also became abundantly clear that the Bible does not represent one sole theological position that could be identified with any specific set of ecclesiastical dogmas, but instead that it contains a multiplicity of theological and ethical viewpoints which supplement, confirm, correct, or refute one another.

The Bible in Eastern Theology

The Bible performs a very specific function in Orthodox theology.[51] In the Eastern churches, the primary focus is not on a historical-critical interpretation of the Bible or on (retrospective) appropriation of the Bible for hermeneutic purposes, but on its spiritual meaning and its significance for the church.[52] The major works of the church fathers—who read the Old Testament as a resolutely Christian text and thought the Bible should shape the life of believers—continue to play a normative role.[53] Consistent with this approach is the way in which biblical scriptures are deployed in the Orthodox liturgy. It is not their interpretation in sermons that occupies a central role, but rather their significance for the ceremonial act of worship in the form of praise, instruction, and above all the Eucharist.[54] Consequently, the Orthodox church adopts an approach to the Bible that is fundamentally different from that of the Western, and especially Protestant, churches. The picture it paints of how the biblical canon came about and how it is to be used in the present day is a fundamentally harmonious one.[55] It regards the Bible as a homogeneous document which, proceeding from a belief in Jesus Christ, is to be used in church life and worship. At root, Orthodox theology is a "theology of experience," which places it directly at odds with the historical-critical perspective of the Western churches. This theology is matched by a religious practice that can be characterized as veneration and adoration of the invisible God made visible in Jesus Christ.[56] Both these aspects—veneration of the triune God in the liturgy and life of the church, and an awareness of the unknowable and transcendent nature of God—are equally characteristic of Orthodox theology and devotional practice. They find clear expression in the veneration of icons. Icons are, so to speak, "windows" through which the transcendent, divine reality becomes visible here below. The object of adoration is not the image itself, but what it represents.

Precisely because of its divergence from the Western and particularly the Protestant approach, the Orthodox approach to the Bible provides important impetus to a dialogue concerning the Bible as seen from different perspectives.[57] For people whose standpoint has been shaped by Enlightenment ideas and a historical-critical reading of the Bible, an interaction with the Bible that is steeped in spirituality and immediacy is at the same time both alien and exciting. Conversely, to Orthodox eyes and ears, a detached, historical interpretation of the Bible is unfamiliar and may be unappealing. But for each group, broadening their horizons to appreciate the other might well prove mutually stimulating and beneficial.[58]

Other Approaches to the Bible

Taking into account the history of the making of the Bible that we have presented in this volume, what might a modern approach to the Bible look like? To summarize our key findings: The Bible is the result of diverse developments that unfolded over many centuries. It is not a homogenous document but reflects a multiplicity of different viewpoints on the God of Israel and his interventions in history. And finally, the Bible generated a rich history of reception and interpretation that Jews and Christians alike should keep constantly in mind when trying to understand the Bible, interpret it, and live with it and according to its precepts.

A common view among scholars today is that there is no single, fixed meaning of "the Bible," but that different interpretations of biblical texts can coexist without there always being a clear consensus on which of them is "correct." At first sight, this might appear to suggest that the Bible has diminished in significance—indeed, this is the conclusion that is often reached. Neither the churches' doctrinal authorities nor biblical scholarship, working from a historical-critical angle, can unequivocally determine the meaning of biblical texts. Church authorities are themselves subject to the forces of changing historical perspectives and human fallibility, even if the Roman Catholic Church (not biblical scholarship) may at times take a different view of this. And for its part, critical biblical scholarship can only offer provisional interpretations of the Bible that reflect the state of knowledge at any given time, as well as the cultural and religious background of those doing the interpreting. In other words, it can never provide an interpretation that holds good irrevocably for all time. Notwithstanding the unquestionably important, indispensable groundwork that it laid for modern approaches to the Bible, the original claim that historical-critical Bible scholarship made to this effect should therefore be qualified. This is certainly the case where Western culture, conditioned as it is by the ideas of the Enlightenment and the science of history, is concerned. Critical biblical scholarship plays a far less significant role in the Orthodox tradition in both Judaism and Christianity. Yet even within Western biblical scholarship, the realization has dawned in recent decades that the only conclusions that can be drawn are provisional, falsifiable, and subject to revision. This does not signify some free-for-all, however, since the historical evidence does not admit of any and every interpretation. But it does mean that in interpreting biblical texts, one must always operate, as with all historical sources, within a certain spectrum of possible readings and interpretations.[59]

Paradoxically, it was historical criticism itself that was the driving force behind this recognition. In questioning ecclesiastical authority and the doctrine of inspiration and establishing in their place human reason and historical knowledge as criteria for judgment, it did away with the conception of the unity of the Bible and of a simple truth inhabiting it, and replaced them with historical conjectures and probabilities.

One outcome of this realization is that historical criticism cannot form the basis of either the Jewish or the Christian faith. Even so, historical knowledge about the circumstances in which biblical texts were written, about the social and political world they came from, and about the religious and ethical standards espoused by their authors does help to provide a better understanding of the contents of the Bible and to break down prejudices. It also prevents any over-hasty or unthinking appeal to the authority of biblical scripture—something that is often primarily designed merely to lend weight to a person's own point of view and interests. In this respect, therefore, historical criticism performs an enlightened and ethical role.

The preceding decades have witnessed the emergence of numerous "engaged" forms of biblical interpretation. Some of these interpretations, which include postcolonial, feminist, Marxist, and liberation-theological readings, have met with great acclaim in many corners. No criticism should attach to such readings in principle. It should be borne in mind, however, that these approaches to the Bible cannot exist in isolation as alternatives to historical Bible criticism, but must integrate its findings into their observations. This critical method is imperative, since the texts of the Bible come from antiquity and need first to be read in a historically enlightened way in order to then make a plausible, cogent case for their new social relevance.

Other, different ways of engaging with the Bible derive from the various media chosen throughout the history of its reception to convey its message. From earliest times, prominent figures and scenes from the Bible have been represented by visual artists, in the form of paintings, frescos, mosaics, and sculptures. Beginning with paintings in the catacombs of Rome and running right up to the present day, Christian and to some extent also Jewish iconography has generated a wealth of depictions of biblical themes and motifs.

Michelangelo's magnificent portrayal of the creation of Adam on the ceiling of the Sistine Chapel in Rome has given rise to many different interpretations. One remarkable feature of the work is the contrast between the languid, passive human figure on the left side and the dynamic way in which God is depicted on the right, moving toward Adam in the company of his heavenly retinue (Figure 42). Moreover, God is shown in human form, an expression of the biblical precept that humans were created in God's image. The tiny gap between the outstretched index fingers of God and Adam has been the cause of much speculation. One interpretation is that Michelangelo was depicting the instant just before the two touch, when God inspires humanity with the breath of life.

One of the most dramatic stories in the Old Testament forms the subject of Caravaggio's *Sacrifice of Isaac* (Figure 43). Abraham is ordered by God to sacrifice his son (Genesis 22). In this way, God puts Abraham's faith in him

Figure 42. Michelangelo Buonarroti, *The Creation of Adam*, ca. 1511, ceiling fresco in the Sistine Chapel in the Vatican.

Figure 43. Caravaggio, *The Sacrifice of Isaac*, ca. 1603, Uffizi Gallery, Florence.

to the test. The painting captures the moment when Abraham has just drawn his dagger to kill his son. A messenger from God (on the left of the picture) prevents Abraham from carrying out the act at the last moment by taking hold of the arm holding the knife. The viewer is transfixed by the expressions on the faces of the three figures: the horrified and tormented look of Isaac, who until now knew nothing about what his father was planning, the astonished Abraham, who cannot understand why he is suddenly being stopped from carrying out God's command, and God's herald, who is pointing by way of explanation at the ram on the right, which Abraham is now meant to sacrifice in place of his son.

A painting of comparable dramatic power, also dating from period of the Italian Baroque, is Artemisia Gentileschi's depiction of a scene from the thirteenth chapter of the apocryphal book of Judith, a scene that Caravaggio also painted. In *Judith Slaying Holofernes,* the Jewish widow Judith is shown in the act of beheading the Assyrian general Holofernes (Figure 44). She does this not only to save the Israelites from a long siege by Nebuchadnezzar's army but also to avoid being raped by Holofernes. The most striking feature of the painting is the determined, powerful demeanor of Judith and her servant as they hold down the general and slit his throat. Lying in his own blood, Holofernes has no way of defending himself or retaliating. It is thought that the painter was processing a dreadful event in her own life when she was raped by a friend of her father, an incident that compromised her reputation despite the fact that she was the innocent victim.

Christ as Lord in the company of his apostles is a motif that is found in many churches (often in the apse). A very early example of this iconography, albeit now incomplete, can be seen in a mosaic in Santa Pudenziana, one of the oldest churches in Rome (Figure 45). The mosaic was partially destroyed by restoration work in the sixteenth and again in the eighteenth century. As a result, only ten of the original twelve apostles have been preserved. Moreover, at the base of the mosaic, below the figure of Christ, there used to be a dove, symbolizing the Holy Spirit, and a lamb with a halo as well as a procession of lambs emerging from the city gates of Jerusalem and Bethlehem. These features of the original mosaic can be reconstructed from a drawing of 1588. They relate the mosaic to similar illustrations that follow the same iconographic program.

Figure 44. Artemisia Gentileschi, *Judith Slaying Holofernes,* ca. 1612–1613, Museo Capodimonte, Naples.

The mosaic is divided into a heavenly and an earthly realm, which are separated by a semicircle of golden bricks. The upper half of the mosaic is a representation of the heavenly Jerusalem, including the twelve city gates mentioned in Revelation 21:12. It also depicts a number of buildings constructed under Constantine and mentioned by Eusebius in his *Vita Constantini,* notably the massive edifice of the Church of the Holy Sepulchre. Constantine's

Figure 45. The apse mosaic in the Church of Santa Pudenziana in Rome, early fifth century.

new building complex, which was constructed opposite the old town, was so extensive that Eusebius refers to it as the "New Jerusalem."

The scene in the foreground of the mosaic is a visualization of the mission of the church by Jesus's apostles. Special prominence is given to the apostles Peter and Paul, who are shown being crowned by two women standing behind them. These women symbolize the churches of the Jewish Christians and the Gentile Christians, to whom the apostles were sent to preach the gospel. Christ himself, seated on a throne in the robe of an emperor and with his right hand raised in a teaching gesture, forms a link between the two parts of the mosaic. His throne is situated among his disciples, whereas his haloed head extends into the upper section of the mosaic. Christ the heavenly ruler is also the protector of his apostles and their teacher, instructing them in their mission. Last but not least, he is also shown as the guardian of the church of Santa Pudenziana; the legend on the book resting on his knees reads, *Dominus Conservator Ecclesiae Pudentianae* ("The Lord, the preserver of the church of Santa Pudenziana").

The cross behind Christ is a gilded gemstone cross set with precious jewels rather than an instrument of martyrdom. It is, however, positioned on a hill—presumably a reference to Golgotha, the site where Jesus was crucified. At the same time, the cross extends up into the vault of heaven, where four figures are depicted, most probably representing the evangelists. The cross likely also refers to the huge cross that Emperor Theodosius II had erected on Golgotha in the early fifth century, shortly before the Santa Pudenziana mosaic was created.

There can scarcely have been a work that has been so extensively quoted, copied, and parodied as Leonardo da Vinci's portrayal of the Last Supper. This mural painting, which measures approximately 4 by 9 meters, shows Jesus and his disciples sitting at a long table, which is presented face-on to the viewer (Figure 46). The pictorial space is reminiscent of the dining room in a monastery, and indeed it is in such a refectory that the picture hangs. Behind Christ and the disciples, the view opens up onto a hilly landscape, over which arches a blue sky. The communal meal has apparently just ended, with scraps of uneaten food spread over the table. Leonardo has not depicted the Last Supper as such—Jesus is not, for instance, shown breaking bread, nor is any chalice of wine visible. Instead, the scene captures the reaction of the disciples to Jesus's prediction that one of his disciples will betray him.

Figure 46. Leonardo da Vinci, *The Last Supper*, 1494–1497, convent of Santa Maria delle Grazie, Milan.

The disciples appear to be in a state of intense agitation, an impression reinforced by the questioning gestures being made and the discussion going on between three disciples on the far right side. Jesus is seated in a strikingly calm pose in the center, with a small gap between him and the groups of figures to his left and right. In the left half of the picture, directly next to Jesus and leaning slightly to one side, we see the unnamed "disciple whom Jesus loved," whom Peter has just asked to inquire of Jesus who the traitor is (John 13:24). Between the two of them sits Judas Iscariot, identifiable from the small money bag he is clutching (a reference to the thirty pieces of silver he received from the Romans for his act of betrayal). The different emotions and reactions to Christ's revelation of his betrayal give the painting a vivid dynamism.

The German Renaissance artist Matthias Grünewald was the creator of a particularly impressive painting of the Crucifixion, a powerful work that exerts a mesmeric pull on the viewer. Grünewald's *Crucifixion* forms the center panel of a triptych known as the Isenheim Altarpiece, named for the Antonite Preceptory (monastery) at Isenheim near Colmar in eastern France that commissioned it in 1512 (Figure 47). It is now housed in the Unterlinden Museum in Colmar. In addition to the Crucifixion, the front of this folding altarpiece, once opened out, has a panel to the left depicting the martyr St. Sebastian, and one to the right showing the hermit St. Anthony. Beneath the Crucifixion, the plinth of the altarpiece is decorated with a portrayal of Christ's deposition in the tomb. The truly striking thing about this work is the highly expressive characterization of the various people: the suffering Christ with his face contorted in pain, his crown of thorns, and his tormented, bloodstained body, the "favorite disciple" (or possibly the Apostle John, who has been identified with this figure), who is shown comforting Jesus's mother in her distress, and the prophetic John the Baptist, shown pointing at the crucified Christ with his right hand while holding a book (the Old Testament) in his left. To the left, beneath the Cross, Mary Magdalene appears, kneeling beside a vessel of ointment and stretching out her hands in despair.

Another motif frequently used by artists is that of the Four Horsemen of the Apocalypse from Revelation 6:1–8. A woodcut on this theme produced in 1498 by the engraver and painter Albrecht Dürer was a milestone in the history of art. The same may be said of pictures on this same theme by the nineteenth-century Swiss symbolist Arnold Böcklin, who painted this motif

Figure 47. Matthias Grünewald, Isenheim Altarpiece, 1512–1516, Musée Unterlinden, Colmar.

twice, under the title *War*. One can be seen in the art museum of Zurich, while the more famous of the two hangs in the Albertinum in Dresden (Figure 48). In the foreground of the picture, on the far right, rides the figure of Death, with a laurel wreath perched on his head. Next to him, clad in a light-colored cape and clutching a sword, with wildly staring eyes and snakes for hair, is the second horseman. Beyond him, and almost totally hidden, is the third rider, a bearded warrior wearing a helmet and a grim expression. Finally, with his head dead-center, comes the fourth horseman, seated on a white horse, dressed in a red cloak, and charging forward with two blazing torches in his hands. Looking from the foreground to the background, we see that Böcklin depicts the four riders in reverse order to the sequence given in Revelation (that is, Conquest, War, Famine, and Death). His portrayal also differs from Dürer's, where the horsemen follow the same sequence as in Böcklin's work but proceed from left to right as our eye travels into the spatial depth of the engraving. The city beneath Böcklin's horsemen is in flames.

Figure 48. Arnold Böcklin, *War*, 1896, Galerie Neue Meister, Albertinum Dresden.

The picture is a striking portrayal of the powerful destructive forces described in John's Apocalypse. The theme of Death was a common one in Böcklin's work. Like his other paintings on this topic, his portrayal of the apocalyptic horsemen can be seen as a dramatic response to the existential threats confronting the artist and humankind in general.

A similarly monumental treatment of biblical subject matter can be found in literature and music. Works that focus on figures and stories from the Bible include Nikos Kazantzakis's *The Last Temptation of Christ*, Richard Beard's *Lazarus Is Dead*, Niall Williams's *John*, Thomas Mann's *Joseph and His Brothers*, Marianne Fredriksson's *According to Mary Magdalene*, Joseph Haydn's *Creation*, George Frideric Handel's *Messiah*, and Leonard Bernstein's Symphony No. 1, "Jeremiah."

Even just this handful of selective and subjective examples demonstrates that biblical themes have been represented and brought to life in a huge variety of different ways in the visual arts, literature, and music. These interpretations form an important part of the history of reception of the Bible, which can result in highly individual encounters with biblical figures and narratives, through looking at paintings, reading books, or listening to music. In their immediacy, these encounters differ from interpretations based on philological and historical analysis and can lead to new, intensive, and sometimes even surprising and provocatively questioning approaches to the Bible.

Biblical texts have from the earliest times been sung, recited, interpreted, and used in ritual acts by Jews and Christians alike in their services of worship. This liturgical use, too, constitutes its own form of reception of the Bible. In this regard, right up to the present day the Bible as a "canonical document" forms the foundation of Judaism and Christianity. Its texts are their life blood, and the two faiths use the Scriptures to come to terms with the ever-changing historical circumstances in which they find themselves. Acknowledging this role necessarily entails seeing the Bible not as a self-contained book from antiquity but as a collection of diverse texts that are open to constant updating and varied interpretation. In this sense it truly has become the Book of Books.[60]

Abbreviations

This list follows the conventions of *Abkürzungen Theologie und Religionswissen-schaft nach RGG⁴*, UTB 2868 (Tübingen: Mohr Siebeck, 2007). For abbreviations not listed in that publication, bibliographical information was obtained from publishers' websites and library catalogs.

ABG	*Archiv für Begriffsgeschichte,* Bonn, 1955–.
ABU	Arbeiten zur Bibel und ihrer Umwelt, Dortmund, 2009–.
ADPV	Abhandlungen des Deutschen Palästina-Vereins, Wiesbaden 1969–.
AJEC	Ancient Judaism and Early Christianity (formerly Arbeiten zur Geschichte des antiken Judentums und des Urchistentums), Leiden, 1970–.
AKG	Arbeiten zur Kirchengeschichte, Berlin et al., 1915–.
ANRW	*Aufstieg und Niedergang der römischen Welt,* Berlin, 1972–.
ANTZ	Arbeiten zur neutestamentlichen Theologie und Zeitgeschichte, Berlin, 1987–.
AOAT	Alter Orient und Altes Testament, Kevelaer et al., 1969–.
ATD	Das Alte Testament Deutsch. Neues Göttinger Bibelwerk, Göttingen, 1949–.
AThANT	Abhandlungen zur Theologie des Alten und Neuen Testaments, Zürich et al., 1944–.
ATM	Altes Testament und Moderne, Münster, 1988–.
BAR	*Biblical Archaeology Review,* Washington, DC, 1975–.
BASOR	*Bulletin of the American Schools of Oriental Research,* Jerusalem et al., 1919–.
BBB	Bonner biblische Beiträge, Bonn, 1950–.
BE	Biblische Enzyklopädie, Stuttgart et al., 1996–.
BEAT	Beiträge zur Erforschung des Alten Testaments und des antiken Judentums, Frankfurt a. M. et al., 1984–.
BEThL	Bibliotheca Ephemeridum Theologicarum Lovaniensium, Leuven et al., 1947–.

BG	Biblische Gestalten, Leipzig, 2001–.
BHTh	Beiträge zur historischen Theologie, Tübingen, 1929–.
BiKi	*Bibel und Kirche,* Stuttgart, 1946–.
BJSt	Brown Judaic Studies, Missoula, MT, et al., 1978–.
BN	*Biblische Notizen: Beiträge zur exegetischen Diskussion,* Bamberg, 1976–.
BThSt	Biblisch-Theologische Studien, Neukirchen-Vluyn, 1977–.
BThZ	*Berliner Theologische Zeitschrift,* Berlin, 1984–.
BWANT	Beiträge zur Wissenschaft vom Alten und Neuen Testament, Stuttgart et al., 1926–.
BZAR	Beihefte zur Zeitschrift für altorientalische und biblische Rechtsgeschichte, Wiesbaden, 2000–.
BZAW	Beihefte zur Zeitschrift für die alttestamentliche Wissenschaft, Berlin et al., 1896–.
BZNW	Beihefte zur Zeitschrift für die neutestamentliche Wissenschaft und die Kunde der älteren Kirche, Berlin et al., 1923–.
CBET	Contribution to Biblical Exegesis and Theology, Kampen, 1990–.
CBQ	*Catholic Biblical Quarterly,* Washington, DC, 1939–.
CHANE	Culture and History of the Ancient Near East, Leiden, 1982–.
COMES	Civitatum Orbis MEditerranei Studia, Tübingen, 2013–.
CRINT	Compendia Rerum Iudaicarum ad Novum Testamentum, Assen et al., 1974–.
CSEL	*Corpus Scriptorum Ecclesiasticorum Latinorum*
CUSAS	Cornell University Studies in Assyriology and Sumerology, Bethesda, MD, 2007–.
DMOA	Documenta et Monumenta Orientis Antiqui, Leiden, 1947–.
DSD	*Dead Sea Discoveries,* Leiden, 1994–.
EC	*Early Christianity,* Tübingen, 2010–.
EHS.T	Europäische Hochschulschriften—Reihe 23: Theologie, Frankfurt a. M., 1970–.
EvTh	*Evangelische Theologie,* München, 1934–1938, 1946–.
FAT	Forschungen zum Alten Testament, Tübingen, 1991–.
FIOTL	Formation and Interpretation of Old Testament Literature, Leiden, 1997–.
FRLANT	Forschungen zur Religion und Literatur des Alten und Neuen Testaments, Göttingen, 1903–.
GAT	Grundrisse zum Alten Testament, Göttingen, 1975–.
GCS NF	Die griechischen christlichen Schriftsteller der ersten drei Jahrhunderte, Berlin, NF, 1995–.
GNT	Grundrisse zum Neuen Testament, Göttingen, 1971–.
HAT	Handbuch zum Alten Testament, Tübingen 1934–.
HBO	Hallesche Beiträge zur Orientwissenschaft, Halle/S., 1979–.

HBS	Herders Biblische Studien, Freiburg i. Br. et al., 1994–.
HeBAI	*Hebrew Bible and Ancient Israel,* Tübingen, 2012–.
HKAT	Handkommentar zum Alten Testament, Göttingen, 1892–.
HThK.AT	Herders theologischer Kommentar zum Alten Testament, Freiburg i. Br., 1999–.
HZ	*Historische Zeitschrift,* München et al., 1859–.
IEJ	*Israel Exploration Journal,* Jerusalem, 1950–.
JAJ	*Journal of Ancient Judaism,* Göttingen, 2010–.
JBL	*Journal of Biblical Literature,* Philadelphia, PA, 1890–.
JBTh	*Jahrbuch für Biblische Theologie,* Neukirchen, 1986–.
JCS	*Journal of Cuneiform Studies,* New Haven, CT, 1947–.
JNSL	*Journal of Northwest Semitic Languages,* Leiden et al., 1971–.
JSHRZ	*Jüdische Schriften aus hellenistisch römischer Zeit,* Gütersloh, 1973–1975, 1995.
JSJ	*Journal for the Study of Judaism in the Persian, Hellenistic and Roman Period,* Leiden, 1960–.
JSJ.S	*Journal for the Study of Judaism in the Persian, Hellenistic and Roman Period,* Supplements, Leiden, 1996–.
JSNT	*Journal for the Study of the New Testament,* Sheffield, 1978–.
JSOT	*Journal for the Study of the Old Testament,* Sheffield, 1976–.
JSOT.S	*Journal for the Study of the Old Testament,* Supplement Series, 1976–.
JSP	*Journal for the Study of the Pseudepigrapha,* London et al. 1987–.
JSRC	Jerusalem Studies in Religion and Culture, Leiden, 2002–.
JTS	*Journal of Theological Studies,* Oxford, 1899–.
KuD	*Kerygma und Dogma,* Göttingen, 1955–.
KUSATU	Kleine Untersuchungen zur Sprache des Alten Testaments und seiner Umwelt, Waltrop, 2000–.
LHB/OTS	The Library of Hebrew Bible/Old Testament Studies, London, 1976–.
LNTS	The Library of New Testament Studies, London, 2004–.
MThS	Münchener theologische Studien, München 1950–.
NT	*Novum Testamentum: An International Quarterly for New Testament and Related Studies,* Leiden, 1956–.
NTOA	Novum Testamentum et Orbis Antiquus, Freiburg (CH) et al., 1986–.
NTP	Novum Testamentum Patristicum, Göttingen, 2007–.
OBO	Orbis Biblicus et Orientalis, Freiburg (CH) et al., 1973–.
ÖBS	Österreichische Biblische Studien, Frankfurt a. M. et al., 1979–.
OLA	Orientalia Lovaniensia Analecta, Leuven, 1975–.
OLB	Orte und Landschaften der Bibel, Zürich et al., 1984–.
OTS	*Oudtestamentische Studiën,* Leiden, 1942–.

PEQ	*Palestine Exploration Quarterly,* London, 1937–.
PNAS	*Proceedings of the National Academy of Sciences of the United States of America,* Washington, DC, 1915–.
PThSt	Paderborner Theologische Studien, Paderborn et al., 1974–.
QD	Quaestiones disputatae, Freiburg i. Br. et al., 1958–.
RAC	*Reallexikon für Antike und Christentum,* Stuttgart, 1985–.
RB	*Revue biblique,* Paris 1892–.
RdQ	*Revue de Qumran,* Paris, 1958/59–.
REJ	*Revue des études juives,* Paris, 1880–.
RHPhR	*Revue d'histoire et de philosophie religieuses,* Strasbourg et al., 1921–.
SBAB	Stuttgarter biblische Aufsatzbände, Stuttgart, 1988–.
SBB	Stuttgarter biblische Beiträge, Stuttgart, 1965–.
SBL.ANEM	Society of Biblical Literature, Ancient Near Eastern Monographs, Atlanta, 2008–.
SBL.SCSt	Society of Biblical Literature—Septuagint and Cognate Studies, Missoula, MT, 1972–.
SBS	Stuttgarter Bibelstudien, Stuttgart, 1965–.
SHANE	Studies in the History of the Ancient Near East, Leiden et al., 1982
SHR	Studies in the History of Religions, Leiden, 1954–.
SJOT	*Scandinavian Journal of the Old Testament,* Oslo 1987–.
SKI.NF	Studien zu Kirche und Israel, Leipzig, NF, 2012–.
SNTSMS	Society for New Testament Studies Monograph Series, Cambridge, 1971–.
SNTW	Studies of the New Testament and Its World, London et al., 1981–.
STAC	Studien und Texte zu Antike und Christentum, Tübingen, 1998–.
STDJ	Studies on the Texts of the Desert of Judah, Leiden, 1957–.
TdT	Themen der Theologie, Tübingen, 2011–.
TEH	Theologische Existenz heute. Eine Schriftenreihe, München 1933–1941; NF, 1946–.
TENTS	Texts and Editions for New Testament Study, Leiden, 2005–.
ThB	Theologische Bücherei, Gütersloh, 1953–.
ThLZ	Theologische Literaturzeitung, Leipzig, 1876–1944, 1947–.
ThPh	*Theologie und Philosophie,* Freiburg i. Br., 1966–.
TSAJ	Texts and Studies in Ancient Judaism / Texte und Studien zum antiken Judentum, Tübingen, 1981–.
ThSt(B)	Theologische Studien, Zürich, 1938–1942, 1997–.
ThW	Theologische Wissenschaft, Stuttgart et al. (1, 1978); 2, 1972–.
ThWNT	Theologisches Wörterbuch zum Neuen Testament, Stuttgart, 1933–1979.

ThZ	*Theologische Zeitschrift.* Theologische Fakultät der Universität Basel, Basel, 1945–.
TUAT	*Texte aus der Umwelt des Alten Testaments,* Gütersloh, 1982–.
UF	*Ugarit-Forschungen,* Neukirchen et al., 1969–.
UTB	Uni-Taschenbücher, Heidelberg et al., 1971–.
VF	*Verkündigung und Forschung,* München, 1940–.
VT	*Vetus Testamentum,* Leiden, 1951–.
VT.S	*Vetus Testamentum,* Supplements, 1953–.
VWGTh	Veröffentlichungen der Wissenschaftlichen Gesellschaft für Theologie, Gütersloh, 1994–.
WdF	Wege der Forschung, Darmstadt, 1956–.
WMANT	Wissenschaftliche Monographien zum Alten und Neuen Testament, Neukirchen, 1960–.
WO	*Die Welt des Orients. Wissenschaftliche Beiträge zur Kunde des Morgenlandes,* Göttingen et al., 1947 / 1952–.
WUNT	Wissenschaftliche Untersuchungen zum Neuen Testament, Tübingen, 1950–.
WUNT II	Wissenschaftliche Untersuchungen zum Neuen Testament, 2. Reihe, 1976–.
ZAR	*Zeitschrift für altorientalische und biblische Rechtsgeschichte,* Wiesbaden, 1995–.
ZAW	*Zeitschrift für die alttestamentliche Wissenschaft,* Berlin, 1881–.
ZDPV	*Zeitschrift des Deutschen Palästina-Vereins,* Wiesbaden et al., 1878–1945, 1953–.
ZThK	*Zeitschrift für Theologie und Kirche,* Tübingen, 1891–.

Notes

1. What Is "the Bible"?

1. See Brandt, *Endgestalten des Kanons;* Finsterbusch and Lange, *What Is Bible?;* Hieke, *Formen des Kanons.*

2. See Dohmen, *Bibel,* 11.

3. See Schrenk, βίβλος, βιβλίον; Spieckermann, "Bible."

4. Jerome, *Letters* V 2.4 (CSEL 54.22): *multis sacrae Bibliothecae codicibus abundamus.*

5. See McDonald, *Formation of the Biblical Canon,* 1:3.

6. See Wallraff, *Kodex und Kanon,* 38–39, including fig. 9, p. 72.

7. See Stern, *Jewish Bible;* Kim, "Vom hellenistischen Kleinrollensystem zum Kodex."

8. Some fragments of apocryphal gospels, for example of the Gospels of Thomas and Mary, come from scrolls. This may have to do with their status as texts intended solely for private reading.

9. See Harnack, *Über den privaten Gebrauch.*

10. See Wallraff, *Kodex und Kanon,* 44–46.

11. The Aramaic texts are primarily parts of the books of Daniel and Ezra.

12. See Mishnah Yadayim 3.5; Megillat Taanit.

13. See Stemberger, "Jabne und der Kanon"; Krieg, "Javne und der Kanon."

14. Martin Luther's definition of the Apocrypha, which introduces a section of the 1534 edition of his bible that is specially devoted to these texts, runs as follows: "Apocrypha: these are books which are not seen as being of the same caliber as Holy Scripture, but which are useful and good to read all the same." (*Apocrypha. Das sind Bücher: so nicht der heiligen Schrift gleich gehalten: und doch nützlich und gut zu lesen sind.*)

15. This is the listing given in the Luther Bible. The precise extent of the Apocrypha can vary between the various ecclesiastical traditions, and it has not always been consistent between the Lutheran and Reformed Church editions of the Bible. On this subject, see the contributions in Meurer, *Apokryphenfrage.*

16. This situation changed after 1947 as a result of the discovery of the Dead Sea Scrolls. Hebrew and Aramaic fragments of the books of Sirach and Tobit were found at Qumran and Masada, meaning that henceforth, parts of these texts also became available in these languages.

17. This restriction of the texts of the Old Testament to the books written in Hebrew, which is already evident among Christian theologians in antiquity, may well have come down to leaders of the Reformation through the works of Jerome. In his prologues to the books of Solomon and his translations of the books of Samuel and Kings, Jerome notes that the books that do not form part of the group of texts he is translating from Hebrew into Latin—namely the books of Wisdom, Sirach, Judith, Tobit, and the Maccabees—are to be counted among the Apocrypha and cannot be regarded as canonical books.

18. See Beckwith, *Old Testament Canon;* Brandt, *Endgestalten des Kanons.*

19. On this topic, see Joosten, "Origin of the Septuagint Canon." The evidence presented by the book of Sirach, which is an important text for early Greek-speaking Judaism in Alexandria, is ambivalent. The prologue reflects the structure of the Jewish Bible that was emerging at the time (Law, Prophets, other texts), whereas the book itself appears to be premised upon the arrangement Law, Wisdom literature, Prophets (Sirach 39:1).

20. See, for example, Schäfer, *Zwei Götter im Himmel.*

21. Other terms are noted by Leiman, *Canonization.*

22. On the designation "Tanakh," see Ilan, "Term and Concept of TaNaKh."

23. Romans 9:4, 11:27; Acts 3:25, 7:8.

24. Unless otherwise indicated, all quotations from the Bible are from the New International Version (NIV), Copyright © 1973, 1978, 1984, 2011 by Biblica, Inc.

25. English translation by Peter Altmann.

26. See also Chapter 6.

27. The tetragrammaton YHWH is the Old Testament name of God, which in all probability was pronounced "Yahweh" (we can deduce this on the basis of ancient transcriptions of the term into Greek). English-language scholarly works have adopted the practice of writing only the consonants of the name, partly because the pronunciation is not certain, and partly out of deference to Jewish tradition, which does not allow utterance of the full name of God.

28. Barnabas 2:4–10.

29. Barnabas 4:8.

30. Barnabas 6:19, 13:1, 14:4.

31. Justin, *Dialogue with Trypho* 11.3–4, 24.1, 34.1, 43.1, 67.9; Irenaeus, *Against Heresies* 4.9.1.

32. Eusebius, *History of the Church* 4.2613–2614.

33. See also the Mishnah Tractate Baba Batra 14b–15a.

34. This is apparent from the fact that the final masorah, which among other things provides information about the number of verses in the preceding book, is missing at the end of the book of Ezra, appearing only at the end of Nehemiah.

35. Not only Melito but also Origen, Eusebius, Athanasius, Cyril of Jerusalem, and Epiphanius all restrict their lists to those books with a Hebrew basis.

36. As for instance in Origen, Athanasius, and Cyril.

37. Toward the end of the first century CE, Flavius Josephus and the fourth book of Ezra also refer, respectively, to a total of twenty-two or twenty-four books.

38. Clement of Alexandria, *Stromata* I 5.28, II 29.2, V 13.85; Origen, *Commentary on John* 10.28, *On the First Principles* 4.1.1. See also von Campenhausen, *Entstehung*, 308–309.

39. This is the view of Kinzig, "Καινὴ διαθήκη."

40. See Markschies, "Haupteinleitung," 23–24.

41. Marcion is discussed at greater length in Chapter 6, with reference to the creation of the New Testament.

42. See Zenger et al., *Einleitung*, 15–17; Sanders, "The 'First' or 'Old' Testament."

43. See Haug, "Zur abweichenden Kapitel- und Verszählung."

44. In an extensive study, O. H. Steck has attempted to ascertain the meaning of the precise textual structuring of the Isaiah Scroll. See Steck, *Die erste Jesajarolle*; Korpel and Oesch, *Delimitation Criticism*. These findings, although they must necessarily remain hypothetical, reveal a definite intention to structure the text.

45. Weippert, *Historisches Textbuch*, 370–372.

46. Examples can also be found in Aland and Aland, *Der Text des Neuen Testaments*, 286–288.

47. See Aland and Aland, *Der Text des Neuen Testaments*, 175.

48. See Aland and Aland, *Der Text des Neuen Testaments*, 89. We are indebted to Holger Strutwolf (Münster) for providing this information.

49. Schenker et al., *Die älteste Zürcherbibel*.

50. The Hebrew University Bible Project, under whose aegis editions of the books of Isaiah, Jeremiah, and Ezekiel have so far appeared, bases its research on the Aleppo Codex, which was written in 950 CE but is incomplete, especially in the area of the Pentateuch. *The Hebrew Bible: A Critical Edition* (edited by Ronald Hendel) presents an eclectic text that combines what are regarded as the best readings into a hybrid text.

51. See Stökl Ben Ezra, *Qumran*.

52. The fragments are reproduced in their entirety in Ulrich, *Biblical Qumran Scrolls*.

53. English translation by Peter Altmann.

54. See Flint, "Daniel Tradition at Qumran."

55. See Renz and Röllig, *Handbuch der althebräischen Epigraphik*.

56. See Berlejung, "Der gesegnete Mensch" and "Ein Programm fürs Leben."

57. See Hurtado, *Earliest Christian Artefacts*, 95–135.

58. These two forms are hard to separate and tended to merge into one another. See Jones, *New Testament Texts on Greek Amulets*, 120–122.

59. P. Oxy. 5073. Publication: G. S. Smith and A. E. Bernhard, "5073," in D. Colomo and J. Chapa (eds.), *The Oxyrhynchus Papyri*, vol. 76 (London, 2011), 19–23.

60. This is the wording that appears on the amulet. Manuscripts of the Gospel of Mark read "The beginning of the Gospel of Jesus Christ." The continuation of this sentence with the words "the son of God," which appears in many manuscripts but is missing in others, is not included on the amulet.

61. P.Ant. 2.54. Publication: J. W. B. Barns, H. Zilliacus, and C. H. Roberts (eds.), *The Antinoopolis Papyri*, part 2 (London, 1960), 6–7 (no. 54).

62. See Kraus, "Manuscripts."

63. See Kraus, "Miniature Codices."

64. Known miniature nonbiblical codices include those with texts from the Shepherd of Hermas, the Acts of Paul and Thecla, the *Didache,* the Protevangelium of James, the Jesus tradition material on Oxyrhynchus Papyrus 840, and a section of the Gospel of Mary.

65. Paul uses the term "canon" (*kanōn* in Greek) in both 2 Corinthians 10:13–16 (three times) and Galatians 6:16.

66. English translation by Peter Altmann.

67. The term is used in this sense in the First Letter of Clement, which was written toward the end of the first century: "you taught them to obey the canon of obedience, and to manage the affairs of their household in seemliness, with all discretion" (1:3); "Let each of you, brothers, in his own order give thanks unto God, maintaining a good conscience and not transgressing the appointed canon of his service, but acting with all seemliness" (41:1). Translation (updated) by J. B. Lightfoot, *The Apostolic Fathers* (London, 1889).

68. For more on the history of this term, see Smith, "Canon."

69. The term is used in this way, for example, by Clement of Alexandria, *Stromata* I 15.69, III 29.1.

70. As for example in Irenaeus, Hippolytus, and Tertullian.

71. These terms are also widely used in publications covering this area of study: there is a *Deuterocanonical and Cognate Literature Yearbook* and a series entitled Deuterocanonical and Cognate Literature Studies, while a German translation of early Jewish texts goes by the name *Jüdische Schriften aus hellenistisch-römischer Zeit* (Jewish Scriptures of the Hellenistic-Roman Period).

72. See Metzger, *Kanon*, 230–234; Walter, "Bücher," 351–363.

73. This phrase appears in Luther's preface to the Letters of James and Jude in the editions of the New Testament from 1522 (the so-called September Testament) and 1530. His famous characterization of the Letter of James as an "epistle of straw"

comes in his preface to the 1522 edition. He did not repeat this phrase subsequently. Furthermore, the statement he made in 1522 ("I cannot therefore include it among the principal books in my Bible") is altered in the 1530 edition to read: "I cannot therefore place it among the principal books." This indicates that Luther later took a somewhat more restrained view concerning the canonicity of the Letter of James.

74. Josephus describes these groups at several places in his works (*The Jewish War* 2.119–166; *Antiquities of the Jews* 13.171–173, 288, 293, 297–298; 18.11–25). The Essenes are also mentioned by Philo and Pliny the Elder. The Pharisees and Sadducees appear in the New Testament as the opponents of Jesus. The term "Pharisees" may mean "the segregated ones" and relates to this group's exceptionally strict observance of the law (although the origin and the meaning of the term are disputed). The Pharisees were the only group to survive the catastrophe of 70 CE. The name "Sadducees" derives from Zadok, the legendary high priest under King David. They were a priestly sect tasked with the maintenance of the Temple in Jerusalem. The etymology of "Essene" is unclear and disputed, while the Zealots were named for their fanatical religious zeal. See Stemberger, *Pharisäer, Sadduzäer, Essener*.

75. See Heiligenthal, "Weltanschauliche Richtungen."

76. See Fabry, *Qumrantexte* and *Umgang*.

2. Scribal Culture

1. See Schmid, *Old Testament*; Carr, *Formation*; van der Toorn, *Scribal Culture*.

2. See Smend, "Mose"; Blum, "Der historische Mose"; S. L. Sanders, *Invention of Hebrew*.

3. See Römer, *Zwischen Urkunden, Fragmenten und Ergänzungen*; Römer et al., *Einleitung*, 120–168.

4. Kleer, *Der liebliche Sänger*; Noam, "Origin."

5. Unless otherwise indicated, English translations of nonbiblical texts are by Peter Lewis.

6. Fischer, "Die literarische Entstehung"; on the era of Jeroboam II and its literary and historical significance, see also Finkelstein, "Corpus."

7. See Huber, *Gab es ein davidisch-salomonisches Großreich*; Gertz, "Konstruierte Erinnerung"; Finkelstein, "A Great United Monarchy?"

8. See McKenzie, *King David*; Dietrich, *David*.

9. See Pietsch, *Kultreform Josias*.

10. English translation by Peter Altmann.

11. See Keel and Uehlinger, *Göttinnen*; Hartenstein and Moxter, *Hermeneutik*, 23–182.

12. See Uehlinger, "Bild JHWHs."

13. *TUAT* I:382. See also Römer, *Erfindung Gottes,* 137–139.

14. Keel and Küchler, *Orte und Landschaften,* 227–233.

15. For a more extensive treatment of this topic, see Schmid, "Canon and the Cult."

16. English translation by Peter Altmann.

17. The titles "Book of the Righteous" and "Book of the Song" probably refer to the same text. The latter title, which has become widely accepted for this lost book but is incomprehensible, is thought to have come about as the result of an incorrect copying of the word *yšr* ("righteous") as *šyr* ("song"). See McDonald, *Formation,* 128–129.

18. Rollston, *Writing;* Grund-Wittenberg, "Literalität."

19. On the life and work of James Breasted, see Abt, *American Egyptologist.*

20. See Parzinger, *Kinder.*

21. Finkelstein and Sass, "West Semitic Alphabetic Inscriptions."

22. See Gzella, *Sprachen.*

23. See Kim, *Early Biblical Hebrew;* Miller-Naudé, *Diachrony;* Hornkohl, "Biblical Hebrew." For a critical view, see Rezetko and Young, *Historical Linguistics.* A very helpful overview of this topic can be found in Gesundheit, "Introduction."

24. The transcriptions of biblical proper names in ancient translations, such as the Septuagint, may provide a clue, yet even here we cannot be sure whether the translator was sufficiently conversant with how these names were originally pronounced.

25. See Porten, *Elephantine Papyri.*

26. A personal name (Abija or Abijahu) appears in the lower left margin of the text, though it may have been added later.

27. See Weippert, *Historisches Textbuch,* 224.

28. Lehmann and Zernecke, "Bemerkungen."

29. McCarter, "Archaic Baʿal Inscription."

30. See Rollston, "Khirbet."

31. See Finkelstein and Fantalkin, "Khirbet"; Schroer and Münger, *Khirbet.*

32. Finkelstein et al., "Writing"; Carr, "Tel Zayit."

33. See Weippert and Weippert, "'Bileam'-Inschrift"; Blum, "Verstehst du dich nicht auf die Schreibkunst?"; Blum, "Kombination."

34. Blum, "Die altaramäischen Wandinschriften."

35. See Weippert, *Historisches Textbuch,* 242–248.

36. Athas, *Tel Dan;* Kottsieper, "Tel Dan."

37. See Weippert, *Historisches Textbuch,* 328–329.

38. See Knauf, "Hezekiah"; Reich, *Excavating the City,* 193–206.

39. See the thoughtful discussion of this question in Richelle, "Elusive Scrolls," which on the one hand quite correctly argues against regarding the eighth century as the strict limit of literary production, but on the other takes a sympathetic view of markedly earlier dates for the production of biblical literature.

40. Wellhausen, "Geschichte Israels," 40. There does not, however, appear to be any historical basis to the figure of Elijah, See Albertz, *Elia.*

41. *TUAT* I:367–409.

42. See, for example, Na'aman, "Canaanite Jerusalem."

43. Weippert, *Historisches Textbuch,* 138–145.

44. Goren et al., "Provenance Study."

45. Fritz, *Entstehung Israels;* also see the contributions in Grabbe, *Land of Canaan.*

46. On female scribes, see Halton and Svärd, *Women's Writing,* and Schroer, "Von zarter Hand."

47. See Carr, *Schrift.*

48. See, for example, 2 Samuel 8:17; 1 Kings 4:3; Jeremiah 32, 36, 43, 45; Ezra 7:6, 7:12, 7:26; Nehemiah 13:12–13; Sirach 38–39.

49. See 2 Kings 12:10 and 2 Chronicles 24:11; also Esther 3:12, 8:9.

50. Faigenbaum-Golovin et al., "Algorithmic Handwriting."

51. See Bosshard-Nepustil, *Schriftwerdung.*

52. For an overview, see Vieweger, *Archäologie.*

53. See, for example, Finkelstein, *Forgotten Kingdom.*

54. See Keel, *Geschichte Jerusalems,* 155.

55. See Finkelstein, "Corpus."

56. See the discussion between Na'aman, "Dismissing the Myth," and Finkelstein, "Migration"; see also Knauf, "Was There a Refugee Crisis?"

57. On the archeological background, see Finkelstein and Singer-Avitz, "Reevaluating Bethel"; Lipschits, "Bethel Revisited." One fundamental question concerns the location of the sanctuary at Bethel. Was it sited within the city itself or outside? Genesis 12:8, 13:3, and 28:19 (in conjunction with Joshua 16:2) appear to indicate the latter.

58. See Blum, *Komposition;* Blum, "Jacob Tradition"; de Pury, "Jacob Story"; Finkelstein and Römer, "Comments on the . . . Jacob Narrative."

59. Even as early a commentator as Wellhausen (*Prolegomena,* 336) is of this opinion: "Here [i.e., in the story of the Patriarchs] the material is not mythical, but national" (*Der Stoff ist hier nicht mythisch, sondern national*). The same applies to the stories of Abraham: Abraham is the father of Isaac, who likewise stands for Israel (see Amos 7:9 and 16), and Lot is the father of Moab and Ammon, who bear the names of the corresponding nations on the east bank of the Jordan River. See Finkelstein and Römer, "Comments on the . . . Abraham Narrative"; the stories of Abraham appear to be of a somewhat more recent date.

60. See Wahl, *Jakobserzählungen.*

61. For an extensive treatment of this topic, see Schmid, "Von Jakob zu Israel."

62. Müller, *Jahwe;* Kratz, "Mythos."

63. See Finkelstein, "Corpus."

64. Smelik, "Origin"; Delcor, "Remarques"; van der Toorn, "Celebrating."

65. See Hensel, *Juda.*

66. See Meshel, *Kuntillet.*

67. See Becker, "Exodus-Credo."

68. See Blum, "Der historische Mose."

69. See Fritz, *Entstehung Israels.*

70. See the wide-ranging discussion in Levy, *Israel's Exodus.*

71. See Donner, "Hier sind deine Götter," 71–75; Römer, *Erfindung Gottes,* 122–123.

72. See Pakkala, "Jeroboam"; Berlejung, "Twisting Traditions." On the question of Dan constituting part of Israel only from the eighth century BCE on, in other words from the time of Jeroboam II, see Finkelstein, "Stages," 230; Arie, "Reconsidering." Hence, King Jeroboam I cannot possibly have established an imperial shrine there in the tenth century BCE.

73. See Lang, "Amos"; Hoffman, "Northern Israelite Typological Myth"; Dozeman, "Hosea."

74. See the attempted reconstruction in Germany, *Exodus-Conquest Narrative.*

75. See de Pury, "Cycle de Jacob"; Schmid, *Erzväter.*

76. See Gerhards, *Aussetzungsgeschichte,* 70–105. Gerhards takes issue with the idea that Exodus 2 was originally written independently of Exodus 1; see ". . . und nahm die Tochter Levis." See also Blum, "Die literarische Verbindung," 146–147.

77. *TUAT Ergänzungslieferung,* 56.

78. See Auzou, *Servitude.*

79. For an exhaustive discussion of this topic, see Keel, *Geschichte Jerusalems.*

80. See Stolz, *Psalmen.*

81. See for example Zenger, "Psalter"; Janowski, "Auf dem Weg."

82. See Janowski, "Freude."

83. Engnell, *Studies,* 176n2; Duhm, *Psalmen,* xxi–xxii. See also Laato, "Biblical Scholarship."

84. See Day, "How Many Pre-Exilic Psalms Are There?"

85. See Keel, "Der salomonische Tempelweihspruch"; Keel, "Sonne der Gerechtigkeit." For a critical view of Keel's thesis, see Rösel, "Salomo." See also Janowski, "JHWH."

86. Steck, *Friedensvorstellungen,* 9: "The Jerusalem Cult Tradition describes the global, self-reflective and closed concept which underpins most of the psalms and which, through a process of reciprocal amendment and reference, is articulated liturgically above all in essential elements of the psalms of Zion, the psalms of creation, and the psalms singing the praises of both YHWH as king and earthly kings."

87. For a comprehensive discussion of Psalm 93, see Jeremias, *Königtum.*

88. See Berges and Beuken, *Das Buch Jesaja;* Berges, "Singt dem Herrn."

89. See Saur, *Einführung.*

90. See Schipper, "Lehre."

91. See Albright, "Ostracon"; Becking, *Fall of Samaria*, 61–73; Becking, "West Semites"; Na'aman, "Population Changes"; Oded, "Observations."

92. See Na'aman and Zadok, "Assyrian Deportations."

93. See Knoppers, *Jews and Samaritans;* Hensel, *Juda.*

94. See Stern and Magen, "Archaeological Evidence"; Magen, "Dating"; Magen et al., *Mount Gerizim Excavations I;* Magen et al., *Mount Gerizim Excavations II,* 167–205.

95. Finkelstein, "Major Saviors," confirms the provenance of these stories in the north but opts for an earlier date of the eighth century BCE, before the fall of the northern kingdom (450). However, the argument that the stories must be based on a situation where the territory of the kingdom was still intact does not weigh very heavily in comparison to the complete absence of a royal figure in the stories of judges in the Bible.

96. See Guillaume, *Waiting for Josiah,* and (albeit with only a small section of literary criticism) Müller, *Königtum,* 93–118.

97. See Steiner, "Moab," especially 772; Dion and Daviau, "Moabites."

98. See Knauf, *Midian,* 31–42.

99. See Na'aman, "Dismissing the Myth"; Finkelstein, "Migration"; Knauf, "Was There a Refugee Crisis?"

100. See Otto, *Das antike Jerusalem.*

101. See Hensel, *Juda,* and Chapter 4 of this work.

102. See on the one side of this argument Kratz, "Israel," and on the other Weingart, *Stämmevolk.*

103. English translation by Peter Altmann.

104. See Blum, "Jesajas prophetisches Testament," 13–16.

105. See Köckert, "YHWH."

106. See Kratz, *Propheten Israels;* Nissinen, *Ancient Prophecy.* See the extensive discussion of prophecy in Schmid, "Prognosen."

107. See *TUAT* II no. 1, 83–93, and *TUAT* II no. 1, 56–82.

108. See Köckert and Nissinen, *Propheten;* Maul, *Wahrsagekunst;* Stökl, *Prophecy;* Nissinen, *Ancient Prophecy.*

109. Weippert, "Aspekte israelitischer Prophetie," 289–290; Weippert, *Götterwort,* 89–90.

110. See Stökl and Carvalho, *Prophets.*

111. See Bosshard and Kratz, "Maleachi."

112. See Bergler, *Joel.*

113. English translation by Peter Altmann.

114. English translation by Peter Altmann.

115. See Müller, *Ausgebliebene Einsicht.*

116. See Jeremias, "Rätsel"; for the alternative view, see Kratz, "Rätsel."

117. See Jeremias, *Prophet Hosea.*

118. See Otto, *Altorientalische und biblische Rechtsgeschichte;* Morrow, *Introduction.*

119. See Römer, "Pentateuch."

120. Assmann, *Herrschaft,* 179.

121. See Borger, "Akkadische Rechtsbücher."

122. English translations of the Laws of Eshnunna and Hammurabi are from Martha T. Roth, *Law Collections from Mesopotamia and Asia Minor* (Atlanta, GA: Scholars Press, 1995).

123. See, for example, Otto, "Bundesbuch."

124. See Jackson, *Wisdom-Laws,* 255–290. Exodus quotation from the New Revised Standard Version Bible, © 1989 National Council of the Churches of Christ in the United States of America.

125. See Albertz, "Theologisierung"; Schmid, "Divine Legislation."

126. See Finsterbusch, *Deuteronomium.*

127. See Stern, *Jewish Bible,* 17.

128. See Crüsemann, "Das 'portative Vaterland.'"

129. Text in Mathys, "Wilhelm Martin Leberecht de Wettes 'Dissertatio critico-exegetica.'"

130. See the exhaustive discussion of this topic in Pietsch, *Kultreform Josias.*

131. See, for example, Frankena, "Vassal-Treaties"; Weinfeld, *Deuteronomy.*

132. See Lauinger, "Esarhaddon's Succession Treaty"; Steymans, "Deuteronomy 28."

133. See, for example, Otto, "Treueid"; Levinson and Stackert, "Between the Covenant Code." Crouch, *Israel,* takes a critical view of the proposition that Deuteronomy represents a reception of New Assyrian vassal treaties, but his argument fails to convince.

134. See Schmid, "Divine Legislation."

135. See Lohfink, "Deuteronomium"; Lohfink, *Studien,* 157–165.

136. See Brague, *Law of God.*

137. See LeFebvre, *Collections;* Fitzpatrick-McKinley, *Transformation.*

138. See Ska, *Introduction,* 52: "The Law was of divine origin, and its validity was therefore 'permanent'; it could not be abrogated. Consequently, a 'new law' was considered to be a form of an old law. It was both identical and different. In practical terms, only a new 'updated' formulation was valid."

139. See Levinson, "Manumission of Hermeneutics." English translation of these verses by Peter Altmann.

140. See Hieke, *Levitikus,* 975–1046.

141. See Levinson, "Birth of the Lemma"; Levinson, *Der kreative Kanon.*

3. Emerging Judaism

1. For a comprehensive overview, see Levin, *Das Alte Testament;* Kratz, "Israel"; also Teeter, "Hebrew Bible." A different conclusion is reached by Hendel and

Joosten, *How Old Is the Hebrew Bible?* 125, who base their judgment primarily on linguistic-historical considerations and only take limited account of the fact that later texts of the Hebrew Bible might have been deliberately written in an archaic manner. Their reconstruction suggests a far greater proximity in time between the narrated world and the world of the authors of the Hebrew Bible than is generally assumed to be the case in recent biblical scholarship. See the critical discussion in Gesundheit, "Introduction"; Blum, "Linguistic Dating."

2. See Keel, *Die Geschichte Jerusalems;* Leuenberger, "Ich bin Jhwh."

3. On circumcision, see Grünwaldt, *Exil;* Ruwe, "Beschneidung"; Wagner, "Profanität"; Römer, Beschneidung." On the Sabbath, see Grund, *Entstehung.*

4. See Gertz, "Mose."

5. See Hahn (ed.), *Zerstörungen.*

6. See Stipp, "Gedalja."

7. Hayajneh, "Götter"; Beyerlin, *Religionsgeschichtliches Textbuch,* 261–262.

8. Of special note here is an Idumaic (i.e., from Edom) ostracon dating from the Hellenistic period that names three temples, dedicated respectively to the deities 'Uzzā, Yahō, and Nabû. As Weippert states, "We may speculate that the temple of 'Uzzā primarily served Idumeans of an Arab background, while that of Yahō catered chiefly to those with a Jewish background, and that of Nabû to those of Aramaic heritage." Weippert, *Historisches Textbuch,* 513n335. Surprisingly, though, there is no mention of Qôs, the national deity of Edom.

9. Other deportation processes took place as well, for example, in Jeremiah 52:28–30. See Lipschits, *Fall and Rise,* 56–62.

10. Pearce, "Looking for Judeans"; Pearce, "Identifying Judeans"; Pearce and Wunsch, *Documents.*

11. See Encel, *Temple.*

12. In recent years, however, the focus of discussion within archeological circles on this question has shifted somewhat. While researchers in the late twentieth century assumed that comparatively large numbers of the rural population remained behind during the Babylonian Exile, more recently it has become the norm to stress the considerable scale of the deportations. Nonetheless, the country continued to have a significant population even during the period of enforced deportation. See Lipschits, "Demographic Changes" and "Rural Settlement"; see also Finkelstein, "Territorial Extent"; Ben Zvi, "Total Exile."

13. See Blanco Wissmann, "Er tat das Rechte."

14. Lamentations 1:1 is longer in the Septuagint than in the Hebrew text and begins with the following words: "And it happened after Israel had been led captive and Jerusalem had been destroyed that Jeremiah sat and lamented with the following lamentation: . . ."

15. See Steck, "Zion als Gelände" and *Gottesknecht,* 126–145; Maier, *Daughter Zion.*

16. See Köckert, "YHWH."

17. See Knauf, "Was There a Refugee Crisis?" which evaluates the disagreement between I. Finkelstein and N. Na'aman.

18. Pearce, "Looking for Judeans" and "Identifying Judeans."

19. See Pichot, *Geburt;* Horowitz, *Mesopotamian Cosmic Geography.*

20. See the classic account given in Nöldeke, "Grundschrift"; de Pury, "Pg as the Absolute Beginning"; de Pury, *Patriarchen,* 13–42; also the discussion in Hartenstein and Schmid (eds.), *Abschied.*

21. Weippert, *Historisches Textbuch,* 425–430.

22. On Enuma Elish, see Gertz, "Antibabylonische Polemik"; Schmid, "Von der Gegenwelt." On Atrahasis and Gilgamesh, see Holloway, "What Ship."

23. In the Hellenistic period, this interaction with the sciences was pursued with considerably greater intensity. A particularly striking example is the compromise between the story of the Creation presented in the Bible and the Platonic dialogue *Timaios* in the Septuagint, the Greek translation of the Old Testament: the terminology and ideas implicit in the Greek text of Genesis 1 are an attempt at harmonizing the cosmology. The Septuagint sees the world described in the Bible as being no different from the one imagined by Greek philosophy and science. The closeness of the biblical account to *Timaios* is evident from Genesis 1:2. There, the Septuagint describes the state of the world prior to the Creation—which is rendered in Hebrew by the phrase *tohu wa bohu* ("chaos")—as "unsightly and unfurnished," a formulation that appears to allude to the concept of a distinction between the world of ideas and the material world, an idea that is central to Plato's *Timaios.* The Greek text's rendition of *rāqiaʿ* ("firmament") in Genesis 1:6 as *steréoma* ("support" or "foundation") may likewise be explained through reference to *Timaios,* which applies the adjective *stereós* ("firm, solid") on many occasions to heavenly bodies (31b, 43c, etc.). See Rösel, *Übersetzung,* 31.36.60.81–87. Karrer, "Septuaginta," also gives a nuanced account of this correspondence.

24. See Pongratz-Leisten, *Ina šulmi irub.*

25. See Ehring, *Rückkehr.*

26. Uehlinger and Müller Trufaut, "Ezekiel."

27. Keel-Leu and Tessier, *Die vorderasiatischen Rollsiegel,* seal no. 236.

28. Hartenstein, *Unzugänglichkeit,* 226; see also Hartenstein, "Wolkendunkel."

29. See Schmid, "Himmelsgott"; Koch, *Gottes himmlische Wohnstatt.*

30. See Levin, "Entstehung"; see also *Encyclopedia of Judaism,* vol. 2 (Leiden, 2005), 1275.

31. *Encyclopedia Judaica,* 2nd ed. (Detroit, 2007), vol. 11, 514; Noth, *Geschichte,* 386.

32. See Brettler, "Judaism"; Mason, "Jews."

33. See Cohen, *Beginnings.*

34. See, for example, Edelman (ed.), *Triumph.*

35. English translations from Maccabees are from the Good News Translation in Today's English Version, Second Edition, Copyright © 1992 by American Bible Society.

36. Wellhausen, *Israelitische und jüdische Geschichte,* 169n1.

37. Wellhausen, *Israelitische und jüdische Geschichte,* 34.

38. See, for example, the material presented in Keel and Uehlinger, *Göttinnen;* Zevit, *Religions;* Hartenstein, "Religionsgeschichte."

39. See Frevel, "Eine"; Frevel and Pyschny, "'Religious' Revolution"; Römer, *Erfindung.*

40. For an extensive account of this feature, see Schmid, "Gibt es."

41. On the question of translation see Weippert, "Synkretismus," 5n15, with reference to Isaiah 49:8.

42. English translation by Peter Altmann.

43. See Sundermeier, *Was ist Religion?* On its application in biblical scholarship, see Wagner, *Primäre und sekundäre Religion.*

44. See 1 Kings 6:2–3 and Ezra 6:3; see also Josephus, *Contra Apionem* I.21–22.

45. However see the balanced account given in Zwickel, *Der salominische Tempel.*

46. See Schaper, *Priester.*

47. On Jerusalem under Persian rule, see Finkelstein, "Jerusalem and Judah" and "Jerusalem in the Persian . . . Period." On composition of texts during this period, see the discussion in Carr, *Formation,* 222–224; Finkelstein, "Jerusalem and Judah," 14. Some commentators have hypothesized that the lack of Hebrew inscriptions during the Persian period—most are Aramaic—means that it is safe to assume that the Hebrew Bible was essentially created in the pre-exile period (Schniedewind, *How the Bible,* 167–172; Hendel and Joosten, *How Old Is the Hebrew Bible?*). However, this assumption runs counter to all historical probability. Of course the inscriptions from the Persian period, almost all of which come from Egypt, are written in what was at the time the lingua franca, Aramaic, whereas the texts of the later Hebrew Bible continued to be written in Hebrew, as befitted the literary product of a scholarly milieu.

48. For a discussion of the momentous religious-historical changes, see Frevel, "Eine."

49. See Plöger, *Theokratie;* see also the discussion in Dörrfuß, *Mose,* 92–115.

50. Frei and Koch, *Reichsidee.*

51. *Translator's note:* see "Behistun," Livius, https://www.livius.org/articles/place /behistun/.

52. See Nöldeke, "Grundschrift"; de Pury, "Pg as the Absolute Beginning"; de Pury, *Patriarchen,* 13–42; Hartenstein and Schmid (eds.), *Abschied.*

53. This term was coined by Dodd, *Parables,* 51, though he used it in the context of Jesus's preaching.

54. English translation by Peter Altmann. "All flesh" includes both humans and animals; see Stipp, "Alles Fleisch." Fish are excluded from this, which is why the flood does not come as a punishment to them.

55. See Mathys, "Erhebung."

56. See Schmid, "Deuteronomistic Image."

57. 1 Kings 8:46–53; Deuteronomy 4:25–31, 28:45–68, 30:1–10; Leviticus 26:32–45; Zechariah 1:2–6; 7; 8; Malachi 3.

58. See Newsom, "Models"; Niditch, *Responsive Self.*

59. The Dead Sea Scrolls represent something of an exception in this regard. In the so-called Damascus Document (CD 14,19) the community regards itself as being part of a "new covenant."

60. See Krüger, "Das menschliche Herz."

61. See Jeremiah 23:5–6, 33:14–26; Ezekiel 17:22–24, 34:23–24, 37:21–25; Amos 9:11–12; Haggai 2:20–23; Zechariah 4:6–10, 6:9–14, 9:9–10. Similar passages in Isaiah 7:14–16, 9:1–6, 11:1–5, and Micah 5:1–5 may even date back to the pre-exile period, though this is disputed. See Schmid (ed.), *Prophetische Heils- und Herrschererwartungen.*

62. See Spans, *Stadtfrau.*

63. See Steck, "Tritojesaja."

64. See Schmid, "Divine Legislation."

65. For details of the current debate on this subject, see Gertz et al. (eds.), *Formation.*

66. See Frevel, "Wiederkehr"; Römer, "From Deuteronomistic History."

67. See Morrow, *Introduction.*

68. See Gertz, "Zusammenhang."

69. See Becker, "Exodus-Credo."

70. See Gertz, "Formation."

71. See, for example, Römer et al. (eds.), *Einleitung,* 120–168; Römer, "Zwischen Urkunden" and "Pentateuch"; Schmid, "Pentateuch."

72. See for example Siegert, *Zwischen Hebräischer Bibel,* 42–43; Görg, "Septuaginta"; Kreuzer, "Entstehung und Entwicklung"; Krauter, "Pentateuch-Septuaginta"; Albrecht, "Die alexandrinische Bibelübersetzung."

73. The oldest manuscript of the Greek Pentateuch is Papyrus Rylands 458, which dates from the mid-second century BCE. See Wevers, "Earliest Witness"; De Troyer, "When Did the Pentateuch," 277; Dorival, "Origines."

74. See Wade, *Consistency.*

75. See 1 Chronicles 16:40, 22:12; 2 Chronicles 12:1, 17:9, 31:3–4, 34:14, 35:26.

76. See Schmid, "Das kosmische Weltgericht."

77. See Schmid, "Persian Imperial Authorization"; Knoppers and Levison (eds.), *Pentateuch.*

78. See Frei and Koch, *Reichsidee.*

79. For a detailed analysis, see Schmid, "Persian Imperial Authorization."

80. See Otto, "Jeremia."

81. See Kratz, "Temple"; Kratz, "Elephantine."

82. See Pearce, "Looking for Judeans" and "Identifying Judeans"; Pearce and Wunsch, *Documents;* Encel, *Temple.*

83. See Donner, "Jesaja LVI 1–7."

84. For a comprehensive overview, see Fishbane, *Biblical Interpretation;* also Kratz, "Innerbiblische Exegese"; Gertz, "Schriftauslegung"; Schmid, "Schrift."

85. Kratz, "Innerbiblische Exegese"; Schmid, *Schriftgelehrte Traditionsliteratur;* Levinson, *Der kreative Kanon;* Gertz, "Schriftauslegung."

86. See Schmid, "Divine Legislation."

87. See Ska, *Introduction,* 52.

88. See Levinson, *Der kreative Kanon.*

89. See Otto, "Techniken."

90. English translation by Peter Altmann.

91. For a more extensive treatment, see Schmid, "Neue Schöpfung."

92. English translation by Peter Altmann.

93. See Newsom, "Models"; Niditch, *Responsive Self.*

94. See Schmid, "Divine Legislation."

95. See Mathys, *Ebenbild,* 35–55; Groß, "Gottebenbildlichkeit"; Janowski, "Die lebendige Statue"; Janowski, *Welt,* 140–171.

96. See Assmann, "Geschichte"; Assman and Stroumsa (eds.), *Transformations;* Assman, "Konstellative Anthropologie."

97. See Schmid, *Hiob;* Schmid, "Gott"; Witte, *Hiobs viele Gesichter.*

98. See the discussion in Oorschot, "Entstehung"; Schmid, "Authors."

99. See Knauf, "Hiobs Heimat."

100. Translation by Peter Altmann.

101. For a detailed account, see Dell and Kynes (eds.), *Reading Job.*

102. Opposing views on this question can be found in Knauf, "Hiobs Heimat," and Dell and Kynes (eds.), *Reading Job.*

4. Scripture in Judaism

1. On the reflections on Alexander the Great in Old Testament literature, see Ego, "Alexander der Große."

2. Droysen, *Geschichte.* An up-to-date survey with important critical notes on the emergence and use of the term "Hellenism" can be found in Markschies, *Hellenisierung.*

3. See, for example, Burkert, *Griechen.*

4. The classic treatment of this theme can be found in Hengel, *Judentum.*

5. See Hengel, "Zum Problem."

6. See Portier-Young, *Apocalypse.*

7. See Tilly, *Apokalyptik;* Förg, *Ursprünge;* Haag, *Das hellenistische Zeitalter;* Beyerle, *Gottesvorstellungen.*

8. See Böttrich, "Urvater."

9. See Albani, *Astronomie.*

10. See Keel and Staub, *Hellenismus.*

11. See van der Toorn, "Revelation."

12. See Krüger, "Rezeption," and Uehlinger, "Qohelet."

13. Some commentators have taken the well-known ending of the book of Ecclesiastes (12:12–14) to be a reference to the conclusion of the Ketuvim; however, the specific way in which it is phrased does not substantiate this.

14. See Schmid, "Abschluss."

15. See Schmitt, "Der heidnische Mantiker"; Witte, "Segen."

16. See the critical discussion in Hendel, "Hasmonean Edition."

17. For use of the expression "canonical process" in biblical scholarship see, for example, Sanders, "Scrolls"; Frey, "Qumran"; Zenger and Frevel, "Bücher," 160–162.

18. See Collins, *Invention*, 184–185.

19. See Kratz, "Temple" and "Elephantine."

20. See Collins, *Invention*, 62–76.

21. See Collins, *Invention*, 76–79.

22. The instruction to take nothing away from a text and to add nothing is designated as a "canonical formula" (see also Jeremiah 26:2 and Proverbs 30:6, which each contain a part of this formula, as well as Revelation 22:18–19). However, when applied to biblical texts, the expression is anachronistic, since the inner-biblical processes of interpretation and updating are clearly more flexible than the expression "canon" and associated terms as they are understood today might suggest. On the religious-historical background, see Levinson, "Die neuassyrischen Ursprünge."

23. See Achenbach, "Prophet."

24. See, for example, Joshua 8:31–32, 23:6; 1 Kings 2:3; 2 Kings 14:6, 18:6, 21:8, 22:8–13, 23:25.

25. English translation by Peter Altmann.

26. English translation by Peter Altmann.

27. See in the Tosefta Sotah 13 and in the Babylonian Talmud Sotah 48b; Yoma 9b; Bava Batra 12a, 14b–15a. See Bosshard and Kratz, "Maleachi."

28. See Gottlieb, "Rabbinic Reception," 403; Petersen, "Rethinking"; Utzschneider, "Schriftprophetie"; Greenspahn, "Why Prophecy Ceased."

29. See Schmid, "Klassische und nachklassische Deutungen."

30. See Steck, *Abschluß*.

31. See Gärtner, *Jesaja 66*.

32. See Grainger, *Syrian War*.

33. See Kratz, "Visions."

34. Flavius Josephus, *Antiquities of the Jews* 12.142, 145. For an overview, see Bickerman, "Charte"; Schröder, *Die "väterlichen Gesetze,"* 82–83; Lefebvre, *Collections*, 174–175; see also Fitzpatrick-McKinley, *Transformation*.

35. See Lange, "Law"; Wright, "Why a Prologue?"

36. English translation by Peter Altmann.

37. See Witte, "Kanon."

38. 2 Maccabees 15:9 reads, "Encouraging them [i.e., the Jews] from the law and the prophets, and reminding them also of the struggles they had won, he [Judas Maccabeus] made them the more eager." 4 Maccabees 18:10 reads, "While he was still with you [the father of the seven brothers who have been martyred], he taught you the law and the prophets." In 2 Maccabees 2:13 it is said that Nehemiah founded a library in which he gathered "the books about the kings and prophets, and the writings of David, and letters of kings about votive offerings."Although the Torah is not mentioned, the other references indicate that the books of the Law and the Prophets, along with the Psalms, were seen as binding for the history and the traditions of Israel. Maccabees quotations from the New Revised Standard Version Bible, copyright © 1989 National Council of the Churches of Christ in the United States of America.

39. In this context, attention should also be drawn to the pseudepigraphic Testament of Levi, 16:2. In a (fictitious) address about the end of days, Levi announces here that Israel will sin against God: "And you will disfigure the law and treat the words of the prophets with disdain." In the form in which it has come down to us, the "Testaments of the 12 Patriarchs" is a Christian text that rests upon Jewish traditions. Yet as regards the phrase "the Law and the Prophets," this is an irrelevance insofar as its usage is attested in both the Jewish and the Christian traditions.

40. On the history and use of this term, see Zsengellér (ed.), *Rewritten Bible;* Feldman and Goldman (eds.), *Scripture.* See also Zahn, "Genre"; Segal, "Qumran Research."

41. Some commentators posit a far later date for Chronicles; see Steins, *Chronik;* Finkelstein, "Rehoboam's Fortified Cities," "Historical Reality," and "Expansion." Thus far, however, this has not become the accepted view among scholars. In particular, attempts to date the inception of Chronicles to the Hasmonean period are hampered by the problem that the cultic, apolitical interpretation of kingship in Chronicles does not square with the self-perception of the Hasmonean king.

42. This is not to claim that a direct connection exists between these phenomena. It is more a case here of simply drawing attention to a literary phenomenon that is encountered in both the Jewish and Christian Bibles.

43. 1 Chronicles 17:5, 21; 2 Chronicles 5:10, 6:5, 7:22, 20:10.

44. The term "opus of historical chronicling" (*chronistisches Geschichtswerk*) was coined by Zunz, *Die gottesdienstlichen Vorträge.*

45. Nickelsburg, "Bible," provides a good summary. See also Siegert, *Einleitung.* The book of Jubilees does, however, form part of the Old Testament in the biblical canon of the Ethiopian Church.

46. See Bernstein, "Genre(s)"; Machiela, *Dead Sea.*

47. This was once incorrectly attributed to Philo of Alexandria; in consequence, its author is now generally referred to as the Pseudo-Philo.

48. See VanderKam, *Einführung*; VanderKam, *Dead Sea Scrolls*; Xeravits and Porzig, *Einführung*; Stökl Ben Ezra, *Qumran*; Magness, *Archaeology*; Schiffman and VanderKam, *Encyclopedia*; Frey, "Qumran."

49. The Qumran fragment 4Q550 was regarded by some researchers as a "proto-Esther" text. This conjecture is not sustainable, though. To date, there is no clear explanation of why the book of Esther was not found among the scrolls at Qumran. See White Crawford, "Has Esther Been Found"; White Crawford, "4QTales"; De Troyer, "Once More."

50. *Translator's note:* Each Dead Sea Scroll manuscript is identified by a manuscript number (for example, 1Q7 denotes the seventh manuscript catalogued from Cave 1 at Qumran). In addition, the manuscript name usually appears in abbreviated form (thus 1Q7 is also referred to as 1QSam, the Samuel scroll).

51. The Essenes are mentioned by Philo in his treatise *Every Good Man Is Free* (*Quod omnis probus liber sit*), 75–91, and by Eusebius in a surviving passage from the *Hypothetica* (Eusebius, Praep. Evang. 8.11.1–18) as well as in his work *On the Contemplative Life* (*De vita contemplativa*). Josephus gives a long description of the Essenes in *The Jewish War* (*De bello Judaico*) 2.119–161. Finally, the Roman author Pliny the Elder includes a note about the Essenes in *Natural History* (*Historia naturalis*) 5.73.

52. Josephus, *The Jewish War* 2.119–161.

53. Josephus, *The Jewish War* 2.160–161. See also the discussion in Rupschus, *Frauen.*

54. See Frey, "Qumran"; Frey, "Qumran und der biblische Kanon," 44–63; Stökl Ben Ezra, *Qumran,* 171–236.

55. Eleven fragments in Aramaic of the constituent parts of the book of Enoch were found in Cave 4, together with one in Greek in Cave 7. It is remarkable that fragments of all the elements that comprise the book of Enoch have been discovered at Qumran, with the exception of the so-called book of Parables (or Similitudes) in 1 Enoch 37–71. The reason for this is not quite clear. It may be that this part of the Enoch literature originated later.

56. See Jain, *Psalmen.*

57. These texts are designated as 4QpalaeoGen, 4QpalaeoExod, and so on. A scroll with the book of Job is also written in Paleo-Hebrew, presumably because the narrative setting of Job is similar to that found in the stories of the Patriarchs in Genesis.

58. See Zahn, "Rethinking"; Perrin, "Variants"; Stökl Ben Ezra, *Qumran,* 208–211; Tigchelaar, "Wie haben die Qumrantexte," 74–76.

59. Greek fragments of the books of Exodus, Leviticus, Numbers, and Deuteronomy were found in Caves 4 and 7. Remarkably, all the fragments found in

Cave 7 were Greek texts. However, the supposition that fragments of New Testament texts will also come to light among them has not been borne out. The Dead Sea texts are uniformly Jewish, not Christian. See Enste, *Kein Markustext.*

60. See CD 5.21–6.1 (4Q266, frg. 3, col. V.21–6.1); 1QS 1.3, 8.15–16; 4Q504, frg. 2, col. III,12–14.

61. This translation is modified by the authors from the reconstruction by García Martinez and Tigchelaar, *Dead Sea Scrolls,* 2: 801.

62. This assumption is made by J. Maier in *Die Qumran-Essener,* his German translation of the Qumran texts.

63. Thus, Pesharim relating to the Psalms have been found at Qumran (e.g. 1QpPs, 4QpPs^a, 4QpPs^b). Likewise, on the basis of the note in 11QPs^a 27.11, which interprets the Psalms of David as "prophecy," it seems clear that the Psalms are not being aggregated to Prophets, but instead singled out and highlighted: "And all these he [David] spoke through prophecy, which was imparted to him by the Highest One."

64. See Bachmann, *Welt.*

65. An informative introduction to the Septuagint, which takes into account all the current research, is provided by Kreuzer, "Entstehung und Überlieferung." See also Tilly, *Einführung.*

66. The term was first applied in this way around the mid-second century by the Christian theologian and philosopher Justin.

67. See Brodersen, *Aristeas,* and Kreuzer, "Entstehung und Überlieferung," 30–49.

68. *Letter of Aristeas* 294.

69. In Eusebius, *Praeparatio Evangelica* 13.12.2.

70. Philo, *Life of Moses* 2.29–43.

71. Josephus, *Antiquities of the Jews* 12.11–118; Justin, 1 *Apologia* 31 (see Dialogue 71); Irenaeus, *Against the Heresies* 3.21.2; Clement of Alexandria, *Stromata* I, 22.148–149; Tertullian, *Apologeticum* 18.

72. According to Justin, the translation was made during the reign of Herod the Great, in other words, very close in time to Jesus's ministry. Furthermore, Justin characterizes the Jewish scriptures that were translated from Hebrew into Greek as "prophetic books," whose meaning the Jews themselves would fail to understand. This clearly reflects Christian polemics against the Jews, which have their basis in Justin's attempt to claim the Jewish scriptures as a testament to Jesus and to dispute their Jewish interpretation.

73. See Nesselrath, "Museion."

74. *Letter of Aristeas* 29–32, quotation at 31.

75. See Tov, "Die griechischen Bibelübersetzungen," and Kreuzer, "Entstehung und Überlieferung."

76. The Targumim are available in Sperber (ed.), *Bible.*

77. The revised edition of the Rahlfs text was produced under the direction of Robert Hanhart and (like its predecessors) was published under the auspices of the German Bible Society in Stuttgart in 2006. The critical edition was completed in 2015. Further volumes are in preparation, with work on the project being conducted by the Kommission zur Edition und Erforschung der Septuaginta of the Academy of Humanities and Sciences in Göttingen.

78. We have already pointed in Chapter 1 to the earliest Christian mention of the books of the "Old Testament" by Melito of Sardes. Further instances are discussed in Chapter 6.

79. See Kartveit, *Origin;* Frey, *Samaritaner;* Knoppers, *Jews;* also see Böhm, "Und sie nahmen ihn nicht auf."

80. A different term, "Samarians," is often used to refer to the population in and around Samaria, which included followers of several different religions.

81. See Tractate Gittin 10a and Tractate Qiddushin 76a (and elsewhere in the Babylonian Talmud).

82. On the explicit identification of "Samaritans" with the "Kutim," see Josephus, *Antiquities of the Jews* 9.290.

83. Even the famous story of the Good Samaritan in Luke 10:30–35 is premised upon a generally negative view of this group: the man who has been waylaid and robbed is passed by—in descending order of importance—by a priest, a Levite, and a Samaritan, and it is the figure with the lowliest social standing, the Samaritan, who stops to help the injured man by the roadside.

84. See Stern and Magen, "Archaeological Evidence"; Magen, "Dating," *Mount Gerizim Excavations I,* and *Mount Gerizim Excavations II,* 167–205.

85. See Hensel, *Juda.*

86. A fundamental problem resides in the fact that the Ten Commandments are not presented as such in either Exodus 20 or Deuteronomy 5, let alone clearly differentiated from one another. For example, Otto (*Mose,* 66) quite rightly maintains that if one adheres strictly to the syntax of the text, Deuteronomy 5 is more of a pentalogue than a decalogue. The first evidence of Jewish numbering of the laws is in the Babylonian Talmud (bMakkot 24a), while the Samaritan amalgamation of the preamble, the commandment against worshipping foreign gods, and the commandment against worshipping graven images is applied in the Masoretes' dotting of the text of Exodus 20:2–7, though this is no older than the Talmud (ca. fifth century CE.).

87. English translation by Peter Altmann.

88. On a corresponding fragment from Qumran, the provenance of which is, however, doubtful, see Kreuzer, *Geschichte,* 151–154.

89. See most recently Nocquet, *Samarie.*

90. See Kratz, "Israel als Staat"; for a critical appraisal, see Weingart, *Stämmevolk.*

91. For a detailed account of the Torah's northern origin, see Schmid, "Pentateuch." See also Nihan, "Torah."

92. Kaiser, *Philo von Alexandrien,* provides a good introduction to the work of Philo. See also Nickelsburg, *Jewish Literature,* 2129–2221. In addition, an exemplary intellectual biography is now available: Niehoff, *Philo of Alexandria.*

93. Josephus, *Antiquities of the Jews* 18.259.

94. Eusebius, *Church History* 2.4.2–3, 2.5.1.6–7. The works of Philo cited by Eusebius have been partially preserved.

95. It is not fully clear whether the "other writings" mentioned alongside the Laws, Prophets, and Psalms refer to other biblical texts or scriptures used specifically by the Therapeutae (such as those named in § 29).

96. *On the Sacrifice of Cain and Abel,* 20–40.

97. Plato, *Phaidros* 253c–256e.

98. See Niehoff, *Philo of Alexandria,* 247–250.

99. *Allegorical Commentary* 1.2–4.

100. *Allegorical Commentary* 2.77–81.

101. *On the Cherubim,* 11–20. The familiar Septuagint text known today states that God "caused *Adam* to dwell over against the Garden of Eden." Philo apparently knew a different version of the text.

102. *Life of Moses* 2.25–44.

103. These include, alongside the previously mentioned *Legatio ad Gaium,* the treatise *Against Flaccus.* In this, Philo describes the anti-Jewish measures undertaken by the Roman governor of Egypt, Aulus Avillius Flaccus, in order to make it clear that God took pity on his people and punished his adversaries. As Philo states at the end of his work, this was borne out by the arrest and death of Flaccus.

5. Ancient Jewish Texts in Early Christianity

1. See the articles by S. Hultgren, L. Doering, and J. K. Zangenberg in Schröter and Jacobi (eds.), *Jesus Handbuch,* 214–245. See also Schröter, *Jesus.*

2. The pronouncedly Jewish character of Galilee has been emphasized many times in recent research, countering some earlier assumptions that the region had a multiethnic character. Archeological studies have ascertained that Galilee was inhabited by Jews from the first century BCE and that there is very little evidence of non-Jewish influence. See Chancey, *Myth of a Gentile Galilee* and *Greco-Roman Culture.*

3. The account given in the Acts of the Apostles forms the basis for this reconstruction. Acts 6 and 7 report that Stephen, one of the Hellenists, adopted an attitude that was critical of the temple and that he was stoned to death as a result by the Jews of Jerusalem. On the Hellenists, see Zugmann, *"Hellenisten."*

4. See Koch, *Geschichte,* 157–223.

5. See, for example, Galatians 3:28: "There is neither Jew nor Gentile, neither slave nor free, nor is there male and female, for you are all one in Christ Jesus." See also Galatians 6:15; 1 Corinthians 7:19, 12:13; Colossians 3:11.

6. See Mark 2:7 par. Luke 5:21; Mark 10:18; John 17:3 ("the only true God"); Galatians 3:20; Romans 3:30; James 2:19.

7. See 1 Thessalonians 1:9; Matthew 16:16; John 6:57.

8. For example, Mark 12:10, 12:24 par. Luke 24:27, 24:32; John 2:22, 5:39, 7:38; Acts 17:11, 18:28; Romans 4:3, 9:17, 10:11; 1 Corinthians 15:3; Galatians 3:8; 1 Timothy 5:18; 1 Peter 2:6 and elsewhere.

9. Romans 3:21; Luke 16:16; Acts 13:15, 24:14, 28:23; Matthew 5:17, 7:12, 11:13 (cited here, oddly, in the order "the Prophets and the Law"), 22:40; John 1:45.

10. English translation by Peter Altmann.

11. Acts 1:16, 1:20, 2:25–36, 4:25, 13:33, 13:35.

12. A similar formulation can be found in line four of the third-century BCE Greek Stoic philosopher Cleanthes's *Hymn to Zeus:* "For we all descend from you . . ." (translation by Stephen Hanselman).

13. See *Didache* 1:5: "Blessed is he who gives . . . but woe unto him to receives"; 4:5; Barnabas 19:9 (see Sirach 4:31).

14. See Pindar's *Pythian Odes* 2.94–96; the same phrase is also used by Aeschylus and Euripides.

15. Paul, for example, does this on several occasions in his Letter to the Romans. In other letters of the New Testament it is also clear that the people being addressed are Gentiles.

16. See, for instance, Mark 14:49; Matthew 26:54, 26:56; Luke 4:21; John 13:16, 17:12, 19:24; Acts 1:16; James 2:23.

17. See Jeska, *Geschichte Israels.*

18. In the case of Hosea and Joel, quotations are taken from the corresponding sections of the twelve Minor Prophets.

19. The reference in Psalm 8:110 is to the human race, to which God has given dominion over the rest of creation. New Testament allusions to it are in Mark 12:36; Matthew 22:44; 1 Corinthians 15:25 and 27; Ephesians 1:20 and 22.

20. Mark 9:12–13 par. Matthew 11:14; Luke 1:17.

21. English translation by Peter Altmann.

22. Origen assumed that this phrase came from the Apocalypse of Elijah. However, that cannot be verified.

23. For example, in the Gospel of Thomas (logion 17) and, loosely translated, in Latin manuscripts of the Ascension of Isaiah (11:34) as well as in the Acts of Peter (chap. 39). The direct influence of 1 Corinthians 2:9 is evident in 1 Clement 34:8 and 2 Clement 11:7.

24. *Abba* appears in Mark 14:36; Romans 8:15; and Galatians 4:6. *Rabbi* or *Rabbouni* as a term of address for Jesus occurs frequently in the Gospels of Mark, Matthew, and John, but not in Luke. The term *Pascha* is found above all in accounts of the events of the Passion in the Gospels and is also used in Acts 12:4; 1 Corinthians 5:7; and Letter to the Hebrews 11:28. The term *Amen,* which was ac-

tually Hebrew, and was used to affirm a wish or a plea, was adopted in Aramaic and occurs frequently in the New Testamament, in the Gospels as well as in the letters and the book of Revelation. In the letters, it invariably comes at the end as a reinforcement of what has previously been said. In the Gospels, it always introduces a pronouncement by Jesus. A peculiarity of the Gospel of John is the double "Amen" introducing the words of Jesus. The names *Barjona* and *Barjesus* are found, respectively, in Matthew 16:17 (as an epithet for Simon Peter) and Acts 13:6. They comprise the Aramaic patronymic prefix *bar*, meaning "son of," and the father's name. Jesus's exclamations *Talitha koum!* and *Ephphata!* appear in Mark 5:41 and 7:34 in the context of stories of healing.

25. It also appears in *Didache* 10:6. The Greek translation appears in Revelation 22:20.

26. For example Mark 5:41, 7:34, 14:36; Matthew 1:23 ("Immanuel" means "God with us"); John 1:41 ("Messiah" translates "the Anointed One").

27. In Acts 6:1 the Hellenists are contrasted with the Hebrews. In both cases, these are Jewish members of the Christian community in Jerusalem, who are distinguished by the language they speak (Greek on the one hand, and Hebrew or Aramaic on the other).

28. This affects, for instance, the meaning of important theological terms like "truth," "righteousness," "covenant," "sin," "glory," "salvation," and so on, which in Jewish Greek texts is frequently influenced by the translation in the Septuagint of the corresponding Hebrew expressions. In addition, there are certain terms that are only attested in Jewish and Christian Greek texts, such as *akrobystía* ("foreskin," "uncircumcised"), *holokaútôma* ("burnt offering"), and *pseudoprophétês* ("false prophet").

29. Galilee was a region overwhelmingly characterized by rural communities, with Sepphoris and Tiberias as the only sizable towns. Magdala may also have had a somewhat urban character. However, the Gospels do not tell of Jesus visiting these locations. Instead, they focus on the village communities, especially the region around the Sea of Galilee. Although the Jewish nature of Galilee has sometimes been questioned, it has been clearly highlighted in more recent research. A prime example of this is the overview by Reed, *Archaeology*.

30. The Synoptic Gospels tell of Jesus visiting Jerusalem for Passover. According to John's gospel, Jesus was in Jerusalem on several occasions to celebrate feast days.

31. On the individual Infancy Gospels, see Markschies and Schröter (eds.), *Antike christliche Apokryphen,* part 2.

32. Mark 1:21, 6:2; Luke 6:6, 13:10; John 6:59; summarizing notes in Matthew 4:23, 9:35; Luke 4:15.

33. English translation by Peter Altmann.

34. English translation by Peter Altmann.

35. Isaiah 26:19, 29:18, 35:5–6, 42:7, 42:18, 61:1.

36. From fragment 4Q521, frg. 2, col. II. Translation from Florentino García Martínez and Eibert J. C. Tigchelaar, *The Dead Sea Scrolls Study Edition,* 2 vols. (Leiden: Brill, 1997, 1998), vol. 2, p. 1045. The text of 4Q521, edited by Émile Puech in 1992, has frequently been studied with regard to its possible relationship to the Jesus tradition. See Becker, "4Q521"; Niebuhr, "Werke."

37. Regulations of this kind can also be found in the texts from Qumran. See CD-A 11,13–17; 4Q265 6,4–8.

38. English translation by Peter Altmann.

39. This precise form of words also appears in its entirety at the beginning of both strophes of the Antitheses in Matthew 5:21 and 33. Yet it is also implied in other cases where only the following abbreviated form is given: "You have heard that it was said. . . ."

40. This view is represented prominently, for instance, by Käsemann, "Problem," 206: "He [Jesus] was certainly a Jew and displayed all the hallmarks of late-Jewish piousness while at the same time, through his claim, making a clear break with this sphere."

41. See, for example, Mark 14:27 (Zechariah 13:7), 14:34 (Psalms 42:6, 42:12; 43:5), 15:24 (Psalm 22:19), 15:33 (Psalm 22:2). See the hint at fulfillment of the scriptures in Mark 15:49.

42. See Matthew 1:22–23, 2:5–6, 2:15, 2:17–18, 2:23, 3:3, 4:14–16, 8:17, 12:17–21, 13:14–15, 13:35, 21:4–5, 24:15, 26:54, 26:56, 27:9–10.

43. See Koch, *Geschichte,* 157–223; Schnelle, *Die ersten 100 Jahre,* 109–222.

44. See Dunn, *Beginning,* 133–240.

45. See Zugmann, *"Hellenisten"*; Kraus, *Zwischen Jerusalem und Antiochia.*

46. See Hengel, "Zwischen Jesus und Paulus."

47. See Riesner, *Frühzeit.* On Paul's Jewish background, see Hengel, *Pre-Christian Paul.*

48. A full account of Paul and Barnabas's missionary activities appears in Acts 13–14.

49. Dunn, *Beginning,* 497–597; Schnelle, *Die ersten 100 Jahre,* 236–303.

50. English translations by Peter Altmann.

51. For more on the material in this section, see Hurtado, *Lord Jesus Christ.*

52. See Fischer, *Tod und Jenseits,* 214–252.

53. English translation by Peter Altmann.

54. English translation by Peter Altmann.

55. English translation by Peter Altmann.

56. English translation by Peter Altmann.

57. Romans 4:24, 8:11; 2 Corinthians 4:14; Galatians 1:1; Colossians 2:12; Ephesians 1:20; 1. Peter 1:21; Acts 17:31.

58. See Joseph and Asenath 8:10, 20:7, and the second benediction of the Jewish Amidah prayer.

59. See 1 Thessalonians 4:14; 1 Corinthians 6:14 and 15:22; 2 Corinthians 4:14; Romans 8:11.

60. The author of the Acts of the Apostles, who frequently takes recourse to the Septuagint and who knew no Hebrew, cites the psalm as it appears in the Septuagint. English translation by Peter Altmann.

61. See for example Galatians 1:4, 3:10–14; 2 Corinthians 5:21; Romans 3:25–26, 4:25; Ephesians 5:25–26; Hebrews 9:15, 10:12; Mark 10:45; Matthew 26:28.

62. English translation by Peter Altmann.

63. See Backhaus, "Kult und Kreuz."

64. See Hofius, "Gottesknechtslied."

65. See Breytenbach, "JesLXX 53,6.12."

66. English translation by Peter Altmann.

67. Translation by Moisés Silva, from *A New English Translation of the Septuagint* © 2007 by the International Organization for Septuagint and Cognate Studies, Inc. http://ccat.sas.upenn.edu/nets/edition/33-esaias-nets.pdf.

68. A specific interpretation of this text can be found in Matthew 8:17. Here, Isaiah 53:4 ("Surely he took up our pain and bore our suffering") is related to the healing ministry of Jesus.

69. English translation by Peter Altmann.

70. See Habermann, *Präexistenzaussagen.*

71. English translation by Peter Altmann.

72. See Koch, *Geschichte,* 249–329.

73. The Letter to the Romans has also been called "an account of the Gospel." In this letter, Paul presents a summary of his view of what it means to believe in Jesus Christ, an account that in large part bears no relation to the actual situation of Roman Christians. In this respect, the epistle differs from all the other letters of Paul.

74. English translation by Peter Altmann.

75. This may be why the quotation is introduced with the phrase "The words of the prophets. . . ."

76. English translation by Peter Altmann.

77. English translation by Peter Altmann.

78. The phrase "from Zion" is used to denote God's act of salvation particularly in Psalms 13:7 (identically in 52:7), 19:3, 49:2, 109:2, 127:5, 133:3, 134:21 (Septuagint). In prophetic texts, the phrase is found in Isaiah 2:3 par. Micah 4:2; Amos 1:2; and Joel 4:16.

79. The same quotation also appears in Acts 2:21.

6. The Formation of the Christian Bible

1. These structures of governance are already reflected in certain texts of the New Testament, such as the First Letter of Peter, the Letter to the Ephesians, and the Pastoral Letters. In the second century, the Letters of Ignatius give further

insight into the development of Christian offices and communities. For an overview of the New Testament texts, see Roloff, *Kirche.* The most important rituals were baptism and the Lord's Supper (or Eucharist). See Ferguson, *Baptism;* Hellholm and Sänger, *Eucharist.* On the question of worship in early Christianity, see the summary by Wick, *Die urchristlichen Gottesdienste.*

2. See Hahn, *Theologie,,* 2:111–142.

3. See Mason, *History of the Jewish War.*

4. On these last two crises, which occurred during the reigns of Trajan and Hadrian respectively, see Horbury, *Jewish War.*

5. Yavne (Jabneh / Jamnia) on the Mediterranean coast became an important site for Judaism in the period between the wars of 66–74 and 132–135. Subsequently, the focus shifted to a number of places in Galilee: Bet She'arim, Sepphoris, and Tiberias.

6. The Jewish polemical attack on Jesus and Christianity may on the one hand be understood by looking at the statements made by ancient Christian theologians like Origen and Tertullian, who, for example, defend themselves against the claim that Jesus was the result of an adulterous relationship on the part of Mary, and on the other through texts such as the Babylonian Talmud and the *Toledot Yeshu,* a Jewish work that originated over a long period and is attested by various sources from the eighth century on, and which presents the life of Yeshu (Jesus) in a polemical way from a Jewish perspective. See Schäfer, *Jesus im Talmud;* also Meerson and Schäfer, *Toledot Yeshu.*

7. The designation of Jesus as a prophet appears, for example, in Mark 6:4 par.; Mark 8:28 par.; Matthew 21:46, 23:37; Luke 13:34, 7:16, 24:19; John 4:19, 4:44, 6:14, 7:40, 9:17. He is referred to as the "Anointed One" (Messiah, Christ) in the sense of God's representative prophesied in Judaism in Mark 8:29 par., 14:62 par. In Mark 11:1–10 par. Jesus is greeted on his entry into Jerusalem with the expectation that he will establish the coming kingdom of David. This and other passages make it clear that those around Jesus used certain designations to try to interpret his ministry. At the same time, the writers of the Gospels stress that these appellations take on a new meaning when they are applied to Jesus: as God's exclusive representative on earth, Jesus is more than a prophet or the Anointed One of Israel; he fulfills these expectations in a unique manner through his death on the cross, his resurrection, and his exaltation.

8. This idea is expressed programmatically in Galatians 3:28: "There is neither Jew nor Gentile, neither slave nor free, nor is there male and female, for you are all one in Christ Jesus." Similar formulations are found in 1 Corinthians 12:13 and Colossians 3:11. This conviction arose in the Christian community at Antioch, where a deliberate policy of reaching out to the Gentiles was implemented for the first time.

9. The title of Peter Schäfer's book *Die Geburt des Judentums aus dem Geist des Christentums* ("The Birth of Judaism from the Spirit of Christianity") succinctly encapsulates this idea.

10. See Dunn, *Partings* and *Jews and Christians.*

11. This criticism is expounded primarily in Lieu, "Parting of the Ways."

12. See Becker and Reed, *The Ways That Never Parted.*

13. See Nicklas, *Jews and Christians?*; also Lieu, "Parting of the Ways," 110–118.

14. As for example in the work *Dissertations* (2.9.19–21) by the cynic and stoic Greek philosopher Epictetus, or the works of the physician Galen: *De Usu Partium* 11.14; *De Differentia Pulsuum* 3.3.

15. In research into Matthew's gospel conducted over the past years, much discussion has centered on whether it represents a viewpoint that is *intra muros* or *extra muros.* In other words, with his story of the life of Jesus, did the writer of Matthew's gospel regard himself as standing inside or outside the "walls" of Judaism? However, using the metaphor of the walls separating Judaism from Christianity or the followers of Jesus risks importing into the Gospel of Matthew a perspective that is in all likelihood not apposite.

16. On distinguishing believers from Jews and Gentiles, see 1 Corinthians 1:21–24; also 1 Corinthians 10:32: ". . . whether Jews, Greeks, or the church of God."

17. For "third way," see Clement of Alexandria, *Stromata* VI 5.41.4–6 (as a quotation from a scripture, which Clement describes as the Sermon of Peter). For "new race," see Diognetus 1; Aristides, *Apologia* 2.2, 15.1, 16.4.

18. See Frey, "Die 'Juden' im Johannesevangelium."

19. Ignatius, *To the Magnesians* 10:3 (see 4; 8:1); *To the Philippians* 6:1 (see 8:2).

20. Barnabas 4:8, 14:3–7.

21. Septuagint references: *Dialogue with Trypho* 120.4, 124.3, 131.1, 137.3 (twice). Justin also refers to the "translation of your seventy elders" (*Dialogue with Trypho* 68.7).

22. English translation by Peter Altmann.

23. Irenaeus, *Against Heresies* 3.21.1.

24. Isaiah 7:14 is not quoted in Luke. However, the tradition of Christ's birth to the Virgin Mary is found in his gospel, too (Luke 1:26–35).

25. English translation by Marcus Dods and George Reith, from *Ante-Nicene Fathers,* vol. 1., ed. Alexander Roberts, James Donaldson, and A. Cleveland Coxe. (Buffalo, NY: 1885), available at https://oll-resources.s3.us-east-2.amazonaws.com /oll3/store/titles/1969/1333.01_Bk.pdf.

26. From a modern perspective, although Justin's interpretation is accurate where the Greek translation of Isaiah 7 is concerned, it is not accurate in the case of the Hebrew original text. See Rösel, "Jungfrauengeburt."

27. See the articles in Alkier and Leppin (eds.), *Juden—Heiden—Christen?*

28. A regulation of this kind might be reflected in the Apostolic Decree, an agreement that was most likely reached in the community of Antioch in order to facilitate the co-existence of Jews and Gentiles within the Christian congregation there. This decree was named by Luke in Acts 15:20, 29 (see also 21:25) and associated there with the Apostolic Council. This is almost certainly not historically

accurate. All the same, the decree provides insight into the situation of Christian communities comprising Jews and Gentiles and the questions that needed to be resolved through regulation in those communities.

29. On the New Testament canon, see von Lips, *Der neutestamentliche Kanon*.

30. Linguistically and theologically, the three letters of John and the Gospel of John are closely intertwined. Biblical scholars disagree about whether all four texts were written by the same author or were edited by the same hand. The question can remain open here. In any event, it is clear that the two "small" letters, the second and third, are the work of the same writer, who in each case introduces himself as the presbyter (elder).

31. See Schröter, "Sammlungen" and *Receptions of Paul*.

32. Eusebius, *Church History* 2.23, 25; 6.14.1.

33. An accessible collection with a translation into German is Lindemann and Paulsen, *Apostolische Väter*.

34. See Gregory and Tuckett, *Reception*; Still and Wilhite, *Apostolic Fathers*.

35. Ancient Christian theologians frequently use the term "apocryphal" in the sense of "falsified" or "heretical." Irenaeus, for instance, talks about a "large number of apocryphal and counterfeit texts, which they [the Valentinians] have produced themselves" (*Against Heresies* 1.20.1). Hippolytus speaks of the "allegedly secret doctrines of Matthew" (*Refutation of All Heresies* 7.20). Tertullian says of the Shepherd of Hermas that it is "counted among the apocryphal and falsified texts" (*On Modesty* 10). According to Eusebius, *Church History* 4.22.9, the early Christian writer Hegesippus claimed of the "so-called Apocrypha" that some had been written by heretics during his lifetime (110–180 CE).

36. See Markschies and Schröter (eds.), *Antike christliche Apokryphen*; also Burke and Landau, *New Testament Apocrypha*.

37. For an English translation of the Nag Hammadi scriptures, see Meyer, *Nag Hammadi Scriptures*.

38. See Schröter and Schwarz, *Die Nag-Hammadi-Schriften*.

39. See the collection by Lührmann, *Fragmente*.

40. The title of Hans-Josef Klauck's book *Die apokryphe Bibel* ("The Apocryphal Bible") therefore gives a misleading impression.

41. See, for example, Hengel and Schwemer, *Der messianische Anspruch Jesu*.

42. See Keith et al. (eds.), *Reception of Jesus*.

43. As evidenced by the presence of certain Aramaic expressions in the Gospels, such as *abba* (Mark 14:36; see Romans 8:15; Galatians 4:6); *rabbouni* (Mark 10:51; John 20:16); *ephphata* (Mark 7:34); *talitha koum* (Mark 5:41); *mammon* (Matthew 6:24; Luke 16:9, 16:11, 16:13), and *Pasha* (used many times). According to Mark 15:31 (see Matthew 27:46), when Jesus was being crucified, he called out in Aramaic, *Eloi, eloi lama sabachthani* ("My God, my God, why have you abandoned me?"), a quotation from Psalm 22:2.

44. The theme of divorce appears in Mark 10:2–12 and Matthew 19:3–12; Matthew 5:27–32; Luke 16:18. The question of support for itinerant missionaries is treated in the mission speeches in the Synoptic Gospels: Mark 6:8–11; Matthew 10:11–14; Luke 9:3–5, 10:5–12.

45. English translation by Peter Altmann.

46. Mark 14:22–25; Matthew 26:26–29; Luke 22:15–20. We do not intend to go into greater detail here regarding the relationship between the slightly differing traditions, which may be split into two distinct lines (Mark and Matthew on the one hand, and Paul and Luke on the other), or on the question of whether an "original form" of the Eucharist tradition might possibly be identified behind them. See Schröter, *Abendmahl*, 124–127.

47. See also 1 Corinthians 11:2: "holding to the traditions just as I passed them on to you."

48. This is clearly enunciated in the confession from Romans 10:9 cited in Chapter 5: The Christian faith is a faith in God, who raised Jesus from the dead, and expresses itself in the affirmation "Jesus is Lord."

49. Passages that are often cited in this regard, namely 1 Thessalonians 4:15 and Romans 14:14, where Paul, respectively, makes reference to "the Lord's word" and says that he is "fully persuaded in the Lord Jesus," are neither quotations of words of Jesus nor allusions to Jesus traditions. Rather, Paul is imparting authority to his own words by making recourse to the "Lord," in much the same way as he does in 1 Corinthians 14:37: "what I am writing to you is the Lord's command." On this topic see Jacobi, *Jesusüberlieferung bei Paulus?*

50. These themes are found in Paul in Romans 14:13–23, 12:14–21 and 1 Thessalonians 5:1–6.

51. Mark 1:1.14–15, 8:35, 10:29, 13:10, 14:9. The term is also used extensively by Paul and the Pauline tradition. But the first time that it is related to the ministry and fate of Jesus is in the Gospel of Mark.

52. Matthew uses the term "gospel" several times in the phrase "gospel of the kingdom (of God)" (e.g., 24:14), whereas the term is not used at all in Luke and John.

53. This is the most widely recognized solution to what is called the "synoptic problem" concerning the relationship of the first three gospels to one another, at least within continental Europe. We do not intend to discuss other models at length here. In the United Kingdom and the United States (represented, for instance, by Francis Watson and Mark Goodacre), the thesis that the author of the Gospel of Luke was familiar with the Gospels of Mark and Matthew is defended as an alternative explanation of the relationships between the Synoptic Gospels. This solution does not need to postulate the existence of a Q source behind Matthew and Luke.

54. Intensive research has been carried out into this supposed source since the nineteenth century. Attempts have been made to reconstruct both the extent

and wording of the source and its precise content and position within the literary and theological history of early Christianity. In the process, some commentators have ventured beyond the bounds of what is actually provable. For a survey of the research on Q, see Kirk, *Q in Matthew,* 151–183.

55. Matthew's gospel represents a partial corrective to the Gospel of Mark. See M. Konradt, "Das Matthäusevangelium als judenchristlicher Gegenentwurf zum Markusevangelium," in Konradt, *Studien,* 43–68.

56. These "reflexive" or "fulfillment" quotations pervade Matthew's portrayal of the life of Jesus, from stories of his birth to the Passion.

57. The most vivid example of Peter's attempt to emulate Jesus is the episode of Jesus's walking on the waters of the Sea of Galilee (Matthew 14:22–33): at first Peter has faith that Jesus will enable him to walk across the water's surface, but then he becomes fearful as a result of the wind and starts to sink.

58. See John 3:14–15, 8:28, 12:32: Jesus's "lifting up"; 8:54, 12:16, 12:23, 13:31–32, 17:1: Jesus's glorification; 7:33–34, 8:14, 8:21, 13:1, 14:3–4: Jesus's "going away."

59. *Didache* 8:2: "as the Lord has commanded you in his gospel" (the Lord's Prayer then follows); 15:3: "Exhort one another, not angrily but peaceably, as you have been commanded in the gospel." The "gospel" is also mentioned in 11:3 and 15:4.

60. A parallel to this story can also be found in Didymus the Blind's commentary on Qohelet 7:21–22a. See Lührmann, *Die apokryph gewordenen Evangelien,* 191–215.

61. See Gregory and Tuckett, *Reception.*

62. Only a few examples from the large stock of apocryphal fragments may be cited here. For a more extensive survey, see Markschies and Schröter (eds.), *Antike christliche Apokryphen.* See also Nicklas, Kruger, Kraus, *Gospel Fragments,* and Schröter, *Die apokryphen Evangelien.*

63. See Kruger, *Gospel of the Savior.*

64. See the in-depth analyses by J. Frey, in Markschies and Schröter (eds.), *Antike christliche Apokryphen,* 560–660.

65. *Stromata* III 93.1.

66. English translation by Arthur Cushman McGiffert, from *Nicene and Post-Nicene Fathers,* 2nd series, vol. 1, ed. Philip Schaff and Henry Wace (Buffalo, NY: Christian Literature Publishing Co., 1890), revised and edited for New Advent by Kevin Knight, http://www.newadvent.org/fathers/250106.htm.

67. See Kraus and Nicklas, *Petrusevangelium;* Foster, *Gospel of Peter.*

68. See the detailed commentary in Gathercole, *Gospel of Thomas.*

69. The fragments in question are the Oxyrhynchus Papyri 1 and 654. Papyrus 654 contains the beginning of the Gospel of Thomas, including logia 1–6. Papyrus 1 contains Greek parallels to logia 26–33 and to logion 77b. Oxyrhynchus Papyrus 655 is also often associated with the Gospel of Thomas. However, because the differences from the Coptic text are much greater, this attribution is far from certain.

70. The Coptic expression may denote both the past and the present. The Greek fragments contain the present-tense form, "Jesus says." Yet some logia presume a narrative situation that lies in the past. Which translation is the more appropriate must therefore be decided on a case-by-case basis.

71. See Tuckett, *Gospel of Mary.*

72. See the commentary by Toepel, *Protevangelium.*

73. This was indeed the case in the Syrian church, where, until the fifth century, Tatian's Diatessaron was regarded as the definitive account of the life and ministry of Jesus.

74. This work in five volumes, which was written in Greek but has only survived in complete form in a Latin translation, is often cited by its Latin title, *Adversus Haereses* (*Against Heresies*). Some passages of the original Greek are known as a result of having been quoted by later authors.

75. *Against Heresies* 1.23–31.

76. *Against Heresies* 4.9.1.

77. Origen, *Homilies on Luke* 1.2.

78. Eusebius, *Church History* 6.14.6–7.

79. See Metzger, *Kanon,* 185–194; Markschies, *Kaiserzeitliche christliche Theologie,* 229–236.

80. English translation by Bruce M. Metzger, from *The Canon of the New Testament* (Oxford, 1987). The Latin phrase *ex opinione* (here rendered as "according to [the general] belief") is difficult to interpret. It can mean "the general view is that [Luke wrote his gospel as a missionary companion of Paul]" or "in Paul's view [Luke wrote his gospel . . .]." Another possibility—entirely plausible in the Muratorian Fragment—is that we are dealing with an error in transcription. The remark might refer to the preface to the (Latin) Gospel of Luke (1:3), where it is stated that the events which are about to be recounted are presented *ex ordine,* that is, "in the proper order."

81. Eusebius, *Church History* 3.39.1. Eusebius cites Irenaeus as the source of this information.

82. See, for example, Leipoldt, *Geschichte,* 145–146; Hengel, *Johanneische Frage,* 86–87. This is sometimes explained by suggesting that the "Presbyter John" mentioned by Papias may be the same person as the author of the Second and Third Letters of John, who also identifies himself as a presbyter. If this individual also wrote the Gospel of John, Papias may have learned of this. However, this matter remains unclear.

83. See Lührmann, *Die apokryph gewordenen Evangelien,* 210–212.

84. The Gospels of Mark and Luke, at least, may well have been known to the writer of the Gospel of John, but this is less certain in the case of the Gospel of Matthew.

85. The only place where the corresponding Greek term *parathêkê* appears is in the two letters to Timothy in the New Testament. Nor is the term used in the Apostolic Fathers.

86. On Marcion, see the excellent monograph by Lieu, *Marcion.*

87. As, for example, in the highly influential monograph on *Markion* by Adolf von Harnack as well as in Hans von Campenhausen's account of the formation of the Christian Bible, *Die Entstehung der christlichen Bibel.*

88. The hypothesis that Marcion was responsible for originating the concept of the "New Testament" was raised by Harnack in *Markion* and was expanded upon by von Campenhausen in *Entstehung.*

89. See Barrett, "The First New Testament."

90. Chapters 2 and 3 of the book of Revelation contain seven short letters to communities in Asia Minor, which were evidently the addressees of the Apocalypse of John.

91. The last letter to be preserved in Papyrus 46 is 1 Thessalonians. The first page and the final seven pages of the codex are missing. It is likely that the codex would have continued with 2 Thessalonians, though this would still have left a few pages over. That space would easily have been large enough for the Letter to Philemon to be included, but not the Pastoral Letters. It is therefore a plausible assumption that the letters to individual addressees were not included. Of course, it is also conceivable that only the Pastoral Letters were left out. We can therefore only speculate about what was on the final seven pages of the codex.

92. Eusebius, *Church History* 6.14.2.

93. Tertullian, *On Modesty* (*De pudicitia*) 20.

94. Eusebius, *Church History* 6.25.14.

95. Origen also occasionally calls individual letter "catholic," for example the Letter of Barnabas (*Against Celsus,* I 63), the First Letter of Peter (Eusebius, *Church History* 6.25.5), the First Letter of John (*Commentary on Matthew* 17, 19) and the Letter of Jude (*Commentary on the Letter to the Romans* VI).

96. Eusebius, *Church History* 2.23.24–25.

97. Eusebius, *Church History* 6.14.1.

98. *Catechetical Lectures* 4.36.

99. See Grünstäudl, "Was lange währt," as well as Merkt, *1. Petrus,* 15–31.

100. Eusebius, *Church History* 3.25.2–3.

101. *Stromata* V 32–55. Clement states that the techniques adopted by the prophetical scriptures are akin to those used by philosophers.

102. Quotation from Hefner, "Theological Methodology," 299.

103. *Against Heresies* 2.20–28.

104. Quotations: *Against Heresies* 2.22.1, 2.27.3, 2.27.1, 1.8.1, 2.27.1, 28.1.

105. *Against Heresies* 1.10.1.

106. The Niceno-Constantinopolitan Creed, or Nicene Creed, is an authoritative statement of the Christian faith formulated by the First Ecumenical Council held at Nicaea in 325.

107. See Athanasius, *Festal Letter* 39; Cyril, *Catechetical Lectures* 4.35–36.

108. Important documents in this context are the Edict of Toleration (Edict of Serdica), issued by Emperor Galerius, and the Edict of Milan, agreed between the emperors Constantine I and Licinius in 313.

109. The production of large Bible codices is often associated with a letter written by Emperor Constantine I, which has come down to us through Eusebius. In this letter, the emperor instructs Eusebius "to order fifty copies of the sacred Scriptures, the provision and use of which you know to be most needful for the instruction of the Church, to be written on prepared parchment in a legible manner, and in a convenient, portable form, by professional transcribers thoroughly practiced in their art" (*Life of Constantine* 4.36); English translation by Arthur Cushman McGiffert, from Schaff and Ware (eds.), *Nicene and Post-Nicene Fathers,* http://www.newadvent.org/fathers/25024.htm. Some commentators have even speculated that the Codex Sinaiticus or the Codex Vaticanus might have been among this batch of fifty codices. However, it is by no means clear whether the books that Constantine commissioned in this letter were fifty *Bibles.* It is also conceivable that Constantine was tasking Eusebius with assembling a collection of the most important texts of the Christian church. In that case, it would not of course have been a question of fifty copies of the same book. See Wallraff, *Kodex und Kanon,* 39–41.

110. See Lührmann, *Die apokryph gewordenen Evangelien,* 1–54.

7. The Jewish Bible, the Mishnah, and the Talmud

1. English translation by Peter Altmann.

2. See, for example, the Qumran fragment 11QPs[a] 27.11: "And all these he [David] spoke through prophecy, which was imparted to him by the Most High." Here, the Psalms are interpreted as a prophecy of David. See also Acts 2:25–36 and elsewhere. In Acts 2:30, David is explicitly described as a prophet.

3. On the Sadducees and the Torah, see Flavius Josephus, *Jewish War* 14.164–165.

4. Flavius Josephus, *Against Apion* 1.8, and in the Babylonian Talmud, Sanhedrin 90b. See Witte, "Kanon," including notes 3–5.

5. See Kratz, "Tora Davids"; Janowski, "Freude an der Tora."

6. For more on the relationship between the Wisdom literature in the Ketuvim and the Torah, see Schipper and Teeter (eds.), *Wisdom and Torah;* Schipper, *Hermeneutik.*

7. See Seybold, "David."

8. See Beckwith, *Old Testament Canon.*

9. See Lang, "Writings"; de Pury, "Zwischen Sophokles und Ijob." See also Steinberg, *Ketuvim.*

10. See Lim, *Formation,* 182: "The closing of the Jewish canon may be seen as a part of the Jewish reaction to knowledge of the books of the New Testament and the increasing influence of Christianity."

11. Lim, "An Indicative Definition," 24, points out that no criteria can be cited that would be authoritative a priori in determining the later canonicity of a text. Instead, the impression of a certain "family resemblance" appears to have been the deciding factor in each case.

12. See Stemberger, "Entstehung," 73–74.

13. See Chapter 4; also Fabry, "Qumrantexte"; Ulrich, *Dead Sea Scrolls;* Lange and Tov (eds.), *Textual History.*

14. See Mason, "Josephus"; Witte, "Kanon," 40n3.

15. From a historical perspective, however, it is unclear who is meant by Artaxerxes, since there were two kings with this regnal name at the time of Ezra and Nehemiah: Artaxerxes I, who ruled from 465 to 425 BCE, and Artaxerxes II, who ruled from 404 to 359 BCE. When the book of Nehemiah (1:1, 2:1) states that Nehemiah came to Jerusalem "in the twentieth year of King Artaxerxes," presumably this means Artaxerxes I, whose twentieth year on the throne was 445 BCE. By contrast, Ezra is said to have come to Jerusalem in the seventh year of the reign of Artaxerxes (Ezra 7:7), in other words, thirteen years before Nehemiah. According to the book of Ezra-Nehemiah, this was unquestionably the same Artaxerxes. However, in historical terms this is hardly possible: Ezra 9:9 states that Jerusalem was already surrounded by a city wall ("wall of protection") at this time in Jerusalem, whereas Nehemiah encounters a broken wall. Conversely, in the political measures he implemented to repopulate Jerusalem, Nehemiah does not appear to have taken the returnees under Ezra into account, who must have already arrived back in the city by this time. Accordingly, Ezra's first appearance must have occurred in the seventh year of the reign of Artaxerxes II, or 398 BCE. In the biblical tradition, however, Ezra as a priest and scribe was accorded a superior position to the political functionary Nehemiah.

16. The fourth book of Ezra dates its own creation to the thirtieth year after the destruction of Jerusalem (4 Ezra 3:1), or 557 BCE. However, this is a literary fiction that is readily identifiable as such: Ezra belongs not to the Babylonian era, but to the Persian period. And in any event, the fourth book of Ezra is even more recent: the date cited in 3:1 signifies the thirtieth year after the *second* destruction of Jerusalem in 70 CE by the Romans. The vision of the eagle in 4 Ezra 11 is also an allusion to the Roman period, with the three heads of the eagle likely symbolizing the emperors Vespasian, Titus, and Domitian. See Schürer, *History,* 297–300; DiTommaso, "Dating the Eagle Vision."

17. See the discussion on this point in Stone, *Fourth Ezra,* 10–11.

18. English translation from Stone, *Fourth Ezra,* 437.

19. See Macholz, "Entstehung"; Becker, "Grenzziehungen."

20. Darshan, "Twenty-four Books," traces the figure of twenty-four back to the Alexandrian tradition, which divided Homer's Iliad and Odyssey into twenty-

four books, reflecting the number of letters in the Greek alphabet (Pseudo-Plutarch, *Vita Homeri* 2.4).

21. See Numbers Rabbah 13.16, 14.4, 14.18, 18.21; Song of Songs Rabbah 4.11; Qohelet Rabbah 12.11–12; see also Leiman, *Canonization,* 54–56.

22. See Stemberger, "Jabne"; Krieg, "Javne." See also Collins, "Before the Canon"; Lim, *Formation,* 179–180.

23. See Rüger, "Werden," 181; Lim, *Formation,* 183.

24. See Neusner, "Role"; Stemberger, "Zum Verständnis der Schrift."

25. See Stemberger, "Rabbinische Schriftauslegung."

26. See Stemberger, *Einleitung;* Krupp, *Einführung.*

27. On the relationship between tradition and innovation in the Talmud, see Vidas, *Tradition.*

28. See the discussion in Schwartz (ed.), *Was 70 CE a Watershed?*

29. See Langer, *Midrasch.*

30. See Kraemer, "Mishnah."

31. On points of contact with Christian literature, see Bar Asher-Siegal, *Early Christian Monastic Literature.*

32. See Krupp, *Einführung,* 90–145.

33. Schwartz, *Imperialism,* 179–202.

34. See also Schäfer, *Geburt.*

35. Edrei and Mendels, "Split Diaspora" and "Split Diaspora II"; in German as Mendels and Edrei, *Zweierlei Diaspora.*

36. See Siegert, *Einleitung;* see also Joosten, "Origin."

37. See Cohen, *Beginnings;* Brettler, "Judaism"; Edelman, *Triumph;* Collins, *Invention.*

38. See Boccaccini, "Introduction" and *Wurzeln.*

39. See Schäfer, *Geburt.*

40. See Schäfer, *Jesus im Talmud;* Lim, *Formation,* 182.

41. See Bar Asher-Siegal, *Early Christian Monastic Literature.*

42. See Vollenweider, "Antijudaismus."

43. See for example Kampling, "Grenzgebiete."

44. See Stemberger, "Rabbinische Schriftauslegung."

8. The Book of Books

1. The *Encyclopedia of the Bible and Its Reception,* which has been published from 2009 by de Gruyter, represents an important first step toward systematic research into the history of the reception of the Bible. See also the related monograph series *Studies of the Bible and Its Reception,* published by de Gruyter as well (from 2013 on).

2. See *Global Scripture Access Report, 2017 Annual Progress,* United Bible Societies, available at https://www.unitedbiblesocieties.org/wp-content/uploads /2018/03/GSAR-2017_UK_brochure_final_lowres_spreads.pdf.

3. For the Hebrew, see Joosten, "Hebrew."

4. See Bechtoldt, *Jüdische deutsche Bibelübersetzungen;* Stern, *Jewish Bible,* 166–195.

5. *Life of Moses* 2.29–43.

6. See Gertz, "Das Alte Testament," 250–251.

7. Indeed, this is the origin of the name Qur'an, which means "recitation, reading." It then came to be applied to the text that was to be read aloud.

8. See Trebolle Barrera, "Vetus Latina."

9. See Graves, "Vulgate."

10. See Rebenich, *Jerome.*

11. See Carbajosa, "Peshitta."

12. See Cox, "Armenian Translations"; Bruni, "Georgian Translations."

13. See Sigismund, "Gothic Translations."

14. See Posset, *Johann Reuchlin.*

15. See Campbell, *Bible;* Burke, Kutsko, and Towner (eds.), *King James Version.*

16. See Bruni, "Old Church Slavonic Translations."

17. See Schmid, "Schrift als Text."

18. See Fishbane, *Biblical Interpretation;* Levinson, *Der kreative Kanon;* see also Schmid, *Schriftgelehrte Traditionsliteratur.*

19. See Ehrlich, "Bibel."

20. Flavius Josephus, *Contra Apionem* 2.275; Philo of Alexandria, *De somniis* 2.127; Acts of the Apostles 15:21. See Perrot, "Reading."

21. See Elbogen, *Der jüdische Gottesdienst,* 159: "From this and several other clauses which determine that precedence should be given to a reading from the Torah over a lection from the Prophets, we may deduce the *terminus ad quem* that we should set when arranging the regular Torah reading; namely, the collection of the prophetic canon. The extenuating exemption applied to the books of the Prophets can only be understood if we bear in mind that the Prophets still has no conclusion within the canon."

22. Ehrlich, "Bibel," 34.

23. See Gesundheit, "Gedanken," 129.

24. See Gesundheit, "Gedanken," 132–133.

25. For a historical perspective on the question of cooking a kid in its mother's milk, see Keel, *Böcklein;* Knauf, "Zur Herkunft und Sozialgeschichte"; also, Lauer, "Kultpolemik"; Petuchowski, "Das rabbinische Verständnis"; Keel, "Replik." On the broadened injunction, see Ehrlich, "Bibel," 39–40.

26. See Kasher, "Interpretation"; Trebolle Barrera, *Jewish Bible,* 468–469.

27. See Krochmalnik, *Im Garten der Schrift.*

28. See Stone, *Compilational History.*

29. See the table in Galley, *Die Hebräische Bibel,* 68–72.

30. See Sperling (ed.), *Students,* and the literature in Ehrlich, "Bibel," 42n37.

31. See Schechter, *Seminary Addresses*, 35–39; Brettler, *How to Read the Jewish Bible*, 4–5.

32. See Smend, "Wellhausen."

33. See Rogerson, "Bibel."

34. See Brettler, *How to Read the Jewish Bible*, 6–7.

35. This factor is clearly in evidence in Martin Luther's famous reply to Holy Roman Emperor Charles V at the Diet of Worms in 1521, after the latter had called on him to recant his 95 Theses: "If, then, I am not convinced by proof from Holy Scripture, or by cogent reasons, if I am not satisfied by the very text I have cited, and if my judgment is not in this way brought into subjection to God's word, I neither can nor will retract anything; for it cannot be either safe or honest for a Christian to speak against his conscience. God help me! Amen."

36. *Bekenntnisschriften der evangelisch-lutherischen Kirche* 769.19–27.

37. Stolt, *Martin Luthers Rhetorik des Herzens.*

38. See Wallraff et al. (eds.), *Basel 1516.*

39. See Porter, *Constantine Tischendorf.*

40. Rogerson, "Bibel."

41. See Semler, *Abhandlung.*

42. See Wrede, "Über Aufgabe und Methode."

43. See, for instance, the examples given in Ebeling, "Bedeutung," 1–3; from a more recent period, see the contributions in Luz, *Zankapfel Bibel;* Linnemann, *Bibelkritik* and *Original.* Further examples can be found in the mission statements of numerous evangelical theological seminaries.

44. See Broer, "Gebremste Exegese."

45. See, from an Old Testament perspective, Ruppert, "Weg"; Seidel, *Erforschung;* Ruppert, "Die historisch-kritische Methode"; from a New Testament standpoint, Klauck, "Die katholische neutestamentliche Exegese."

46. See Hahn, "Beitrag."

47. See Breytenbach, "Das II. Vatikanische Konzil."

48. In his foreword to the first volume (10–23), Ratzinger emphasizes the limits of the historical-critical method, which it is his aim to transcend through "canonical exegesis" and a revival of the doctrine of inspiration. That would amount de facto to a relativization of historical criticism of the ecclesiastical teaching profession.

49. See Legaspi, *Death of Scripture.* The term "theology" is used somewhat tentatively in Judaism. See, for instance, Gesundheit, "Gibt es eine jüdische Theologie . . . ?"; Sommer, "Dialogical Biblical Theology"; Kalimi, *Jewish Bible Theology;* Sommer, "Jewish Concepts"; Sweeney, *Tanak;* Fishbane, *Jewish Hermeneutical Theology.* There is no evidence in Judaism of the creation of the kind of theological doctrinal edifice that is found in Christian denominations. Indeed, such a thing is sometimes explicitly rejected; see Levenson, "Warum Juden."

50. Troeltsch, "Über historische und dogmatische Methode," 8.

51. A brief but informative overview can be found in Luz, *Theologische Herme-neutik,* 71–81.

52. See Pentiuc, *Old Testament.*

53. See Karakolis, "Erwägungen."

54. See Stylianopoulos, *New Testament.*

55. See Stylianopoulos, *Making of the New Testament.* This brief study presents the emergence of the New Testament as a continual process from Jesus through the early Christians to the completion of the New Testament canon in the fourth century. This way of viewing things is fundamentally different from the historical-critical approach customarily adopted in the "Western" tradition.

56. See Felmy, *Einführung.* The first two chapters of this work describe Orthodox theology as a "theology of experience" and "apophatic" (i.e., a theology of negation).

57. See the reflections on this subject in Luz, "Significance" and *Theologische Hermeneutik,* 511–515.

58. To this end, joint conferences of Orthodox and Western theologians have been held in several Eastern European countries in recent years. Their themes have included: the Old Testament (2001), Church Unity (2005), Prayer (2007), the Holy Spirit and the Church in the Testament (2013), History and Theology in the Gospels (2016).

59. Reinhart Koselleck has put it thus: "Strictly speaking, a source can never tell us what we should say. But it certainly can prevent us from making statements that we shouldn't make. The sources have a right of veto. They stop us from attempting or allowing interpretations that can easily be debunked on the basis of the source as downright wrong or inadmissible. . . . Sources protect us from making errors, but they don't tell us what we should say" (*Vergangene Zukunft,* 206).

60. For overviews of the topic of sacred scriptures, see Tworuschka (ed.), *Hei-lige Schriften;* Bultmann et al. (eds.), *Heilige Schriften.*

Bibliography

Abt, J. *American Egyptologist: The Life of James Henry Breasted and the Creation of His Oriental Institute* (Chicago, 2012).

Achenbach, R. "'A Prophet Like Moses' (Deuteronomy 18:15)—'No Prophet Like Moses' (Deuteronomy 34:10): Some Observations on the Relation between the Pentateuch and the Latter Prophets," in T. B. Dozeman et al. (eds.), *The Pentateuch: International Perspectives on Current Research*, FAT 78 (Tübingen, 2011), 435–458.

Aland, K., and B. Aland. *Der Text des Neuen Testaments: Einführung in die wissenschaftlichen Ausgaben sowie in Theorie und Praxis der modernen Textkritik*, 2nd ed. (Stuttgart, 1989).

Albani, M. *Astronomie und Schöpfungsglaube: Untersuchungen zum astronomischen Henochbuch*, WMANT 68 (Neukirchen-Vluyn, 1994).

Albertz, R. *Elia: Ein feuriger Kämpfer für Gott*, BG 13 (Leipzig, 2006).

Albertz, R. "Die Theologisierung des Rechts im Alten Israel," in R. Albertz, *Geschichte und Theologie: Studien zur Exegese des Alten Testaments und zur Religionsgeschichte Israels*, BZAW 326 (Berlin, 2003), 187–207.

Albrecht, F. "Die alexandrinische Bibelübersetzung. Einsichten zur Entstehungs-, Überlieferungs und Wirkungsgeschichte der Septuaginta," in T. Georges et al. (eds.), *Alexandria*, COMES 1 (Tübingen, 2013), 209–243.

Albright, W. F. "An Ostracon from Calah and the North-Israelite Diaspora," *BASOR* 149 (1958), 33–36.

Alkier, S., and H. Leppin (eds.). *Juden—Heiden—Christen? Religiöse Inklusion und Exklusion in Kleinasien bis Decius*, WUNT 400 (Tübingen, 2018).

Arie, E. "Reconsidering the Iron Age II Strata at Tel Dan: Archaeological and Historical Implications," *Tel Aviv* 35 (2008), 6–64.

Assmann, J. *Herrschaft und Heil* (Darmstadt, 2000).

Assmann, J. "Konstellative Anthropologie: Zum Bild des Menschen im alten Ägypten," in B. Janowski and K. Liess (eds.), *Der Mensch im alten Israel: Neue Forschungen zur alttestamentlichen Anthropologie* (Freiburg, 2009), 95–120.

Assmann, J. "Zur Geschichte des Herzens im Alten Ägypten," in J. Assmann and T. Sundermeier (eds.), *Die Erfindung des inneren Menschen: Studien zur religiösen Anthropologie* (Gütersloh, 1993), 81–112.

Assmann, J., and G. G. Stroumsa (eds.). *Transformations of the Inner Self in Ancient Religions,* SHR 83 (Leiden, 1999).

Athas, G. *The Tel Dan Inscription: A Reappraisal and a New Interpretation* (London, 2005).

Auzou, G. *De la servitude au service: Étude du livre de l'Exode,* Connaissance de la Bible 3 (Paris, 1961).

Bachmann, V. *Die Welt im Ausnahmezustand: Eine Untersuchung zu Aussagegehalt und Theologie des Wächterbuches (1 Hen 1–36),* BZAW 409 (Berlin, 2009).

Backhaus, K. "Kult und Kreuz," in K. Backhaus, *Der sprechende Gott: Gesammelte Studien zum Hebräerbrief,* WUNT 240 (Tübingen, 2009), 239–261.

Bar Asher-Siegal, M. *Early Christian Monastic Literature and the Babylonian Talmud* (Cambridge, 2013).

Bar Asher-Siegal, M., W. Grünstäudl, and M. Thiessen, (eds.). *Perceiving the Other in Ancient Judaism and Early Christianity,* WUNT 394 (Tübingen, 2017).

Barrett, C. K. "The First New Testament," *NT* 38 (1996), 94–104.

Barth, K. *Das Evangelium in der Gegenwart,* TEH 25 (Munich, 1935).

Bechtoldt, H.-J. *Jüdische deutsche Bibelübersetzungen vom ausgehenden 18. bis zum Beginn des 20. Jahrhunderts* (Stuttgart, 2005).

Becker, A. H., and A. Y. Reed (eds.). *The Ways That Never Parted: Jews and Christians in Late Antiquity and the Early Middle Ages,* TSAJ 95 (Tübingen, 2003).

Becker, M. "4Q521 und die Gesalbten," *RdQ* 18/69 (1997), 73–96.

Becker, M. "Grenzziehungen des Kanons im frühen Judentum und die Neuschrift der Bibel nach 4. Buch Esra," in M. Becker and J. Frey (eds.), *Qumran und der biblische Kanon,* BThSt 92 (Neukirchen-Vluyn, 2009), 195–253.

Becker, M., and J. Frey (eds.). *Qumran und der biblische Kanon,* BThSt 92 (Neukirchen-Vluyn, 2009).

Becker, U. "Das Exodus-Credo. Historischer Haftpunkt und Geschichte einer alttestamentlichen Glaubensformel," in U. Becker and J. van Oorschot (eds.), *Das Alte Testament—ein Geschichtsbuch?! Geschichtsschreibung und Geschichtsüberlieferung im antiken Israel,* ABG 17 (Leipzig, 2005), 81–100.

Becking, B. *The Fall of Samaria: A Historical and Archaeological Study,* SHANE 2 (Leiden, 1992).

Becking, B. "West Semites at Tell Sekh Hamad: Evidence for the Israelite Exile?," in U. Hübner and E. A. Knauf (eds.), *Kein Land für sich allein Studien zum Kulturkontakt in Kanaan, Israel/Palästina und Ebirnari für Manfred Weippert zum 65. Geburtstag,* OBO 186 (Fribourg/Göttingen, 2002), 153–166.

Beckwith, T. *The Old Testament Canon of the New Testament Church and Its Background in Early Judaism* (Grand Rapids, MI, 1985).

Ben Zvi, E. "Total Exile, Empty Land and the General Intellectual Discourse in Yehud," in E. Ben Zvi and C. Levin (eds.), *The Concept of Exile in Ancient Israel and Its Historical Contexts*, BZAW 404 (Berlin, 2010), 155–168.

Berges, U. "'Singt dem Herrn ein neues Lied': Zu den Trägerkreisen von Jesajabuch und Psalter," in F.-L. Hossfeld et al. (eds.), *Trägerkreise in den Psalmen*, BBB 178 (Göttingen, 2017), 11–33.

Berges, U., and W. A. M. Beuken. *Das Buch Jesaja: Eine Einführung*, UTB 4647 (Göttingen, 2016).

Bergler, S. *Joel als Schriftinterpret*, BEAT 16 (Frankfurt a. M., 1988).

Berlejung, A. "Der gesegnete Mensch. Text und Kontext von Num 6, 22–27 und den Silberamuletten von Ketef Hinnom," in A. Berlejung and R. Heckl (eds.), *Mensch und König: Studien zur Anthropologie des Alten Testaments: Rüdiger Lux zum 60. Geburtstag*, HBS 53 (Freiburg i. Br., 2008), 37–62.

Berlejung, A. "Ein Programm fürs Leben: Theologisches Wort und anthropologischer Ort der Silberamulette von Ketef Hinnom," *ZAW* 120 (2008), 204–230.

Berlejung, A. "Twisting Traditions: Programmatic Absence-Theology for the Northern Kingdom in 1 Kgs 12:26–33* (the 'Sin of Jeroboam')," *JNSL* 35 (2009), 1–42.

Bernstein, M. J. "The Genre(s) of the Genesis Apocryphon," in M. J. Bernstein, *Reading and Rereading Scripture at Qumran*, vol. 1: *Genesis and Its Interpretation*, STDJ 107 / 1 (Leiden, 2013), 217–238.

Beyerle, S. *Die Gottesvorstellungen in der antik-jüdischen Apokalyptik*, JSJ.S 103 (Leiden, 2005).

Beyerlin, W. *Religionsgeschichtliches Textbuch zum Alten Testament*, GAT 1 (Göttingen, 1975).

Bickerman, E. "La charte séleucide de Jérusalem," *REJ* 100 (1935), 4–35; also published in *Studies in Jewish and Christian History II*, AGJU 9 (Leiden, 1980), 44–85.

Blanco Wissmann, F. *'Er tat das Rechte . . .': Beurteilungskriterien und Deuteronomismus in 1Kön 12–2Kön 25*, AThANT 93 (Zurich, 2008).

Blum, E. "Die altaramäischen Wandinschriften aus Tell Deir 'Alla und ihr institutioneller Kontext," in F.-E. Focken and M. Ott (eds.), *Meta-Texte: Erzählungen von schrifttragenden Artefakten in der alttestamentlichen und mittelalterlichen Literatur*, Materiale Textkulturen 15 (Berlin / Boston 2016), 21–52.

Blum, E. "Der historische Mose und die Frühgeschichte Israels," *HeBAI* 1 (2012), 37–63.

Blum, E. "The Jacob Tradition," in C. A. Evans et al. (eds.), *The Book of Genesis: Composition, Reception, and Interpretation*, VT.S 152 (Leiden, 2012), 181–211.

Blum, E. "Jesajas prophetisches Testament," *ZAW* 109 (1997), 12–29.

Blum, E. "Die Kombination I der Wandinschrift vom Tell Deir 'Alla: Vorschläge zur Rekonstruktion mit historisch-kritischen Anmerkungen," in I. Kottsieper et al. (eds.), *Berührungspunkte: Studien zur Sozial- und Religionsgeschichte Israels und seiner Umwelt*. Festschrift für Rainer Albertz zu seinem 65. Geburtstag, AOAT 350 (Münster, 2008), 573–601.

Blum, E. *Die Komposition der Vätergeschichte*, WMANT 57 (Neukirchen-Vluyn, 1984).

Blum, E. "The Linguistic Dating of Biblical Texts—An Approach with Methodological Limitations," in J. C. Gertz et al. (eds.), *The Formation of the Pentateuch: Bridging the Academic Cultures of Europe, Israel, and North America*, FAT 111 (Tübingen, 2016), 295–302, 303–326.

Blum, E. "Die literarische Verbindung von Erzvätern und Exodus: Ein Gespräch mit neueren Endredaktionshypothesen," in J. C. Gertz et al. (eds.), *Abschied vom Jahwisten: Die Komposition des Hexateuch in der jüngsten Diskussion*, BZAW 315 (Berlin / New York, 2002), 119–156.

Blum, E. "'Verstehst du dich nicht auf die Schreibkunst . . . ?' Ein weisheitlicher Dialog über Vergänglichkeit und Verantwortung: Kombination II der Wandinschrift vom Tell Deir 'Alla," in M. Bauks et al. (eds.), *Was ist der Mensch, dass du seiner gedenkst? (Psalm 8,5): Aspekte einer theologischen Anthropologie*, Festschrift für Bernd Janowski zum 65. Geburtstag (Neukirchen-Vluyn, 2008), 33–53.

Boccaccini, G. "Introduction: From the Enoch Literature to Enochic Judaism," in G. Boccaccini, *Enoch and Qumran Origins: New Light on a Forgotten Connection* (Grand Rapids, MI, 2005), 1–14.

Boccaccini, G. *Wurzeln des rabbinischen Judentums: Eine Geistesgeschichte von Ezechiel bis Daniel* (Berlin, 2014).

Böhm, M. "'Und sie nahmen ihn nicht auf, weil sein Gesicht nach Jerusalem zu ging' (Lk 9:53): Samaritaner und Juden zwischen dem 4. Jh. v. und 1. Jh. n. Chr.," in W. Beltz and J. Tubach (eds.), *Regionale Systeme koexistierender Religionsgemeinschaften*, HBO 34 (Halle 2002), 113–127.

Borger, R. "Akkadische Rechtsbücher: Die mittelassyrischen Gesetze," *TUAT* I / 1 (Gütersloh, 1982), 80–92.

Bosshard, E., and R. G. Kratz. "Maleachi im Zwölfprophetenbuch," *BN* 52 (1990), 27–46.

Bosshard-Nepustil, E. *Schriftwerdung der Hebräischen Bibel: Thematisierungen der Schriftlichkeit biblischer Texte im Rahmen ihrer Literaturgeschichte*, AThANT 106 (Zurich, 2015).

Böttrich, C. "Der Urvater und die offenbarte Weisheit Gottes: Die Henoch-Schriften," *Welt und Umwelt der Bibel* 71 (2014), 36–41.

Brague, R. *The Law of God: The Philosophical History of an Idea*, trans. L. G. Cochrane (Chicago, 2007).

Brandt, P. *Endgestalten des Kanons: Das Arrangement der Schriften Israels in der jüdischen und christlichen Bibel*, BBB 131 (Berlin / Vienna, 2001).

Brettler, M. Z. *How to Read the Jewish Bible* (Oxford, 2006).

Brettler, M. Z. "Judaism in the Hebrew Bible? The Transition from Ancient Israelite Religion to Judaism," *CBQ* 61 (1999), 429–447.

Breytenbach, C. "Das II. Vatikanische Konzil und 'evangelische' Exegese des Neuen Testaments," *BThZ* 31 (2014), 342–358.

Breytenbach, C. "JesLXX 53,6.12 als Interpretatio Graeca und die urchristlichen Hingabeformeln," in W. Kraus and M. Karrer (eds., with the assistance of Martin Meiser), *Die Septuaginta—Texte, Theologien, Einflüsse,* WUNT 252 (Tübingen, 2010), 655–670.

Brodersen, K. *Aristeas: Der König und die Bibel* (Stuttgart, 2008).

Broer, I. "Gebremste Exegese: Katholische Neutestamentler in der ersten Hälfte des 20. Jahrhunderts," in C. Breytenbach and R. Hoppe (eds.), *Neutestamentliche Wissenschaft nach 1945: Hauptvertreter der deutschsprachigen Exegese in der Darstellung ihrer Schüler* (Neukirchen-Vluyn, 2008), 59–112.

Bruni, A. M. "Georgian Translations," in A. Lange and E. Tov (eds.), *Textual History of the Bible: The Hebrew Bible,* vol. 1a: *Overview Articles* (Leiden, 2016), 375–385.

Bruni, A. M. "Old Church Slavonic Translations," in A. Lange and E. Tov (eds.), *Textual History of the Bible: The Hebrew Bible,* vol. 1a: *Overview Articles* (Leiden, 2016), 393–408.

Bultmann, C., et al. (eds.). *Heilige Schriften: Ursprung, Geltung und Gebrauch* (Münster, 2005).

Burke, D. G., J. F. Kutsko, and P. H. Towner (eds.). *The King James Version at 400: Assessing Its Genius as Bible Translation and Its Literary Influence* (Atlanta, GA, 2013).

Burke, T., and B. Landau. *New Testament Apocrypha: More Noncanonical Scriptures* (Grand Rapids, MI, 2016).

Burkert, W. *Die Griechen und der Orient: Von Homer bis zu den Magiern* (Munich, 2003).

Campbell, G. *Bible: The Story of the King James Version, 1611–2011* (Oxford, 2010).

Carbajosa, I. "Peshitta," in A. Lange and E. Tov (eds.), *Textual History of the Bible: The Hebrew Bible,* vol. 1a: *Overview Articles* (Leiden, 2016), 262–278.

Carr, D. M. *The Formation of the Hebrew Bible: A New Reconstruction* (New York, 2011).

Carr, D. M. *Schrift und Erinnerungskultur: Die Entstehung der Bibel und der antiken Literatur im Rahmen der Schreiberausbildung,* AThANT 107 (Zurich, 2015).

Carr, D. M. "The Tel Zayit Abecedary in (Social) Context," in R. E. Tappy and P. Kyle McCarter (eds.), *Literate Culture and Tenth-Century Canaan: The Tel Zayit Abecedary in Context* (Winona Lake, IN, 2008), 113–129.

Chancey, M. A. *Greco-Roman Culture and the Galilee of Jesus,* SNTSMS 134 (Cambridge, 2005).

Chancey, M. A. *The Myth of a Gentile Galilee,* SNTSMS 118 (Cambridge, 2002).

Cohen, S. D. *The Beginnings of Jewishness: Boundaries, Varieties, Uncertainties* (Berkeley, CA, 1999).

Collins, J. J. "Before the Canon: Scriptures in Second Temple Judaism," in J. L. Mays et al. (eds.), *Old Testament Interpretation: Past, Present, and Future* (Nashville, TN, 1995), 225–241.

Collins, J. J. *The Invention of Judaism: Torah and Jewish Identity from Deuteronomy to Paul* (Oakland, CA, 2017).

Cox, C. "Armenian Translations," in A. Lange and E. Tov (eds.), *Textual History of the Bible: The Hebrew Bible,* vol. 1a: *Overview Articles* (Leiden, 2016), 370–375.

Crouch, C. L. *Israel and the Assyrians: Deuteronomy, the Succession Treaty of Esarhaddon, and the Nature of Subversion,* SBL Ancient Near East Monographs 8 (Atlanta, GA, 2014).

Crüsemann, F. "Das 'portative Vaterland': Struktur und Genese des alttestamentlichen Kanons," in A. Assmann and J. Assmann (eds.), *Kanon und Zensur* (Munich, 1987), 63–79.

Darshan, G. "The Twenty-four Books of the Hebrew Bible and Alexandrian Scribal Methods," in M. R. Niehoff (ed.), *Homer and the Bible in the Eyes of Ancient Interpreters: Between Literary and Religious Concerns,* JSRC 16 (Leiden, 2012), 221–244.

Day, J. "How Many Pre-Exilic Psalms Are There?" in J. Day (ed.), *In Search of Pre-Exilic Israel: Proceedings of the Oxford Old Testament Seminar,* JSOT.S 406 (London, 2004), 225–250.

Delcor, M. "Remarques sur la datation du Ps 20 comparée à celle du psaume araméen apparenté dans le papyrus Amherst 63," in M. Dietrich and O. Loretz (eds.), *Mesopotamica—Ugaritica—Biblica,* Festschrift für Kurt Bergerhof zur Vollendung seines 70. Lebensjahres am 7. Mai 1992, AOAT 232 (Kevelaer, 1993), 25–43.

Dell, K., and W. Kynes (eds.). *Reading Job Intertextually,* LHB / OTS 574 (New York, 2013).

de Pury, A. "Le cycle de Jacob comme légende autonome des origines d'Israël," in J. A. Emerton (ed.), *Congress Volume Leuven 1989,* VT.S 43 (Leiden, 1991), 78–96.

de Pury, A. "The Jacob Story and the Beginning of the Formation of the Pentateuch," in A. de Pury, *Die Patriarchen und die Priesterschrift: Gesammelte Studien zu seinem 70. Geburtstag / Les patriarches et le document sacerdotal: Recueil d'articles, à l'occasion de son 70e anniversaire,* ed. J.-D. Macchi et al., AThANT 99 (Zurich, 2010), 147–169.

de Pury, A. *Die Patriarchen und die Priesterschrift,* AThANT 99 (Zurich, 2010).

de Pury, A. "Pg as the Absolute Beginning," in T. Römer and K. Schmid (eds.), *Les dernières rédactions du Pentateuque, de l'Hexateuque et de l'Ennéateuque,* BEThL 203 (Leuven, 2007), 99–128.

de Pury, A. "Zwischen Sophokles und Ijob: Die Schriften (Ketubim): ein jüdischer Literatur- Kanon," *Welt und Umwelt der Bibel* 28 (2003), 24–27.

De Troyer, K. "Once More, the So-called Esther Fragments of Cave 4," *RdQ* 19 (2000), 401–422.

De Troyer, K. "When Did the Pentateuch Come into Existence? An Uncomfortable Perspective," in M. Karrer and W. Kraus (eds.), *Die Septuaginta: Texte, Kontexte, Lebenswelten.* Internationale Fachtagung veranstaltet von Septuaginta Deutsch (LXX.D), Wuppertal 20.-23. Juli 2006, WUNT I / 219 (Tübingen, 2008), 269–286.

Dietrich, W. *David: Der Herrscher mit der Harfe* (Leipzig, 2006).

Dion, P.-E. and M. Daviau. "The Moabites," in A. Lemaire et al. (eds.), *The Books of Kings: Sources, Composition, Historiography and Reception,* VT.S 129 (Leiden, 2010), 205–224.

DiTommaso, L. "Dating the Eagle Vision of 4 Ezra: A New Look at an Old Theory," *JSP* 20 (1999), 3–38.

Dodd, C. H. *The Parables of the Kingdom* (London, 1935).

Dohmen, C. *Die Bibel und ihre Auslegung* (Munich, 2011).

Donner, H. "Hier sind deine Götter, Israel!," in H. Donner, *Aufsätze zum Alten Testament aus vier Jahrzehnten,* BZAW 224 (Berlin / New York, 1994), 67–75.

Donner, H. "Jesaja LVI 1-7: Ein Abrogationsfall innerhalb des Kanons— Implikationen und Konsequenzen," in J. A. Emerton (ed.), *Congress Volume Salamanca,* VT.S 36, (Leiden, 1985), 81–95, reprinted in H. Donner, *Aufsätze zum Alten Testament aus vier Jahrzehnten,* BZAW 224 (Berlin, 1994), 165–179.

Dorival, G. "Les origines de la Septante: La traduction en grec des cinq livres de la Torah," in M. Harl (ed.), *La Bible grecque de Septante* (Paris, 1988), 39–82.

Dörrfuß, E. M. *Mose in den Chronikbüchern: Garant theokratischer Zukunftserwartung,* BZAW 219 (Berlin, 2012).

Dozeman, T. B. "Hosea and the Wilderness Wandering Tradition," in S. L. McKenzie et al. (eds.), *Rethinking the Foundations: Historiography in the Ancient World and in the Bible: Essays in Honour of John van Seters,* BZAW 294 (Berlin / New York, 2000), 55–70.

Droysen, J. G. *Geschichte des Hellenismus (1833–1843),* ed. K.-M. Guth (Norderstedt, 2014).

Duhm, B. *Das Buch Jesaja,* HKAT III / 1 (Göttingen, 1892).

Duhm, B. *Die Psalmen,* HAT 14, 2nd ed. (Freiburg im Breisgau, 1922).

Dunn, J. D. G. *Beginning from Jerusalem,* Christianity in the Making, vol. 2 (Grand Rapids, MI, 2009).

Dunn, J. D. G. (ed.). *Jews and Christians: The Parting of the Ways A.D. 70 to 135,* WUNT 66 (Tübingen, 1992).

Dunn, J. D. G. *The Partings of the Ways between Christianity and Judaism and Their Significance for the Character of Christianity,* 2nd ed. (London, 2006).

Ebeling, G. "Die Bedeutung der historisch-kritischen Methode für die protestantische Theologie und Kirche," *ZThK* 47 (1950), 1–46; also published in G. Ebeling, *Wort und Glaube,* vol. 1, 3rd ed. (Tübingen, 1967), 1–49.

Edelman, D. (ed.). *The Triumph of Elohim: From Yahwisms to Judaisms,* CBET 13 (Kampen, 1995).

Edrei, A., and D. Mendels. "A Split Jewish Diaspora: Its Dramatic Consequences," *Journal for the Study of the Pseudepigrapha* 16 (2007), 91–137.

Edrei, A., and D. Mendels. "A Split Jewish Diaspora: Its Dramatic Consequences II," *Journal for the Study of Pseudepigrapha* 17 (2008), 163–187.

Ego, B. "Alexander der Große in der alttestamentlichen Überlieferung—eine Spurensuche und ihre theologischen Implikationen," in C. Maier (ed.), *Congress Volume Munich 2013,* VT.S 163 (Leiden, 2014), 18–39.

Ego, B. "Targumim," in A. Lange and E. Tov (eds.), *Textual History of the Bible. The Hebrew Bible,* vol. 1a: *Overview Articles* (Leiden, 2016), 239–262.

Ehring, C. *Die Rückkehr JHWHs: Traditions- und religionsgeschichtliche Untersuchungen zu Jesaja 40,1–11, Jesaja 52,7–10 und verwandten Texten,* WMANT 116 (Neukirchen-Vluyn, 2007).

Ehrlich, C. S. "Die Bibel im Judentum," in C. S. Ehrlich, *Bibel und Judentum: Beiträge aus dem christlich-jüdischen Gespräch* (Zurich, 2004), 31–46.

Elbogen, I. *Der jüdische Gottesdienst in seiner geschichtlichen Entwicklung,* 3rd ed. (Frankfurt a. M., 1931; repr. Hildesheim, 1995).

Encel, S. *Temple et temples dans le judaïsme antique,* Bibliothèque d'études juives 48 (Paris, 2012).

Engnell, I. *Studies in Divine Kingship in the Ancient Near East,* 2nd ed. (1943; Oxford, 1967).

Enste, S. *Kein Markustext in Qumran: Eine Untersuchung der These: Qumran-Fragment 7Q5 = Mk 6,52–53,* NTOA 45 (Fribourg, 2000).

Fabry, H.-J. "Die Qumrantexte und das biblische Kanonproblem," in S. Beyerle et al. (eds.), *Recht und Ethos im Alten Testament—Gestalt und Wirkung* (Neukirchen-Vluyn, 1999), 251–271.

Fabry, H.-J. "Der Umgang mit der kanonisierten Tora in Qumran," in E. Zenger (ed.), *Die Tora als Kanon für Juden und Christen,* HBS 10 (Freiburg, 1996), 293–327.

Faigenbaum-Golovin, S., et al. "Algorithmic Handwriting Analysis of Judah's Military Correspondence Sheds Light on Composition of Biblical Texts," *PNAS* 113 (2016), 4664–4669.

Feldman, A., and L. Goldman (eds.). *Scripture and Interpretation: Qumran Texts That Rework the Bible,* BZAW 449 (Berlin 2014).

Felmy, K. C. *Einführung in die orthodoxe Theologie der Gegenwart,* 2nd ed. (Berlin, 2011).

Ferguson, E. *Baptism in the Early Church: History, Theology, and Liturgy in the First Five Centuries* (Grand Rapids, MI, 2009).

Finkelstein, I. "A Corpus of North Israelite Texts in the Days of Jeroboam II?," *HeBAI* 6 (2017), 262–289.

Finkelstein, I. "The Expansion of Judah in II Chronicles: Territorial Legitimation for the Hasmoneans?'" *ZAW* 127 (2015), 669–695.

Finkelstein, I. *The Forgotten Kingdom: The Archaeology and History of Northern Israel,* Society of Biblical Literature, Ancient Near East Monographs 5 (Atlanta, GA, 2013).

Finkelstein, I. "A Great United Monarchy? Archaeological and Historical Perspectives," in R. G. Kratz and H. Spieckermann (eds.), *One God—One Cult—One Nation: Archaeological and Biblical Perspectives,* BZAW 405 (Berlin, 2010), 3–28.

Finkelstein, I. "The Historical Reality behind the Genealogical Lists in 1 Chronicles," *JBL* 131 (2012), 65–83.

Finkelstein, I. "Jerusalem and Judah 600–200 BCE: Implications for Understanding Pentateuchal Texts," in P. Dubovsky et al. (eds.), *The Fall of Jerusalem and the Rise of the Torah,* FAT 107 (Tübingen, 2016), 3–18.

Finkelstein, I. "Jerusalem in the Persian (and Early Hellenistic) Period and the Wall of Nehemiah," *JSOT* 32 (2008), 501–520.

Finkelstein, I. "Major Saviors, Minor Judges: The Historical Background of the Northern Accounts in the Book of Judges," *JSOT* 41 (2017), 431–449.

Finkelstein, I. "Migration of Israelites into Judah after 720 BCE: An Answer and an Update," *ZAW* 127 (2015), 188–206.

Finkelstein, I. "Rehoboam's Fortified Cities (II Chr 11,5–12). A Hasmonean Reality?," *ZAW* 123 (2011), 92–107.

Finkelstein, I. "Stages in the Territorial Expansion of the Northern Kingdom," *VT* 61 (2011), 227–242.

Finkelstein, I. "The Territorial Extent and Demography of Yehud / Judea in the Persian and Early Hellenistic Periods," *RB* 117 (2010), 39–54.

Finkelstein, I., and A. Fantalkin. "Khirbet Qeiyafa: An Unsensational Archaeological and Historical Interpretation," *Tel Aviv* 39 (2012), 38–63.

Finkelstein, I., and T. Römer. "Comments on the Historical Background of the Abraham Narrative: Between 'Realia' and 'Exegetica,'" *HeBAI* 3 (2014), 3–23.

Finkelstein, I., and T. Römer. "Comments on the Historical Background of the Jacob Narrative in Genesis," *ZAW* 126 (2014), 317–338.

Finkelstein, I., and B. Sass. "The West Semitic Alphabetic Inscriptions, Late Bronze II to Iron IIA: Archeological Context, Distribution and Chronology," *Hebrew Bible and Ancient Israel 2* (2013), 149–220.

Finkelstein, I., B. Sass, and L. Singer-Avitz. "Writing in Iron IIA Philistia in the Light of the Ṭell Zayit / Zētā abecedary," *ZDPV* 124 (2008), 1–14.

Finkelstein, I., and L. Singer-Avitz. "Reevaluating Bethel," *ZDPV* 125 (2009), 33–48.

Finsterbusch, K. *Das Deuteronomium: Eine Einführung* (Göttingen, 2012).

Finsterbusch, K., and A. Lange (eds.). *What Is Bible?,* CBET 67 (Leuven, 2012).

Fischer, A. A. "Die literarische Entstehung des Großreichs Davids und ihr geschichtlicher Hintergrund: Zur Darstellung der Kriegschronik in 2Sam 8,1–14 (15)," in U. Becker and J. van Oorschot (eds.), *Das Alte Testament—ein Geschichtsbuch?!*, ABG 17 (Leipzig, 2005), 101–128.

Fischer, A. A. *Der Text des Alten Testaments: Neubearbeitung der Einführung in die Biblia Hebraica von Ernst Würthwein* (Stuttgart, 2009).

Fischer, A. A. *Tod und Jenseits im Alten Orient und im Alten Testament: Eine Reise durch antike Vorstellungs- und Textwelten*, SKI.NF 7 (Leipzig, 2014).

Fishbane, M. *Biblical Interpretation in Ancient Israel* (Oxford, 1985).

Fishbane, M. *Jewish Hermeneutical Theology* (Leiden, 2015).

Fitzpatrick-McKinley, A. *The Transformation of Torah from Scribal Advice to Law*, JSOT.S 287 (Sheffield, 1993).

Flint, P. W. "The Daniel Tradition at Qumran," in J. J. Collins and P. W. Flint. (eds.), *The Book of Daniel: Composition and Reception*, FIOTL 2,2 / VTS 83 / 2 (Leiden, 2001), 329–367.

Förg, F. *Die Ursprünge der alttestamentlichen Apokalyptik*, ABG 45 (Leipzig, 2013).

Foster, P. *The Gospel of Peter: Introduction, Critical Edition and Commentary*, TENTS 4 (Leiden, 2010).

Frankena, R. "The Vassal-Treaties of Esarhaddon and the Dating of Deuteronomy," *OTS* 14 (Leiden, 1965), 122–154.

Frei, P., and K. Koch. *Reichsidee und Reichsorganisation im Perserreich*, OBO 337, 2nd ed. (Fribourg, 1996).

Frevel, C. "Der Eine oder die Vielen? Monotheismus und materielle Kultur in der Perserzeit," in C. Schwöbel (ed.), *Gott—Götter—Götzen. XIV. Europäischer Kongress für Theologie, 11–15 September 2011, Zurich* (Leipzig, 2013), 238–265.

Frevel, C. "Die Wiederkehr der Hexateuchperspektive: Eine Herausforderung für die These vom deuteronomistischen Geschichtswerk," in H.-J. Stipp (ed.), *Das deuteronomistische Geschichtswerk*, ÖBS 39 (Frankfurt a. M., 2011), 13–53.

Frevel, C., and K. Pyschny. "A 'Religious Revolution' in Yehûd? The Material Culture of the Persian Period as a Test Case: Introduction," in C. Frevel, K. Pyschny, and I. Cornelius (eds.), *A 'Religious Revolution' in Yehûd? The Material Culture of the Persian Period as a Test Case*, OBO 267 (Fribourg, 2014), 1–22.

Frey, J. "Die 'Juden' im Johannesevangelium und die Frage nach der 'Trennung der Wege' zwischen der johanneischen Gemeinde und der Synagoge," in J. Frey, *Die Herrlichkeit des Gekreuzigten: Studien zu den johanneischen Schriften I*, WUNT 307 (Tübingen, 2013), 339–377.

Frey, J. "Qumran," *RAC* 28 (Stuttgart, 2017), 550–591.

Frey, J. "Qumran und der biblische Kanon: Eine thematische Einführung," in M. Becker and J. Frey (eds.), *Qumran und der biblische Kanon*, BThSt 92 (Neukirchen-Vluyn, 2009), 1–63.

Frey, J. *Die Samaritaner und die Bibel: Historische und literarische Wechselwirkungen zwischen biblischen und samaritanischen Traditionen / The Samaritans and the Bible: Historical and Literary Interactions between Biblical and Samaritan Traditions*, Studia Judaica / Studia Samaritana 7 (Berlin, 2012).

Frey, J., et al. (eds.). *Qumran und die Archäologie*, WUNT 278 (Tübingen, 2011).

Fritz, V. *Die Entstehung Israels im 12. und 11. Jahrhundert v. Chr.*, BE 2 (Stuttgart, 1996).

Furey, C. M., et al. (eds.). *Studies of the Bible and Its Reception*, SBR (Berlin, 2013).

Galley, S., et al. *Die Hebräische Bibel: Eine Einführung* (Darmstadt, 2004).

Gamble, H. Y. *Books and Readers in the Early Church: A History of Early Christian Texts* (New Haven, CT, 1995).

García Martínez, F., and E. J. C. Tigchelaar. *The Dead Sea Scrolls Study Edition*, 2 vols. (Leiden, 1997, 1998).

Gärtner, J. *Jesaja 66 und Sacharja 14 als Summe der Prophetie: Eine traditions- und redaktionsgeschichtliche Untersuchung zum Abschluss des Jesaja- und Zwölfprophetenbuchs*, WMANT 114 (Neukirchen-Vluyn, 2006).

Gathercole, S. *The Gospel of Thomas: Introduction and Commentary*, TENTS 11 (Leiden, 2014).

Georges, T., F. Albrecht, and R. Feldmeier (eds.). *Alexandria*, COMES 1 (Tübingen, 2013).

Gerhards, M. *Die Aussetzungsgeschichte des Mose: Literatur- und traditionsgeschichtliche Untersuchungen zu einem Schlüsseltext des nichtpriesterschriftlichen Tetrateuch*, WMANT 109 (Neukirchen-Vluyn, 2006).

Gerhards, M. "'. . . und nahm die Tochter Levis': Noch einmal zu Ex 2,1 als Motivation der Aussetzung des Mose: 'Seine Geburt war unordentlich . . .'—wirklich?," *BN* 154 (2012), 103–122.

Germany, S. *The Exodus-Conquest Narrative: The Composition of the Non-Priestly Narratives in Exodus-Joshua*, FAT 115 (Tübingen, 2018).

Gertz, J. C. "Das Alte Testament—Heilige Schrift des Urchristentums und Teil der christlichen Bibel," in F. W. Graf and K. Wiegandt (eds.), *Die Anfänge des Christentums* (Frankfurt a. M., 2009), 231–260.

Gertz, J. C. "Antibabylonische Polemik im priesterlichen Schöpfungsbericht?" *ZThK* 106 (2009), 137–155.

Gertz, J. C. "The Formation of the Primeval History," in C. A. Evans, J. Lohr, and D. L. Petersen (eds.), *The Book of Genesis. Composition, Reception, and Interpretation*, VT.S 152 (Leiden, 2012), 107–136.

Gertz, J. C. "Konstruierte Erinnerung: Alttestamentliche Historiographie im Spiegel von Archäologie und literarhistorischer Kritik am Fallbeispiel des salomonischen Königtums," *BThZ* 21 (2004), 3–29.

Gertz, J. C. "Mose und die Anfänge der jüdischen Religion," *ZThK* 99 (2002), 3–20.

Gertz, J. C. "Schriftauslegung in alttestamentlicher Perspektive," in F. Nüssel (ed.), *Schriftauslegung*, TdT 8 (Tübingen, 2014), 9–41.

388

Bibliography

Gertz, J. C. "Zusammenhang, Trennung und Selbständigkeit der Bücher Genesis
und Exodus im priesterlichen und nachpriesterlichen Pentateuch," in F. Giun-
toli and K. Schmid (eds.), *The Post-Priestly Pentateuch: New Perspectives on Its
Redactional Development and Theological Profiles,* FAT 101 (Tübingen, 2015),
233–251.

Gertz, J. C., B. M. Levinson, D. Rom-Shiloni, and K. Schmid (eds.). *The Formation
of the Pentateuch: Bridging the Academic Cultures of Europe, Israel, and North
America,* FAT 111 (Tübingen, 2016).

Gesundheit, S. "Gedanken zum jüdischen Offenbarungsverständnis," ZThK 115
(2018), 125–136.

Gesundheit, S. "Gibt es eine jüdische Theologie der Hebräischen Bibel?," in
B. Janowski (ed.), *Theologie und Exegese des Alten Testaments / der Hebräischen
Bibel: Zwischenbilanz und Zukunftsperspektiven,* SBS 200 (Stuttgart, 2005),
73–86.

Gesundheit, S. "Introduction: The Strengths and Weaknesses of Linguistic Dating,"
in J. C. Gertz et al. (eds.), *The Formation of the Pentateuch: Bridging the Academic Cultures of Europe, Israel, and North America,* FAT 111 (Tübingen,
2016), 295–302.

Goren, Y., et al. "A Provenance Study of the Gilgamesh Fragment from Megiddo,"
Archaeometry 51 (2009), 763–773.

Görg, M. "Die Septuaginta im Kontext spätägyptischer Kultur: Beispiele lokaler
Inspiration bei der Übersetzungsarbeit am Pentateuch," in H.-J. Fabry and
U. Offerhaus (eds.), *Im Brennpunkt: Die Septuaginta: Studien zur Entstehung
und Bedeutung der Griechischen Bibel,* BWANT 153 (Stuttgart, 2001), 115–130.

Gottlieb, I. B. "Rabbinic Reception of the Prophets," in C. J. Sharp (ed.), *The Oxford Handbook of the Prophets* (Oxford, 2016), 388–406.

Grabbe, L. L. (ed.). *The Land of Canaan in the Late Bronze Age,* LHB/OTS 636
(London, 2016).

Grainger, J. D. *The Syrian War,* Mnemosyne Supplements 320 (Leiden, 2010).

Graves, M. "Vulgate," in A. Lange and E. Tov (eds.), *Textual History of the Bible:
The Hebrew Bible,* vol. 1a: *Overview Articles* (Leiden, 2016), 278–289.

Greenspahn, F. E. "Why Prophecy Ceased," *JBL* 108 (1989), 37–49.

Gregory, A. F., and C. M. Tuckett. *The Reception of the New Testament in the
Apostolic Fathers* (Oxford, 2005).

Groß, W. "Die Gottebenbildlichkeit des Menschen nach Gen 1,26.27 in der Diskussion des letzten Jahrzehnts," in W. Groß, *Studien zur Priesterschrift und
zu alttestamentlichen Gottesbildern,* SBAB 30 (Stuttgart, 1999), 37–54.

Grund, A. *Die Entstehung des Sabbats: Seine Bedeutung für Israels Zeitkonzept und
Erinnerungskultur,* FAT 75 (Tübingen, 2011).

Grund-Wittenberg, A. "Literalität und Institution: Auf der Suche nach lebensweltli-
chen Kontexten der Literaturwerdung im alten Israel," *ZAW* 129 (2017),
327–345.

Grünstäudl, W. "Was lange währt . . . : Die Katholischen Briefe und die Formung des neutestamentlichen Kanons," *Early Christianity* 7 (2016), 71–94.

Grünwaldt, K. *Exil und Identität: Beschneidung, Passa und Sabbat in der Priesterschrift,* BBB 85 (Frankfurt a. M., 1992).

Guillaume, P. *Waiting for Josiah: The Judges,* JSOT.S 385 (London, 2004), 55–72.

Gzella, H. (ed.). *Sprachen aus der Welt des Alten Testaments,* 2nd ed. (Darmstadt, 2012).

Haag, E. *Das hellenistische Zeitalter: Israel und die Bibel im 4. bis 1. Jahrhundert v. Chr.,* BE 9 (Stuttgart, 2003).

Habermann, J. *Präexistenzaussagen im Neuen Testament,* EHS.T 362 (Frankfurt a. M., 1990).

Hahn, F. "Der Beitrag der katholischen Exegese zur neutestamentlichen Forschung," *VF* 18 / 2 (1973), 83–98.

Hahn, F. *Theologie des Neuen Testaments,* vol. 2: *Die Einheit des Neuen Testaments* (Tübingen, 2002).

Hahn, J. (ed.). *Zerstörungen des Jerusalemer Tempels: Geschehen—Wahrnehmung—Bewältigung,* WUNT 147 (Tübingen, 2002).

Halton, C., and S. Svärd. *Women's Writing of Ancient Mesopotamia: An Anthology of the Earliest Female Authors* (Cambridge, 2017).

Harnack, A. von. *Markion: Das Evangelium vom fremden Gott. Eine Monographie zur Geschichte der Grundlegung der katholischen Kirche,* 2nd ed. (Leipzig, 1924).

Harnack, A. von. *Über den privaten Gebrauch der Heiligen Schriften in der Alten Kirche,* Beiträge zur Einleitung in das Neue Testament 5 (Leipzig, 1912).

Hartenstein, F. *Die Unzugänglichkeit Gottes im Heiligtum. Jesaja 6 und der Wohnort JHWHs in der Jerusalemer Kulttradition,* WMANT 75 (Neukirchen-Vluyn, 1997).

Hartenstein, F. "Religionsgeschichte Israels—ein Überblick über die Forschung seit 1990," *VF* 48 (2003), 2–28.

Hartenstein, F. "Wolkendunkel und Himmelsfeste: Zur Genese und Kosmologie der Vorstellung des himmlischen Heiligtums JHWHs," in B. Janowski and B. Ego (eds.), *Das biblische Weltbild und seine altorientalischen Kontexte,* FAT 32 (Tübingen, 2001), 126–179.

Hartenstein, F., and M. Moxter. *Hermeneutik des Bilderverbots: Exegetische und systematisch-theologische Annäherungen,* ThLZ. F. 26 (Leipzig, 2016).

Hartenstein, F., and K. Schmid (eds.). *Abschied von der Priesterschrift? Zum Stand der Pentateuchdebatte,* VWGTh 40 (Leipzig, 2015).

Haug, H. "Zur abweichenden Kapitel- und Verszählung im Alten Testament: Ein Fund aus der Hinterlassenschaft von Eberhard Nestle," *ZAW* 113 (2001), 618–623.

Hayajneh, H., et al. "Die Götter von Ammon, Moab und Edom in einer frühnordarabischen Inschrift aus Südost-Jordanien," in V. Golinets et al. (eds.), *Neue*

Beiträge zur Semitistik. Fünftes Treffen der Arbeitsgemeinschaft Semitistik in der Deutschen Morgenländischen Gesellschaft vom 15.–17. Februar 2012 an der Universität Basel, AOAT 425 (Münster, 2015), 79–106.

Hefner, Philip. "Theological Methodology and St. Irenaeus," *Journal of Religion* 44, no. 4 (1964), 294–309.

Heiligenthal, R. "Weltanschauliche Richtungen und Gruppen: Die religiöse Vielfalt Palästinas. Sadduzäer," in K. Erlemann et al. (eds.), *Neues Testament und Antike Kultur,* vol. 3: *Weltauffassung—Kult—Ethos* (Neukirchen-Vluyn, 2011), 34–36.

Hellholm, D., and D. Sänger (eds.). *The Eucharist—Its Origins and Contexts,* 3 vols., WUNT 376 (Tübingen, 2017).

Hendel, R. "A Hasmonean Edition of MT Genesis? The Implications of the Editions of the Chronology in Genesis 5," *HeBAI* 1 (2012), 448–464.

Hendel, R., and J. Joosten. *How Old is the Hebrew Bible? A Linguistic, Textual, and Historical Study* (New Haven, CT, 2018).

Hengel, M. *Die johanneische Frage: Ein Lösungsversuch,* WUNT 67 (Tübingen, 1993).

Hengel, M. *Judentum und Hellenismus: Studien zu ihrer Begegnung unter besonderer Berücksichtigung Palästinas bis zur Mitte des 2. Jh.s v. Chr.* (Tübingen, 1969; 3rd rev. ed., 1988).

Hengel, M. (with R. Deines), *The Pre-Christian Paul* (Philadelphia, 1991).

Hengel, M. (with C. Markschies), "Zum Problem der 'Hellenisierung' Judäas im 1. Jahrhundert nach Christus," in M. Hengel, *Judaica et Hellenistica, Kleine Schriften I,* WUNT 90 (Tübingen, 1996), 1–90.

Hengel, M. "Zwischen Jesus und Paulus: Die 'Hellenisten,' die Sieben und Stephanus," in M. Hengel, *Paulus und Jakobus. Kleine Schriften III,* WUNT 141 (Tübingen, 2002), 1–67.

Hengel, M., and A. M. Schwemer. *Der messianische Anspruch Jesu und die Anfänge der Christologie: Vier Studien,* WUNT 138 (Tübingen, 2001).

Hensel, B. *Juda und Samaria: Zum Verhältnis zweier nach-exilischer Jahwismen,* FAT 110 (Tübingen, 2016).

Hieke, T. *Levitikus 16–27,* HThK.AT (Freiburg im Breisgau, 2014).

Hieke, T. (ed.). *Formen des Kanons: Studien zu Ausprägungen des biblischen Kanons von der Antike bis zum 19. Jahrhundert,* SBS 229 (Stuttgart, 2013).

Hoffman Y. "A North Israelite Typological Myth and a Judaean Historical Tradition: The Exodus in Hosea and Amos," *VT* 39 (1989), 169–182.

Hofius, O. "Das vierte Gottesknechtslied in den Briefen des Neuen Testaments," in O. Hofius, *Neutestamentliche Studien,* WUNT 132 (Tübingen, 2000), 340–360.

Holloway, S. W. "What Ship Goes There? The Flood Narratives in the Gilgamesh Epic and Genesis Considered in Light of Ancient Near Eastern Temple Ideology," *ZAW* 103 (1991), 328–355.

Horbury, W. *Jewish War under Trajan and Hadrian* (Cambridge, 2014).

Hornkohl, A. "Biblical Hebrew: Periodization," in G. Khan (ed.), *Encyclopedia of Hebrew Language and Linguistics,* vol. 1 (Leiden, 2014), 315–325.

Horowitz, W. *Mesopotamian Cosmic Geography* (Philadelphia, PA, 1998).

Huber, M. *Gab es ein davidisch-salomonisches Großreich? Forschungsgeschichte und neuere Argumentationen aus der Sicht der Archäologie,* SBB 64 (Stuttgart, 2010).

Hurtado, L. W. *The Earliest Christian Artefacts: Manuscripts and Christian Origins* (Grand Rapids, MI, 2006).

Hurtado, L. W. *Lord Jesus Christ: Devotion to Jesus in Earliest Christianity* (Grand Rapids, MI, 2003).

Ilan, T. "The Term and Concept of TaNaKh," in K. Finsterbusch and A. Lange (eds.), *What Is Bible?,* CBET 67 (Leuven, 2012), 219–234.

Jackson, B. *Wisdom-Laws: A Study of the Mishpatim in Exodus 21:1–22:16* (Oxford, 2006).

Jacobi, C. *Jesusüberlieferung bei Paulus? Analogien zwischen den echten Paulusbriefen und den synoptischen Evangelien,* BZNW 213 (Berlin, 2015).

Jain, E. *Psalmen oder Psalter? Materielle Rekonstruktion und inhaltliche Untersuchung der Psalmenhandschriften aus der Wüste Juda,* STDJ 109 (Leiden, 2014).

Janowski, B. "Auf dem Weg zur Buchreligion: Transformation des Kultischen im Psalter," in F.-L. Hossfeld et al. (eds.), *Trägerkreise in den Psalmen,* BBB 178 (Göttingen, 2017), 223–261.

Janowski, B. "Freude an der Tora: Psalm 1 als Tor zum Psalter," *EvTh* 67 (2007), 18–31.

Janowski, B. "JHWH und der Sonnengott: Aspekte der Solarisierung JHWHs in vorexilischer Zeit," in J. Mehlhausen (ed.), *Pluralismus und Identität* (Gütersloh, 1995), 214–241; also published in *Die rettende Gerechtigkeit: Beiträge zur Theologie des Alten Testaments 2* (Neukirchen-Vluyn, 1999), 192–219.

Janowski, B. "Die lebendige Statue Gottes: Zur Anthropologie der priesterlichen Urgeschichte," in M. Witte (ed.), *Gott und Mensch im Dialog.* Festschrift für Otto Kaiser zum 80. Geburtstag, vol. 1, BZAW 345/I (Berlin, 2004), 183–214.

Janowski, B. *Die Welt als Schöpfung,* Beiträge zur Theologie des Alten Testaments 4 (Neukirchen-Vluyn, 2008).

Jeremias, J. *Das Königtum Gottes in den Psalmen: Israels Begegnung mit dem kanaanäischen Mythos in den Jahwe-König-Psalmen,* FRLANT 141 (Göttingen, 1987).

Jeremias, J. *Der Prophet Hosea,* ATD 24,1 (Göttingen, 1983).

Jeremias, J. "Das Rätsel der Schriftprophetie," *ZAW* 125 (2013), 93–117.

Jeska, J. *Die Geschichte Israels in der Sicht des Lukas: Apg 7,2b–53 und 13,17–25 im Kontext antik-jüdischer Summarien der Geschichte Israels,* FRLANT 195 (Göttingen, 2001).

Jones, B. C. New Testament Texts on Greek Amulets from Late Antiquity, LNTS 554 (London / New York, 2016).

Joosten, J. "How Hebrew Became a Holy Language," BAR 43 (2017), 44–49, 62.

Joosten, J. "The Origin of the Septuagint Canon," in Siegfried Kreuzer et al. (eds.), Die Septuaginta—Orte und Intentionen, WUNT 361 (Tübingen, 2016), 688–699.

Kaiser, O. Philo von Alexandrien: Denkender Glaube. Eine Einführung, FRLANT 259 (Göttingen, 2015).

Kalimi, I. (ed.). Jewish Bible Theology: Perspectives and Case Studies (Winona Lake, IN, 2012).

Kampling, R. "Grenzgebiete—Zu Strukturelementen des spätantiken Antijuda-ismus," in H. Frankemölle and J. Wohlmuth (eds.), Das Heil der Anderen. Problemfeld: "Judenmission," QD 238 (Freiburg im Breisgau, 2010), 337–357.

Karakolis, C. "Erwägungen zur Exegese des Alten Testaments bei den griechischen Kirchenvätern," in I. Z. Dimitrov et al. (eds.), Das Alte Testament als christ-liche Bibel in orthodoxer und westlicher Sicht, WUNT 174 (Tübingen, 2004), 21–38.

Karrer, M. "Septuaginta und Philosophie," in U. Dahmen and J. Schnocks (eds.), Juda und Jerusalem in der Seleukidenzeit. Herrschaft—Widerstand—Identität, Festschrift für Heinz-Josef Fabry, BBB 159 (Göttingen, 2010), 191–212.

Kartveit, M. The Origin of the Samaritans, VT.S 128 (Leiden, 2009).

Käsemann, E. "Das Problem des historischen Jesus," in E. Käsemann, Exegetische Versuche und Besinnungen (Göttingen, 1964), 187–214.

Kasher, R. "The Interpretation of Scripture in Rabbinic Literature," in M. J. Mulder (ed.), Mikra: Text, Translation, Reading, and Interpretation of the Hebrew Bible in Ancient Judaism and Early Christianity, CRINT II / 1 (Assen / Philadelphia, PA, 1990), 547–594.

Keel, O. Das Böcklein in der Milch seiner Mutter und Verwandtes: Im Lichte eines altorientalischen Bildmotivs, OBO 33 (Göttingen, 1980).

Keel, O. Die Geschichte Jerusalems und die Entstehung des Monotheismus, 2 vols., OLB VI, 1 (Göttingen, 2007).

Keel, O. "Eine Replik auf die Stellungnahme von Dr. S. Lauer und Prof. Petuchowski zum 'Böcklein in der Milch seiner Mutter,'" Judaica 37 (1981), 234–235.

Keel, O. "Der salomonische Tempelweihspruch: Beobachtungen zum religionsge-schichtlichen Kontext des Ersten Jerusalemer Tempels," in O. Keel and E. Zenger (eds.), Gottesstadt und Gottesgarten: Zur Geschichte und Theologie des Jerusalemer Tempels, QD 191 (Freiburg im Breisgau, 2002), 9–23.

Keel, O. "Sonne der Gerechtigkeit: Jerusalemer Traditionen vom Sonnen- und Richtergott," BiKi 63 (2008), 215–218.

Keel, O., and M. Küchler. Orte und Landschaften der Bibel: Ein Handbuch und Stu-dienreiseführer zum Heiligen Land, vol. 2: Der Süden (Göttingen, 1982).

Keel, O., and U. Staub. *Hellenismus und Judentum: Vier Studien zu Daniel 7 und zur Religionsnot unter Antiochus IV.*, OBO 178 (Freiburg, 2000).

Keel, O., and C. Uehlinger. *Göttinnen, Götter und Gottessymbole: Neue Erkenntnisse zur Religionsgeschichte Kanaans und Israels aufgrund bislang unerschlossener ikonographischer Quellen*, 6th ed. (Fribourg, 2010).

Keel-Leu, H., and B. Teissier. *Die vorderasiatischen Rollsiegel der Sammlungen 'Bibel + Orient' der Universität Fribourg*, OBO 200 (Fribourg, 2000).

Keith, C. L., et al. (eds.). *The Reception of Jesus in the First Three Centuries*, 3 vols. (London, 2019).

Kim, D.-H. *Early Biblical Hebrew, Late Biblical Hebrew, and Linguistic Variability: A Sociolinguistic Evaluation of the Linguistic Dating of Biblical Texts*, VT.S 156 (Leiden, 2013).

Kim, J.-H. "Vom hellenistischen Kleinrollensystem zum Kodex: Beobachtungen zur Textgestalt der griechischen Samuel- und Königebücher," in M. K. H. Peters (ed.), *XIV. Congress of the IOSCS, Helsinki 2010*, SBL.SCSt 59 (Atlanta, GA, 2013), 231–242.

Kinzig, W. "Καινὴ διαθήκη: The Title of the New Testament in the Second and Third Centuries," *JTS* 45 (1994), 519–544.

Kirk, A. *Q in Matthew: Ancient Media, Memory, and Early Scribal Transmission of the Jesus Tradition*, LNTS 564 (London, 2016).

Klauck, H.-J. "Alle Jubeljahre: Zum neuen Dokument der Päpstlichen Bibelkommission," in H.-J. Klauck, *Religion und Gesellschaft im frühen Christentum*, *Neutestamentliche Studien*, WUNT 152 (Tübingen, 2003), 394–420.

Klauck, H.-J. *Die apokryphe Bibel: Ein anderer Zugang zum frühen Christentum*, Tria Corda 4 (Tübingen, 2008).

Klauck, H.-J. "Die katholische neutestamentliche Exegese zwischen Vatikanum I und II," in H.-J. Klauck, *Religion und Gesellschaft im frühen Christentum: Neutestamentliche Studien*, WUNT 152 (Tübingen, 2003), 360–393.

Kleer, M. *Der liebliche Sänger der Psalmen Israels: Untersuchungen zu David als Dichter und Beter der Psalmen*, BBB 108 (Bodenheim, 1996).

Knauf, E. A. "Hezekiah or Manasseh? A Reconsideration of the Siloam Tunnel and Inscription," *Tel Aviv* 28 (2001): 281–287.

Knauf, E. A. "Hiobs Heimat," *WO* 19 (1988), 65–83.

Knauf, E. A. *Midian: Untersuchungen zur Geschichte Palästinas und Nordarabiens am Ende des 2. Jahrtausends v. Chr.*, ADPV (Wiesbaden, 1988).

Knauf, E. A. "Was There a Refugee Crisis in the 8th / 7th Centuries BCE?," in O. Lipschits et al. (eds.), *Rethinking Israel: Studies in the History and Archaeology of Ancient Israel in Honor of Israel Finkelstein* (Winona Lake, IN, 2017), 159–172.

Knauf, E. A. "Zur Herkunft und Sozialgeschichte Israels: 'Das Böckchen in der Milch seiner Mutter,'" *Biblica* 69 (1988), 153–169; also published in E. A.

Knauf, *Data and Debates: Essays in the History and Culture of Israel and Its Neighbors in Antiquity,* AOAT 407 (Münster, 2013), 37–47.

Knoppers, G. N. *Jews and Samaritans: The Origins and History of Their Early Relations* (Oxford, 2013).

Knoppers, G. N., and B. M. Levinson (eds.). *The Pentateuch as Torah: New Models for Understanding Its Promulgation and Acceptance* (Winona Lake, IN, 2007).

Koch, C. *Gottes himmlische Wohnstatt: Transformationen im Verhältnis von Gott und Himmel in tempeltheologischen Entwürfen des Alten Testaments in der Exilszeit,* FAT 119 (Tübingen, 2018).

Koch, D.-A. *Geschichte des Urchristentums: Ein Lehrbuch,* 2nd ed. (Göttingen, 2014).

Köckert, M. "YHWH in the Northern and Southern Kingdom," in R. G. Kratz and H. Spieckermann (eds.), *One God—One Cult—One Nation: Archaeological and Biblical Perspectives,* BZAW 405 (Berlin, 2010), 357–394.

Köckert, M., and M. Nissinen (eds.). *Propheten in Mari, Assyrien und Israel,* FRLANT 201 (Göttingen, 2003).

Konradt, M. *Studien zum Matthäusevangelium,* WUNT 358 (Tübingen, 2016).

Korpel, M., and J. Oesch (eds.). *Delimitation Criticism: A New Tool in Biblical Scholarship* (Leiden, 2000).

Koselleck, R. *Vergangene Zukunft: Zur Semantik geschichtlicher Zeiten* (Frankfurt a. M., 1979).

Kottsieper, I. "The Tel Dan Inscription (KAI 310) and the Political Relations between Aram-Damascus and Israel in the First Half of the First Millennium BCE," in L. L. Grabbe (ed.), *Ahab Agonistes: The Rise and Fall of the Omri Dynasty* (London, 2007), 104–134.

Kraemer, D. "The Mishnah," in S. Katz. (ed.), *The Cambridge History of Judaism,* vol. 4: *The Late Roman-Rabbinic Period* (Cambridge, 2006), 299–315.

Kratz, R. G. "Elephantine und Alexandria: Nicht-biblisches und biblisches Judentum in Ägypten," in T. Georges et al. (eds.), *Alexandria,* COMES 1 (Tübingen, 2013), 193–208.

Kratz, R. G. *Historisches und biblisches Israel: Drei Überblicke zum Alten Testament* (Tübingen, 2013).

Kratz, R. G. "Innerbiblische Exegese und Redaktionsgeschichte im Lichte empirischer Evidenz," in R. G. Kratz, *Das Judentum im Zeitalter des Zweiten Tempels,* FAT 42 (Tübingen, 2004), 126–156.

Kratz, R. G. "Israel als Staat und als Volk," *ZThK* 97 (2000), 1–17.

Kratz, R. G. "Der Mythos vom Königtum Gottes in Kanaan und Israel," *ZThK* 100 (2003), 147–162.

Kratz, R. G. *Die Propheten Israels* (Munich, 2003).

Kratz, R. G. "Das Rätsel der Schriftprophetie. Eine Replik," *ZAW* 125 (2013), 635–639.

Kratz, R. G. "Temple and Torah: Reflections on the Legal Status of the Pentateuch between Elephantine and Qumran," in G. N. Knoppers and B. M. Levinson (eds.), *The Pentateuch as Torah: New Models for Understanding Its Promulgation and Acceptance* (Winona Lake, IN, 2007), 77–103.

Kratz, R. G. "Die Tora Davids: Ps 1 und die doxologische Fünfteilung des Psalters," *ZThK* 93 (1996), 1–34.

Kratz, R. G. "The Visions of Daniel," in J. J. Collins and P. W. Flint (eds.), *The Book of Daniel: Composition and Reception*, VT.S 83 / 1 (Leiden, 2001), 91–113.

Kraus, T. J. "Manuscripts with the Lord's Prayer—They Are More Than Simply Witnesses to That Text Itself," in T. J. Kraus and T. Nicklas (eds.), *New Testament Manuscripts: Their Texts and Their World*, TENTS 2 (Leiden / Boston, 2006), 227–266.

Kraus, T. J. "Miniature Codices in Late Antiquity: Preliminary Remarks and Tendencies about a Specific Book Format," *EC* 7 (2016), 134–152.

Kraus, T. J., and T. Nicklas. *Das Petrusevangelium und die Petrusapokalypse: Die griechischen Fragmente mit deutscher und englischer Übersetzung*, GCS NF 11 (Berlin, 2004).

Kraus, W. *Zwischen Jerusalem und Antiochia: Die 'Hellenisten,' Paulus und die Aufnahme der Heiden in das endzeitliche Gottesvolk*, SBS 179 (Stuttgart, 1999).

Kraus, W., and M. Karrer (eds.). *Septuaginta Deutsch: Das griechische Alte Testament in deutscher Übersetzung* (Stuttgart, 2009; 2nd ed., 2010).

Krauter, S. "Die Pentateuch-Septuaginta als Übersetzung in der Literaturgeschichte der Antike," in T. S. Caulley and H. Lichtenberger (eds.), *Die Septuaginta und das frühe Christentum / The Septuagint and Christian Origins*, WUNT 277 (Tübingen, 2011), 26–46.

Kreuzer, S. "Entstehung und Entwicklung der Septuaginta im Kontext alexandrinischer und frühjüdischer Kultur und Bildung," in M. Karrer and W. Kraus (eds.), *Septuaginta Deutsch: Erläuterungen und Kommentare zum griechischen Alten Testament* (Stuttgart, 2011), 3–39.

Kreuzer, S. "Entstehung und Überlieferung der Septuaginta," in S. Kreuzer. (ed.), *Handbuch zur Septuaginta, LXX.H*, vol. 1: *Einleitung in die Septuaginta* (Gütersloh, 2016), 29–88.

Kreuzer, S. *Geschichte, Sprache und Text: Studien zum Alten Testament und seiner Umwelt*, BZAW 479 (Berlin, 2015).

Krieg, C. "Javne und der Kanon. Klärungen," in G. Steins and J. Taschner (eds.), *Kanonisierung—die Hebräische Bibel im Werden*, BThSt 110 (Neukirchen-Vluyn, 2010), 133–152.

Krochmalnik, D. *Im Garten der Schrift: Wie Juden die Bibel lesen* (Augsburg, 2006).

Kruger, M. J. *The Gospel of the Savior: An Analysis of P.Oxy. 840 and Its Place in the Gospel Traditions of Early Christianity*, TENTS 1 (Leiden, 2005).

Krüger, T. "Das menschliche Herz und die Weisung Gottes: Elemente einer Diskussion über Möglichkeiten und Grenzen der Tora-Rezeption im Alten Testament," in T. Krüger, *Das menschliche Herz und die Weisung Gottes: Studien zur alttestamentlichen Anthropologie und Ethik*, AThANT 96 (Zurich, 2009), 107–136.

Krüger, T. "Die Rezeption der Tora im Buch Kohelet," in L. Schwienhorst-Schönberger (ed.), *Das Buch Kohelet: Studien zur Struktur, Geschichte, Rezeption und Theologie*, BZAW 254 (Berlin, 1997), 173–193.

Krupp, M. *Einführung in die Mischna* (Frankfurt a. M., 2007).

Laato, A. "Biblical Scholarship in Northern Europe," in M. Sæbø (ed.), *Hebrew Bible / Old Testament. The History of Its Interpretation*, vol. 3: *From Modernism to Post-Modernism (the Nineteenth and Twentieth Centuries)*, part 2: *The Twentieth Century—from Modernism to Post-Modernism* (Göttingen, 2015), 336–370.

Lang, B. "The 'Writings': A Hellenistic Literary Canon in the Hebrew Bible," in A. van der Kooij and K. van der Toorn (eds.), *Canonization and Decanonization: Papers Presented to the International Conference of the Leiden Institute for the Study of Religion (LISOR)*, held at Leiden, 9–10 January 1997, SHR 82 (Leiden, 1997), 41–65.

Lang, M. "Amos und Exodus: Einige Überlegungen zu Am 3–6," *BN* 119/120 (2003), 27–29.

Lange, A. "The Law, the Prophets, and the Other Books of the Fathers (Sir, Prologue): Canonical Lists in Ben Sira and Elsewhere?," in G. G. Xeravits and J. Zsengellér (eds.), *Studies in the Book of Ben Sira: Papers of the Third International Conference on the Deuterocanonical Books*, Shime'on Centre, Pápa, Hungary, 18–20 May 2006, JSJ.S 127 (Leiden, 2008), 55–80.

Lange, A., and E. Tov (eds.). *Textual History of the Bible: The Hebrew Bible*, vol. 1A: *Overview Articles* (Leiden, 2016).

Langer, G. *Midrasch*, UTB 4675 (Tübingen, 2016).

Lauer, S. "Kultpolemik—Theorie und / oder Heiligkeitsgesetz. Zu O. Keel, 'Das Böcklein in der Milch seiner Mutter und Verwandtes,'" *Judaica* 37 (1981), 161–162.

Lauinger, J. "Esarhaddon's Succession Treaty at Tell Tayinat: Text and Commentary," *JCS* 64 (2012), 87–123.

LeFebvre, M. *Collections, Codes, and Torah: The Re-characterization of Israel's Written Law*, LHB / OTS 451 (London, 2006).

Legaspi, M. *The Death of Scripture and the Rise of Biblical Studies* (Oxford, 2010).

Lehmann, R. G., and A. E. Zernecke. "Bemerkungen und Beobachtungen zu der neuen Ophel-Pithosinschrift," in R. G. Lehmann and A. E. Zernecke (eds.), *Schrift und Sprache: Papers Read at the 10th Mainz International Colloquium on Ancient Hebrew, Mainz, 28–30 October 2011*, KUSATU 15 (Waltrop, 2013), 437–450.

Leiman, S. Z. *The Canonization of Hebrew Scripture: The Talmudic and Midrashic Evidence*, 2nd ed. (New Haven, CT, 1991).

Leipoldt, J. *Geschichte des neutestamentlichen Kanons. Erster Teil: Die Entstehung* (Leipzig, 1907).

Leuenberger, M. *"Ich bin Jhwh und keiner sonst": Der exklusive Monotheismus des Kyros-Orakels Jesaja 45,1-7*, SBS 224 (Stuttgart, 2010).

Levenson, J. D. "Warum Juden sich nicht für biblische Theologie interessieren," *EvTh* 51 (1991), 402–430.

Levin, C. *Das Alte Testament*, 5th ed. (Munich, 2018).

Levin, C. "Die Entstehung des Judentums als Gegenstand der alttestamentlichen Wissenschaft," in C. M. Maier (ed.), *Congress Volume Munich 2013*, VT.S 163 (Leiden, 2014), 1–17.

Levinson, B. M. "The Birth of the Lemma: The Restrictive Reinterpretation of the Covenant Code's Manumission Law by the Holiness Code (Leviticus 25:44–46)," *JBL* 124 (2005), 617–639.

Levinson, B. M. *Der kreative Kanon: Innerbiblische Schriftauslegung und religionsgeschichtlicher Wandel im alten Israel* (Tübingen, 2012).

Levinson, B. M. "The Manumission of Hermeneutics: The Slave Laws of the Pentateuch as a Challenge to Contemporary Pentateuch Theory," in A. Lemaire (ed.), *Congress Volume Leiden 2004*, VT.S 109 (Leiden, 2006), 281–324.

Levinson, B. M. "Die neuassyrischen Ursprünge der Kanonformel in Deuteronomium 13,1," in S. Beyerle et al. (eds.), *Viele Wege zu dem Einen: Historische Bibelkritik—die Vitalität der Glaubensüberlieferung in der Moderne*, BThSt 121 (Neukirchen-Vluyn, 2012), 23–59.

Levinson, B. M., and J. Stackert. "Between the Covenant Code and Esarhaddon's Succession Treaty: Deuteronomy 13 and the Composition of Deuteronomy," *JAJ* (2012), 123–140.

Levy, T. E., et al. (eds.). *Israel's Exodus in Transdisciplinary Perspective: Text, Archaeology, Culture, and Geoscience* (Heidelberg, 2015).

Lieu, J. *Christian Identity in the Jewish and Graeco-Roman World* (Oxford, 2004).

Lieu, J. *Marcion and the Making of a Heretic: God and Scripture in the Second Century* (Cambridge, 2015).

Lieu, J. "'The Parting of the Ways': Theological Construct or Historical Reality?," *JSNT* 56 (1994), 101–119; also published in J. Lieu, *Neither Jew nor Greek? Constructing Christian Identity*, SNTW (London, 2002), 11–29.

Lim, T. *The Formation of the Jewish Canon* (New Haven, CT, 2013).

Lim, T. "An Indicative Definition of Canon," in T. Lim (ed.), *When Texts Are Canonized*, BJSt 359 (Providence, RI, 2017), 1–24.

Lindemann, A., and H. Paulsen. *Die Apostolischen Väter: Griechisch-deutsche Parallelausgabe* (Tübingen, 1992).

Linnemann, E. *Bibelkritik auf dem Prüfstand—Wie wissenschaftlich ist die "wissenschaftliche Theologie"?* (Nuremberg, 1998).

Linnemann, E. *Original oder Fälschung: Historisch-kritische Theologie im Licht der Bibel*, 2nd ed. (Bielefeld, 1999).

Lipschits, O. "Bethel Revisited," in O. Lipschits, Y. Gadot, and M. J. Adams (eds.), *Rethinking Israel: Studies in the History and Archaeology of Ancient Israel in Honor of Israel Finkelstein* (Winona Lake, IN, 2017), 233–246.

Lipschits, O. "Demographic Changes in Judah between the Seventh and the Fifth Centuries B.C.E.," in O. Lipschits and J. Blenkinsopp (eds.), *Judah and the Judeans in the Neo-Babylonian Period* (Winona Lake, IN, 2003), 323–376.

Lipschits, O. *The Fall and Rise of Jerusalem: Judah under Babylonian Rule* (Winona Lake, IN, 2005).

Lipschits, O. "The Rural Settlement in Judah in the Sixth Century B.C.E: A Rejoinder," *PEQ* 136 (2004), 99–107.

Lohfink, N. "Das Deuteronomium: Jahwegesetz oder Mosegesetz?," *ThPh* 65 (1990), 387–391.

Lohfink, N. *Studien zum Deuteronomium und zur deuteronomistischen Literatur III*, SBAB 20 (Stuttgart, 1995).

Lührmann, D. *Die apokryph gewordenen Evangelien: Studien zu neuen Texten und zu neuen Fragen*, NovTestSuppl. 112 (Leiden, 2004).

Lührmann, D. *Fragmente apokryph gewordener Evangelien in griechischer und lateinischer Sprache*, MThS 59 (Marburg, 2000).

Luz, U. "The Significance of the Church Fathers for Biblical Interpretation in Western Protestant Perspective," in U. Luz, *Studies in Matthew* (Grand Rapids, MI, 2005), 290–312.

Luz, U. *Theologische Hermeneutik des Neuen Testaments* (Neukirchen-Vluyn, 2014).

Luz, U. (ed.). *Zankapfel Bibel: Eine Bibel—viele Zugänge* (Zurich, 1992).

Machiela, D. A. *The Dead Sea Genesis Apocryphon: A New Text and Translation with Introduction and Special Treatment of Columns 13–17*, STDJ 79 (Leiden, 2009).

Macholz, C. "Die Entstehung des hebräischen Bibelkanons nach 4 Esra 14," in E. Blum (ed.), *Die hebräische Bibel und ihre zweifache Nachgeschichte: Festschrift für Rolf Rendtorff zum 65. Geburtstag* (Neukirchen-Vluyn, 1990), 379–391.

Magen, Y. "The Dating of the First Phase of the Samaritan Temple on Mount Gerizim in Light of the Archaeological Evidence," in O. Lipschits et al., *Judah and the Judeans in the Fourth Century B.C.E.* (Winona Lake, IN, 2007), 157–211.

Magen, Y., et al. (eds.). *Mount Gerizim Excavations I: The Aramaic, Hebrew and Samaritan Inscriptions* (Jerusalem, 2004).

Magen, Y., et al. (eds.). *Mount Gerizim Excavations II: A Temple City* (Jerusalem, 2008).

Magness, J. *The Archaeology of Qumran and the Dead Sea Scrolls* (Grand Rapids, MI, 2002).

Maier, C. *Daughter Zion, Mother Zion: Gender, Space, and the Sacred in Ancient Israel* (Minneapolis, MN, 2008).

Maier, J. *Die Qumran-Essener: Die Texte vom Toten Meer,* vol. 2: *Die Texte der Höhle 4* (Munich, 1995).

Markschies, C. "Haupteinleitung," in C. Markschies and J. Schröter (eds.), *Antike christliche Apokryphen in deutscher Übersetzung,* vol. 1: *Evangelien und Verwandtes* (Tübingen, 2012), 1–180.

Markschies, C. *Hellenisierung des Christentums: Sinn und Unsinn einer historischen Deutungskategorie* (Leipzig, 2012).

Markschies, C. *Kaiserzeitliche christliche Theologie und ihre Institutionen* (Tübingen, 2007).

Markschies, C., and J. Schröter (eds.). *Antike christliche Apokryphen in deutscher Übersetzung,* vol. 1: *Evangelien und Verwandtes* (Tübingen, 2012).

Mason, S. *A History of the Jewish War A.D. 66–74* (Cambridge, 2016).

Mason, S. "Jews, Judaeans, Judaizing, Judaism: Problems of Categorization in Ancient History," *JSJ* 38 (2007), 457–512.

Mason, S. "Josephus and His Twenty-Two Book Canon," in L. M. McDonald and J. A. Sanders (eds.), *The Canon Debate* (Peabody, MA, 2002), 110–127.

Mathys, H.-P. "Die Erhebung Davids zum König nach der Darstellung der Chronik," *RHPhR* 93 (2013), 29–47.

Mathys, H.-P. "Wilhelm Martin Leberecht de Wettes 'Dissertatio critico-exegetica' von 1805," in M. Kessler and M. Wallraff (eds.), *Biblische Theologie und historisches Denken: Wissenschaftsgeschichtliche Studien aus Anlass der 50. Wiederkehr der Basler Promotion von Rudolf Smend* (Basel, 2008), 171–211.

Mathys, H.-P. (ed.). *Ebenbild Gottes—Herrscher über die Welt,* BThSt 33 (Neukirchen-Vluyn, 1998).

Maul, S. M. *Die Wahrsagekunst im Alten Orient: Zeichen des Himmels und der Erde* (Munich, 2013).

McCarter, P. K., et al. "An Archaic Ba'al Inscription from Tel Beth-Shemesh," *Tel Aviv* 38 (2011), 179–193.

McDonald, L. M. *The Formation of the Biblical Canon,* vol. 1: *The Old Testament: Its Authority and Canonicity;* vol. 2: *The New Testament: Its Authority and Canonicity* (London, 2017).

McKenzie, S. L. *King David: A Biography* (New York, 2000).

McKenzie, S. L., T. Römer, et al. (eds.). *The Encyclopedia of the Bible and Its Reception,* EBR (Berlin, 2009).

Meerson, M., and P. Schäfer. *Toledot Yeshu: The Life Story of Jesus,* 2 vols. and database, TSAJ 159 (Tübingen, 2014).

Meisner, N. "Aristeasbrief," in *JSHRZ* II / 1 (Gütersloh, 1973), 35–87.

Mendels, D., and A. Edrei. *Zweierlei Diaspora: Zur Spaltung der antiken jüdischen Welt,* Toldot 8 (Göttingen, 2010).

Merkt, A. *1. Petrus,* part 1, NTP 21 / 1 (Göttingen, 2015).

Meshel, Z. (ed.). *Kuntillet 'Ajrud (Horvat Teman): An Iron Age II Religious Site on the Judah-Sinai Border* (Jerusalem, 2012).

Metzger, B. M. *Der Kanon des Neuen Testaments. Entstehung—Entwicklung—Bedeutung* (Düsseldorf, 1993) (Engl. ed., *The Canon of the New Testament,* Oxford, 1987).

Meurer, S. (ed.). *Die Apokryphenfrage im ökumenischen Horizont,* 2nd ed. (Stuttgart, 1993).

Meyer, Marvin (ed.). *The Nag Hammadi Scriptures: The Revised and Updated Translation of Sacred Gnostic Texts* (New York, 2007).

Milik, J. T. "Les modèles araméens du livre d'Esther dans la Grotte 4 de Qumran," *RdQ* 15 (1992), 321–404.

Miller-Naudé, C., and Z. Zevit, (eds.). *Diachrony in Biblical Hebrew,* Linguistic Studies in Ancient West Semitic 8 (Winona Lake, IN, 2012).

Morrow, W. S. *An Introduction to Biblical Law* (Grand Rapids, MI, 2017).

Mosis, R. "Die Bücher des 'Alten Bundes' bei Melito von Sardes," in A. Moenikes (ed.), *Schätze der Schrift: Festgabe für Hans F. Fuhs zur Vollendung seines 65. Lebensjahres,* PThSt 47 (Paderborn, 2007), 131–176.

Müller, R. *Ausgebliebene Einsicht: Jesajas "Verstockungsauftrag" (Jes 6,9–11) und die judäische Politik am Ende des 8.Jahrhunderts,* BThSt 124 (Neukirchen-Vluyn, 2012).

Müller, R. *Jahwe als Wettergott: Studien zur althebräischen Kultlyrik anhand ausgewählter Psalmen,* BZAW 387 (Berlin, 2008).

Müller, R. *Königtum und Gottesherrschaft: Untersuchungen zur alttestamentlichen Monarchiekritik,* FAT II / 3 (Tübingen, 2004).

Müller-Kessler, C. "Christian Palestinian Aramaic Translation," in A. Lange and E. Tov (eds.), *Textual History of the Bible: The Hebrew Bible,* vol. 1a: *Overview Articles* (Leiden, 2016), 385–393.

Na'aman, N. "Canaanite Jerusalem and Its Central Hill Country Neighbours in the Second Millennium B.C.E." *UF* 24 (1992), 275–291.

Na'aman, N. "Dismissing the Myth of a Flood of Israelite Refugees in the Late Eighth Century BCE," *ZAW* 126 (2014), 1–14.

Na'aman, N. "Population Changes in Palestine Following Assyrian Deportations," *Tel Aviv* 20 (1993), 104–124.

Na'aman, N., and R. Zadok. "Assyrian Deportations to the Province of Samerina in the Light of Two Cuneiform Tablets from Tel Hadid," *Tel Aviv* 27 (2000), 159–188.

Nesselrath, H.-G. "Das Museion und die Große Bibliothek von Alexandria," in T. Georges, F. Albrecht, and R. Feldmeier (eds.), with the collaboration of M. Kaden and C. Martsch, *Alexandria,* Civitatum Orbis MEditarranei Studia 1 (Tübingen, 2013), 65–90.

Neusner, J. "The Role of Scripture in the Torah: Is Judaism a 'Biblical Religion'?," in H. Merklein et al. (eds.), *Bibel in jüdischer und christlicher Tradition* (Frankfurt a. M., 1993), 192–211.

Newsom, C. A. "Models of the Moral Self: Hebrew Bible and Second Temple Judaism," *JBL* 131 (2012), 5–25.

Nickelsburg, G. W. E. "The Bible Rewritten and Expanded," in M. E. Stone (ed.), *Jewish Writings of the Second Temple Period: Apocrypha, Pseudepigrapha, Qumran Sectarian Writings, Philo, Josephus*, CRINT II/2 (Assen/Philadelphia, 1984), 89–156.

Nickelsburg, G. W. E. *Jewish Literature between the Bible and the Mishnah: A Historical and Literary Introduction*, 2nd ed. (Minneapolis, 2005).

Nickelsburg, G. W. E. *Jüdische Literatur zwischen Bibel und Mischna: Eine historische und literarische Einführung*, ANTZ 13 / ABU 4 (Berlin/Dortmund, 2018).

Nicklas, T. *Jews and Christians? Second Century "Christian" Perspectives on the "Parting of the Ways,"* Annual Deichmann Lectures 2013 (Tübingen, 2014).

Nicklas, T. "Parting of the Ways? Probleme eines Konzepts," in S. Alkier and H. Leppin (eds.), *Juden—Christen—Heiden? Religiöse Inklusion und Exklusion in Kleinasien bis Decius*, WUNT 400 (Tübingen, 2018), 21–42.

Nicklas, T., M., J. Kruger, and T. J. Kraus. *Gospel Fragments*, Oxford Early Christian Gospel Texts (Oxford, 2009).

Niditch, S. *The Responsive Self: Personal Religion in Biblical Literature of the Neo-Babylonian and Persian Periods* (New Haven, CT, 2015).

Niebuhr, K.-W. "Die Werke des eschatologischen Freudenboten: 4Q521 und die Jesusüberlieferung," in C. M. Tuckett (ed.), *The Scriptures in the Gospels*, BETL 131 (Leuven, 1997), 637–646.

Niehoff, M. *Philo of Alexandria: An Intellectual Biography* (New Haven, 2018).

Nihan, C. "The Torah between Samaria and Judah: Shechem and Gerizim in Deuteronomy and Joshua," in B. M. Levinson and G. N. Knoppers (eds.), *The Pentateuch as Torah: New Models for Understanding Its Promulgence and Its Acceptance* (Winona Lake, IN, 2007), 187–223.

Nissinen, M. *Ancient Prophecy: Near Eastern, Biblical, and Greek Perspectives* (Oxford, 2018).

Noam, V. "The Origin of the List of David's Songs in 'David's Compositions,'" *DSD* 13 (2006), 134–149.

Nocquet, D. *La Samarie, la Diaspora et l'achèvement de la Torah*, OBO 284 (Fribourg, 2017).

Nöldeke, T. "Die s. g. Grundschrift des Pentateuchs," in T. Nöldeke, *Untersuchungen zur Kritik des Alten Testaments* (Kiel, 1869), 1–144.

Noth, M. *Geschichte Israels* (Göttingen, 1950).

Oded, B. "Observations on the Israelite/Judaean Exiles in Mesopotamia during the Eighth–Sixth Centuries BCE," in K. Van Lerberghe and A. Schoors (eds.), *Immigration and Emigration within the Ancient Near East*, Festschrift für E. Lipinski, OLA 65 (Leuven, 1995), 205–212.

Öhler, M., and F. Wilk (eds.). *Paulinische Schriftrezeption: Grundlagen— Ausprägungen—Wirkungen—Wertungen,* FRLANT 268 (Göttingen, 2017).

Oorschot, J. van. "Die Entstehung des Hiobbuches," in T. Krüger et al. (eds.), *Das Buch Hiob und seine Interpretationen.* Beiträge zum Hiob-Symposium auf dem Monte Verità vom 14.–19. August 2005, AThANT 88 (Zurich, 2007), 165–184.

Otto, E. *Altorientalische und biblische Rechtsgeschichte: Gesammelte Studien,* BZAR 8 (Wiesbaden 2008).

Otto, E. *Das antike Jerusalem: Archäologie und Geschichte,* Beck'sche Reihe 2418 (Munich, 2008).

Otto, E. "Das Bundesbuch und der 'Kodex' Hammurapi: Das biblische Recht zwischen positiver und subversiver Rezeption von Keilschriftrecht," *ZAR* 16 (2010), 1–26.

Otto, E. "Jeremia und die Tora: Ein nachexilischer Diskurs," in E. Otto, *Die Tora. Studien zum Pentateuch: Gesammelte Schriften,* BZAR 9 (Wiesbaden, 2009), 515–560.

Otto, E. *Mose: Geschichte und Legende* (Munich, 2006).

Otto, E. "Techniken der Rechtssatzredaktion israelitischer Rechtsbücher in der Redaktion des Prophetenbuches Micha," *SJOT* 5 (1991), 119–150.

Otto, E. "Treueid und Gesetz: Die Ursprünge des Deuteronomiums im Horizont neuassyrischen Vertragsrechts," *ZAR* 2 (1996), 1–52.

Pakkala, J. "Jeroboam without Bulls," *ZAW* 120 (2008), 501–525.

Parker, D. C. *An Introduction to the New Testament Manuscripts and Their Texts* (Cambridge 2008), 13–20.

Parzinger, H. *Die Kinder des Prometheus: Eine Geschichte der Menschheit vor der Erfindung der Schrift,* 5th ed. (Munich, 2016).

Pearce, L. E. "Identifying Judeans and Judean Identity in the Babylonian Evidence," in C. Waerzeggers and J. Stökl (eds.), *Exile and Return: The Babylonian Context,* BZAW 478 (Berlin, 2015), 7–32.

Pearce, L. E. "Looking for Judeans in Babylonia's Core and Periphery," in E. Ben Zvi and C. Levin (eds.), *Centres and Peripheries in the Early Second Temple Period,* FAT 108 (Tübingen, 2016), 43–64.

Pearce, L. E., and C. Wunsch. *Documents of Judean Exiles and West Semites in Babylonia in the Collection of David Sofer,* CUSAS 28 (Bethesda, MD, 2014).

Pentiuc, E. J. *The Old Testament in Eastern Orthodox Tradition* (Oxford, 2014).

Perrin, A. B. "The Variants of 4Q (Reworked) Pentateuch: A Comprehensive List of the Textual Variants in 4Q158, 4Q364–7 in Biblical Sequence," *Journal of Jewish Studies* 63 (2012), 127–157.

Perrot, C. "The Reading of the Bible in the Ancient Synagogue," in M. J. Mulder (ed.), *Mikra: Text, Translation, Reading, and Interpretation of the Hebrew Bible in Ancient Judaism and Early Christianity,* CRINT II / 1 (Assen / Philadelphia, PA, 1990), 137–159.

Petersen, D. L. "Rethinking the End of Prophecy," in M. Augustin and K.-D. Schunck (eds.), *Wünschet Jerusalem Frieden,* BEAT 13 (Frankfurt a. M., 1988), 65–71.

Petuchowski, J. J. "Das rabbinische Verständnis vom 'Böcklein in der Milch seiner Mutter.' Zu O. Keel, 'Das Böcklein in der Milch seiner Mutter und Verwandtes,'" *Judaica* 37 (1981), 163–165.

Pichot, A. *Die Geburt der Wissenschaft: Von den Babyloniern zu den frühen Griechen* (Frankfurt a. M., 1995).

Pietsch, M. *Die Kultreform Josias: Studien zur Religionsgeschichte Israels in der späten Königszeit,* FAT 86 (Tübingen, 2013).

Plöger, O. *Theokratie und Eschatologie,* WMANT 2, 2nd ed. (Neukirchen-Vluyn, 1962).

Polliack, M. "Jewish Arabic Translations," in A. Lange and E. Tov (eds.), *Textual History of the Bible. The Hebrew Bible,* vol. 1a: *Overview Articles* (Leiden, 2016), 289–309.

Pongratz-Leisten, B. *Ina šulmi irub: Die kulttopographische und ideologische Programmatik der akitu-Prozession in Babylonien und Assyrien im 1. Jahrtausend vor Christus* (Mainz, 1994).

Porten, B. *The Elephantine Papyri in English: Three Millennia of Cross-Cultural Continuity and Change,* DMOA 22 (Leiden, 1996).

Porter, S. E. *Constantine Tischendorf: The Life and Work of a 19th Century Bible Hunter. Including Constantine Tischendorf's When Were Our Gospels Written?* (London, 2015).

Portier-Young, A. *Apocalypse against Empire: Theologies of Resistance in Early Judaism* (2010; Grand Rapids, MI, 2014).

Posset, F. *Johann Reuchlin (1455–1522): A Theological Biography,* AKG 129 (Berlin, 2015).

Rebenich, S. *Jerome* (Abingdon, 2002).

Reed, J. L. *Archaeology and the Galilean Jesus: A Re-Examination of the Evidence* (Harrisburg, PA, 2000).

Reich, R. *Excavating the City of David: Where Jerusalem's History Began* (Jerusalem, 2011).

Renz, J., and W. Röllig. *Handbuch der althebräischen Epigraphik,* 3 vols. (Darmstadt, 1995–2003).

Rezetko, R., and I. Young. *Historical Linguistics and Biblical Hebrew: Steps toward an Integrated Approach,* SBL.ANEM 9 (Atlanta, GA, 2014).

Richelle, M. "Elusive Scrolls: Could Any Hebrew Literature Have Been Written Prior to the Eighth Century BCE?," *VT* 66 (2016), 556–594.

Riesner, R. *Die Frühzeit des Apostels Paulus: Studien zu Chronologie, Missionsstrategie und Theologie,* WUNT 71 (Tübingen, 1994).

Rogerson, J. W. "Die Bibel lesen wie jedes andere Buch? Auseinandersetzungen um die Autorität der Bibel vom 18. Jahrhundert an bis heute," in S. Chapman et al.

(eds.), *Biblischer Text und theologische Theoriebildung,* BThSt 44 (Neukirchen-Vluyn, 2001), 211–234.

Rollston, C. "The Khirbet Qeiyafa Ostracon: Methodological Musings and Caveats," *Tel Aviv* 38 (2011), 67–82.

Rollston, C. *Writing and Literacy in the World of Ancient Israel* (Atlanta, GA, 2010).

Roloff, J. *Die Kirche im Neuen Testament,* GNT 10 (Göttingen, 1993).

Römer, T. "Beschneidung in der Hebräischen Bibel und ihre literarische Begründung in Genesis 17," in M. Jung et al. (eds.), *Dem Körper eingeschrieben: Verkörperung zwischen Leiberleben und kulturellem Sinn* (Heidelberg, 2016), 227–241.

Römer, T. *Die Erfindung Gottes: Eine Reise zu den Quellen des Monotheismus* (Darmstadt, 2018).

Römer, T. "From Deuteronomistic History to Nebiim and Torah," in I. Himbaza (ed.), *Making the Biblical Text: Textual Studies in the Hebrew and Greek Bible,* OBO 275 (Fribourg, 2015), 1–18.

Römer, T. "Der Pentateuch," in W. Dietrich et al. (eds.), *Die Entstehung des Alten Testaments,* ThW 1,1 (Stuttgart, 2014), 52–166.

Römer, T. "Zwischen Urkunden, Fragmenten und Ergänzungen: Zum Stand der Pentateuchforschung," *ZAW* 125 (2013), 2–24.

Römer, T., J.-D. Macchi, and C. Nihan (eds.). *Einleitung in das Alte Testament: Die Bücher der Hebräischen Bibel und die alttestamentlichen Schriften der katholischen, protestantischen und orthodoxen Kirchen* (Zurich, 2013).

Rösel, M. "Die Jungfrauengeburt des endzeitlichen Immanuel. Jesaja 7 in der Übersetzung der Septuaginta," *JBTh* 6 (1991), 135–151.

Rösel, M. "Salomo und die Sonne. Zur Rekonstruktion des Tempelweihspruchs I Reg 8,12 f.," *ZAW* 121 (2009), 402–417.

Rösel, M. *Übersetzung als Vollendung der Auslegung: Studien zur Genesis-Septuaginta,* BZAW 223 (Berlin, 1994).

Rüger, H. P. "Das Werden des christlichen Alten Testaments," *JBTh* 3 (1988), 175–189.

Ruppert, L. "Die historisch-kritische Methode der Bibelexegese im deutschen Sprachraum: Vorgeschichte, gegenwärtige Entwicklungen, Tendenzen, Aufbrüche," in L. Ruppert, *Studien zur Literaturgeschichte des Alten Testaments,* SBAB 18 (Stuttgart, 1994), 266–307.

Ruppert, L. "Der Weg der neueren katholischen Exegese vornehmlich im Bereich des Alten Testaments," in G. Kaufmann (ed.), *Tendenzen der katholischen Theologie nach dem Zweiten Vatikanischen Konzil* (Munich, 1979), 43–63.

Rupschus, N. *Frauen in Qumran,* WUNT II/457 (Tübingen, 2017).

Ruwe, A. "Beschneidung als interkultureller Brauch und Friedenszeichen Israels. Religionsgeschichtliche Überlegungen zu Genesis 17, Genesis 34, Exodus 4 und Josua 5," *ThZ* 64 (2008), 309–342.

Sanders, J. A. "The 'First' or 'Old' Testament: What to Call the First Christian Testament," in L. M. McDonald (ed.), *The Formation of the Biblical Canon,* vol. 1: *The Old Testament: Its Authority and Canonicity* (London, 2017), 36–38.

Sanders, J. A. "The Scrolls and the Canonical Process," in J. C. VanderKam and P. W. Flint (eds.), *The Dead Sea Scrolls after Fifty Years II* (Leiden, 1999), 1–22.

Sanders, S. L. *The Invention of Hebrew* (Champaign, IL, 2009).

Saur, M. *Einführung in die alttestamentliche Weisheitsliteratur* (Darmstadt, 2012).

Schäfer, P. *Die Geburt des Judentums aus dem Geist des Christentums: Fünf Vorlesungen zur Entstehung des rabbinischen Judentums,* Tria Corda 6 (Tübingen, 2010).

Schäfer, P. *Jesus im Talmud,* 2nd ed. (Tübingen, 2010).

Schäfer, P. *Zwei Götter im Himmel: Gottesvorstellungen in der jüdischen Antike* (Munich, 2017).

Schaper, J. *Priester und Leviten im achämenidischen Juda: Studien zur Kult- und Sozialgeschichte Israels in persischer Zeit,* FAT 31 (Tübingen, 2000).

Schechter, S. *Seminary Addressees and Other Papers* (Cincinnati, OH, 1915).

Schenke, H.-M., H.-G. Bethge, and U. U. Kaiser. *Nag Hammadi Deutsch,* 2 vols., GCS NF 8 (2001; Berlin, 2003).

Schenker, A., et al. (eds.). *Die älteste Zürcherbibel: Erstmalige teilweise Ausgabe und Übersetzung der ältesten vollständig erhaltenen Bibel in deutscher Sprache* (Fribourg, 2016).

Schiffman, L., and J. C. VanderKam (eds.). *Encyclopedia of the Dead Sea Scrolls* (Oxford, 2008).

Schipper, B. U. *Hermeneutik der Tora: Studien zur Traditionsgeschichte von Prov 2 und zur Komposition von Prov 1–9,* BZAW 432 (Berlin, 2012).

Schipper, B. U. "Die Lehre des Amenemope und Prov 22,17–24,22: Eine Neubestimmung des literarischen Verhältnisses," *ZAW* 117 (2005), 53–72, 232–248.

Schipper, B. U., and D. A. Teeter (eds.). *Wisdom and Torah: Reception of "Torah" in the Wisdom Literature of the Second Temple Period,* JSJ.S 163 (Leiden, 2013).

Schmid, K. "Der Abschluss der Tora als exegetisches und historisches Problem," in K. Schmid, *Schriftgelehrte Traditionsliteratur: Fallstudien zur innerbiblischen Schriftauslegung im Alten Testament,* FAT 77 (Tübingen, 2011), 159–184.

Schmid, K. "The Authors of the Book of Job and the Problem of Their Historical and Social Settings," in L. Perdue (ed.), *Scribes, Sages and Seers: The Sage in the Mediterranean World,* FRLANT 219 (Göttingen, 2008), 145–153.

Schmid, K. "The Canon and the Cult: The Emergence of Book Religion in Ancient Israel and the Gradual Sublimation of the Temple Cult," *JBL* 131, no. 2 (2012), 291–307.

Schmid, K. "The Deuteronomistic Image of History as Interpretive Device in the Second Temple Period: Towards a Long-Term Interpretation of 'Deuteronomism,'" in M. Nissinen (ed.), *Congress Volume Helsinki 2010*, VT.S 148 (Leiden, 2012), 369–388.

Schmid, K. "Divine Legislation in the Pentateuch in Its Late Judean and Neo-Babylonian Context," in P. Dubovský et al. (eds.), *The Fall of Jerusalem and the Rise of the Torah*, FAT 107 (Tübingen, 2016), 129–153.

Schmid, K. *Erzväter und Exodus: Untersuchungen zur doppelten Begründung der Ursprünge Israels innerhalb der Geschichtsbücher des Alten Testaments*, WMANT 81 (Neukirchen-Vluyn, 1999).

Schmid, K. "Gibt es 'Reste hebräischen Heidentums' im Alten Testament? Methodische Überlegungen anhand von Dtn 32,8 f. und Ps 82," in A. Wagner (ed.), *Primäre und sekundäre Religion als Kategorie der Religionsgeschichte des Alten Testaments*, BZAW 364 (Berlin, 2006), 105–120.

Schmid, K. "Gott als Angeklagter, Anwalt und Richter: Zur Religionsgeschichte und Theologie juridischer Interpretationen Gottes im Hiobbuch," in L. Ratschow and H. von Sass (eds.), *Die Anfechtung Gottes: Exegetische und systematisch-theologische Beiträge zur Theologie des Hiobbuches*, ABG 54 (Leipzig, 2016), 105–135.

Schmid, K. "Himmelsgott, Weltgott und Schöpfer: 'Gott' und der 'Himmel' in der Literatur der Zeit des Zweiten Tempels," *JBTh* 20 (2005), 111–148.

Schmid, K. *Hiob als biblisches und antikes Buch: Historische und intellektuelle Kontexte seiner Theologie*, SBS 219 (Stuttgart, 2010).

Schmid, K. "Klassische und nachklassische Deutungen der alttestamentlichen Prophetie," *Zeitschrift für neuere Theologiegeschichte* 3 (1996), 225–250.

Schmid, K. "Das kosmische Weltgericht in den Prophetenbüchern und seine historischen Kontexte," in H. Jenni et al. (eds.), *Nächstenliebe und Gottesfurcht. Beiträge aus alttestamentlicher, semitistischer und altorientalischer Wissenschaft für Hans-Peter Mathys zum 65. Geburtstag*, AOAT 439 (Münster, 2016), 409–434.

Schmid, K. *Literaturgeschichte des Alten Testaments: Eine Einführung*, 2nd ed. (Darmstadt, 2014).

Schmid, K. "Neue Schöpfung als Überbietung des neuen Exodus: Die Tritojesajanische Aktualisierung der Deuterojesajanischen Theologie und der Tora," in K. Schmid, *Schriftgelehrte Traditionsliteratur: Fallstudien zur innerbiblischen Schriftauslegung im Alten Testament*, FAT 77 (Tübingen, 2011), 185–205.

Schmid, K. *The Old Testament: A Literary History*, trans. Linda M. Maloney (Minneapolis, MN, 2012).

Schmid, K. "Der Pentateuch und seine Theologiegeschichte," *ZThK* 111 (2014), 239–271.

Schmid, K. "The Persian Imperial Authorization as Historical Problem and as Biblical Construct: A Plea for Differentiations in the Current Debate," in G. N. Knoppers and B. M. Levinson (eds), *The Pentateuch as Torah: New Models for Understanding Its Promulgation and Acceptance* (Winona Lake, IN, 2007), 22–38.

Schmid, K. "Prognosen und Postgnosen in der biblischen Prophetie," *EvTh* 74 (2014), 462–476.

Schmid, K. "Die Schrift als Text und Kommentar verstehen: Theologische Konsequenzen der neuesten literaturgeschichtlichen Forschung an der Hebräischen Bibel," *JBTh* 31 (2016), 47–63.

Schmid, K. *Schriftgelehrte Traditionsliteratur: Fallstudien zur innerbiblischen Schriftauslegung im Alten Testament*, FAT 77 (Tübingen, 2011; Study edition, 2015).

Schmid, K. "Von der Gegenwelt zur Lebenswelt: Evolutionäre Kosmologie und Theologie im Buch Genesis," in Th. Fuhrer, M. Erler et al. (eds.), *Cosmologies et cosmogonies dans la littérature antique: Huit exposés suivis de discussions et d'un épilogue*, Fondation Hardt: Entretiens sur l'Antiquité classique LXI (Geneva, 2015), 51–104.

Schmid, K. "Von Jakob zu Israel: Das antike Israel auf dem Weg zum Judentum im Spiegel der Fortschreibungsgeschichte der Jakobüberlieferungen der Genesis," in M. Grohmann (ed.), *Identität und Schrift: Fortschreibungsprozesse als Mittel religiöser Identitätsbildung*, BThSt 169 (Neukirchen-Vluyn, 2017), 33–67.

Schmid, K. (ed.). *Prophetische Heils- und Herrschererwartungen*, SBS 194 (Stuttgart, 2005).

Schmid, K. (ed.). *Schöpfung*, TdT 4 (Tübingen, 2012).

Schmitt, H.-C. "Der heidnische Mantiker als eschatologischer Jahweprophet: Zum Verständnis Bileams in der Endgestalt von Num 22–24," in I. Kottsieper et al. (eds.), *"Wer ist wie du, Herr, unter den Göttern?"* (Göttingen, 1994), 180–198.

Schnelle, U. *Die ersten 100 Jahre des Christentums 30–130 n. Chr.: Die Entstehungsgeschichte einer Weltreligion*, 2nd ed. (Göttingen, 2016).

Schniedewind, W. M. *How the Bible Became a Book: The Textualization of Ancient Israel* (Cambridge, 2004).

Schrenk, G. βίβλος, βιβλίον, ThWNT I (Stuttgart, 1933), 613–620.

Schröder, B. *Die "väterlichen Gesetze": Flavius Josephus als Vermittler von Halachah an Griechen und Römer*, TSAJ 53 (Tübingen, 1996).

Schroer, S. "Von zarter Hand geschrieben: Autorinnen in der Bibel," *Welt und Umwelt der Bibel* 8, (2003), 28–30.

Schroer, S., and S. Münger (eds.). *Khirbet Qeiyafa in the Shephelah*, Papers Presented at a Colloquium of the Swiss Society for Ancient Near Eastern Studies Held at the University of Bern, September 6, 2014, OBO 282 (Fribourg / Göttingen, 2017).

Schröter, J. *Das Abendmahl: Frühchristliche Deutungen und Impulse für die Gegenwart*, SBS 210 (Stuttgart, 2006).

Schröter, J. *Die apokryphen Evangelien: Jesusüberlieferungen außerhalb der Bibel* (Munich, 2020).

Schröter, J. *Jesus: Leben und Wirkung* (Munich, 2020).

Schröter, J. "Sammlungen der Paulusbriefe und die Entstehung des neutestamentlichen Kanons," in J. Schröter, S. Butticaz, and A. Dettwiler (eds.), *Receptions of Paul in Early Christianity*, BZNW 234 (Berlin, 2018), 799–822.

Schröter, J., and C. Jacobi (eds.). *Jesus Handbuch* (Tübingen, 2017).

Schröter, J., and K. Schwarz (eds.). *Die Nag-Hammadi-Schriften in der Literatur- und Theologiegeschichte des frühen Christentums*, STAC 106 (Tübingen, 2017).

Schröter, J., et al. (eds.). *Receptions of Paul in Early Christianity: The Person of Paul and His Writings through the Eyes of His Early Interpreters* (Berlin/Boston, 2018).

Schulz, H. *Leviten im vorstaatlichen Israel und im Mittleren Osten* (Munich, 1987).

Schürer, E. *The History of the Jewish People in the Age of Jesus Christ (175 B.C.–A.D. 135), III/1*, ed. G. Vermes, F. Millar, and M. Goodman (Edinburgh, 1986).

Schwartz, D. R. (ed.). *Was 70 CE a Watershed in Jewish History? On Jews and Judaism before and after the Destruction of the Second Temple*, AJEC 78 (Leiden, 2012).

Schwartz, S. *Imperialism and Jewish Society 200 B.C.E. to 640 C.E.* (Princeton, NJ, 2001).

Segal, M. "Qumran Research in Israel: Rewritten Bible and Biblical Interpretation," in D. Dimant (ed.), *The Dead Sea Scrolls in Scholarly Perspective: A History of Research*, STDJ 99 (Leiden, 2012), 315–333.

Seidel, H. W. *Die Erforschung des Alten Testaments in der katholischen Theologie seit der Jahrhundertwende (1962)*, ed. C. Dohmen, Athenäums Monographien Theologie 86 (Frankfurt a. M., 1993).

Semler, J. S. *Abhandlung von freier Untersuchung des Canon*, 4 vols. (Halle, 1771–1775).

Seybold, K. "David als Psalmsänger in der Bibel: Entstehung einer Symbolfigur," in W. Dietrich and H. Herkommer (eds.), *König David—biblische Schlüsselfigur und europäische Leitgestalt* (Fribourg, 2003), 145–163.

Siegert, F. *Einleitung in die hellenistisch-jüdische Literatur: Apokrypha, Pseudepigrapha und Fragmente verlorener Autorenwerke* (Berlin, 2016).

Siegert, F. *Zwischen Hebräischer Bibel und Altem Testament: Eine Einführung in die Septuaginta* (Münster, 2001).

Sigismund, M. "Gothic Translations, " in A. Lange and E. Tov (eds.), *Textual History of the Bible: The Hebrew Bible*, vol. 1a: *Overview Articles* (Leiden, 2016), 416–419.

Ska, J. L. *Introduction to Reading the Pentateuch* (Winona Lake, IN, 2006).

Smelik, K. A. D. "The Origin of Psalm 20," *JSOT* 31 (1985), 75–81.

Smend, R. "Mose als geschichtliche Gestalt," *HZ* 260 (1995), 1–19.

Smend, R. "Wellhausen und das Judentum," *ZThK* 79 (1982), 249–282.

Smith, J. Z. "Canon, Catalogues, and Classic," in A. van der Kooij and K. van der Toorn (eds.), *Canonization and Decanonization: Papers Presented to the International Conference of the Leiden Institute for the Study of Religions (LISOR)*, held at Leiden 9–10 January 1997, SHR 82 (Leiden, 1998), 295–311.

Sommer, B. "Dialogical Biblical Theology: A Jewish Approach to Reading Scripture Theologically," in Leo G. Perdue et al. (eds.), *Biblical Theology. Introduction and Conversation* (Nashville, TN, 2009), 1–53.

Sommer, B. *Jewish Concepts of Scripture: A Comparative Introduction* (New York, 2012).

Spans, A. *Die Stadtfrau Zion im Zentrum der Welt: Exegese und Theologie von Jesaja 60–62*, BBB 175 (Göttingen, 2015).

Sperber, A. (ed.), *The Bible in Aramaic Based on Old Manuscripts and Reprinted Texts*, 4 vols. in 5 parts (Leiden, 1959–1973).

Sperling, D. S. (ed.), *Students of the Covenant: A History of Jewish Biblical Scholarship in North America* (Atlanta, GA, 1992).

Spieckermann, H. "Bible," in *Encyclopedia of the Bible and Its Reception*, vol. 1 (Berlin / Boston 2011), 1067–1068.

Steck, O. H. *Der Abschluß der Prophetie im Alten Testament: Ein Versuch zur Frage der Vorgeschichte des Kanons*, BThSt 17 (Neukirchen-Vluyn, 1991).

Steck, O. H. *Die erste Jesajarolle von Qumran (1QIsᵃ), Schreibweise als Leseanleitung für ein Prophetenbuch*, SBS 173 / 1.2 (Stuttgart, 1998).

Steck, O. H. *Friedensvorstellungen im alten Jerusalem* (Zurich, 1972).

Steck, O. H. *Gottesknecht und Zion: Gesammelte Aufsätze zu Deuterojesaja*, FAT 4 (Tübingen, 1992).

Steck, O. H. "Tritojesaja im Jesajabuch," in O. H. Steck, *Studien zu Tritojesaja*, BZAW 203 (Berlin, 1991), 3–45.

Steck, O. H. "Zion als Gelände und Gestalt: Überlegungen zur Wahrnehmung Jerusalems als Stadt und Frau im Alten Testament," *ZThK* 86 (1989), 261–281.

Steinberg, J. *Die Ketuvim—ihr Aufbau und ihre Botschaft*, BBB 152 (Hamburg, 2006).

Steiner, M. L. "Moab during the Iron Age II Period," in M. L. Steiner and A. E. Killebrew (eds.), *The Oxford Handbook of the Archaeology of the Levant* (Oxford, 2014), 770–781.

Steins, G. *Die Chronik als kanonisches Abschlußphänomen: Studien zur Entstehung und Theologie von 1 / 2 Chronik*, BBB 93 (Weinheim, 1995).

Stemberger, G. *Einleitung in Talmud und Midrasch*, 2nd ed. (Munich, 2011).

Stemberger, G. "Entstehung und Auffassung des Kanons im rabbinischen Denken," in G. Stemberger, *Judaica Minora*, part 1: *Biblische Traditionen im rabbinischen Judentum*, TSAJ 133 (Tübingen, 2010), 69–87.

Stemberger, G. "Jabne und der Kanon," in G. Stemberger, *Studien zum rabbinischen Judentum*, SBAB 10 (Stuttgart, 1990), 375–389.

Stemberger, G. *Pharisäer, Sadduzäer, Essener: Fragen—Fakten—Hintergründe* (Stuttgart, 2013).

Stemberger, G. "Rabbinische Schriftauslegung und mündliche Tradition," *JBTh* 31 (2016), 137–148.

Stemberger, G. "Zum Verständnis der Schrift im rabbinischen Judentum," in G. Stemberger, *Judaica Minora*, part 1: *Biblische Traditionen im rabbinischen Judentum*, TSAJ 133 (Tübingen, 2010), 15–26.

Stern, D. *The Jewish Bible: A Material History* (Seattle, 2017).

Stern, E., and Y. Magen. "Archaeological Evidence for the First Stage of the Samaritan Temple on Mount Gerizim," *IEJ* 52 (2002), 49–57.

Steymans, H. U. "Deuteronomy 28 and Tell Tayinat," *Verbum et Ecclesia* 34 (2013), 1–13.

Still, T. D., and D. E. Wilhite. *The Apostolic Fathers and Paul* (London, 2017).

Stipp, H.-J. "'Alles Fleisch hatte seinen Wandel auf der Erde verdorben' (Gen 6,12): Die Mitverantwortung der Tierwelt an der Sintflut nach der Priesterschrift," in H.-J. Stipp, *Alttestamentliche Studien: Arbeiten zu Priesterschrift, Deuteronomistischem Geschichtswerk und Prophetie*, BZAW 442 (Berlin,) 2013, 95–116.

Stipp, H.-J. "Gedalja und die Kolonie von Mizpa," in H.-J. Stipp, *Studien zum Jeremiabuch: Text und Redaktion*, FAT 96 (Tübingen, 2015), 409–432.

Stökl, J. *Prophecy in the Ancient Near East. A Philological and Sociological Comparison*, CHANE 56 (Leiden, 2012).

Stökl, J., and C. L. Carvalho (eds.). *Prophets Male and Female: Gender and Prophecy in the Hebrew Bible, the Eastern Mediterranean, and the Ancient Near East* (Atlanta, GA, 2013).

Stökl Ben Ezra, D. *Qumran: Die Texte vom Toten Meer und das antike Judentum*, UTB 4681 (Tübingen, 2016).

Stolt, B. *Martin Luthers Rhetorik des Herzens* (Stuttgart, 2000).

Stolz, F. *Psalmen im nachkultischen Raum*, ThSt(B) 129 (Zurich, 1983).

Stone, M. *Fourth Ezra: A Commentary on the Book of Fourth Ezra*, ed. F. M. Cross, Hermeneia (Minneapolis, MN, 1990).

Stone, T. J. *The Compilational History of the Megilloth: Canon, Contoured Intertextuality and Meaning in the Writings*, FAT II / 59 (Tübingen, 2013).

Stylianopoulos, T. G. *The Making of the New Testament: Church, Gospel, and Canon* (Brookline, MA, 2014).

Stylianopoulos, T. G. *The New Testament: An Orthodox Perspective*, vol. 1: *Scripture, Tradition, Hermeneutics* (Brookline, MA, 1997; repr. 2004).

Sundermeier, T. *Was ist Religion? Religionswissenschaft im theologischen Kontext*, ThB 96 (Gütersloh, 1999).

Sweeney, M. A. *Tanak: A Theological and Critical Introduction to the Jewish Bible* (Minneapolis, MN, 2012).

Talmon, S. "Was the Book of Esther Known at Qumran?," *DSD* 2 (1995), 249–267.

Teeter, D. A. "The Hebrew Bible and / as Second Temple Literature. Methodological Reflections," *DSD* 20 (2013), 349–377.

Tigchelaar, E. "Wie haben die Qumrantexte unsere Sicht des kanonischen Prozesses verändert?," in M. Becker and J. Frey (eds.), *Qumran und der biblische Kanon,* BThSt 92 (Neukirchen-Vluyn, 2009), 65–87.

Tilly, M. *Apokalyptik,* UTB 3651 (Tübingen, 2012).

Tilly, M. *Einführung in die Septuaginta* (Darmstadt, 2005).

Tilly, M. "Paulus und die antike jüdische Schriftauslegung," *KuD* 63 (2017), 157–181.

Toepel, A. *Das Protevangelium des Jakobus: Ein Beitrag zur neueren Diskussion um Herkunft, Auslegung und theologische Einordnung,* FThS 71 (Münster, 2014).

Tov, E. "Die griechischen Bibelübersetzungen," in ANRW II.20 / 1 (Berlin, 1987), 121–189.

Tov, E. *Der Text der Hebräischen Bibel: Handbuch der Textkritik* (Stuttgart, 1997).

Trebolle Barrera, J. *The Jewish Bible and the Christian Bible: An Introduction to the History of the Bible* (Leiden / Grand Rapids, MI, 1998).

Trebolle Barrera, J. "Vetus Latina," in A. Lange and E. Tov (eds.), *Textual History of the Bible: The Hebrew Bible,* vol. 1a: *Overview Articles* (Leiden, 2016), 319–331.

Troeltsch, E. "Über historische und dogmatische Methode in der Theologie (1900)," in F. Voigt (ed.), *Ernst Troeltsch Lesebuch,* UTB 2452 (Tübingen, 2003), 2–25.

Tuckett, C. M. *The Gospel of Mary,* Oxford Early Christian Gospel Texts (Oxford, 2007).

Tworuschka, U. (ed.). *Heilige Schriften: Eine Einführung* (Darmstadt, 2000).

Uehlinger, C. "Ein Bild JHWHs und seiner Aschera? Nein! Vielleicht!," *Welt und Umwelt der Bibel 11* (1999), 50.

Uehlinger, C. "Qohelet im Horizont der mesopotamischen, levantinischen und ägyptischen Weisheit der persischen und hellenistischen Zeit," in L. Schwienhorst-Schönberger (ed.), *Das Buch Kohelet: Studien zur Struktur, Geschichte, Rezeption und Theologie,* BZAW 254 (Berlin, 1996), 155–247.

Uehlinger, C., and S. Müller Trufaut. "Ezekiel 1, Babylonian Cosmological Scholarship and Iconography: Attempts at Further Refinement," *ThZ* 57 (2001), 140–171.

Ulrich, E. *The Biblical Qumran Scrolls: Transcriptions and Textual Variants,* VT.S 134 (Leiden, 2010).

Ulrich, E. C. *The Dead Sea Scrolls and the Developmental Composition of the Bible,* VT.S 169 (Leiden, 2015).

Utzschneider, H. "Die Schriftprophetie und die Frage nach dem Ende der Prophetie: Überlegungen anhand von Mal 1,6–2,16," *ZAW* 104 (1992), 377–394.

VanderKam, J. C. *The Dead Sea Scrolls and the Bible* (Grand Rapids, MI, 2012).

VanderKam, J. C. *Einführung in die Qumranforschung,* UTB 1998 (Göttingen, 1998).

VanderKam, J. C., and P. W. Flint (eds.). *The Dead Sea Scrolls after Fifty Years II* (Leiden, 1999).

van der Toorn, K. "Celebrating the New Year with the Israelites: Three Extrabiblical Psalms from Papyrus Amherst 63," *JBL* 136 (2017), 633–649.

van der Toorn, K. "Revelation as a Scholarly Construct in Israel and Mesopotamia," in M. Oeming et al. (eds.), *Theologie in Israel und in den Nachbarkulturen.* Beiträge des Symposiums "Das Alte Testament und die Kultur der Moderne" anlässlich des 100. Geburtstags Gerhard von Rads (1901–1971), Heidelberg, 18–21 October 2001, ATM 9 (Münster, 2004), 125–138.

van der Toorn, K. *Scribal Culture and the Making of the Hebrew Bible* (Cambridge, MA, 2017).

Vidas, M. *Tradition and the Formation of the Talmud* (Princeton, NJ, 2014).

Vieweger, D. *Archäologie der biblischen Welt* (Gütersloh, 2012).

Vollandt, R. "Arabic (Christian) Translations," in A. Lange and E. Tov (eds.), *Textual History of the Bible. The Hebrew Bible,* vol. 1a: *Overview Articles* (Leiden, 2016), 408–416.

Vollenweider, S. "Antijudaismus im Neuen Testament. Der Anfang einer unseligen Tradition," in S. Vollenweider, *Horizonte neutestamentlicher Christologie. Studien zu Paulus und zur frühchristlichen Theologie,* WUNT 144 (Tübingen, 2002), 125–140.

von Campenhausen, H. *Die Entstehung der christlichen Bibel,* BHTh 39 (Tübingen, 1968; new ed. 2003).

von Campenhausen, H. *The Formation of the Christian Bible,* trans. J. A. Baker (Philadelphia, 1972).

von Lips, H. *Der neutestamentliche Kanon: Seine Geschichte und Bedeutung* (Zurich, 2004).

Wade, M. L. *Consistency of Translation Techniques in the Tabernacle Accounts of Exodus in the Old Greek* (Atlanta, GA, 2003).

Wagner, A. (ed.). *Primäre und sekundäre Religion als Kategorie der Religionsgeschichte des Alten Testaments,* BZAW 364 (Berlin, 2006).

Wagner, V. "Profanität und Sakralisierung der Beschneidung im Alten Testament," *VT* 60 (2010), 447–464.

Wahl, H. M. *Die Jakobserzählungen: Studien zu ihrer mündlichen Überlieferung, Verschriftung und Historizität,* BZAW 258 (Berlin, 1997).

Wallraff, M. *Kodex und Kanon: Das Buch im frühen Christentum,* Hans-Lietzmann-Vorlesungen 12 (Berlin, 2012).

Wallraff, M., et al. (eds.). *Basel 1516: Erasmus' Edition of the New Testament,* Spätmittelalter, Humanismus, Reformation 91 (Tübingen, 2016).

Walter, N. "'Bücher: so nicht der Heiligen Schrifft gleich gehalten . . .'? Karlstadt, Luther—und die Folgen," in N. Walter, *Praeparatio Evangelica: Studien zur*

Umwelt, Exegese und Hermeneutik des Neuen Testaments, ed. von W. Kraus und F. Wilk, WUNT 98 (Tübingen, 1997), 341–369.

Weinfeld, M. *Deuteronomy and the Deuteronomic School* (Oxford, 1972).

Weingart K. *Stämmevolk—Staatsvolk—Gottesvolk? Studien zur Verwendung des Israel-Namens im Alten Testament,* FAT II / 68 (Tübingen, 2014).

Weippert, H., and M. Weippert. "Die 'Bileam'-Inschrift von Tell Der 'Alla," *ZDPV* 98 (1982), 77–103.

Weippert, M. "Aspekte israelitischer Prophetie im Lichte verwandter Erscheinungen des Alten Orients," in G. Mauer and U. Magen (eds.), *Ad bene et fideliter seminandum,* Festschrift für K. Deller, AOAT 220 (Neukirchen-Vluyn, 1988), 287–319.

Weippert, M. *Götterwort in Menschenmund: Studien zur Prophetie in Assyrien, Israel und Juda,* FRLANT 252 (Göttingen, 2014).

Weippert, M. *Historisches Textbuch zum Alten Testament,* GAT 10 (Göttingen, 2010).

Weippert, M. "Synkretismus und Monotheismus: Religionsinterne Konfliktbewältigung im alten Israel (1990)," in M. Weippert, *Jahwe und die anderen Götter: Studien zur Religionsgeschichte des antiken Israel in ihrem syrisch-palästinischen Kontext,* FAT 18 (Tübingen, 1997), 1–24.

Wellhausen, J. "Geschichte Israels" (1880), in J. Wellhausen, *Grundrisse zum Alten Testament,* ed. R. Smend, ThB 27 (Munich, 1965), 13–64.

Wellhausen, J. *Israelitische und jüdische Geschichte* (Berlin, 1894).

Wellhausen, J. *Prolegomena zur Geschichte Israels* (Berlin, 1883).

Wevers, J. W. "The Earliest Witness to the LXX Deuteronomy," *CBQ* 39 (1977), 240–244.

White Crawford, S. "4QTales of the Persian Court (4Q550a–e) and Its Relation to Biblical Royal Courtier Tales, Especially Esther, Daniel and Joseph," in E. D. Herbert and E. Tov (eds.), *The Bible as Book: The Hebrew Bible and the Judaean Desert Discoveries* (London, 2002), 121–137.

White Crawford, S. "Has Esther Been Found at Qumran? 4QProto-Esther and the Esther Corpus," *RdQ* 17 (1996), 307–325.

Wick, P. *Die urchristlichen Gottesdienste: Entstehung und Entwicklung im Rahmen der frühjüdischen Tempel-, Synagogen- und Hausfrömmigkeit,* BWANT 150 (Stuttgart, 2002).

Witte, M. *Hiobs viele Gesichter: Studien zur Komposition, Tradition und frühen Rezeption des Hiobbuches,* FRLANT 267 (Göttingen, 2018).

Witte, M. "Der 'Kanon' heiliger Schriften des antiken Judentums," in M. Witte, *Texte und Kontexte des Sirachbuches,* FAT 98 (Tübingen, 2015), 39–58.

Witte, M. "Der Segen Bileams—eine redaktionsgeschichtliche Problemanzeige zum 'Jahwisten' in Num 22–24," in J. C. Gertz et al. (eds.), *Abschied vom Jahwisten. Die Komposition des Hexateuch in der jüngsten Diskussion,* BZAW 315 (Berlin, 2002), 191–213.

Wrede, W. "Über Aufgabe und Methode der sogenannten Neutestamentlichen Theologie," in G. Strecker (ed.), *Das Problem der Theologie des Neuen Testaments,* WdF 367 (Darmstadt, 1975), 81–154 (first published 1897).

Wright, B. G. "Why a Prologue? Ben Sira's Grandson and His Greek Translation," in S. Paul et al. (eds.), *Emanuel: Studies in Hebrew Bible, Septuagint and Dead Sea Scrolls in Honor of Emanuel Tov,* VT.S 94 (Leiden, 2003), 633–644.

Xeravits, G., and P. Porzig. *Einführung in die Qumranliteratur* (Berlin, 2015).

Zahn, M. M. "Genre and Rewritten Scripture: A Reassessment," *JBL* 131 (2012), 271–288.

Zahn, M. M. *Rethinking Rewritten Scripture: Composition and Exegesis in the 4Q Reworked Pentateuch Manuscripts,* STDJ 95 (Leiden, 2011).

Zenger, E. *Einleitung in das Alte Testament.* 8th rev. ed., ed. Christian Frevel (Stuttgart, 2012).

Zenger, E. "Der Psalter als Buch: Beobachtungen zu seiner Entstehung, Komposition und Funktion," in E. Zenger (ed.), *Der Psalter in Judentum und Christentum,* Herders biblische Studien 18 (Freiburg im Breisgau, 1998), 1–57.

Zenger, E., and C. Frevel. "Die Bücher der Tora / des Pentateuch," in E. Zenger and C. Frevel, *Einleitung in das Alte Testament.* 8th rev. ed. (Stuttgart, 2012), 67–232.

Zenger, E., et al. *Einleitung in das Alte Testament,* 9th updated ed. by C. Frevel (Stuttgart, 2016).

Zevit, Z. *The Religions of Ancient Israel: A Synthesis of Parallactic Approaches* (London, 2001).

Zewi, T. "Samaritan Arabic Translations," in A. Lange and E. Tov (eds.), *Textual History of the Bible. The Hebrew Bible,* vol. 1a: *Overview Articles* (Leiden, 2016), 309–315.

Zsengellér, J. (ed.). *Rewritten Bible after Fifty Years: Texts, Terms, or Techniques? A Last Dialogue with Geza Vermes,* JSJ.S 166 (Leiden, 2014).

Zugmann, M. *"Hellenisten" in der Apostelgeschichte. Historische und exegetische Untersuchungen zu Apg 6,1; 9,29; 11,20,* WUNT 2.264 (Tübingen, 2009).

Zunz, L. *Die gottesdienstlichen Vorträge der Juden, historisch entwickelt: Ein Beitrag zur Alterthumskunde und biblischen Kritik, zur Literatur- und Religionsgeschichte (1892),* 2nd ed., ed. N. Brüll (Frankfurt a. M., 1992).

Zwickel, W. *Der salomonische Tempel* (Mainz, 1999).

Acknowledgments

This book came to fruition over the course of many weekends of intensive face-to-face discussions, several conference meetings, and countless hours of online conversation. We focused our efforts on mapping out, reworking, amending, and modifying the layout of the work as a whole and its individual chapters. As a result of our endeavors, the book in its current configuration gradually took shape. Although we incorporated the latest research and most recent findings, our aim from the very beginning was to present the creation of the Jewish and Christian Bibles in such a way as to make our account accessible to readers who do not have an intimate knowledge of biblical scholarship.

Right from the inception of this project, Ulrich Nolte, senior editor at C. H. Beck, has been our constant, attentive guide and companion. Our lively exchange of ideas on questions of the book's concept and content, copyediting of the manuscript, production details, and even the design of the cover and how the illustrations should appear took place in a cooperative, convivial atmosphere. Our common goal was to produce a book that was intellectually stimulating and readable in equal measure. We are enormously grateful to him for his helpful input. We likewise owe Petra Rehder our sincere thanks for her painstaking work on the manuscript and her invaluable suggestions on amending certain passages. Our thanks are also due to all the other staff members at Beck who took part in editing and producing the book with great care and reliability.

We would like to thank Peter Altmann, who provided draft English translations of the individual chapters which were used especially for the biblical citations.

Finally, we would like to express our gratitude to Harvard University Press, most especially the editorial director, Sharmila Sen, for opening up our book to an even wider readership by proposing an English translation. Our translator, Peter Lewis, has produced a sensitive rendition of our text, and we have enjoyed a very collegial relationship with him during this undertaking. We also want to thank Louise E. Robbins for her careful revision of the English text and the very helpful correspondence about remaining questions. Our thanks are also due to HUP editor Joseph

Pomp for his helpful input on the translation and to Associate Editor Heather Hughes for guiding the work through its production phases.

We very much hope that our book will resonate with readers and contribute to the ongoing discussion about the making of the Jewish and Christian Bibles.

Illustration Credits

Figure 1: Biblioteca Medicea Laurenziana, Florence. © bpk-images / Scala.

Figures 2 and 24: Johannes Renz and Wolfgang Röllig, *Handbuch der althebräischen Epigraphik,* vol. 3 (Darmstadt: WBG, 1995), plate 38, no. 8; plate 1, no. 1.

Figures 3, 6, 7, 12, 13, 15, and 41: Kurt Aland and Barbara Aland, *Der Text des Neuen Testaments,* 2nd ed. (Stuttgart: Deutsche Bibelges, 1989), pp. 99, 23, 25, 98, 104, 101, 15.

Figures 4, 5, 8, 9a and 9b, 10, 16, 20, 21, 22, 23, 30, and 40: Alexander Achilles Fischer, *Der Text des Alten Testaments* (Stuttgart: Deutsche Bibelges, 2009), ill. 26, 24, 6, 9, 11, 1, 13, 14, 48, 5, 3, 47.

Figures 11 and 19: Emanuel Tov, *Textual Criticism of the Hebrew Bible,* 3rd ed., revised and expanded (Minneapolis: Fortress Press, 2011), p. 383 (plate 1), p. 400 (plate 17).

Figure 14: Biblioteca Apostolica Vaticana / Wikimedia Commons.

Figures 17, 18a and 18b: © BIBEL + ORIENT Foundation, Freiburg, Switzerland.

Figure 25: Eilat Mazar, David Ben-Shlomo, and Shmuel Aḥituv, "An Inscribed Pithos from the Ophel, Jerusalem," *Israel Exploration Journal* 63, no. 1 (2013): 39–49, fig. 3 left.

Figure 26: P. Kyle McCarter, Shlomo Bunimovitz, and Zvi Lederman, "An Archaic Baʻal Inscription from Tel Beth-Shemesh," *Tel Aviv* 38, no. 2 (2011): 179–193, fig. 1b.

Figure 27: Yosef Garfinkel, "Khirbet Qeiyafa in the Shephelah: Data and Interpretations," in Silvia Schroer and Stefan Münger (eds.), *Khirbet Qeiyafa in the Shephelah: Papers Presented at a Colloquium of the Swiss Society for Ancient Near Eastern Studies Held at the University of Bern, September 6, 2014* (Fribourg / Göttingen: Academic Press / Vandenhoeck & Ruprecht, 2017), fig. 35.

Figure 28: Helga Weippert and Manfred Weippert, "Die 'Bileam'-Inschrift von Tell Dēr ʼAllā," *Zeitschrift des Deutschen Palästina-Vereins* 98 (1982): 77–103, fig. 1.

Figure 29: Ze'ev Meshel, *Kuntillet 'Ajrud (Horvat Teman): An Iron Age II Religious Site on the Judah-Sinai Border* (Jerusalem: Israel Exploration Society, 2012), p. 115.

Figure 31: Cuneiform Digital Library Initiative, University of California, Los Angeles, http://cdli.ucla.edu.

Figure 32: Wayne Horowitz and Takayoshi Oshima, *Cuneiform in Canaan* (Jerusalem: Israel Exploration Society, 2006), p. 232, Megiddo 1.

Figure 33: Louvre Museum / Mbzt / Wikimedia Commons / GNU Free Documentation License.

Figure 34: Jacob Lauinger, "Esarhaddon's Succession Treaty at Tell Tayinat: Text and Commentary," *Journal of Cuneiform Studies* 64 (2012): 87–123, p. 89.

Figure 35: Laurie E. Pearce and Cornelia Wunsch, *Documents of Judean Exiles and West Semites in Babylonia in the Collection of David Sofer* (Bethesda: CDL Press, 2014), plate 1.

Figure 36: Jan Christian Gertz (ed.), *Grundinformation Altes Testament,* 5th ed. (Göttingen: Vandenhoeck & Ruprecht, 2016), p. 367.

Figure 37: biblical-data.org/Wikimedia Commons.

Figure 38: Sotheby's / Wikimedia Commons.

Figure 39: Emile Schrijver and Falk Wiesemann (eds.), *Schöne Seiten: Jüdische Schriftkultur aus der Braginsky Collection* (Zurich: Scheidegger & Spiess, 2011), p. 306, detail from ill. 99.

Figure 42: Reproduced from Volker Reinhardt, *Der Göttliche. Das Leben des Michelangelo* (Munich: C. H. Beck Verlag, 2010), plate 2.

Figure 43: Reproduced from Navid Kermani, *Ungläubiges Staunen: Über das Christentum* (Munich: C. H. Beck Verlag, 2015), pp. 200–201.

Figure 44: National Museum of Capodimonte / Web Gallery of Art / Wikimedia Commons.

Figure 45: Sixtus / Wikimedia Commons.

Figure 46: Reproduced from Volker Reinhardt, *Leonardo da Vinci: Das Auge der Welt* (Munich: C. H. Beck Verlag, 2018), pp. 128–129.

Figure 47: Unterlinden Museum / Wikimedia Commons.

Figure 48: Gallerie Neue Meister / Wikimedia Commons.

Maps © Peter Palm, Berlin / Germany.

Scripture Index

Verses from the Septuagint are labeled LXX. The Dead Sea Scrolls and writings not referred to by chapter and verse in the text are listed in the General Index.

General Index